F

AUG '08

CH

WATER BABY

Published by DC Comics,

1700 Broadway,

New York, NY 10019.

The stories, characters and incidents mentioned in this

book are entirely fictional.

Printed in Canada.

DC Comics, a Warner Bros.

Entertainment Company.

ISBN: 978-1-4012-1147-9

COVER BY ROSS CAMPBELL

Karen Berger, Sr. VP-Executive Editor Shelly Bond, Editor Angela Rufino, Assistant Editor Robbin Brosterman, Sr. Art Director
Paul Levitz, President & Publisher Georg Brewer, VP-Design & DC Direct Creative Richard Bruning, Sr. VP-Creative Director
Patrick Caldon, Exec. VP-Finance & Operations Chris Caramalis, VP-Finance John Cunningham, VP-Marketing Terri Cunningham, VP-Managing Editor
Alison Gill, VP-Manufacturing Hank Kanalz, VP-General Manager, WildStorm Jim Lee, Editorial Director-WildStorm
Paula Lowitt, Sr. VP-Business & Legal Affairs MaryEllen McLaughlin, VP-Advertising & Custom Publishing John Nee, Sr.VP-Business Development
Gregory Noveck, Sr. VP-Creative Affairs Sue Pohja, VP-Book Trade Sales Steve Rotterdam, Sr. VP-Sales & Marketing
Cheryl Rubin, Sr. VP-Brand Management Jeff Trojan, VP-Business Development, DC Direct Bob Wayne, VP-Sales

WATER BABY

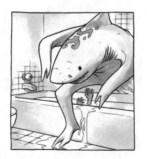

Written & Illustrated by **Ross Campbell**

Lettering by **Jared K. Fletcher**

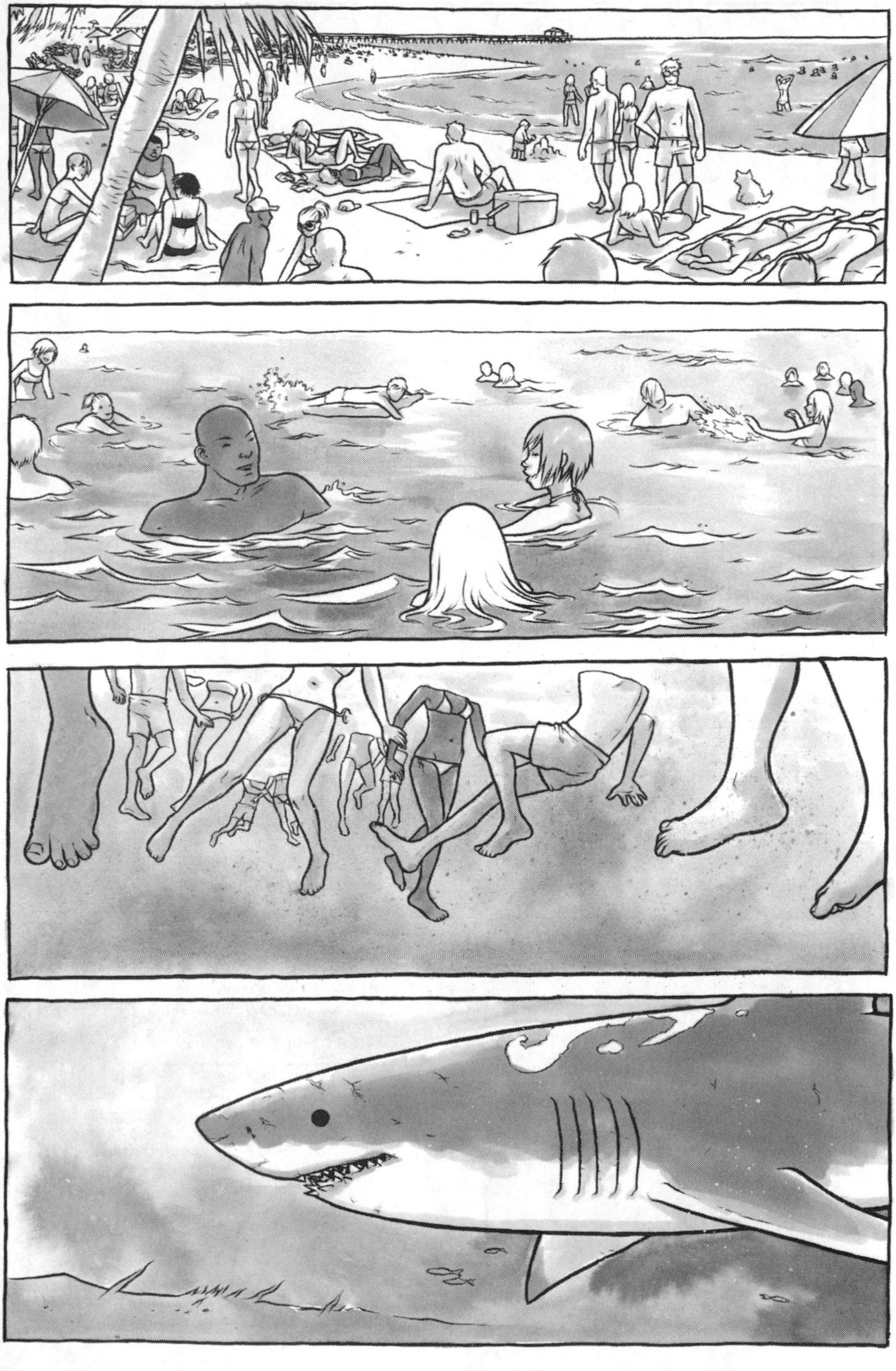

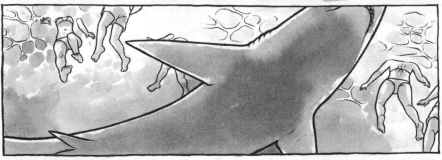

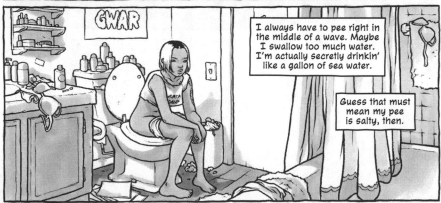

I always have to pee right in the middle of a wave. Maybe I swallow too much water. I'm actually secretly drinkin' like a gallon of sea water.

Guess that must mean my pee is salty, then.

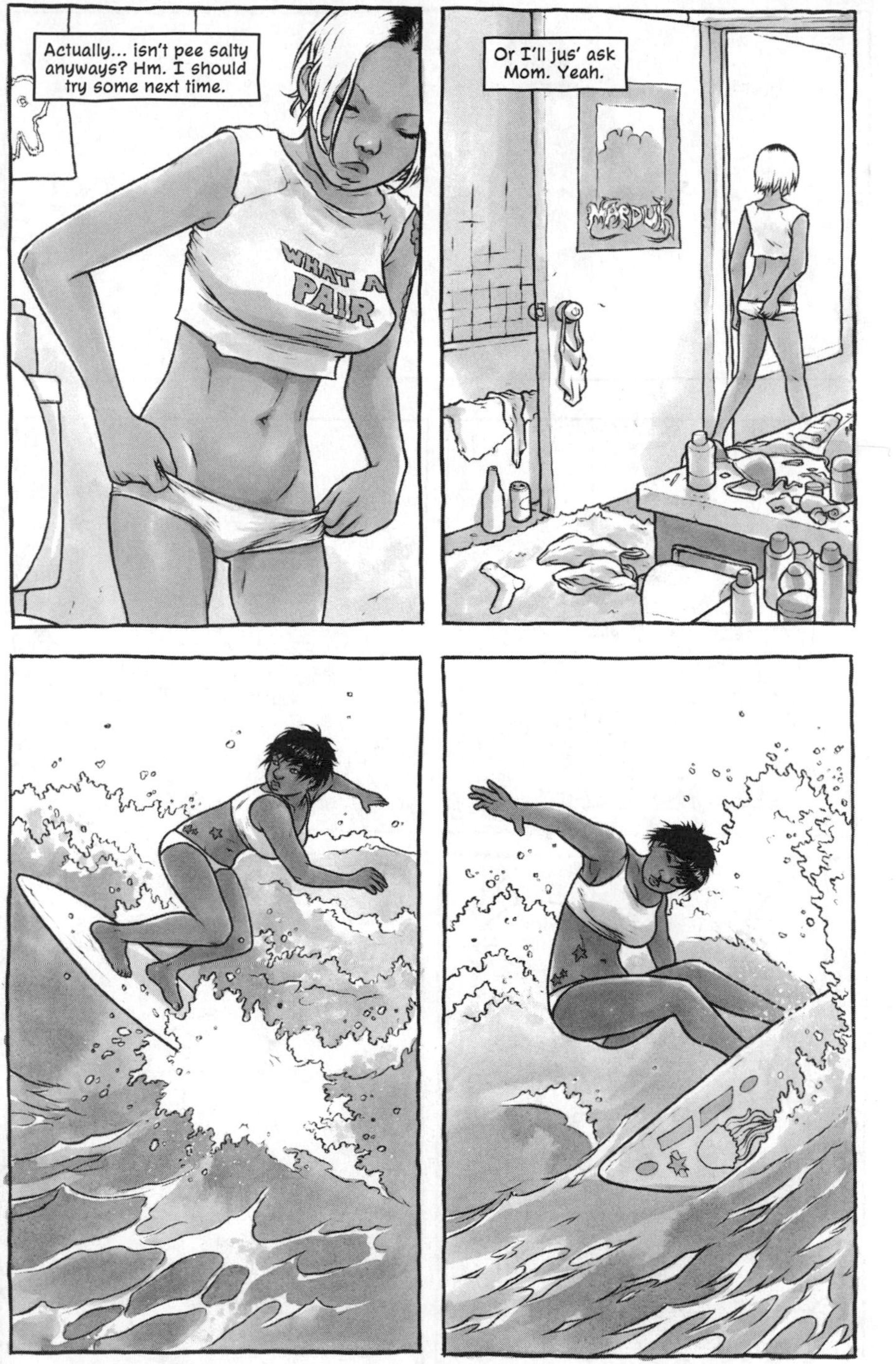
Actually... isn't pee salty anyways? Hm. I should try some next time.
WHAT A PAIR
Or I'll jus' ask Mom. Yeah.
MARDUK

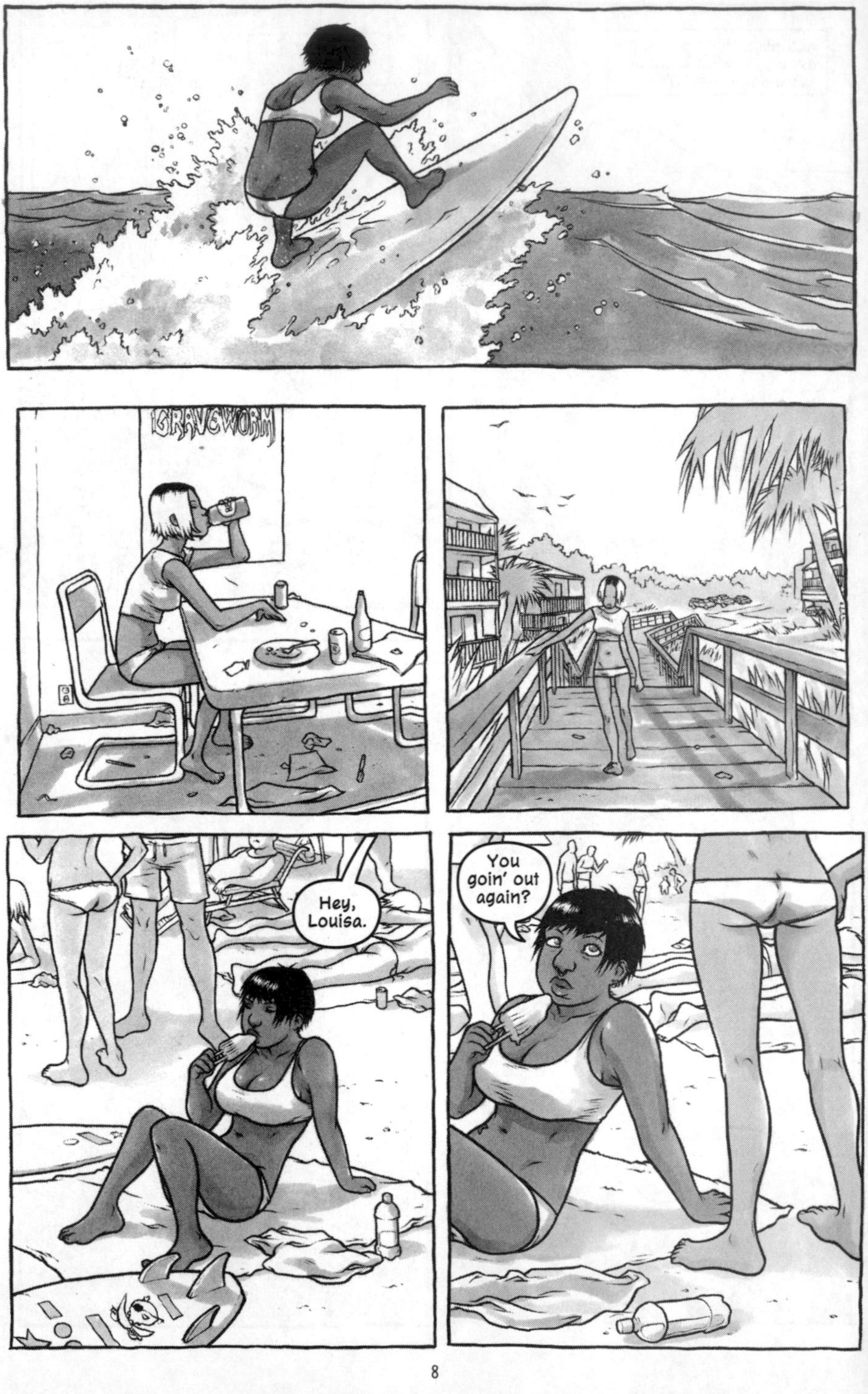
GRAVEWORM
Hey, Louisa.
You goin' out again?

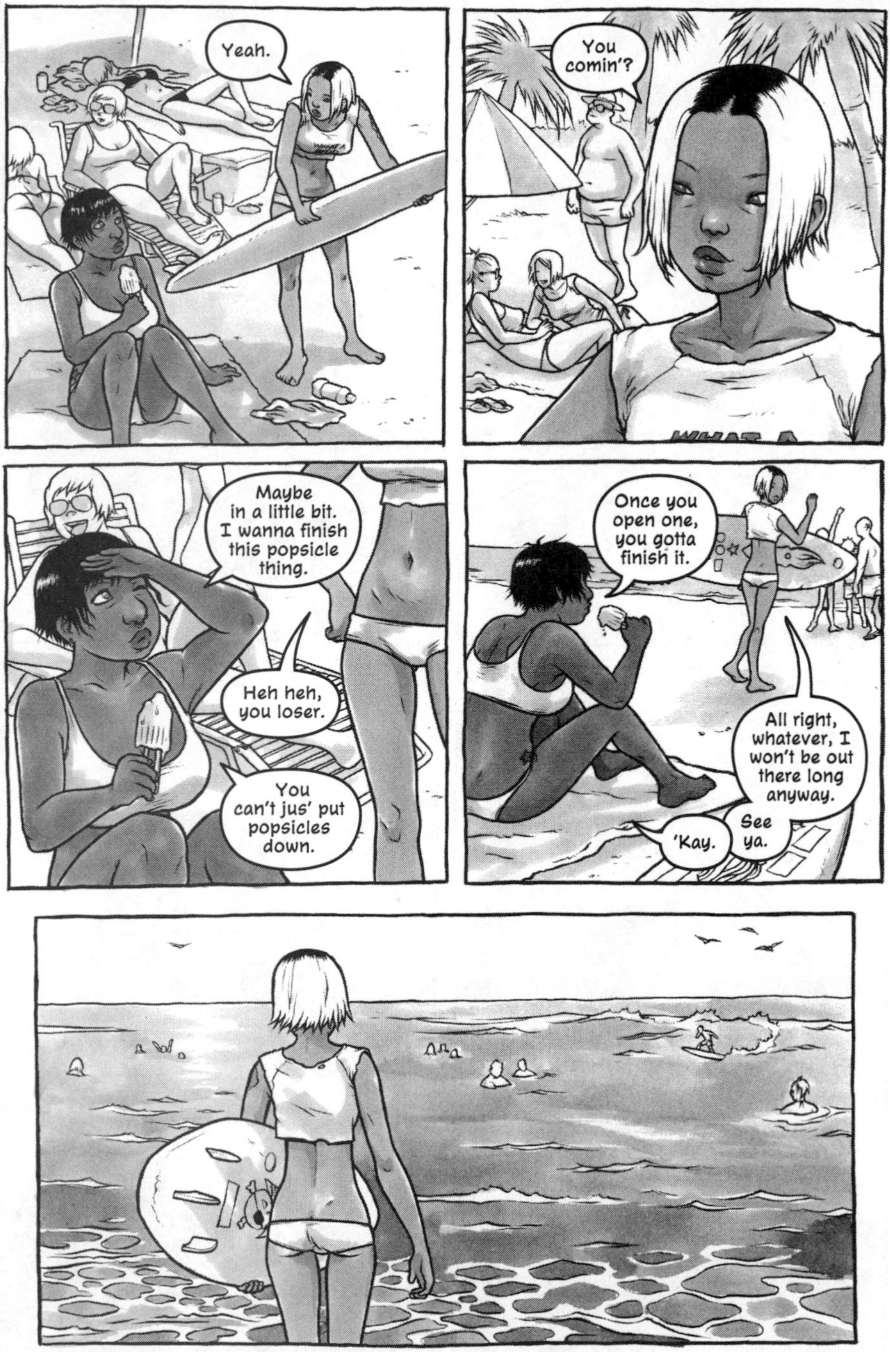
Yeah.
You comin'?
Maybe in a little bit. I wanna finish this popsicle thing.
Heh heh, you loser.
You can't jus' put popsicles down.
Once you open one, you gotta finish it.
All right, whatever, I won't be out there long anyway.
See ya.
'Kay.

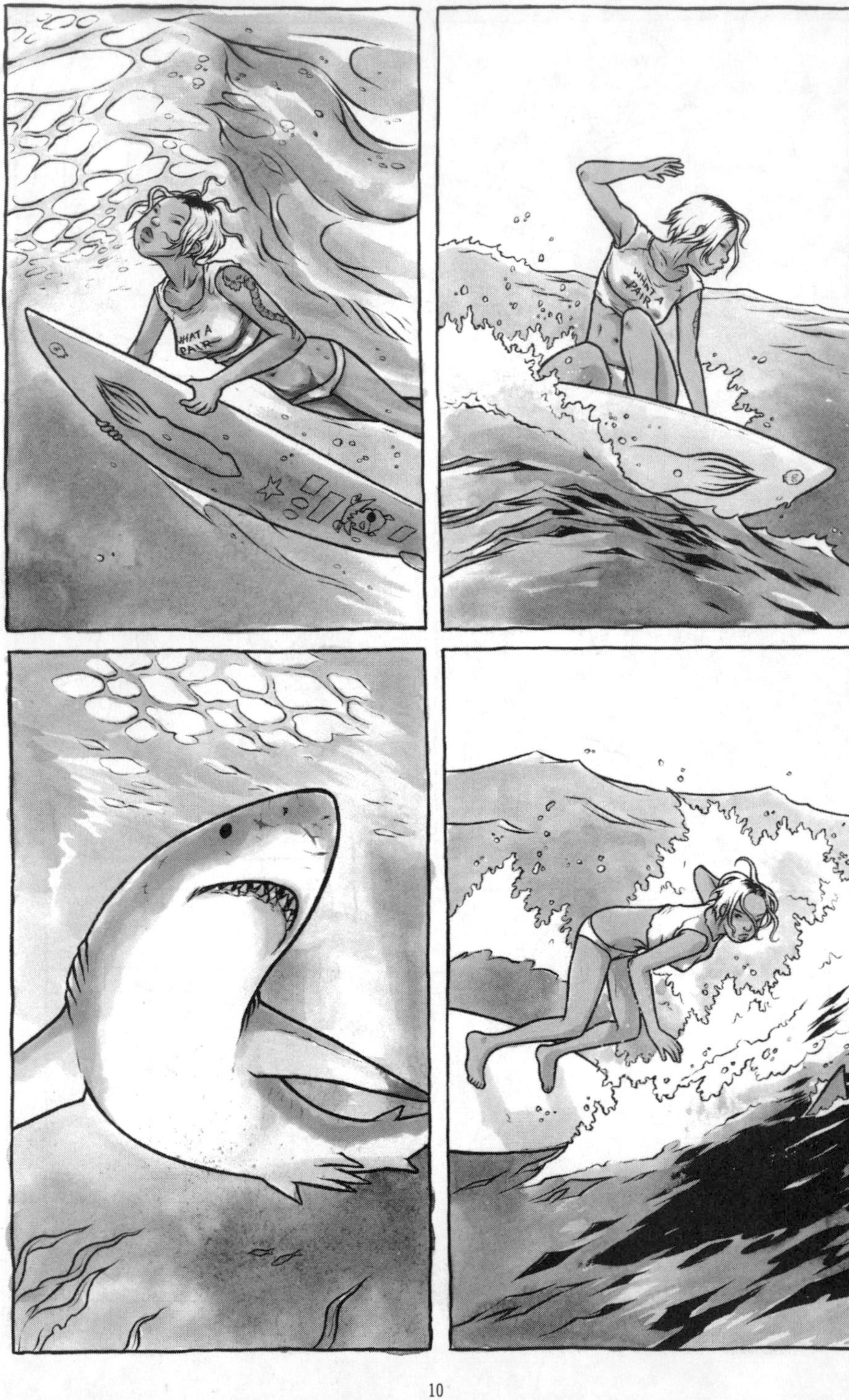
WHAT A PAIR
WHAT A PAIR

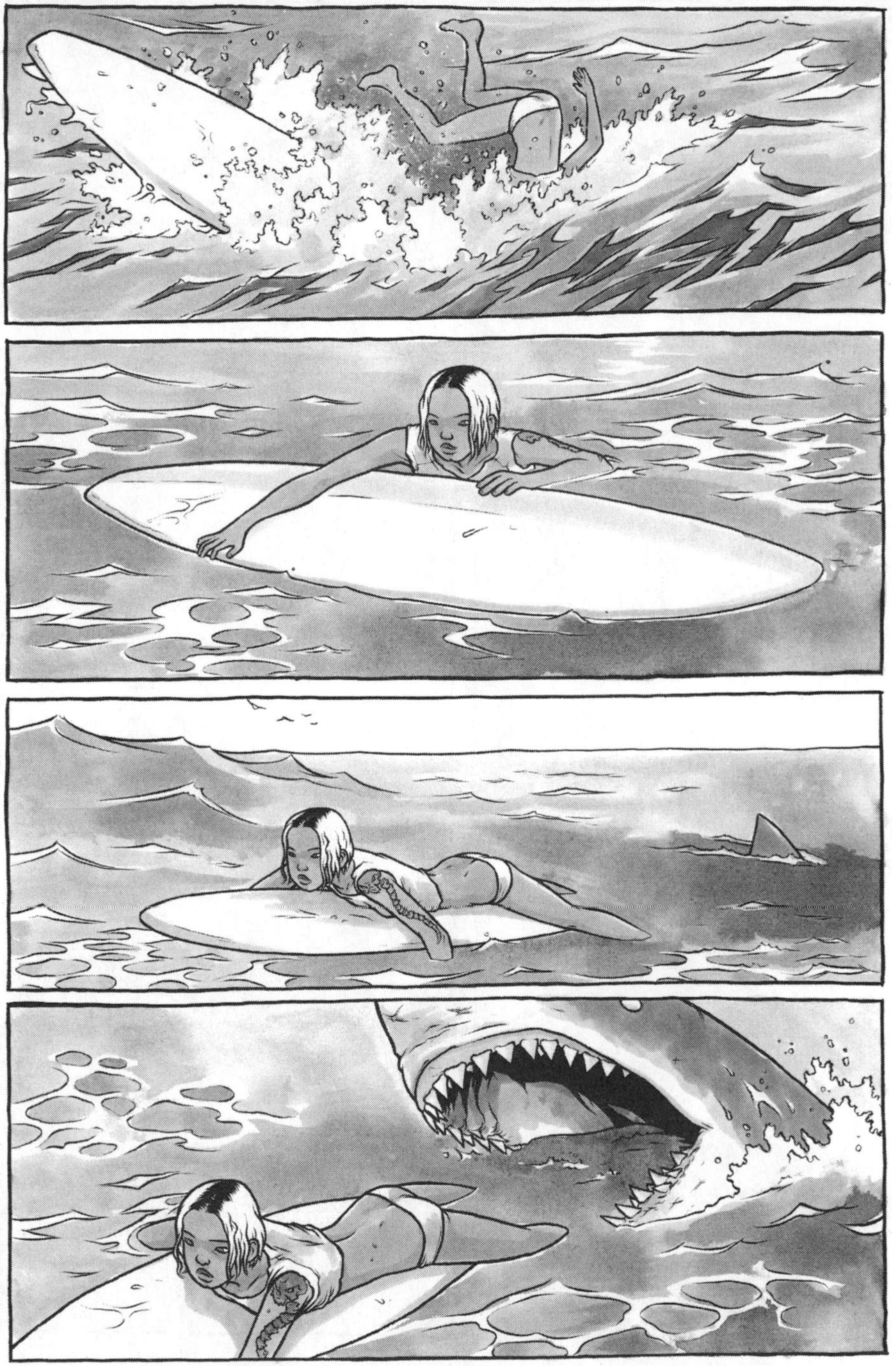

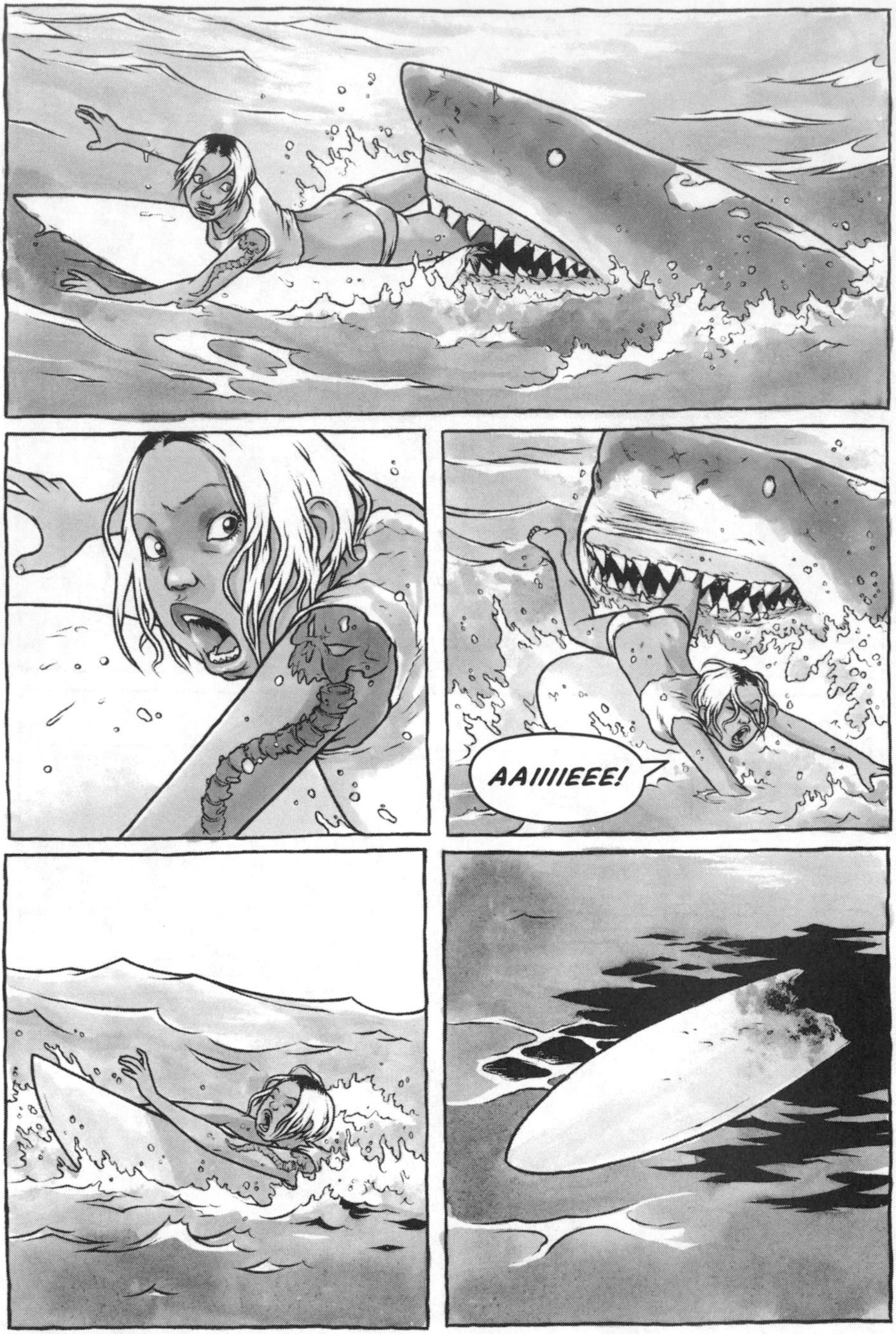
AAIIIIEEE!

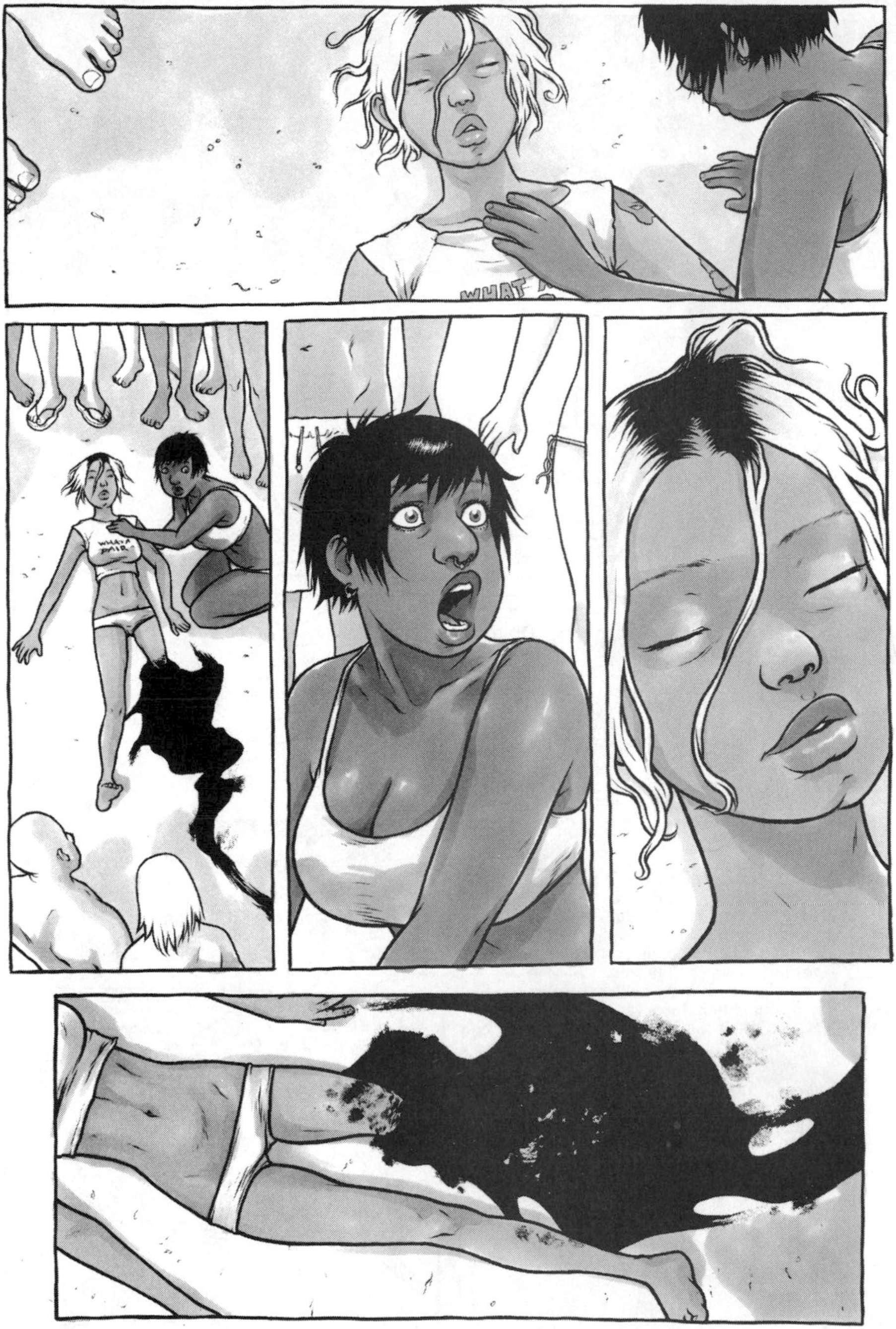
WHAT A PAIR

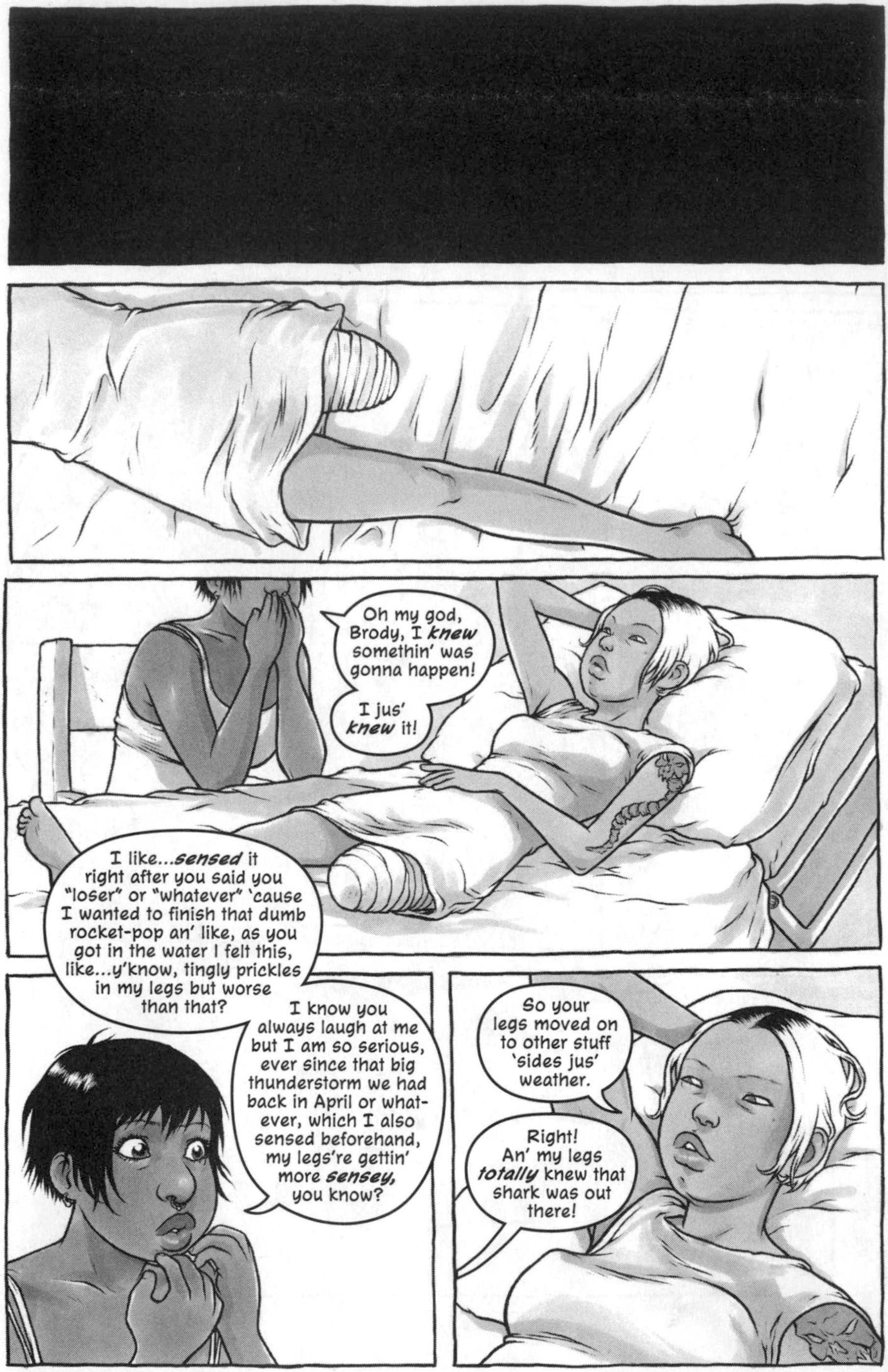

Oh my god, Brody, I *knew* somethin' was gonna happen!
I jus' *knew* it!
I like...*sensed* it right after you said you "loser" or "whatever" 'cause I wanted to finish that dumb rocket-pop an' like, as you got in the water I felt this, like...y'know, tingly prickles in my legs but worse than that?
I know you always laugh at me but I am so serious, ever since that big thunderstorm we had back in April or whatever, which I also sensed beforehand, my legs're gettin' more *sensey,* you know?
So your legs moved on to other stuff 'sides jus' weather.
Right! An' my legs *totally* knew that shark was out there!

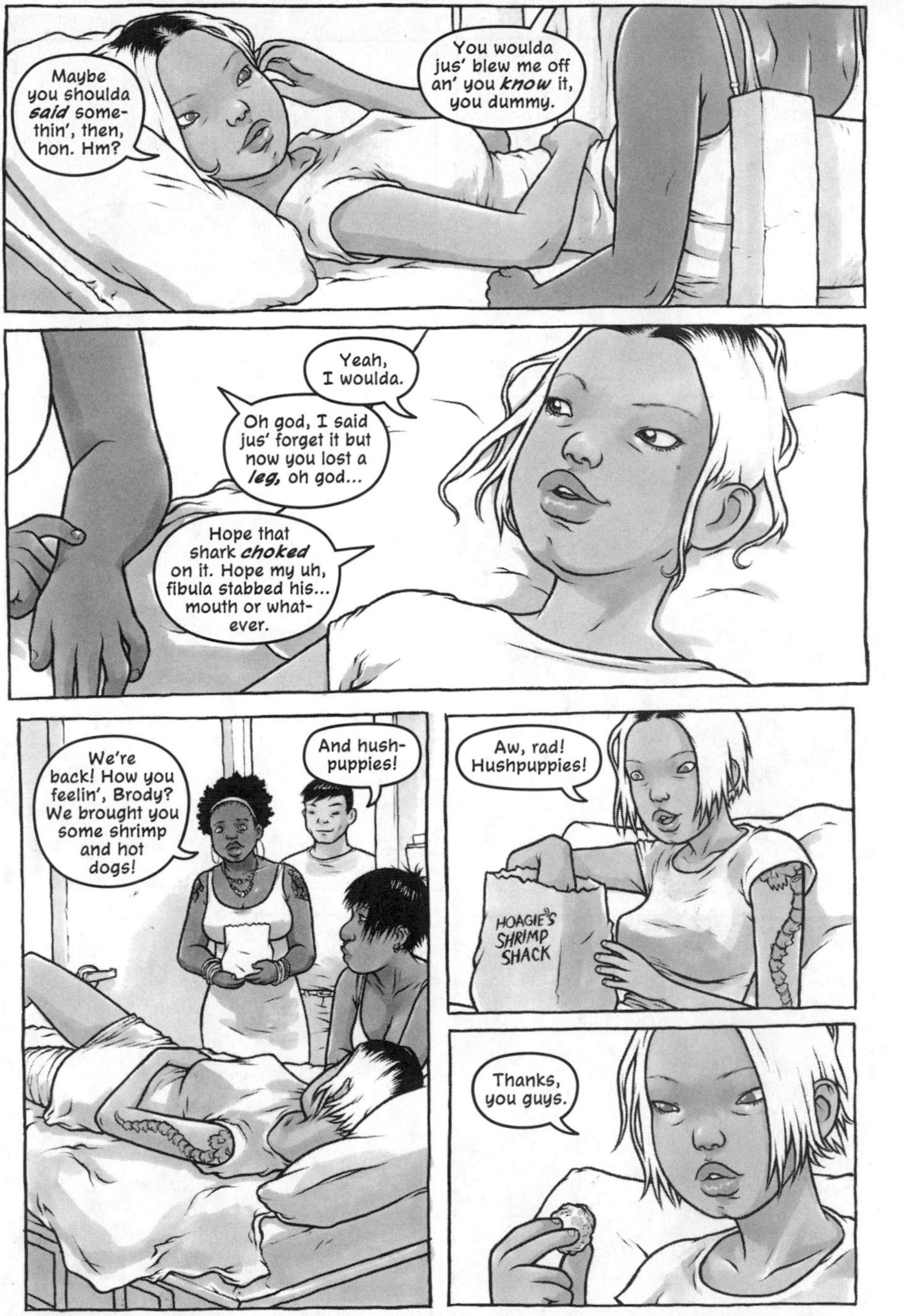
Maybe you shoulda said somethin', then, hon. Hm?
You woulda jus' blew me off an' you know it, you dummy.
Yeah, I woulda.
Oh god, I said jus' forget it but now you lost a leg, oh god...
Hope that shark choked on it. Hope my uh, fibula stabbed his... mouth or whatever.
We're back! How you feelin', Brody? We brought you some shrimp and hot dogs!
And hushpuppies!
Aw, rad! Hushpuppies!
HOAGIE'S SHRIMP SHACK
Thanks, you guys.

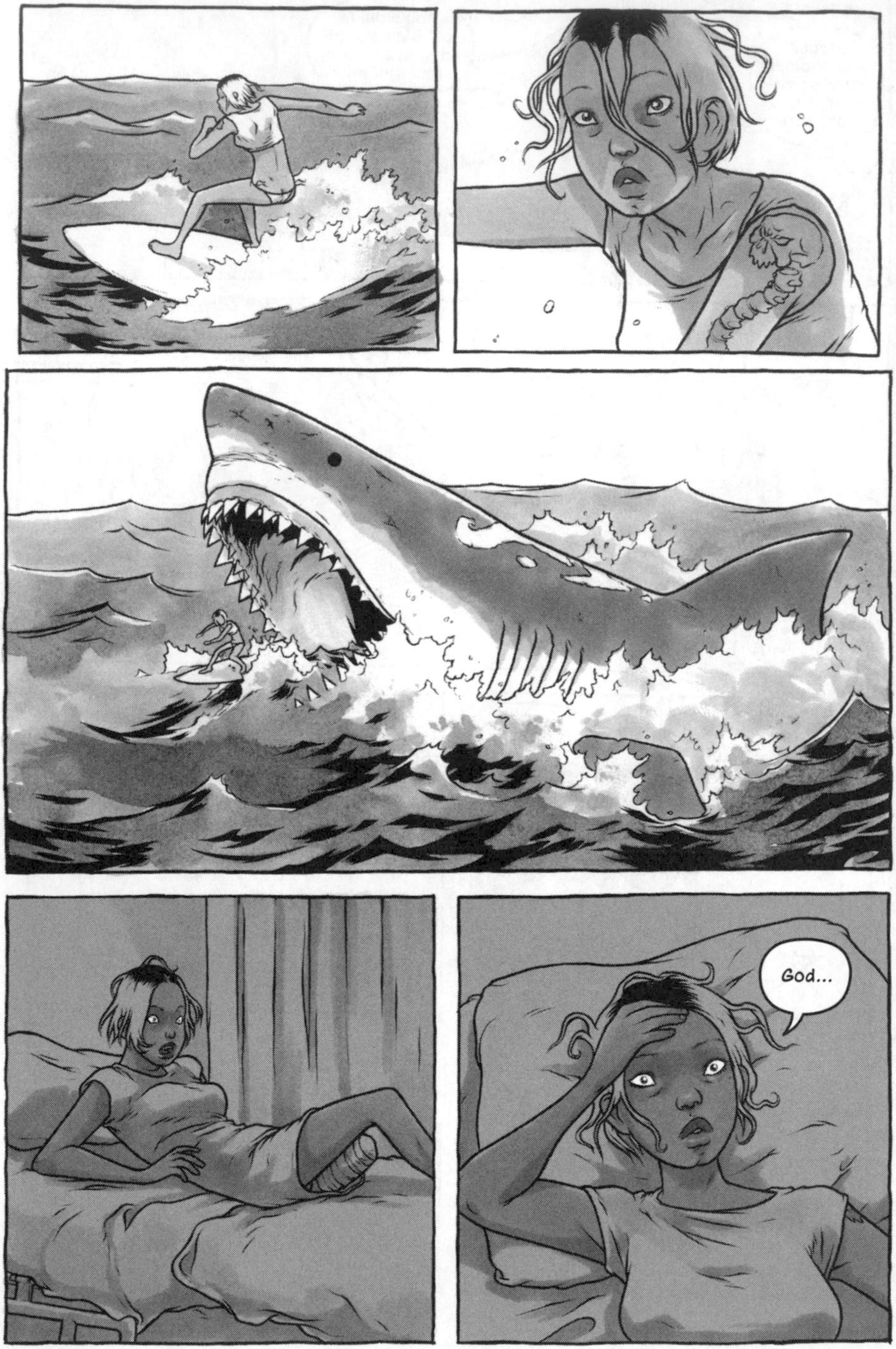
God...

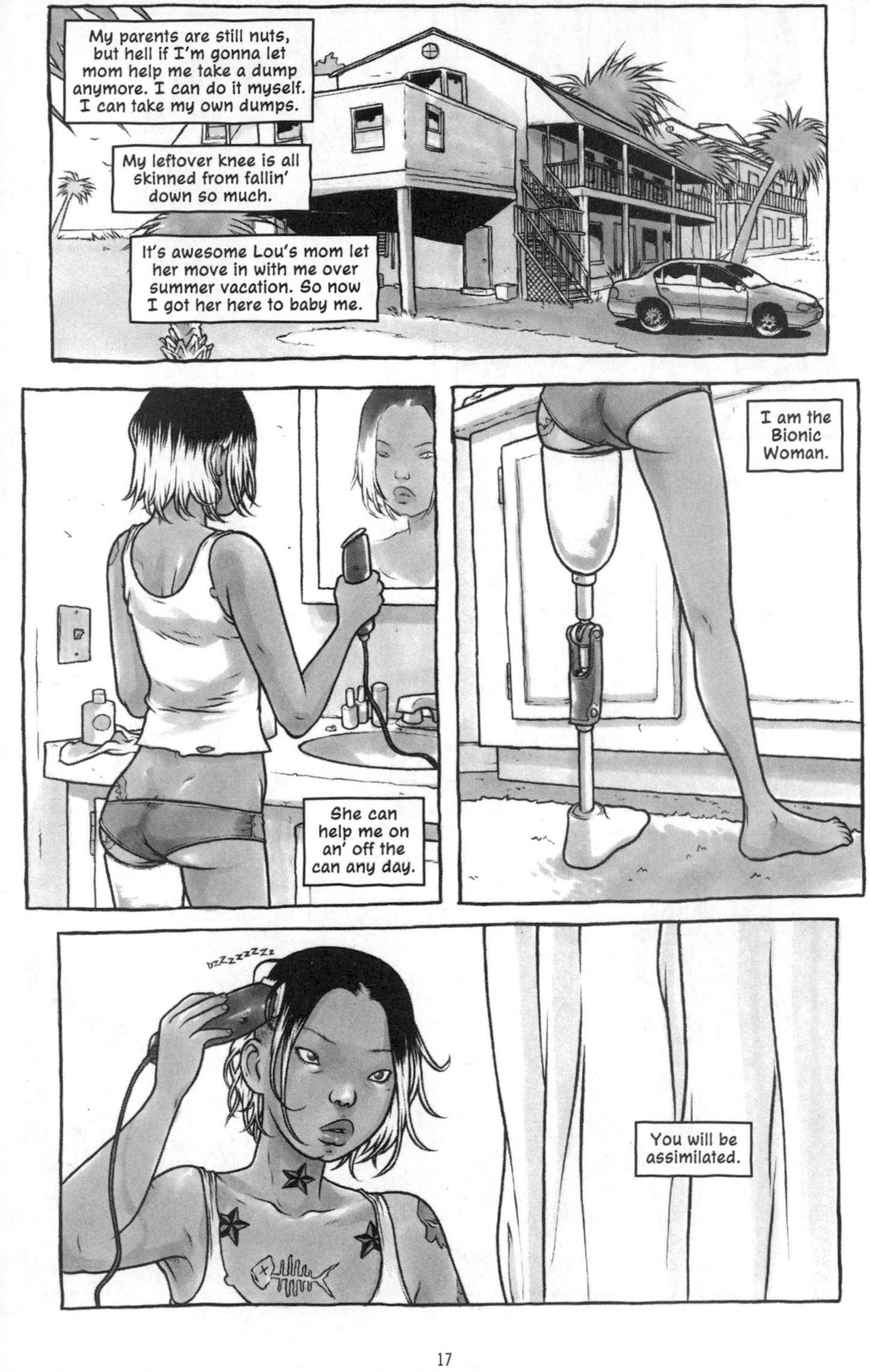
My parents are still nuts, but hell if I'm gonna let mom help me take a dump anymore. I can do it myself. I can take my own dumps.
My leftover knee is all skinned from fallin' down so much.
It's awesome Lou's mom let her move in with me over summer vacation. So now I got her here to baby me.
She can help me on an' off the can any day.
I am the Bionic Woman.
You will be assimilated.

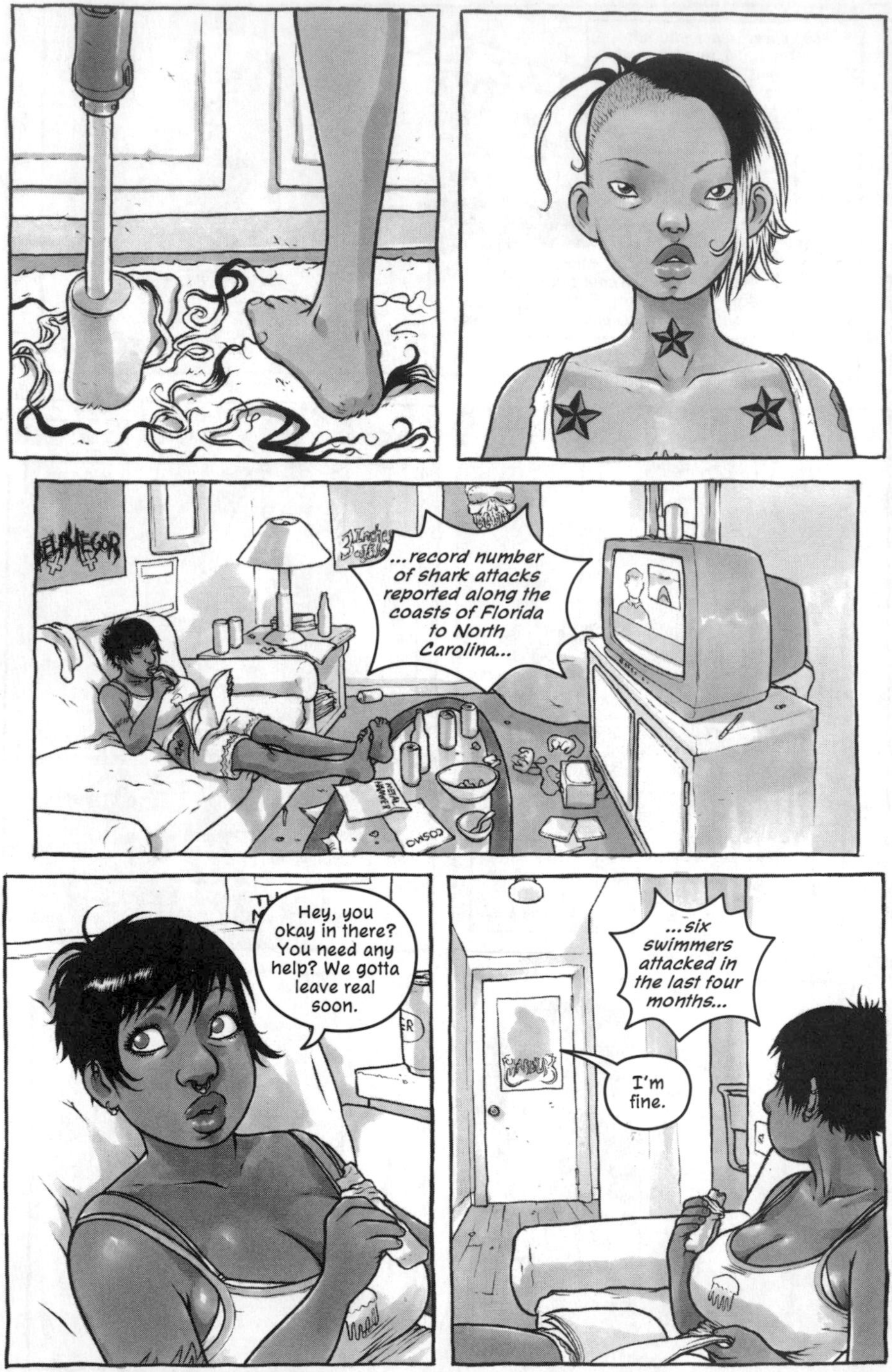
...record number of shark attacks reported along the coasts of Florida to North Carolina...
Hey, you okay in there? You need any help? We gotta leave real soon.
...six swimmers attacked in the last four months...
I'm fine.

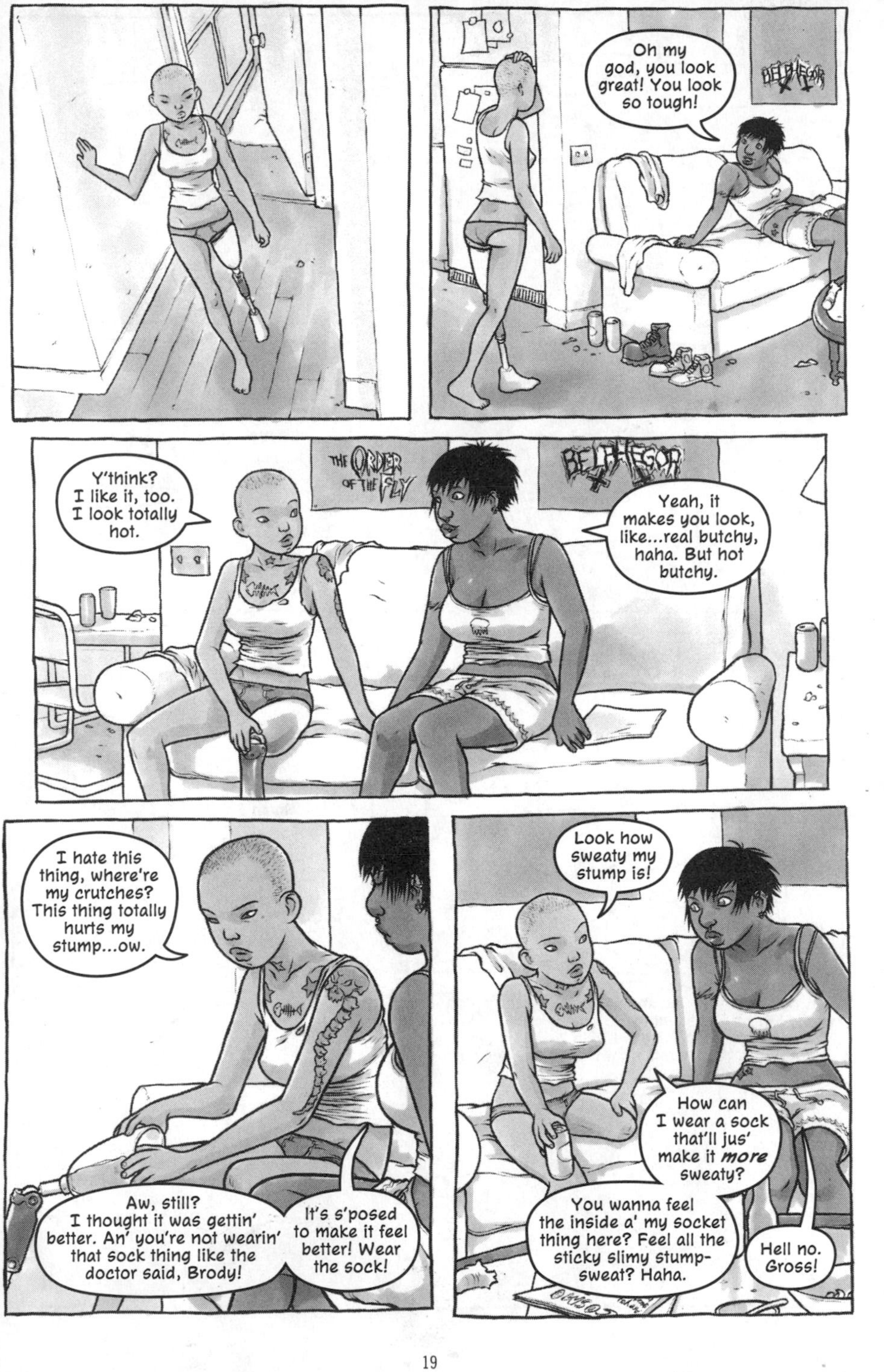
Oh my god, you look great! You look so tough!
BELPHEGOR
THE ORDER OF THE FLY
BELPHEGOR
Y'think? I like it, too. I look totally hot.
Yeah, it makes you look, like...real butchy, haha. But hot butchy.
I hate this thing, where're my crutches? This thing totally hurts my stump...ow.
Aw, still? I thought it was gettin' better. An' you're not wearin' that sock thing like the doctor said, Brody!
It's s'posed to make it feel better! Wear the sock!
Look how sweaty my stump is!
How can I wear a sock that'll jus' make it *more* sweaty?
You wanna feel the inside a' my socket thing here? Feel all the sticky slimy stump-sweat? Haha.
Hell no. Gross!

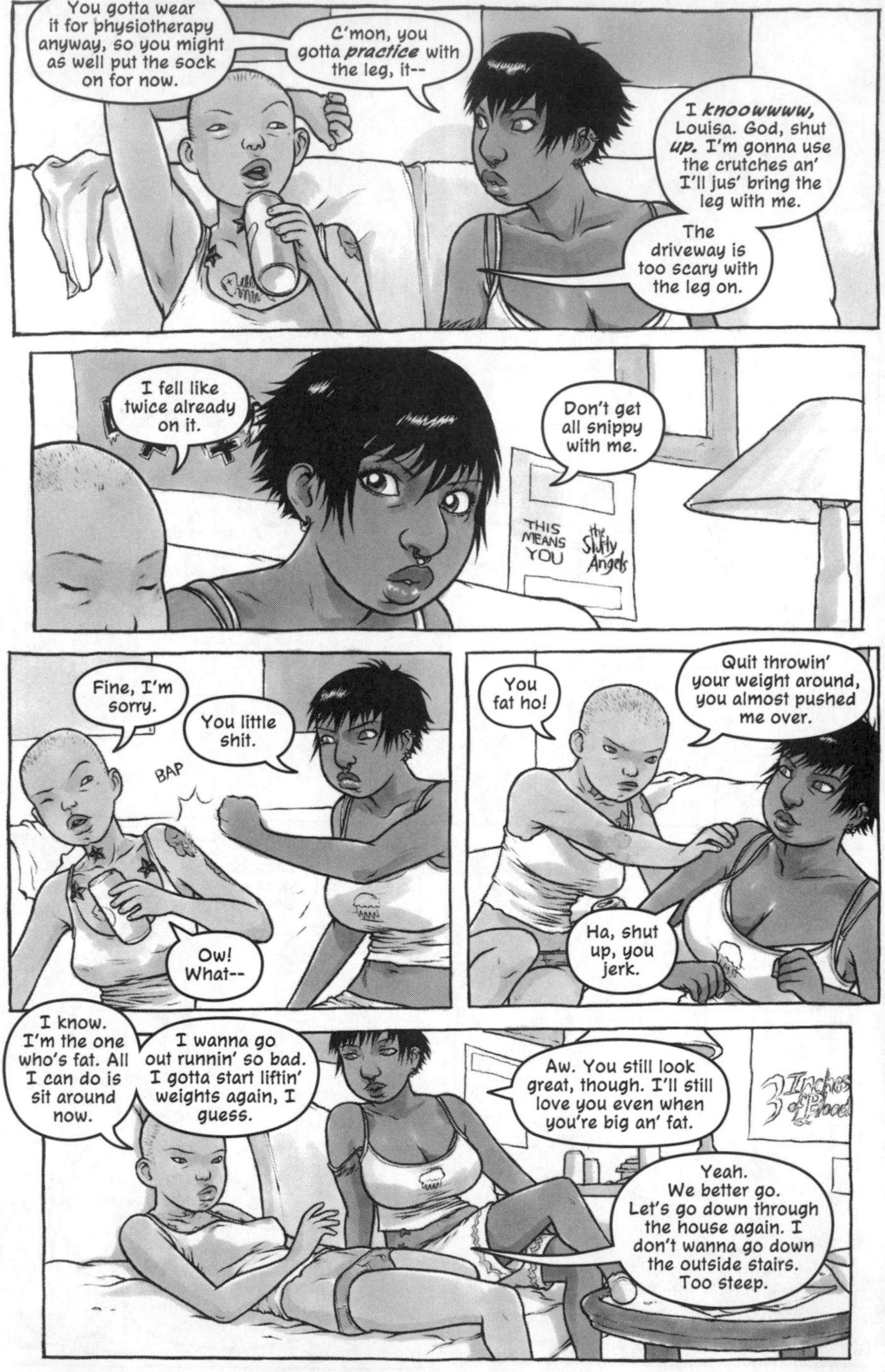
You gotta wear it for physiotherapy anyway, so you might as well put the sock on for now.
C'mon, you gotta *practice* with the leg, it--
I *knoowwww,* Louisa. God, shut *up.* I'm gonna use the crutches an' I'll jus' bring the leg with me.
The driveway is too scary with the leg on.
I fell like twice already on it.
Don't get all snippy with me.
THIS MEANS YOU
the Slutty Angels
Fine, I'm sorry.
You little shit.
BAP
Ow! What--
You fat ho!
Quit throwin' your weight around, you almost pushed me over.
Ha, shut up, you jerk.
I know. I'm the one who's fat. All I can do is sit around now.
I wanna go out runnin' so bad. I gotta start liftin' weights again, I guess.
Aw. You still look great, though. I'll still love you even when you're big an' fat.
Yeah. We better go. Let's go down through the house again. I don't wanna go down the outside stairs. Too steep.

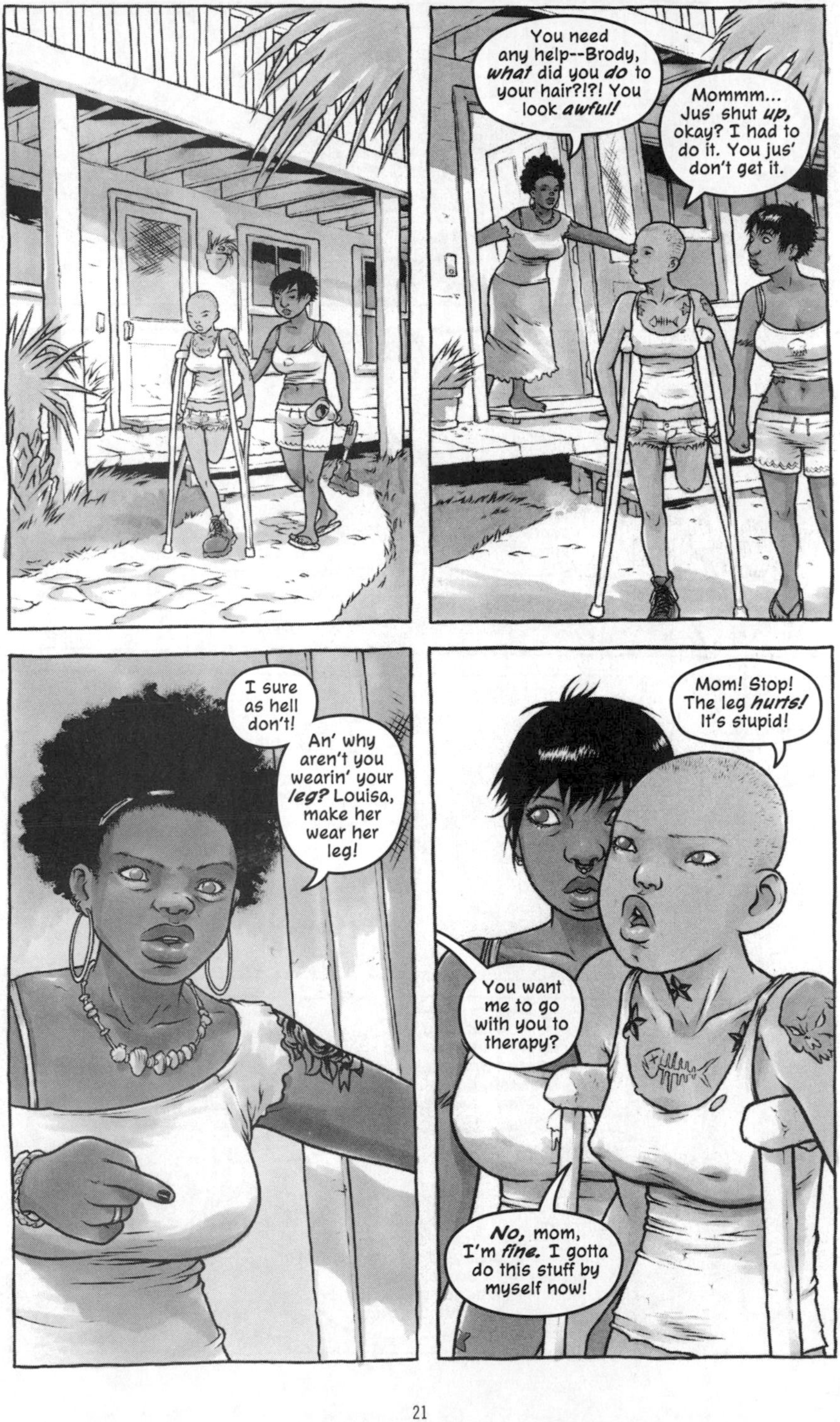
You need any help--Brody, *what* did you *do* to your hair?!?! You look *awful!*
Mommm... Jus' shut *up,* okay? I had to do it. You jus' don't get it.
I sure as hell don't!
An' why aren't you wearin' your *leg?* Louisa, make her wear her leg!
Mom! Stop! The leg *hurts!* It's stupid!
You want me to go with you to therapy?
No, mom, I'm *fine.* I gotta do this stuff by myself now!

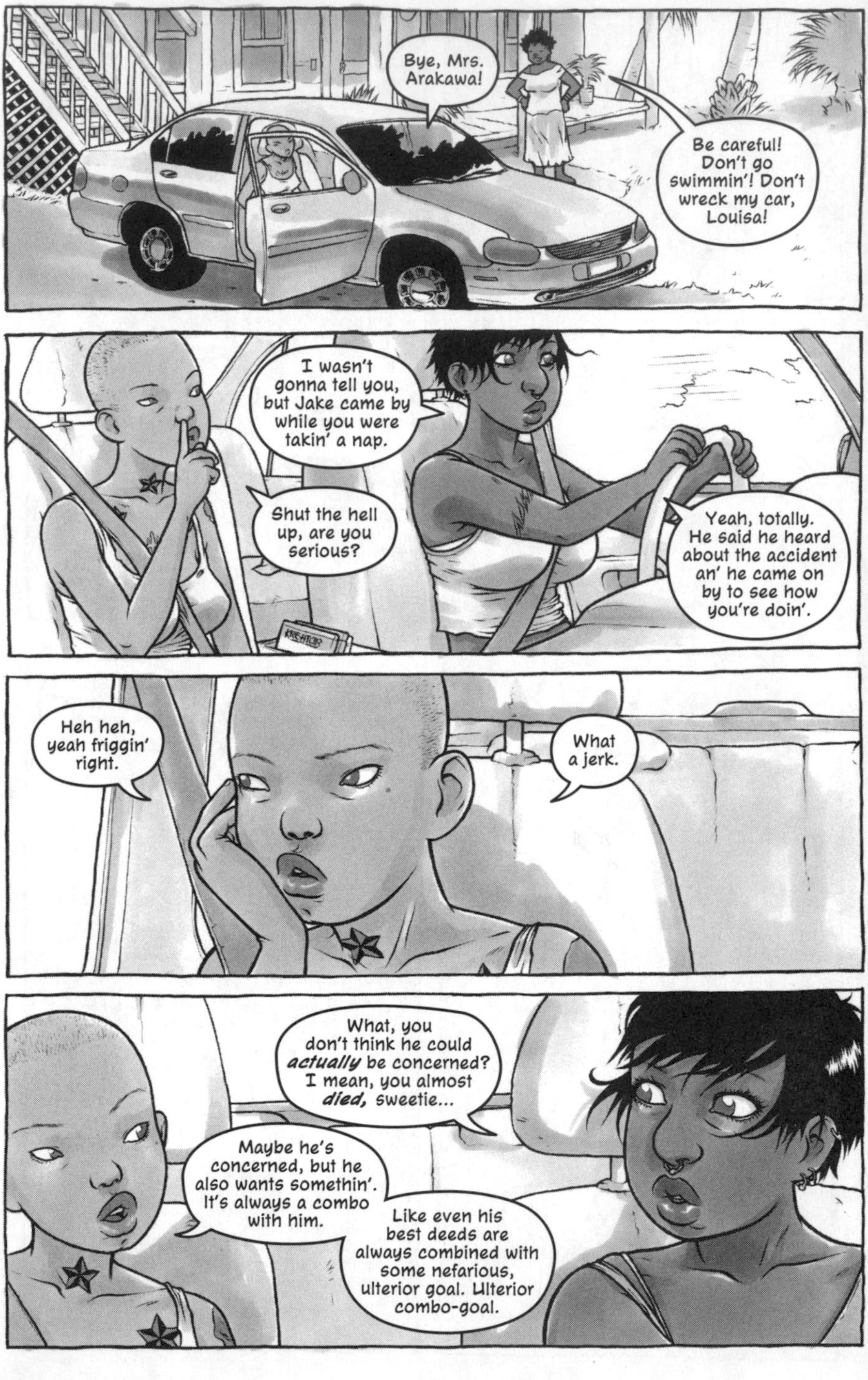
Bye, Mrs. Arakawa!
Be careful! Don't go swimmin'! Don't wreck my car, Louisa!
I wasn't gonna tell you, but Jake came by while you were takin' a nap.
Shut the hell up, are you serious?
Yeah, totally. He said he heard about the accident an' he came on by to see how you're doin'.
Heh heh, yeah friggin' right.
What a jerk.
What, you don't think he could *actually* be concerned? I mean, you almost *died,* sweetie...
Maybe he's concerned, but he also wants somethin'. It's always a combo with him.
Like even his best deeds are always combined with some nefarious, ulterior goal. Ulterior combo-goal.

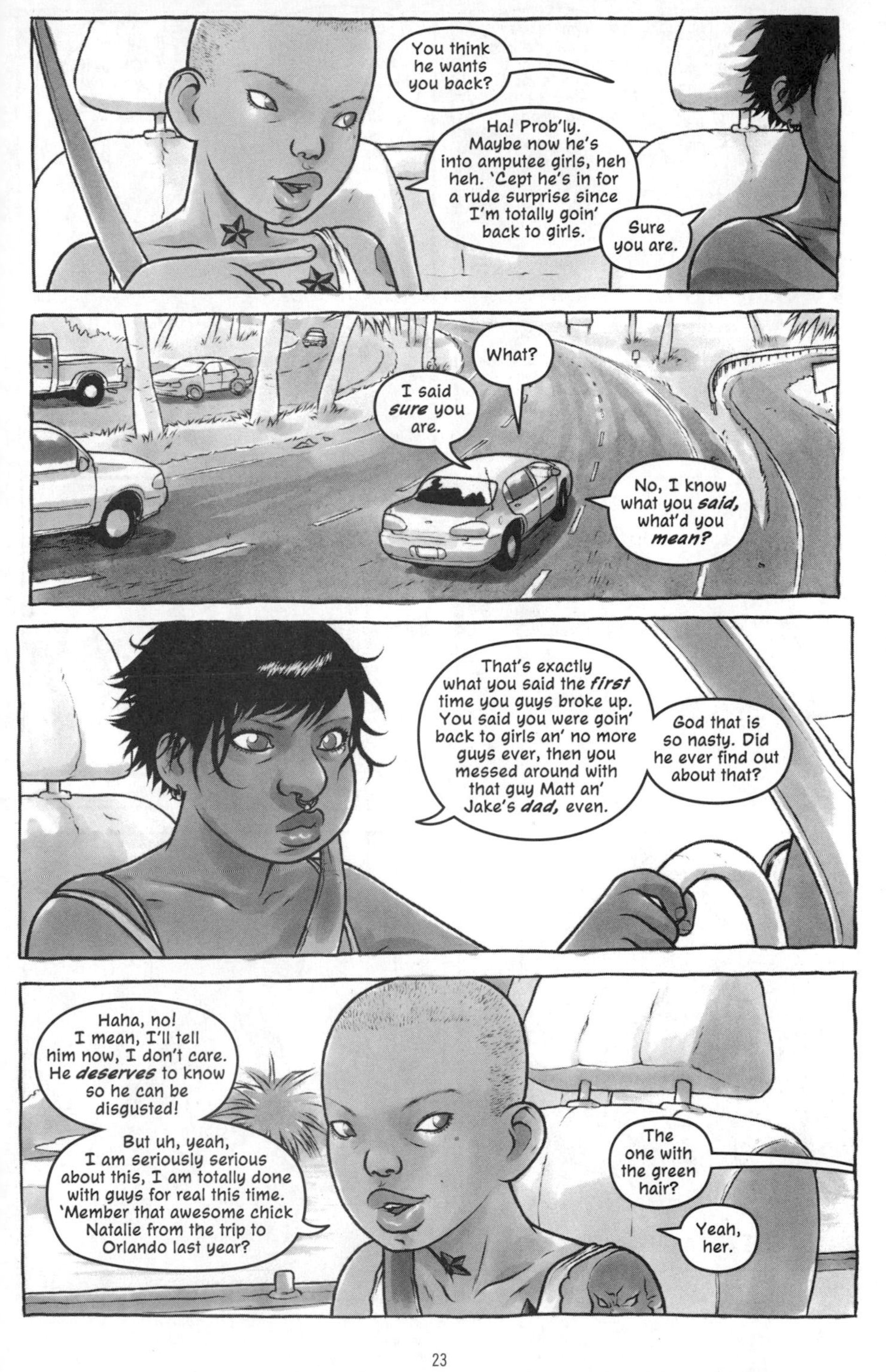
You think he wants you back?
Ha! Prob'ly. Maybe now he's into amputee girls, heh heh. 'Cept he's in for a rude surprise since I'm totally goin' back to girls.
Sure you are.
What?
I said sure you are.
No, I know what you said, what'd you mean?
That's exactly what you said the first time you guys broke up. You said you were goin' back to girls an' no more guys ever, then you messed around with that guy Matt an' Jake's dad, even.
God that is so nasty. Did he ever find out about that?
Haha, no! I mean, I'll tell him now, I don't care. He deserves to know so he can be disgusted!
But uh, yeah, I am seriously serious about this, I am totally done with guys for real this time. 'Member that awesome chick Natalie from the trip to Orlando last year?
The one with the green hair?
Yeah, her.

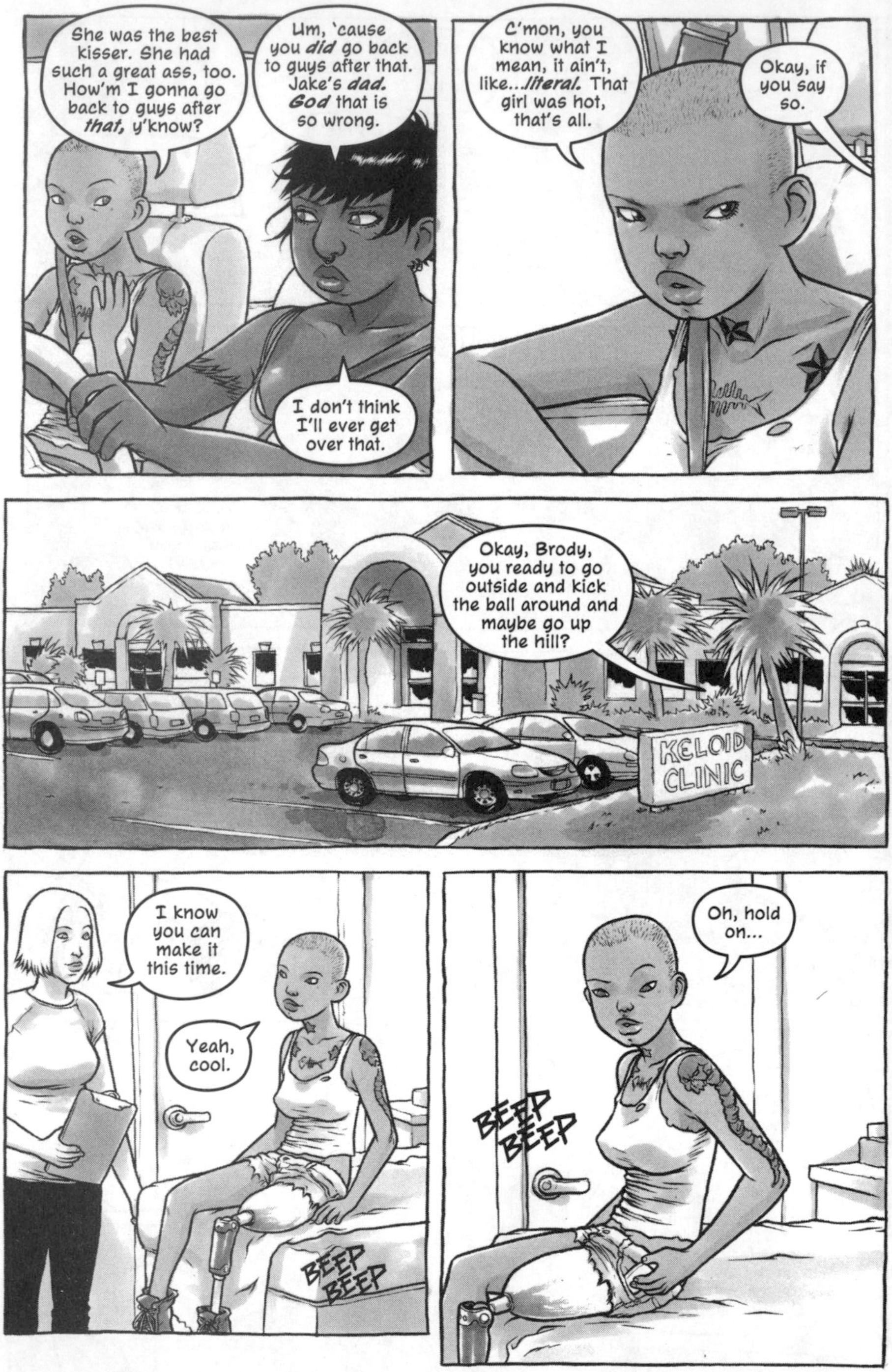
She was the best kisser. She had such a great ass, too. How'm I gonna go back to guys after *that,* y'know?
Um, 'cause you *did* go back to guys after that. Jake's *dad. God* that is so wrong.
I don't think I'll ever get over that.
C'mon, you know what I mean, it ain't, like...*literal.* That girl was hot, that's all.
Okay, if you say so.
Okay, Brody, you ready to go outside and kick the ball around and maybe go up the hill?
KELOID CLINIC
I know you can make it this time.
Yeah, cool.
BEEP BEEP
Oh, hold on...
BEEP BEEP

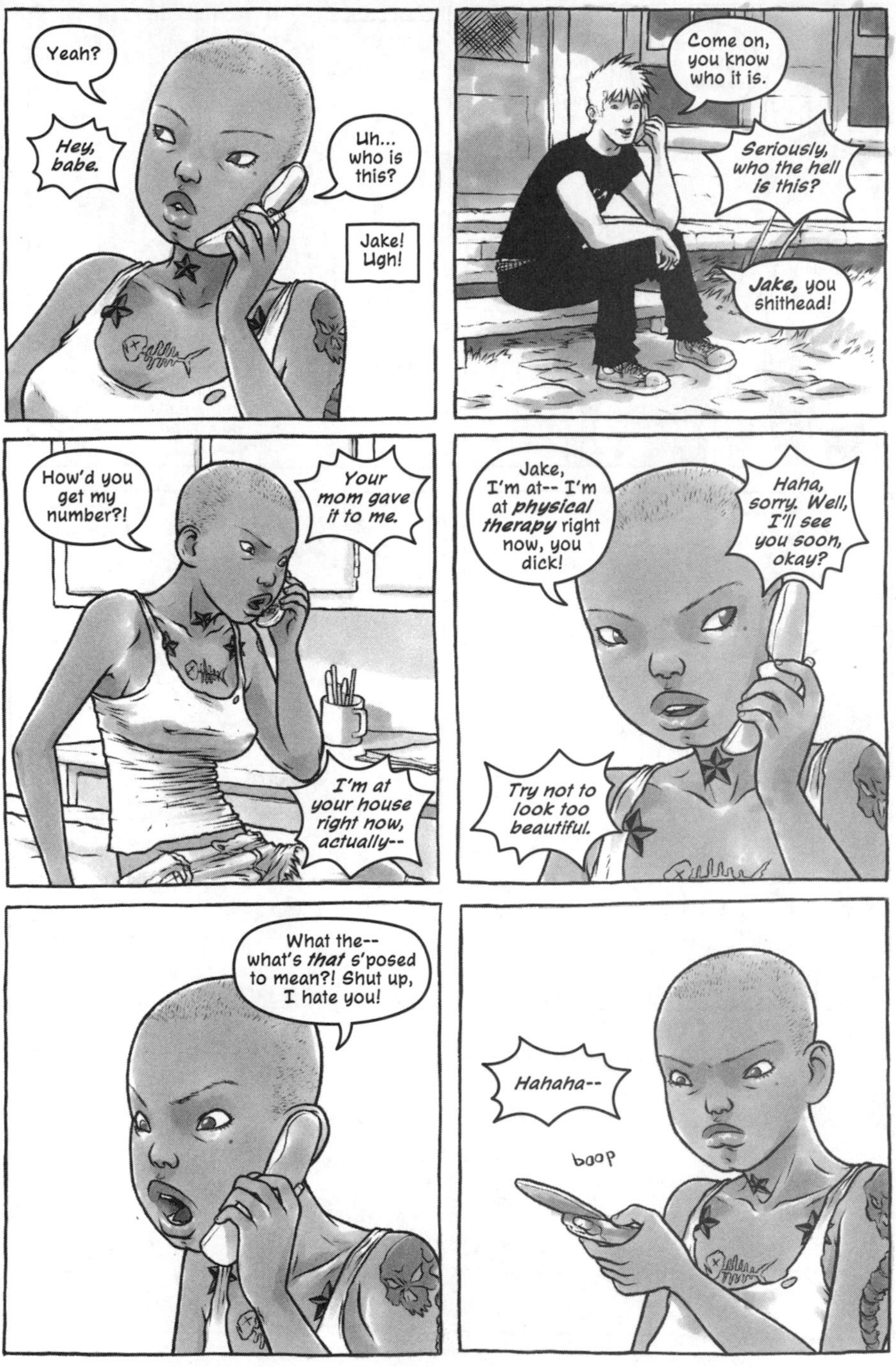

Yeah?
Hey, babe.
Uh... who is this?
Jake! Ugh!
Come on, you know who it is.
Seriously, who the hell is this?
Jake, you shithead!
How'd you get my number?!
Your mom gave it to me.
I'm at your house right now, actually--
Jake, I'm at-- I'm at physical therapy right now, you dick!
Haha, sorry. Well, I'll see you soon, okay?
Try not to look too beautiful.
What the-- what's that s'posed to mean?! Shut up, I hate you!
Hahaha--
boop

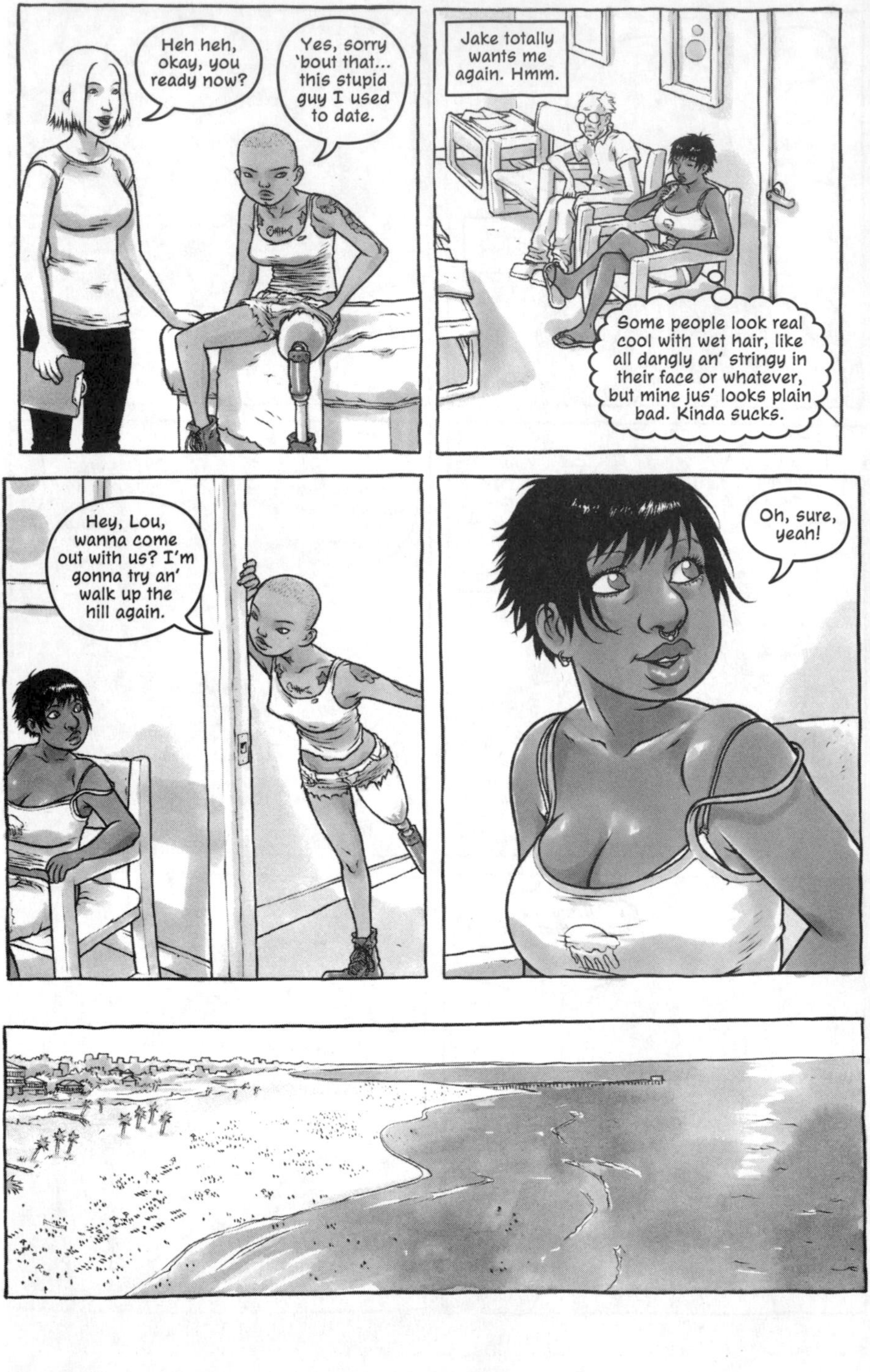
Heh heh, okay, you ready now?
Yes, sorry 'bout that... this stupid guy I used to date.
Jake totally wants me again. Hmm.
Some people look real cool with wet hair, like all dangly an' stringy in their face or whatever, but mine jus' looks plain bad. Kinda sucks.
Hey, Lou, wanna come out with us? I'm gonna try an' walk up the hill again.
Oh, sure, yeah!

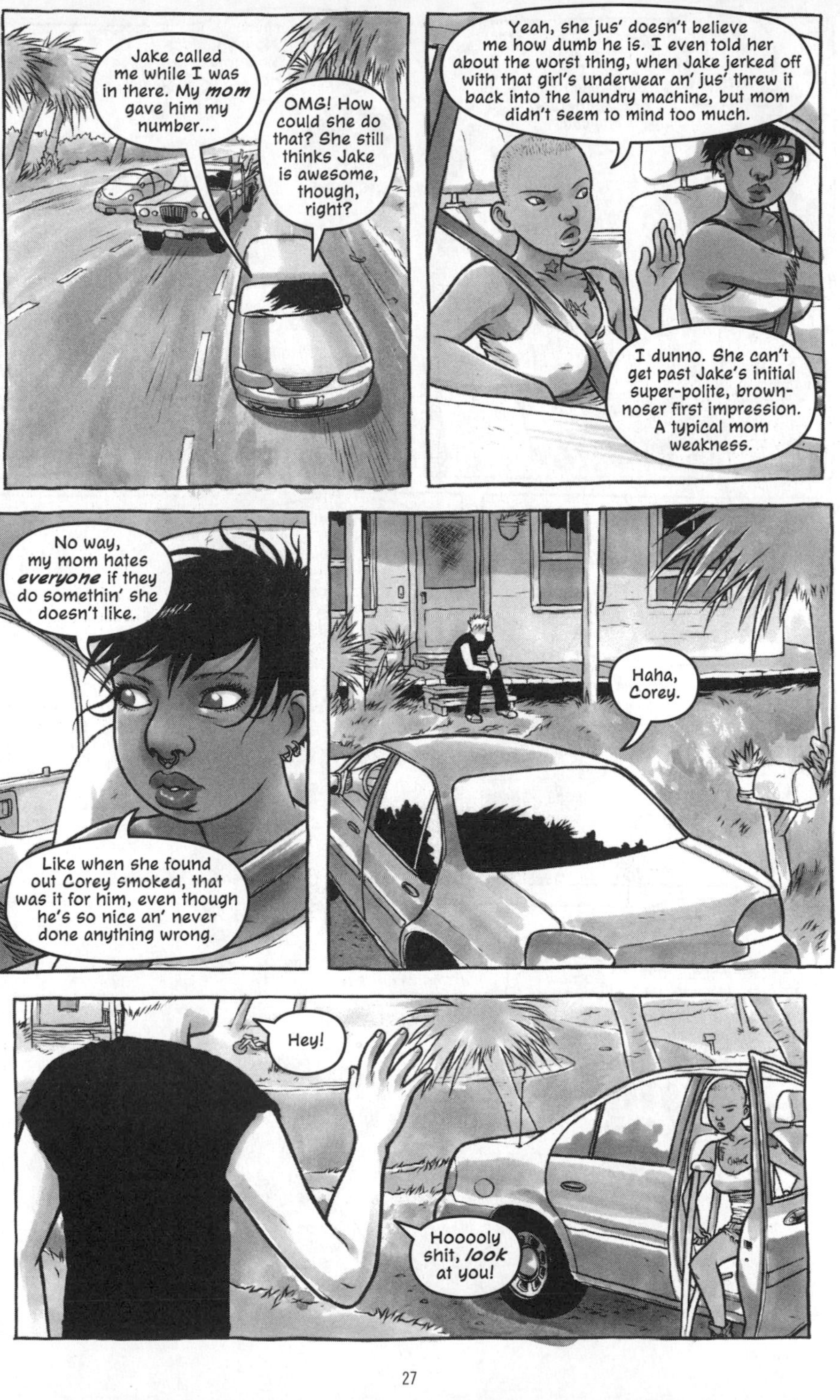
Jake called me while I was in there. My *mom* gave him my number...
OMG! How could she do that? She still thinks Jake is awesome, though, right?
Yeah, she jus' doesn't believe me how dumb he is. I even told her about the worst thing, when Jake jerked off with that girl's underwear an' jus' threw it back into the laundry machine, but mom didn't seem to mind too much.
I dunno. She can't get past Jake's initial super-polite, brown-noser first impression. A typical mom weakness.
No way, my mom hates *everyone* if they do somethin' she doesn't like.
Like when she found out Corey smoked, that was it for him, even though he's so nice an' never done anything wrong.
Haha, Corey.
Hey!
Hoooooly shit, *look* at you!

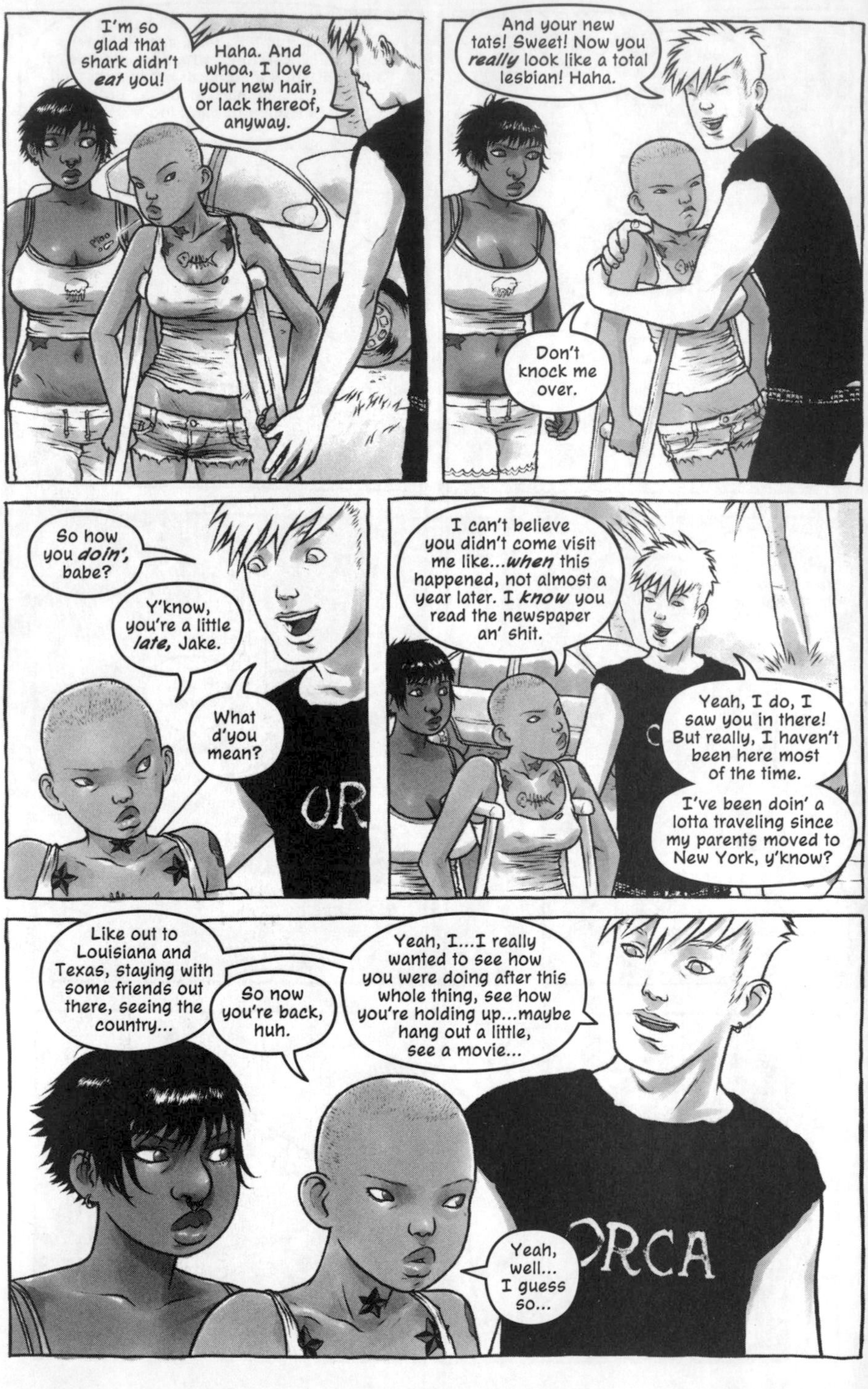
I'm so glad that shark didn't *eat* you!
Haha. And whoa, I love your new hair, or lack thereof, anyway.
And your new tats! Sweet! Now you *really* look like a total lesbian! Haha.
Don't knock me over.
So how you *doin'*, babe?
Y'know, you're a little *late*, Jake.
What d'you mean?
ORC
I can't believe you didn't come visit me like...*when* this happened, not almost a year later. I *know* you read the newspaper an' shit.
Yeah, I do, I saw you in there! But really, I haven't been here most of the time.
I've been doin' a lotta traveling since my parents moved to New York, y'know?
Like out to Louisiana and Texas, staying with some friends out there, seeing the country...
So now you're back, huh.
Yeah, I...I really wanted to see how you were doing after this whole thing, see how you're holding up...maybe hang out a little, see a movie...
ORCA
Yeah, well... I guess so...

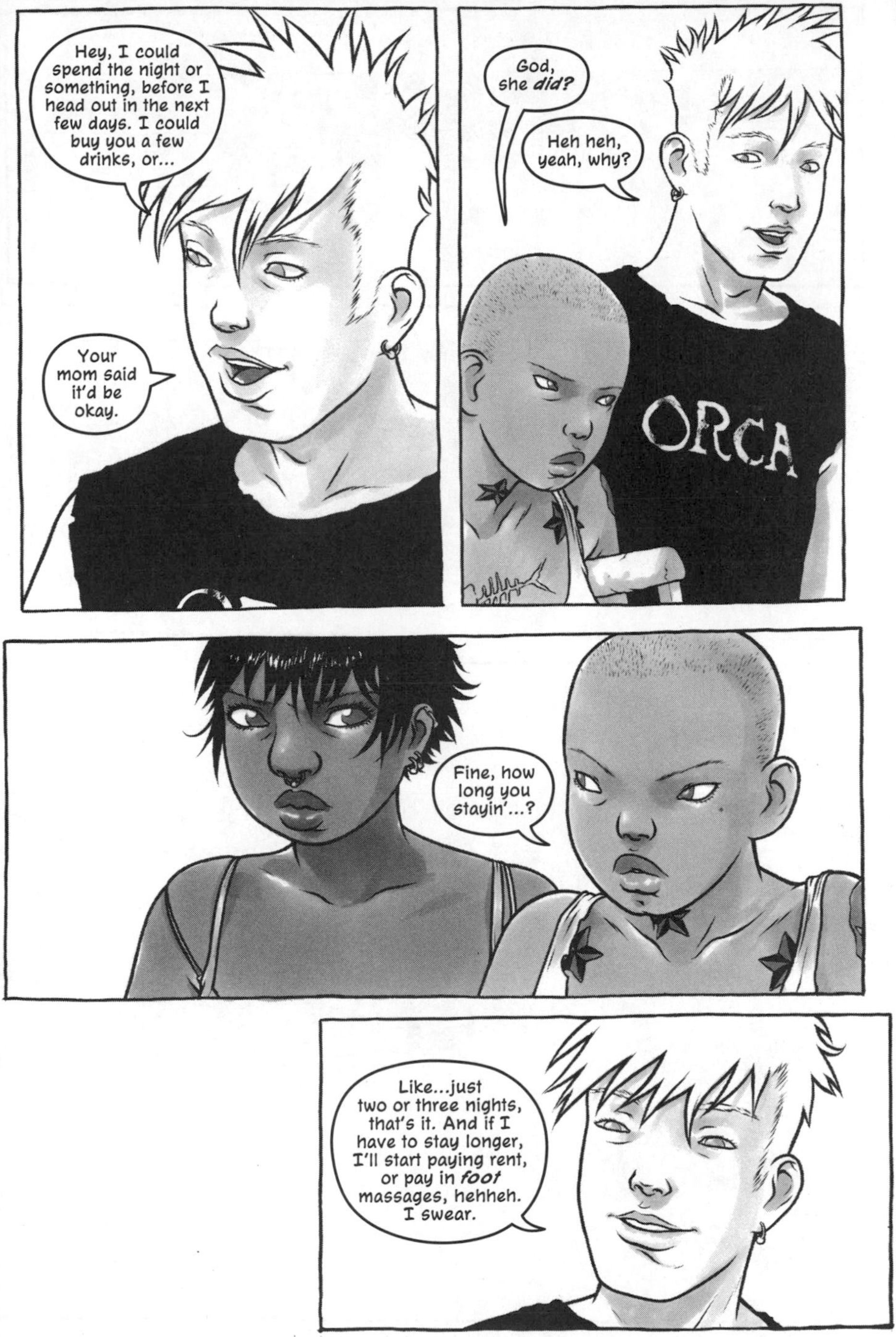
Hey, I could spend the night or something, before I head out in the next few days. I could buy you a few drinks, or...
Your mom said it'd be okay.
God, she *did?*
Heh heh, yeah, why?
ORCA
Fine, how long you stayin'...?
Like...just two or three nights, that's it. And if I have to stay longer, I'll start paying rent, or pay in *foot* massages, hehheh. I swear.

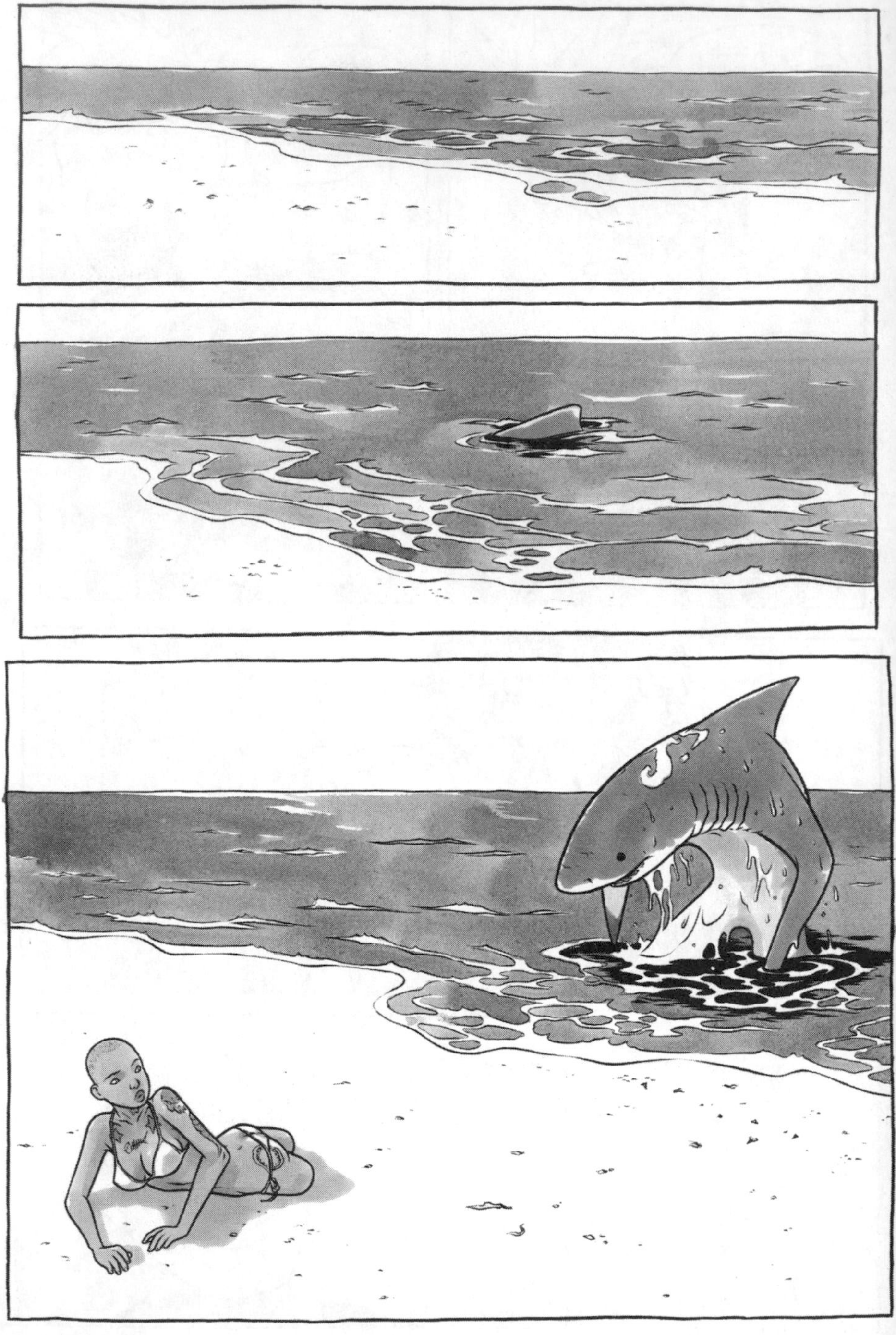

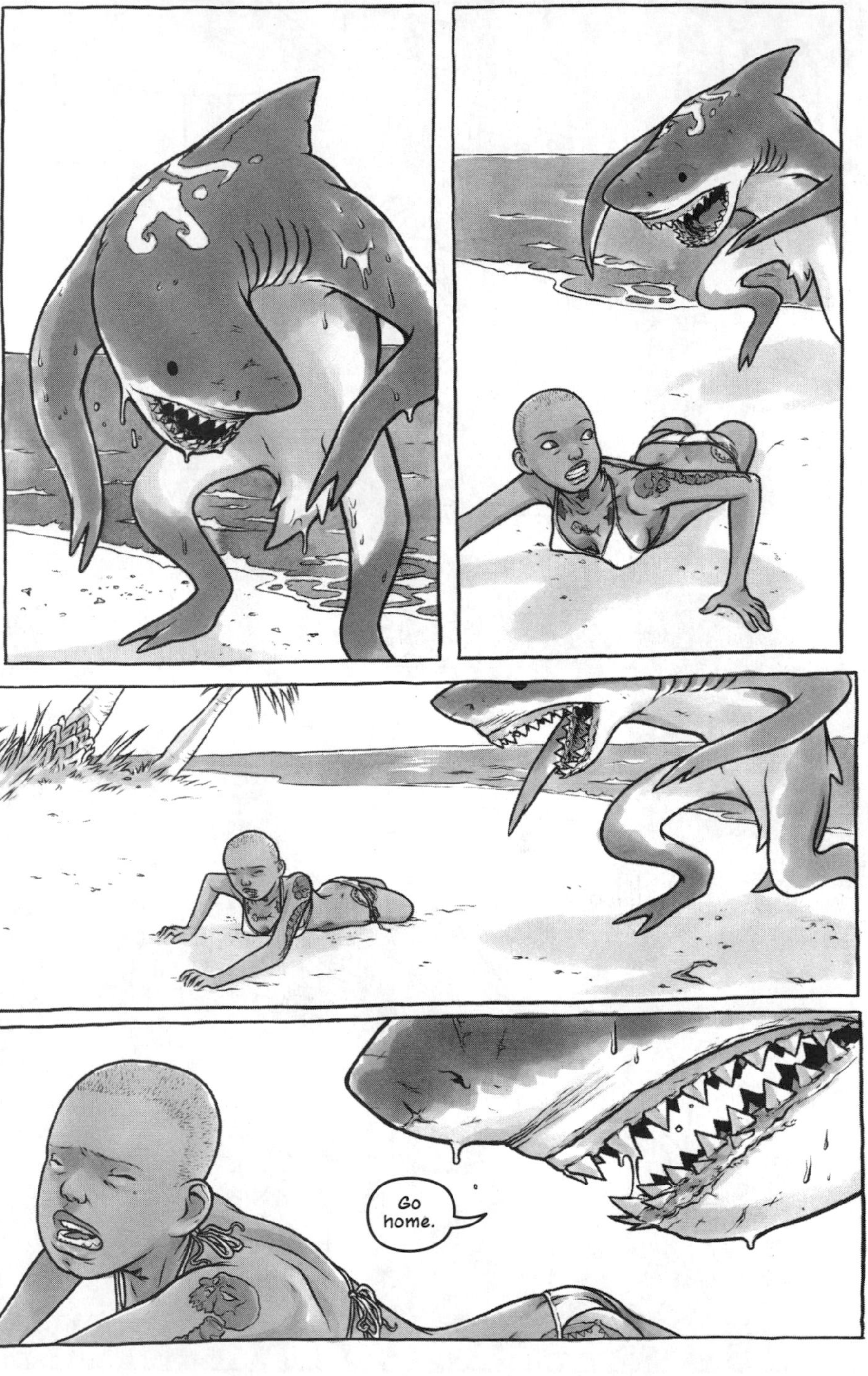
Go home.

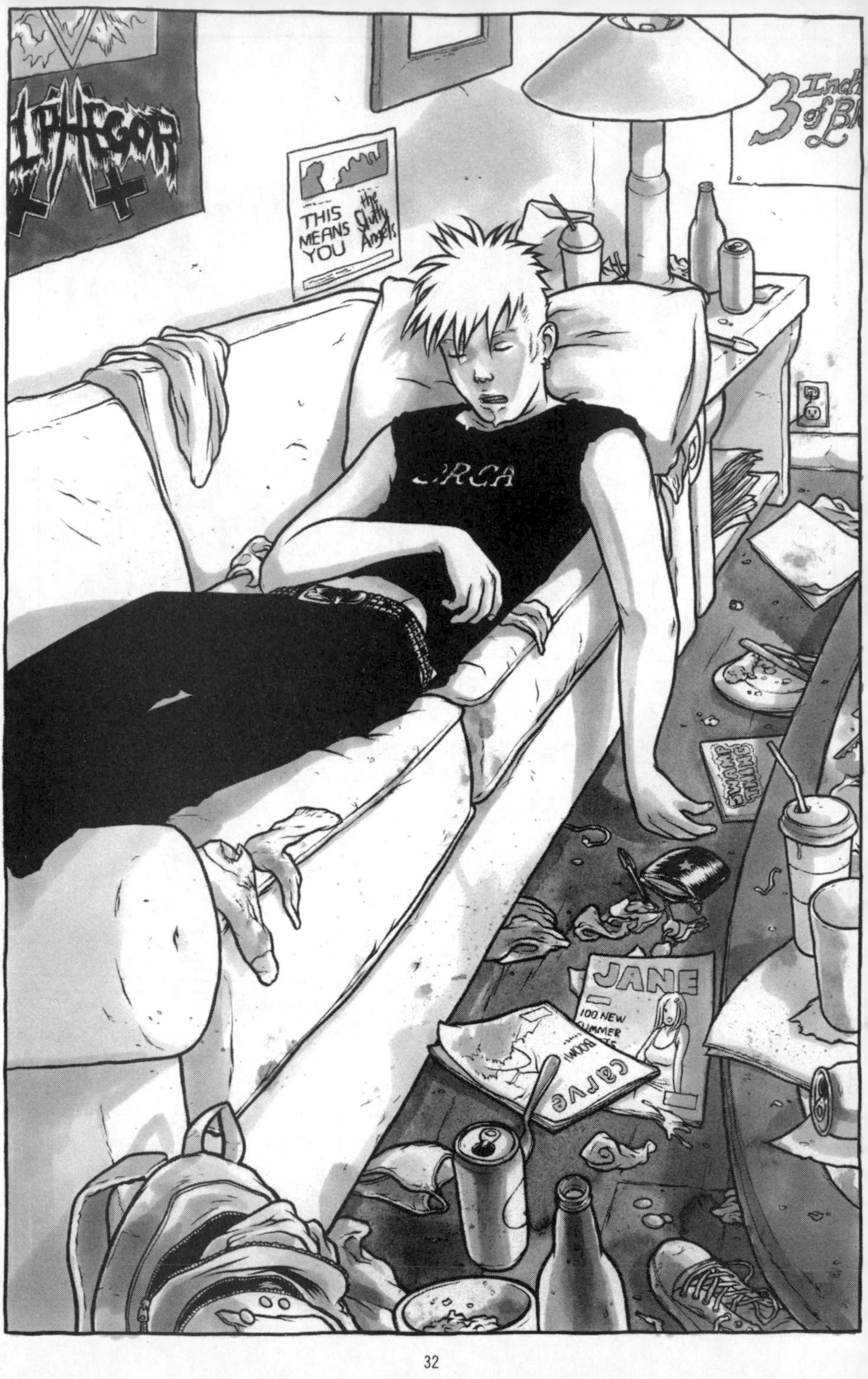
THIS
MEANS
YOU
the Slutty Angels
SWAMP THING
JANE
100 NEW
carve
BOOM!

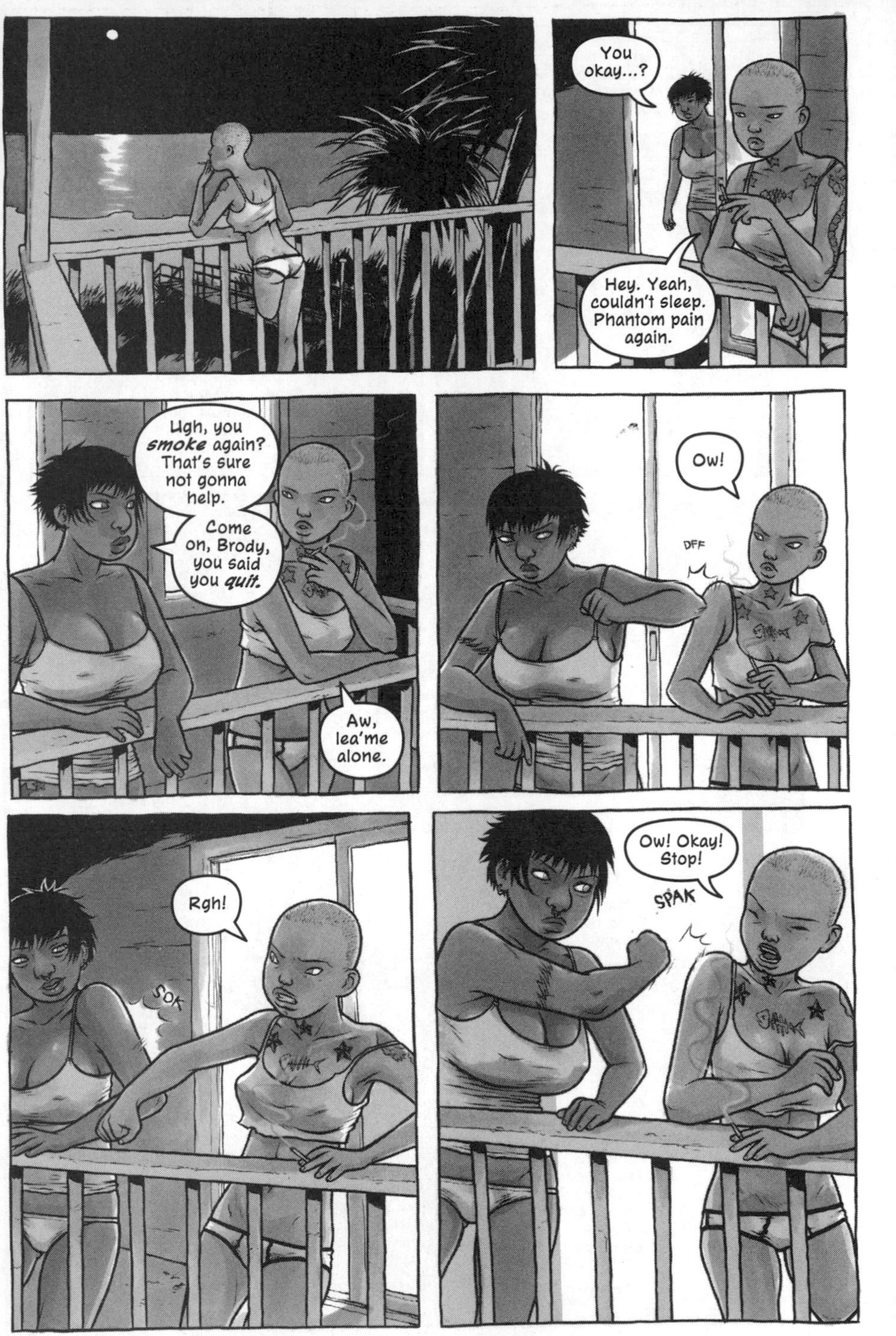
You okay...?
Hey. Yeah, couldn't sleep. Phantom pain again.
Ugh, you smoke again? That's sure not gonna help.
Come on, Brody, you said you quit.
Aw, lea'me alone.
Ow!
DFF
Rgh!
SOK
Ow! Okay! Stop!
SPAK

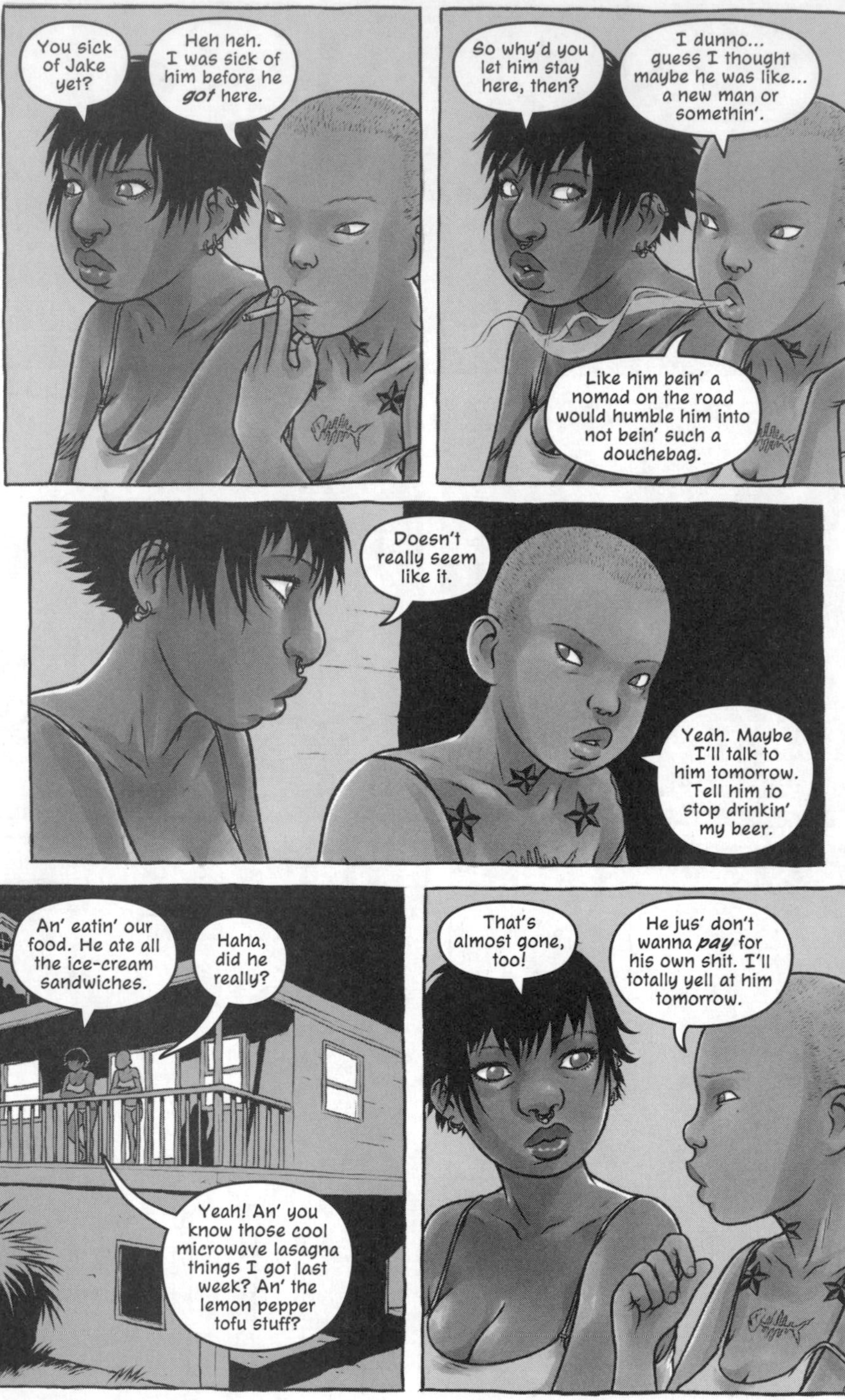
You sick of Jake yet?
Heh heh. I was sick of him before he *got* here.
So why'd you let him stay here, then?
I dunno... guess I thought maybe he was like... a new man or somethin'.
Like him bein' a nomad on the road would humble him into not bein' such a douchebag.
Doesn't really seem like it.
Yeah. Maybe I'll talk to him tomorrow. Tell him to stop drinkin' my beer.
An' eatin' our food. He ate all the ice-cream sandwiches.
Haha, did he really?
Yeah! An' you know those cool microwave lasagna things I got last week? An' the lemon pepper tofu stuff?
That's almost gone, too!
He jus' don't wanna *pay* for his own shit. I'll totally yell at him tomorrow.

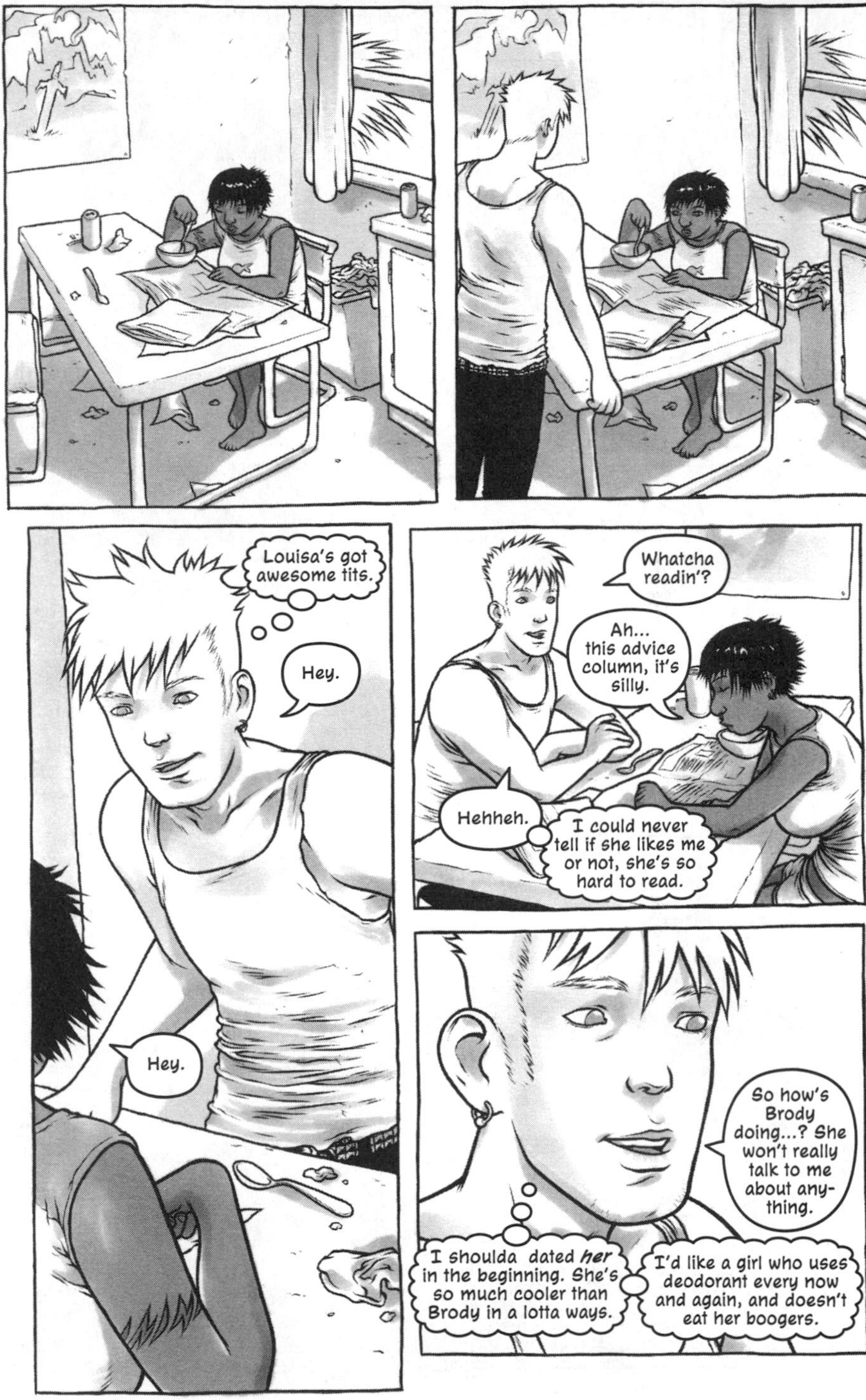
Louisa's got awesome tits.
Hey.
Hey.
Whatcha readin'?
Ah... this advice column, it's silly.
Hehheh.
I could never tell if she likes me or not, she's so hard to read.
So how's Brody doing...? She won't really talk to me about any-thing.
I shoulda dated *her* in the beginning. She's so much cooler than Brody in a lotta ways.
I'd like a girl who uses deodorant every now and again, and doesn't eat her boogers.

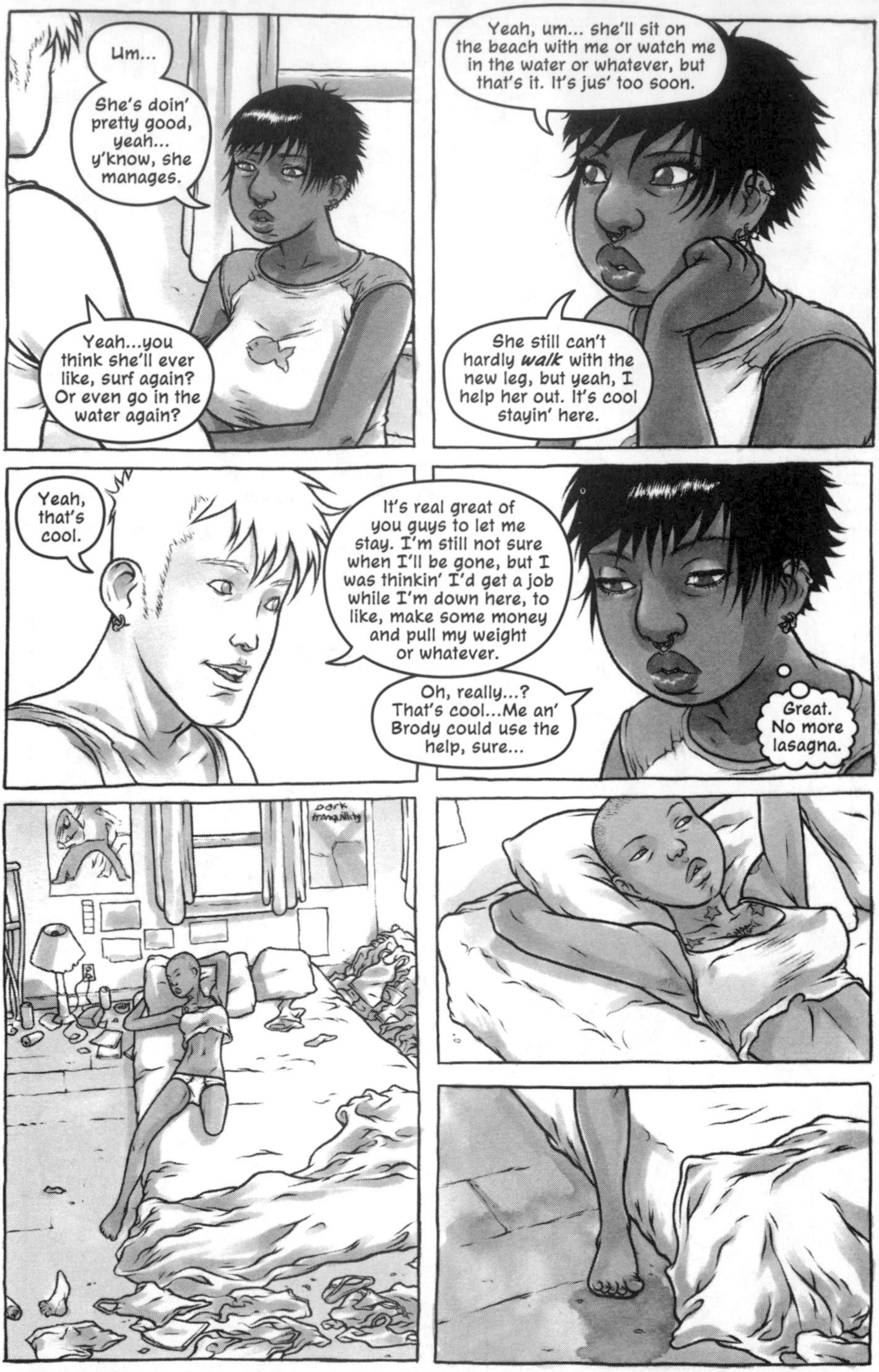
Um...
She's doin' pretty good, yeah... y'know, she manages.
Yeah...you think she'll ever like, surf again? Or even go in the water again?
Yeah, um... she'll sit on the beach with me or watch me in the water or whatever, but that's it. It's jus' too soon.
She still can't hardly *walk* with the new leg, but yeah, I help her out. It's cool stayin' here.
Yeah, that's cool.
It's real great of you guys to let me stay. I'm still not sure when I'll be gone, but I was thinkin' I'd get a job while I'm down here, to like, make some money and pull my weight or whatever.
Oh, really...? That's cool...Me an' Brody could use the help, sure...
Great. No more lasagna.

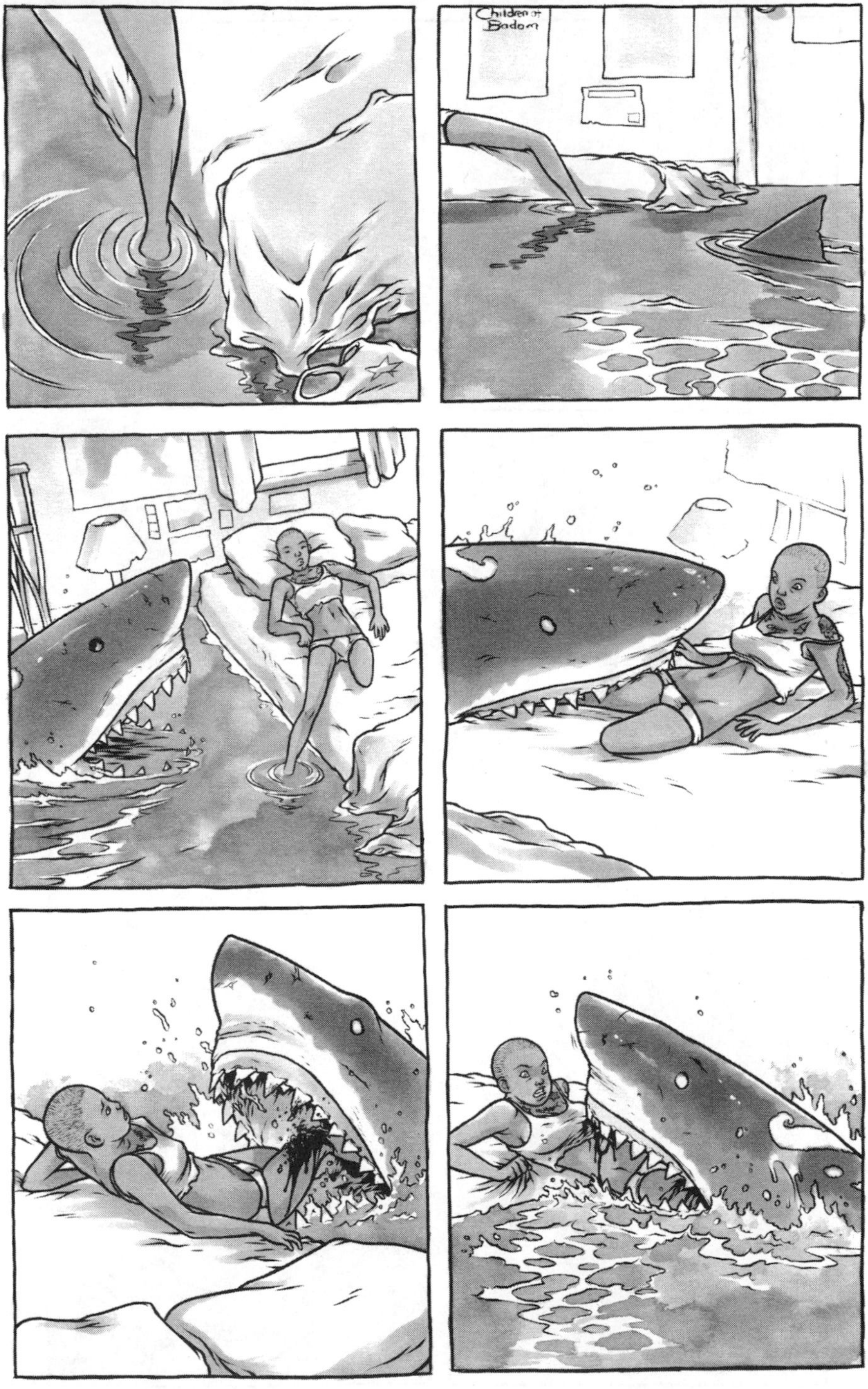
Children of Bodom

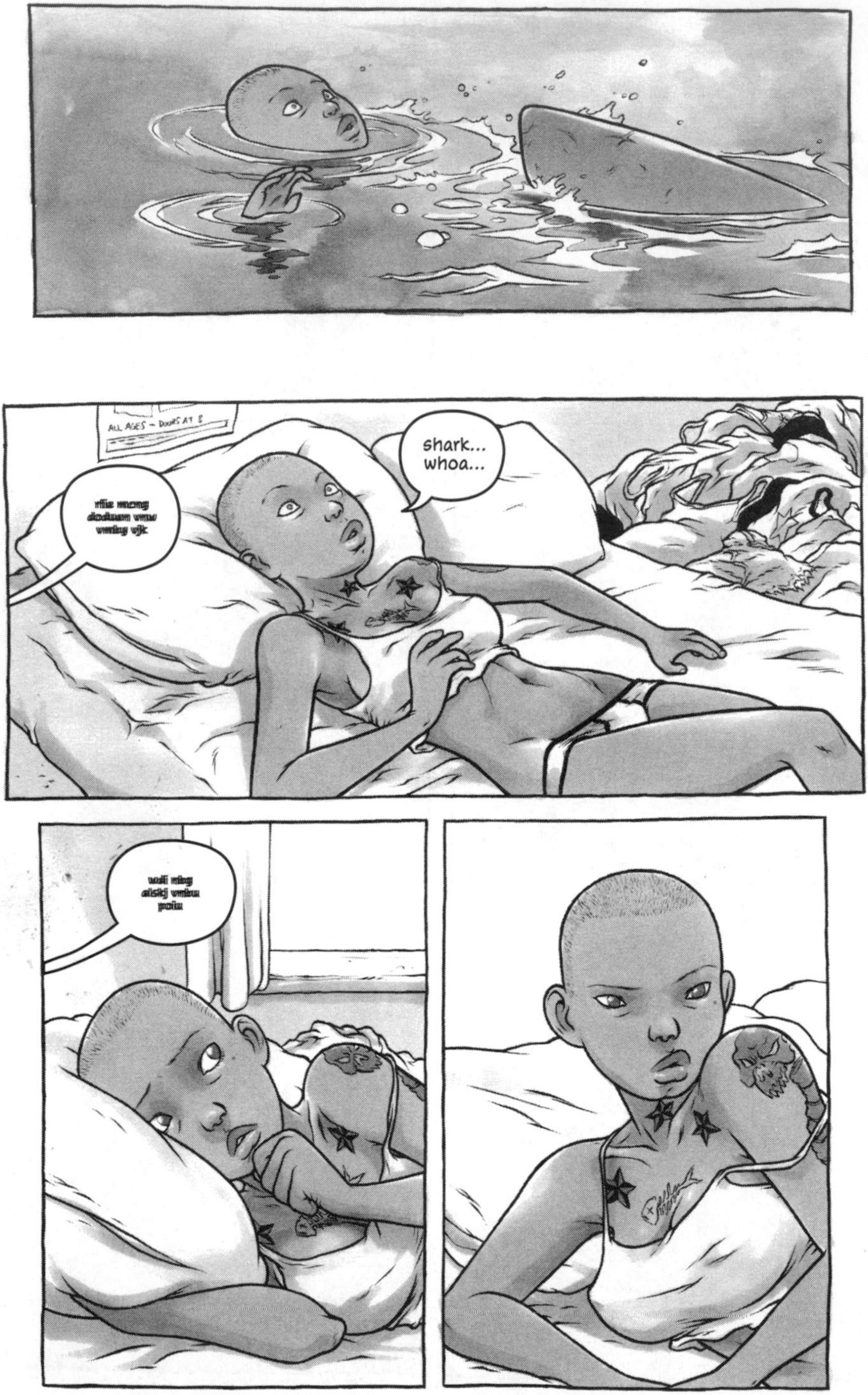
ALL AGES – DOORS AT 8
shark... whoa...

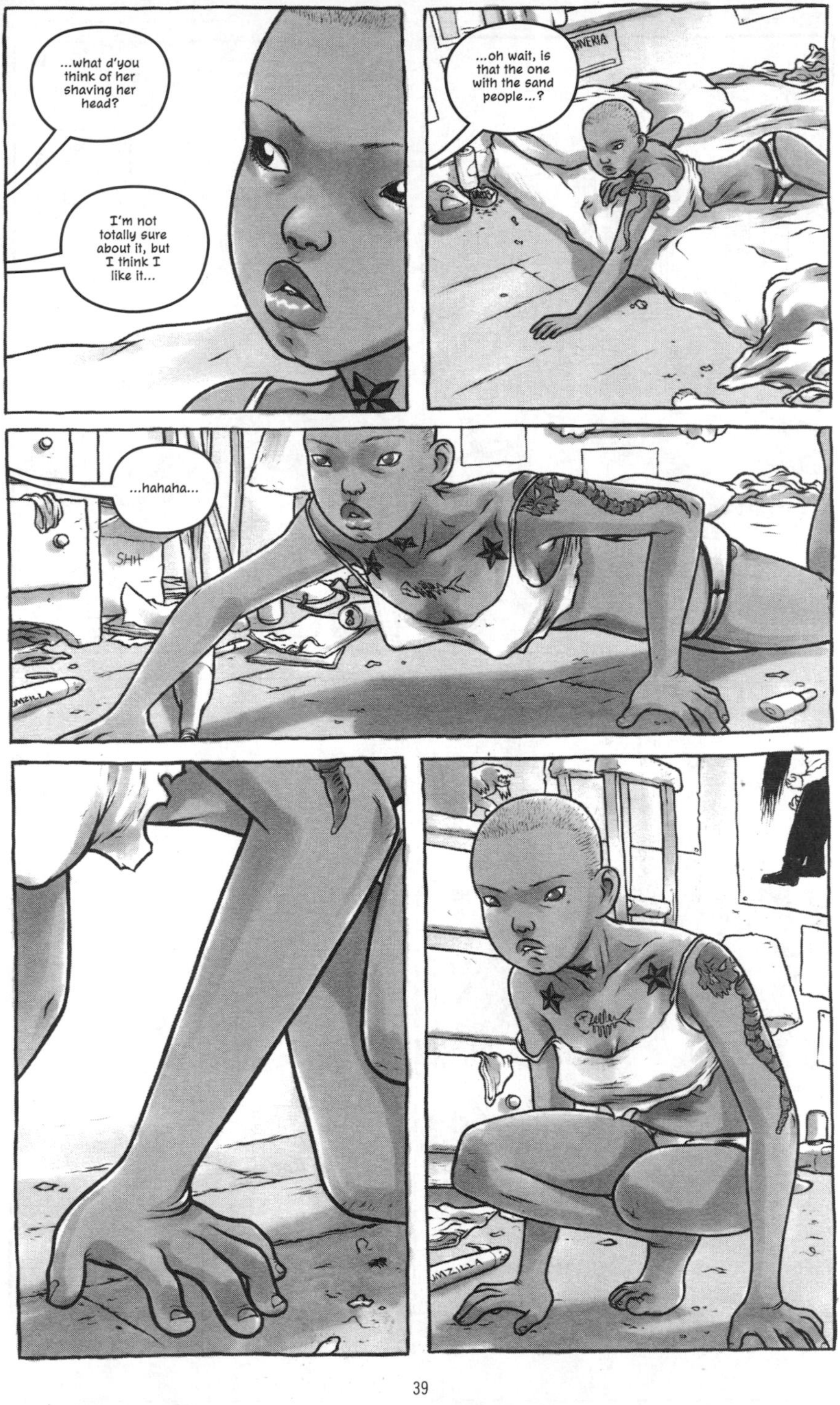
...what d'you think of her shaving her head?
I'm not totally sure about it, but I think I like it...
...oh wait, is that the one with the sand people...?
...hahaha...

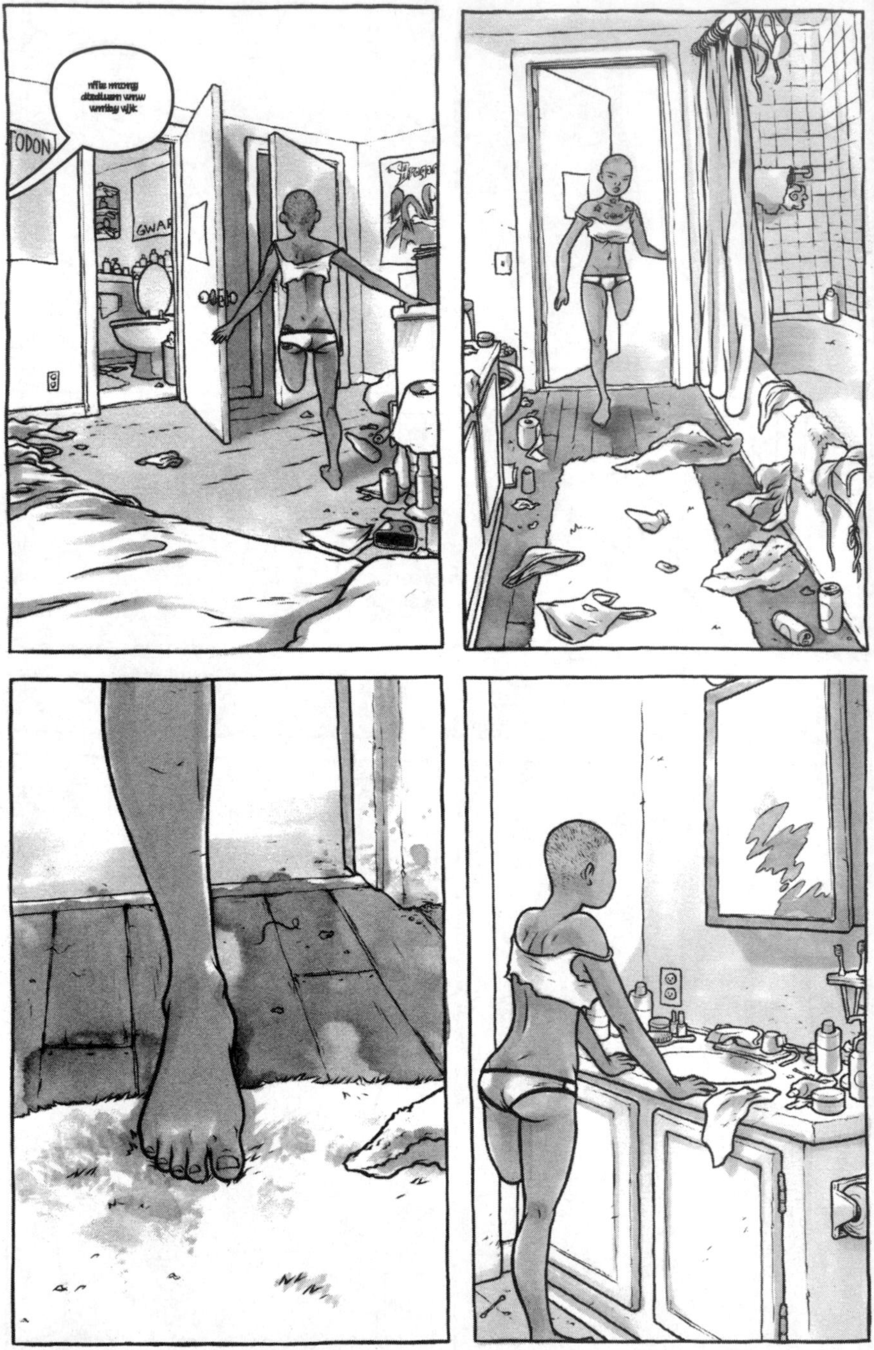
TODON
GWAR

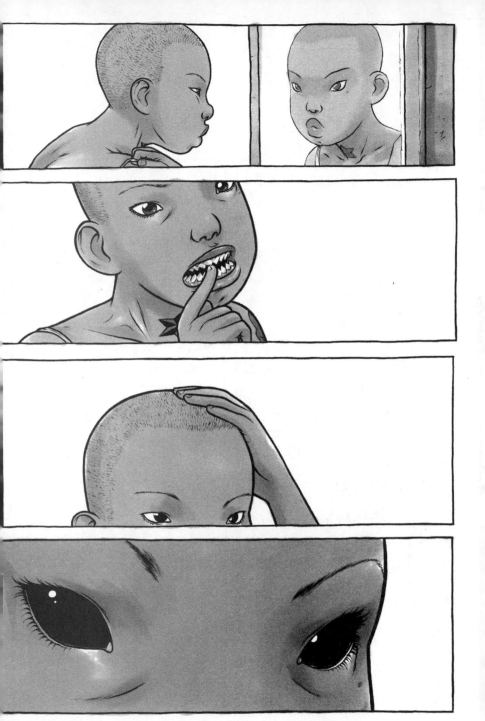

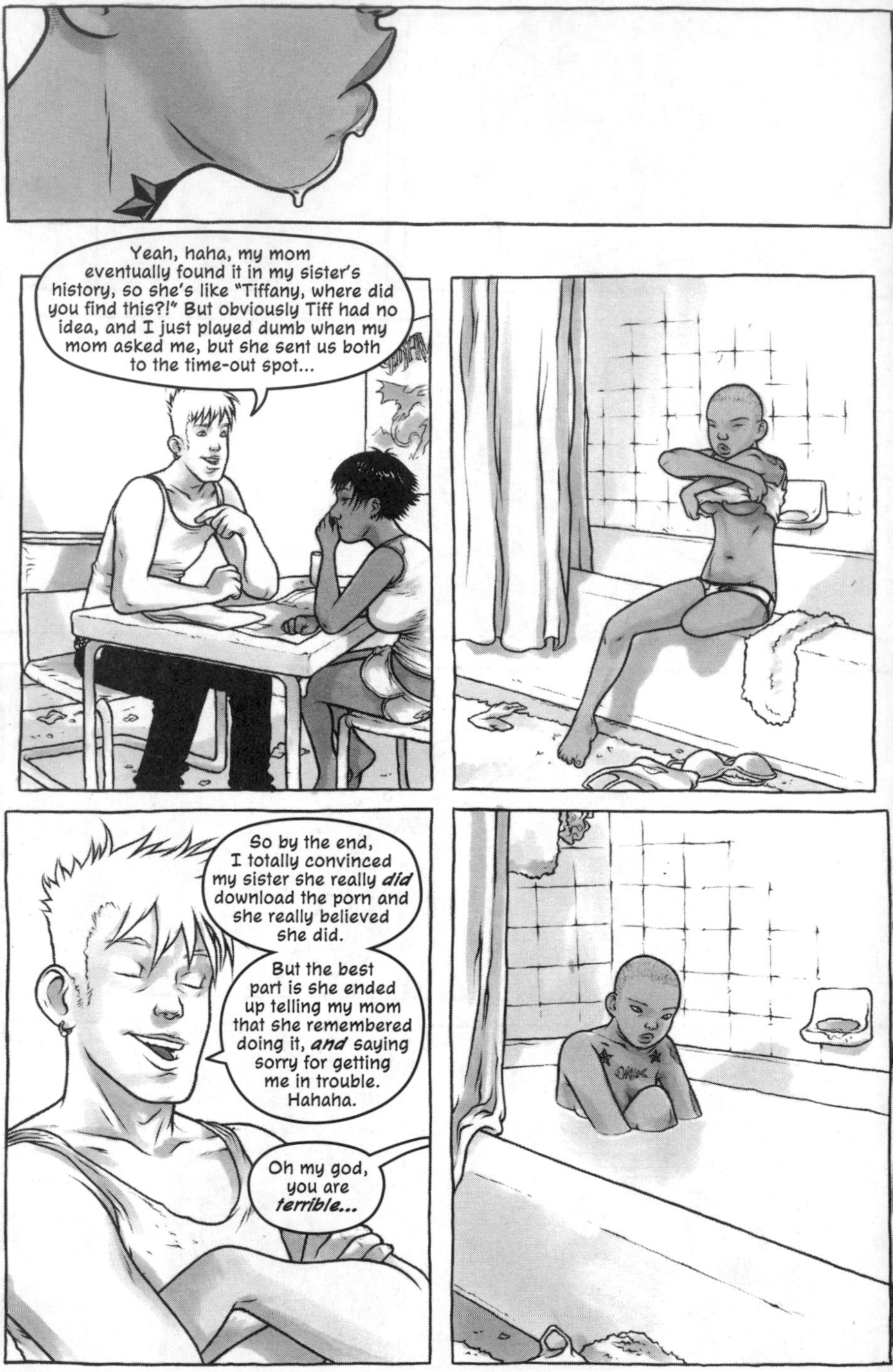

Yeah, haha, my mom eventually found it in my sister's history, so she's like "Tiffany, where did you find this?!" But obviously Tiff had no idea, and I just played dumb when my mom asked me, but she sent us both to the time-out spot...
So by the end, I totally convinced my sister she really *did* download the porn and she really believed she did.
But the best part is she ended up telling my mom that she remembered doing it, *and* saying sorry for getting me in trouble. Hahaha.
Oh my god, you are *terrible...*

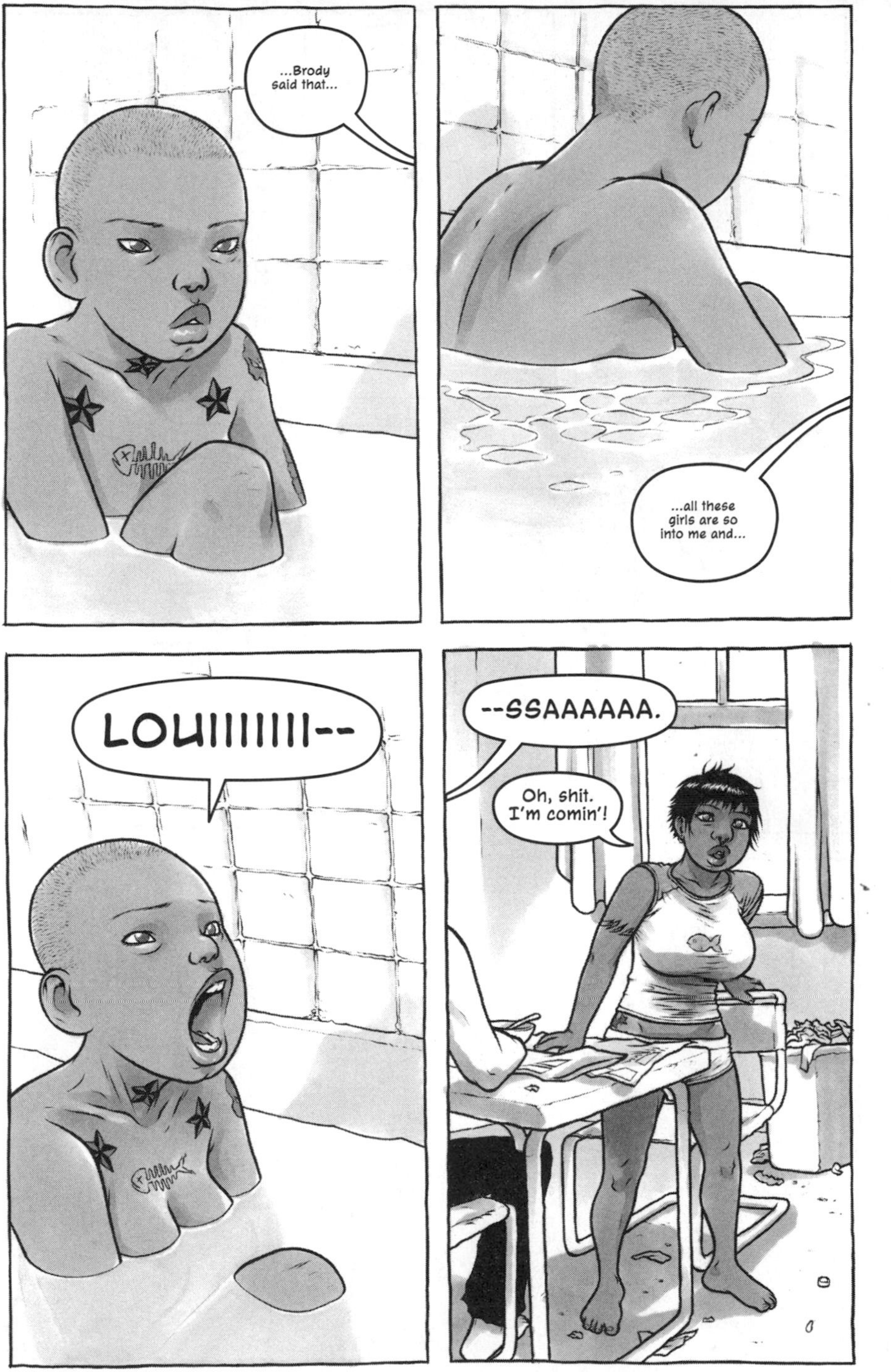
...Brody said that...
...all these girls are so into me and...
LOUIIIIIII--
--SSAAAAAA.
Oh, shit. I'm comin'!

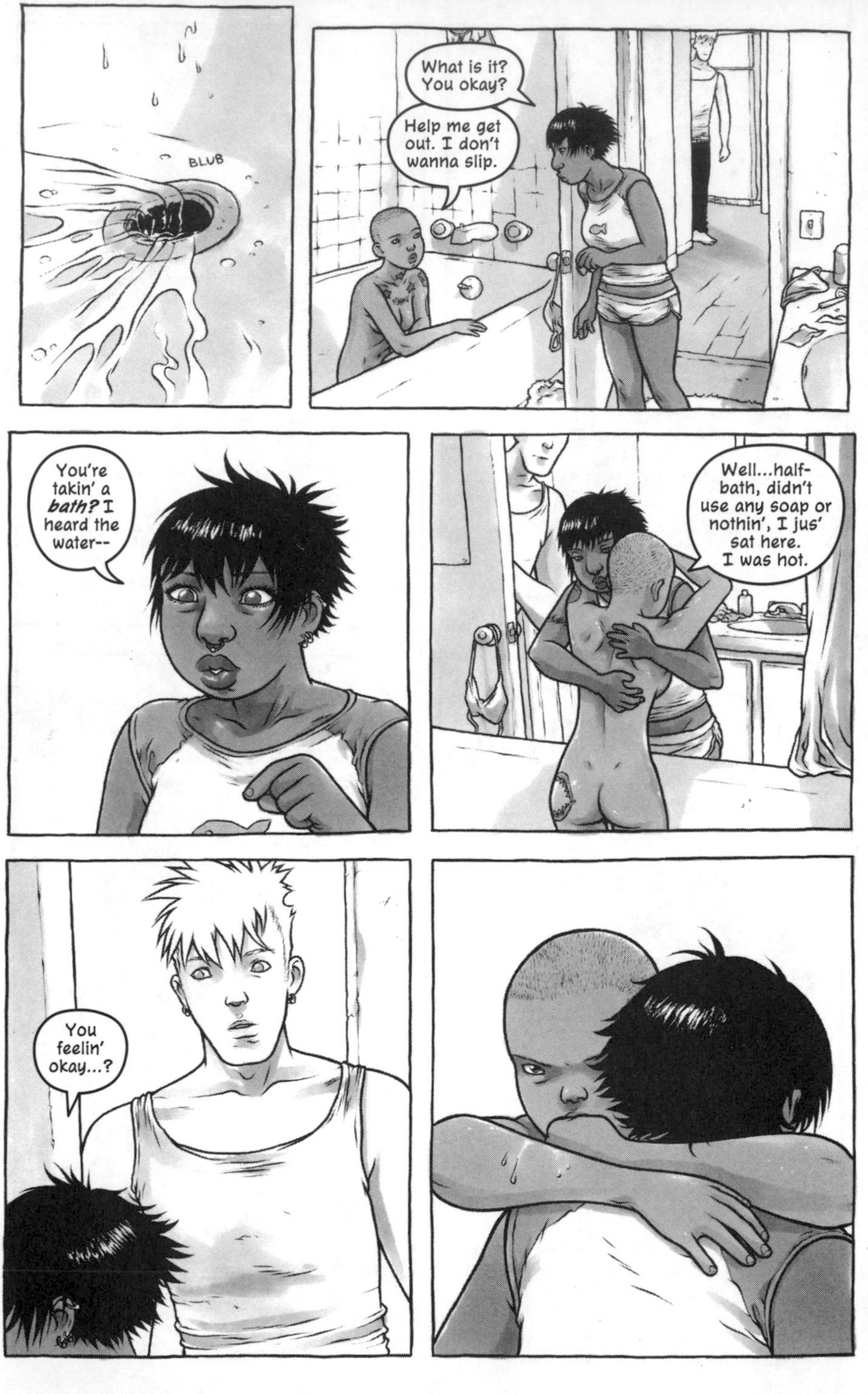
BLUB
What is it? You okay?
Help me get out. I don't wanna slip.
You're takin' a **bath?** I heard the water--
Well...half-bath, didn't use any soap or nothin', I jus' sat here. I was hot.
You feelin' okay...?

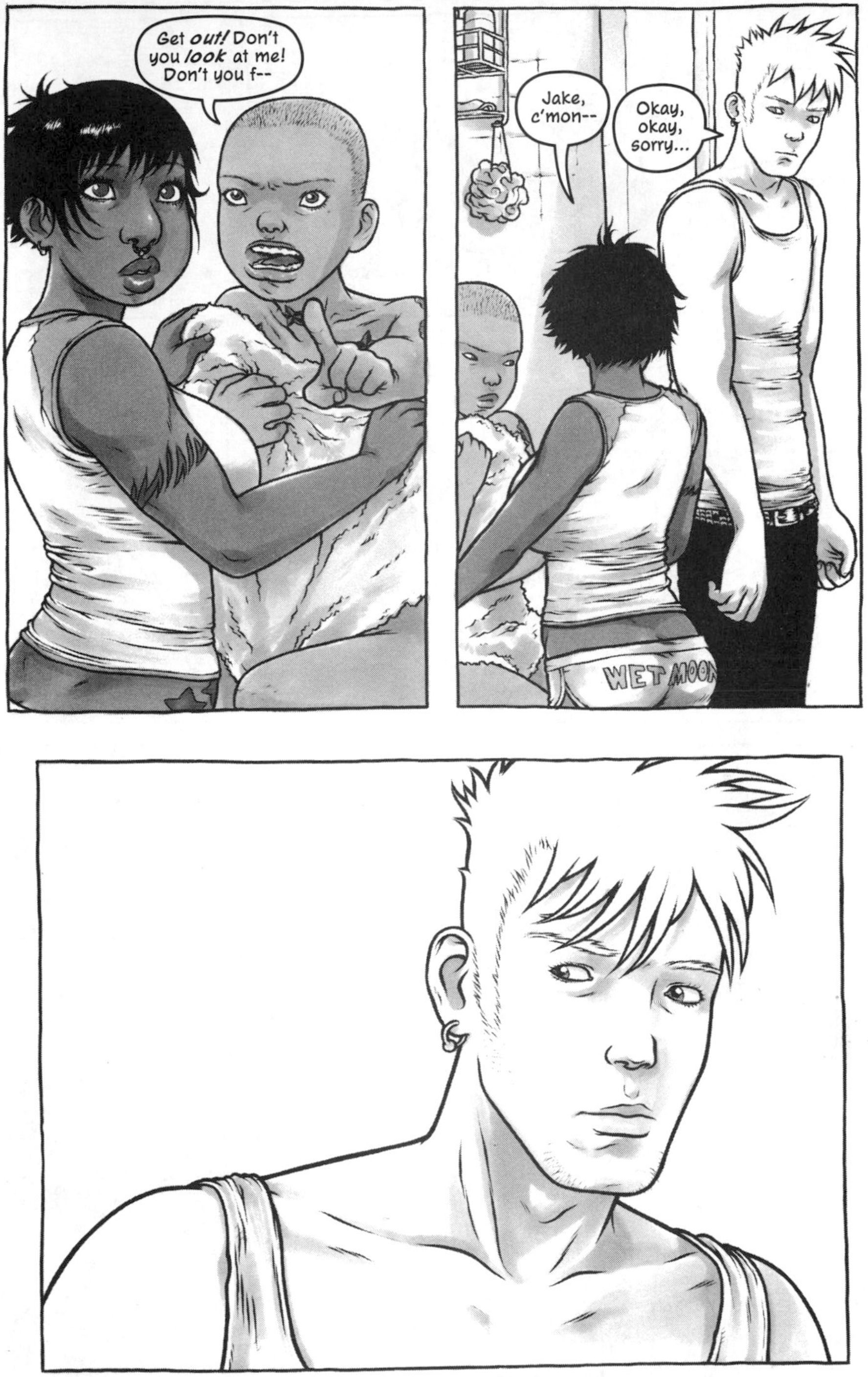
Get *out!* Don't you *look* at me! Don't you f--
Jake, c'mon--
Okay, okay, sorry...
WET MOON

Heh heh.

Hey.

Oh, hey, babe.

C'mon, don't call me that.

Heh, okay, whatever. I won't.

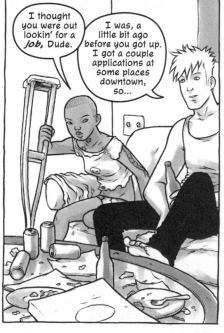

I thought you were out lookin' for a *job,* Dude.

I was, a little bit ago before you got up. I got a couple applications at some places downtown, so...

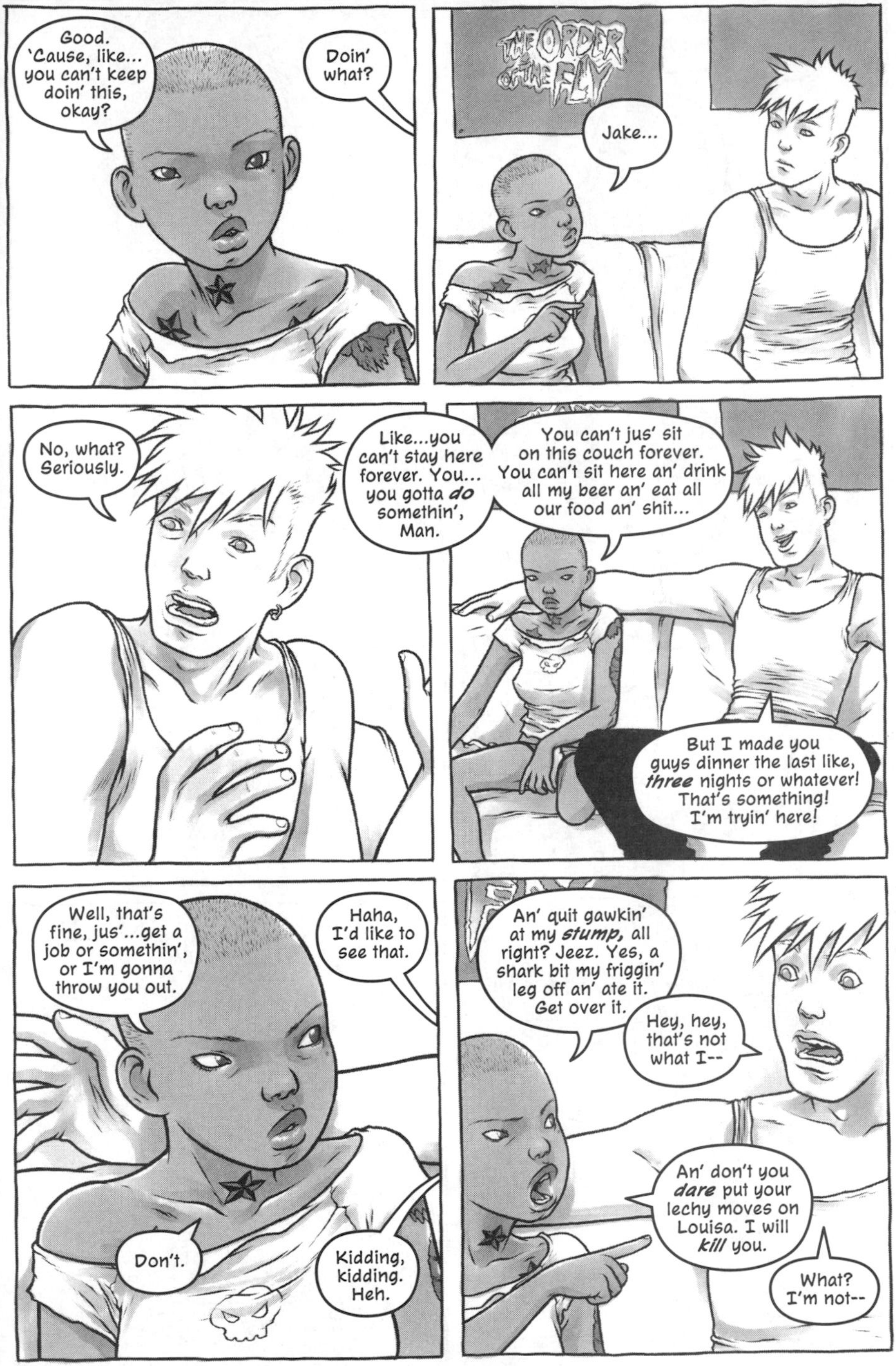
Good. 'Cause, like... you can't keep doin' this, okay?
Doin' what?
THE ORDER OF THE FLY
Jake...
No, what? Seriously.
Like...you can't stay here forever. You... you gotta *do* somethin', Man.
You can't jus' sit on this couch forever. You can't sit here an' drink all my beer an' eat all our food an' shit...
But I made you guys dinner the last like, *three* nights or whatever! That's something! I'm tryin' here!
Well, that's fine, jus'...get a job or somethin', or I'm gonna throw you out.
Haha, I'd like to see that.
Don't.
Kidding, kidding. Heh.
An' quit gawkin' at my *stump,* all right? Jeez. Yes, a shark bit my friggin' leg off an' ate it. Get over it.
Hey, hey, that's not what I--
An' don't you *dare* put your lechy moves on Louisa. I will *kill* you.
What? I'm not--

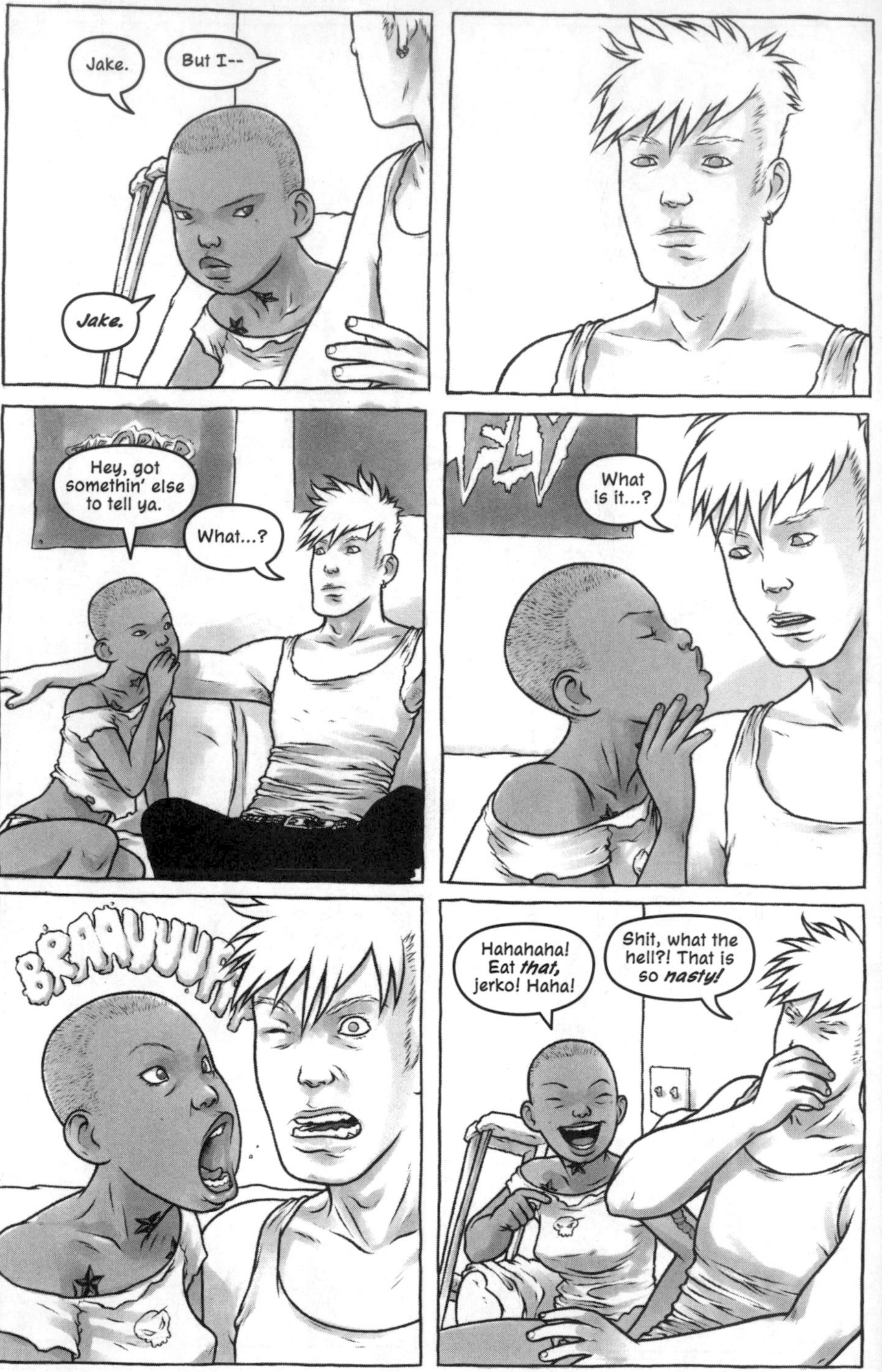
Jake.
But I--
Jake.
Hey, got somethin' else to tell ya.
What...?
What is it...?
BRAAUUUP
Hahahaha! Eat *that,* jerko! Haha!
Shit, what the hell?! That is so *nasty!*

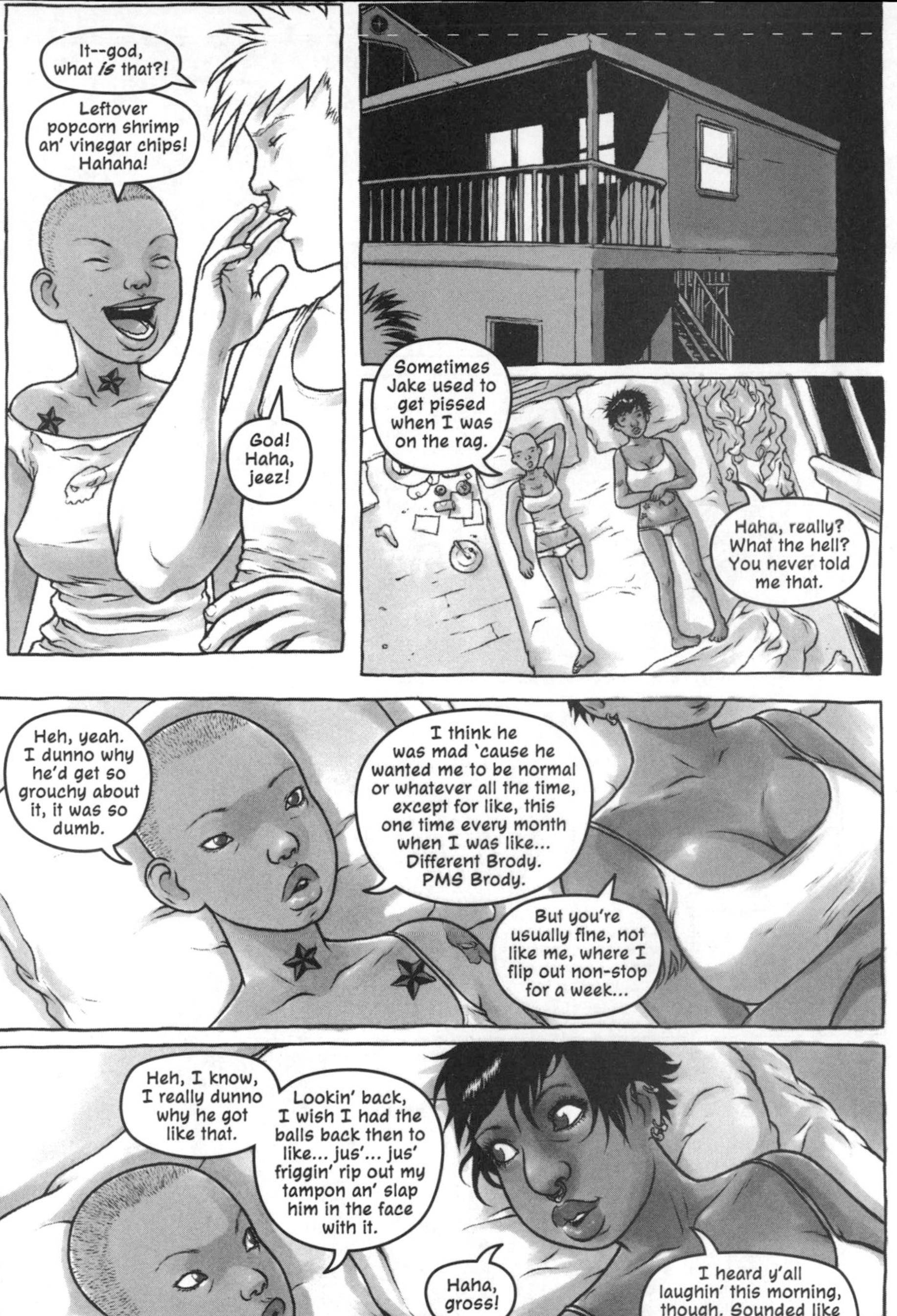
It--god, what *is* that?!
Leftover popcorn shrimp an' vinegar chips! Hahaha!
God! Haha, jeez!
Sometimes Jake used to get pissed when I was on the rag.
Haha, really? What the hell? You never told me that.
Heh, yeah. I dunno why he'd get so grouchy about it, it was so dumb.
I think he was mad 'cause he wanted me to be normal or whatever all the time, except for like, this one time every month when I was like... Different Brody. PMS Brody.
But you're usually fine, not like me, where I flip out non-stop for a week...
Heh, I know, I really dunno why he got like that.
Lookin' back, I wish I had the balls back then to like... jus'... jus' friggin' rip out my tampon an' slap him in the face with it.
Haha, gross!
I heard y'all laughin' this morning, though. Sounded like you were havin' a good time, for a little bit at least.

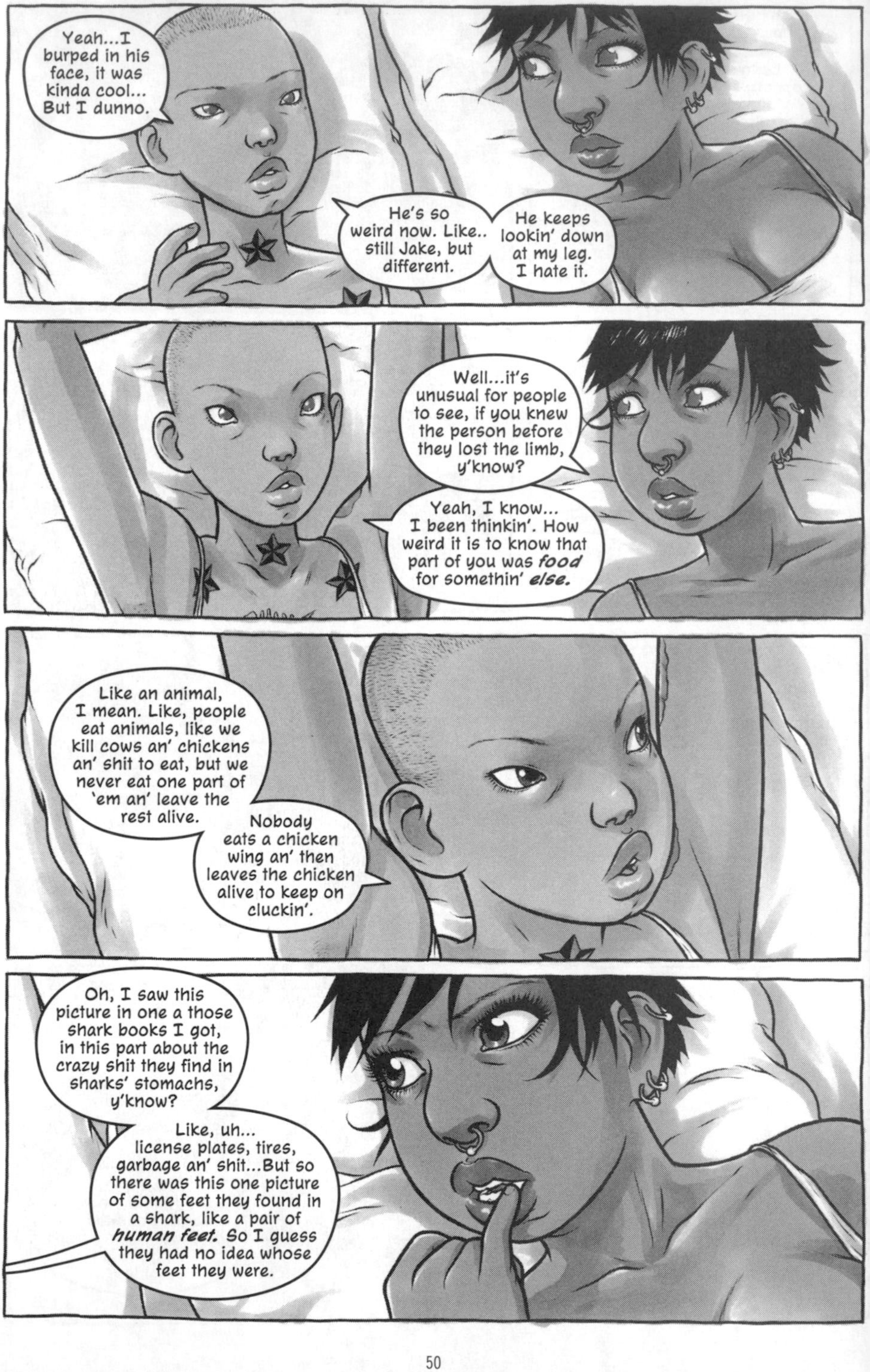
Yeah...I burped in his face, it was kinda cool... But I dunno.
He's so weird now. Like.. still Jake, but different.
He keeps lookin' down at my leg. I hate it.
Well...it's unusual for people to see, if you knew the person before they lost the limb, y'know?
Yeah, I know... I been thinkin'. How weird it is to know that part of you was *food* for somethin' *else.*
Like an animal, I mean. Like, people eat animals, like we kill cows an' chickens an' shit to eat, but we never eat one part of 'em an' leave the rest alive.
Nobody eats a chicken wing an' then leaves the chicken alive to keep on cluckin'.
Oh, I saw this picture in one a those shark books I got, in this part about the crazy shit they find in sharks' stomachs, y'know?
Like, uh... license plates, tires, garbage an' shit...But so there was this one picture of some feet they found in a shark, like a pair of ***human feet.*** So I guess they had no idea whose feet they were.

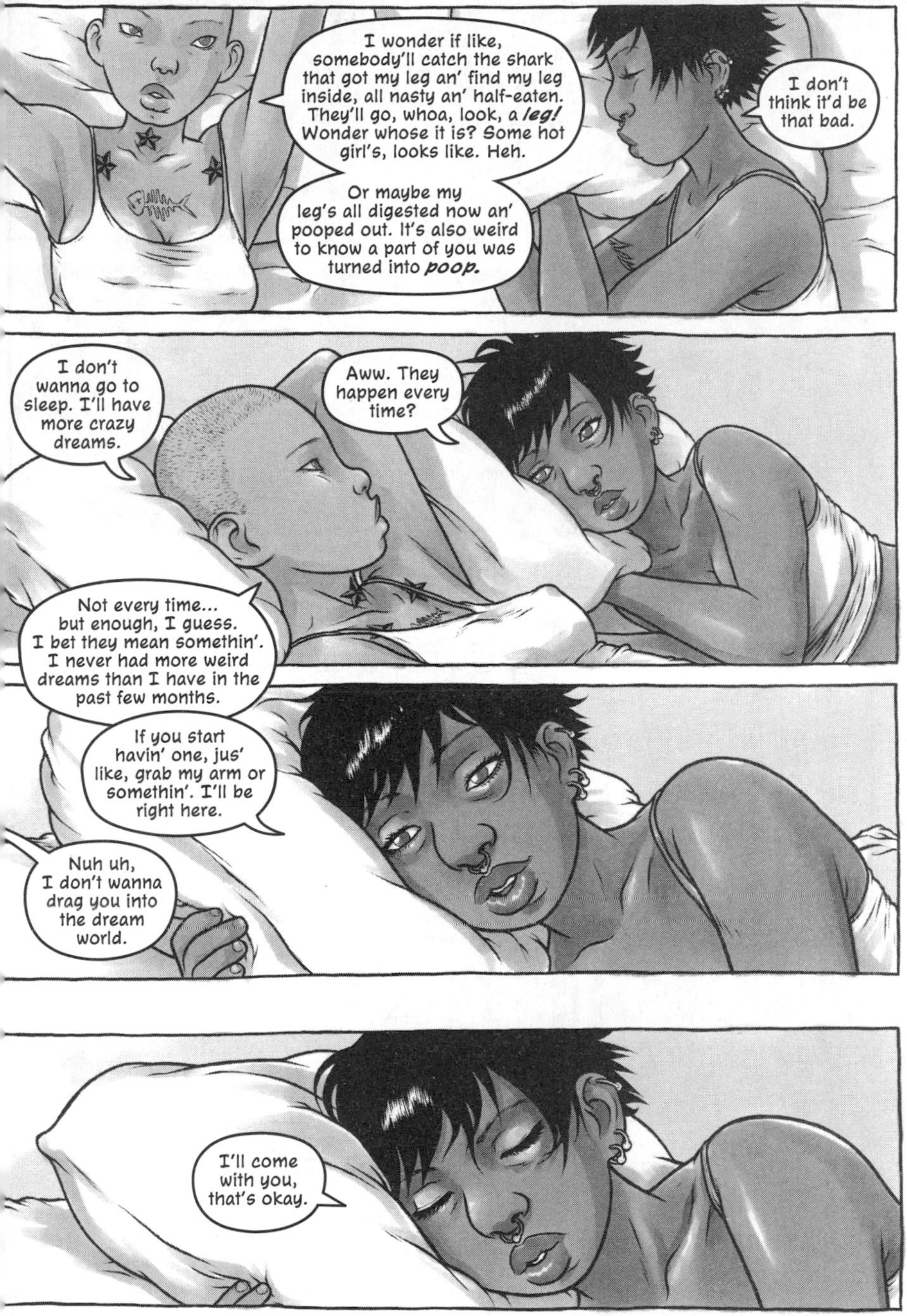
I wonder if like, somebody'll catch the shark that got my leg an' find my leg inside, all nasty an' half-eaten. They'll go, whoa, look, a *leg!* Wonder whose it is? Some hot girl's, looks like. Heh.
Or maybe my leg's all digested now an' pooped out. It's also weird to know a part of you was turned into *poop.*
I don't think it'd be that bad.
I don't wanna go to sleep. I'll have more crazy dreams.
Aww. They happen every time?
Not every time... but enough, I guess. I bet they mean somethin'. I never had more weird dreams than I have in the past few months.
If you start havin' one, jus' like, grab my arm or somethin'. I'll be right here.
Nuh uh, I don't wanna drag you into the dream world.
I'll come with you, that's okay.

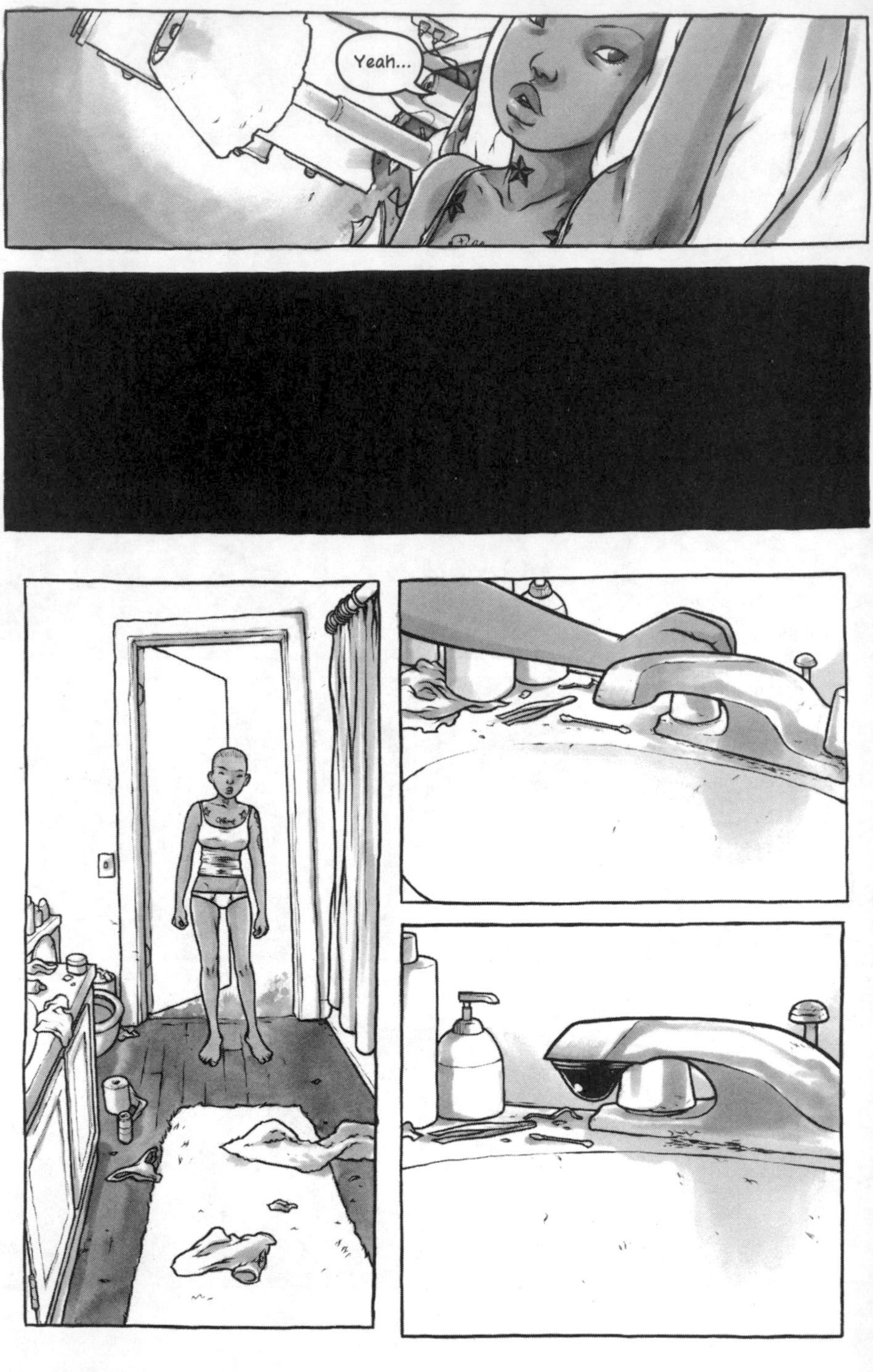
Yeah...

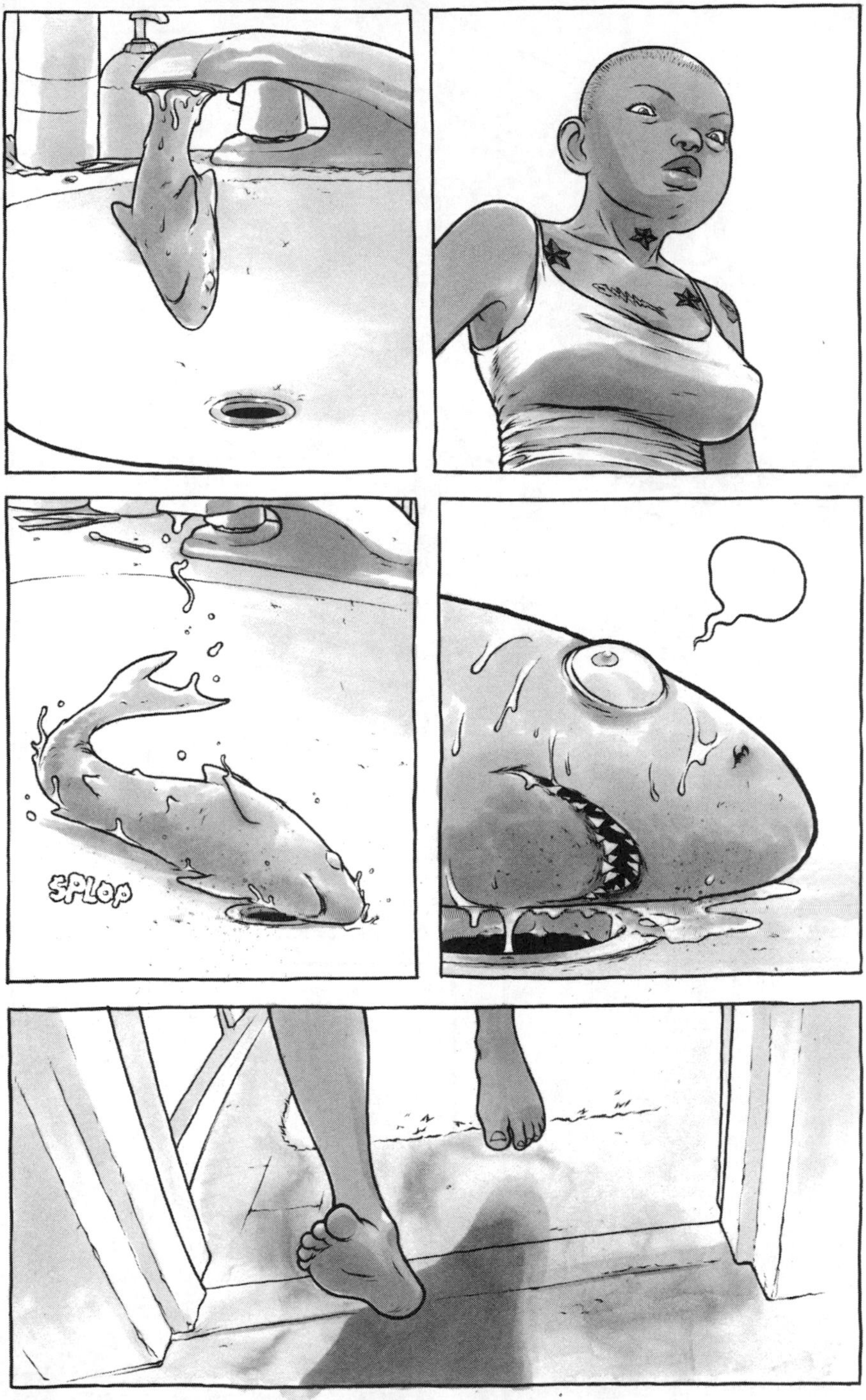
SPLOP

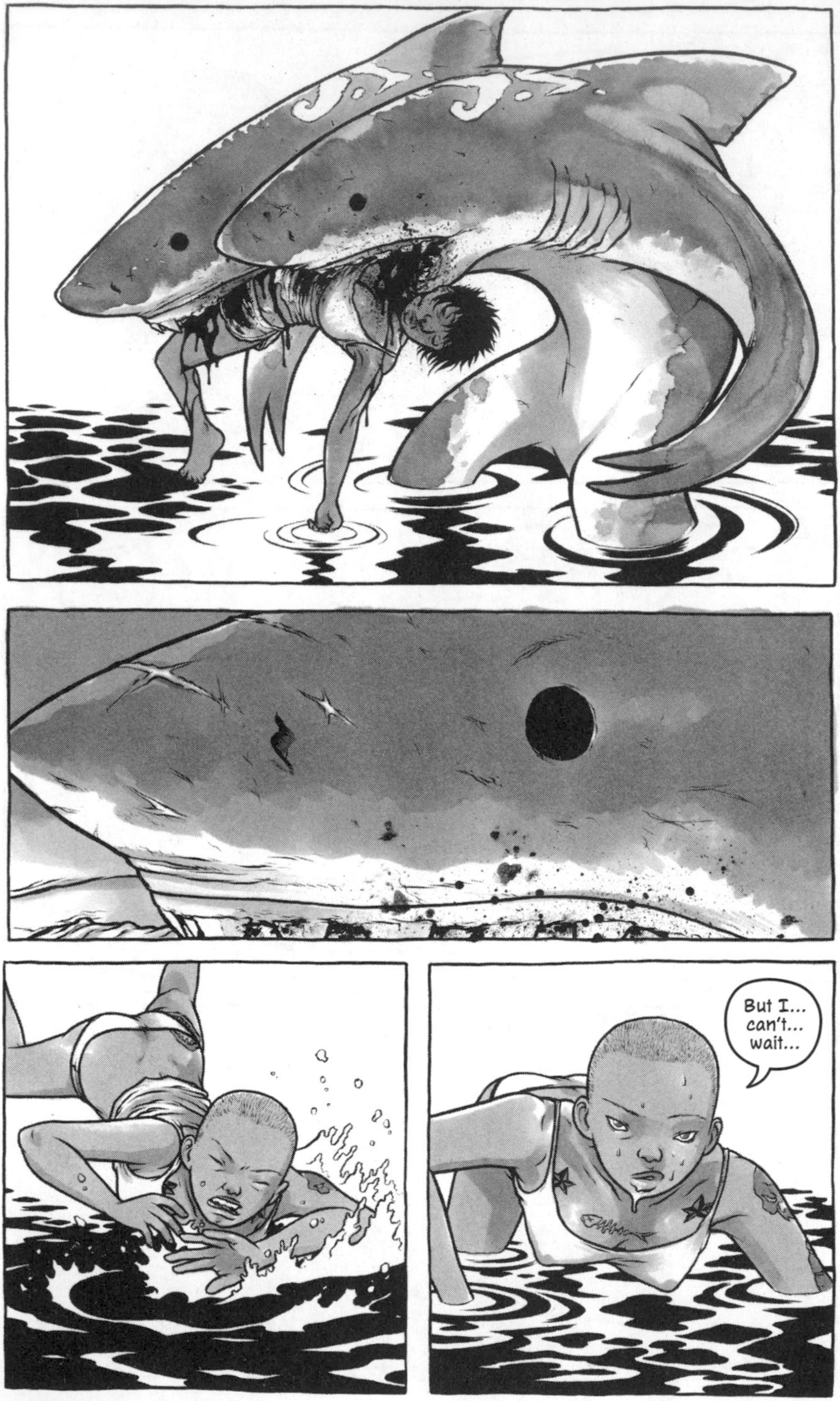
But I... can't... wait...

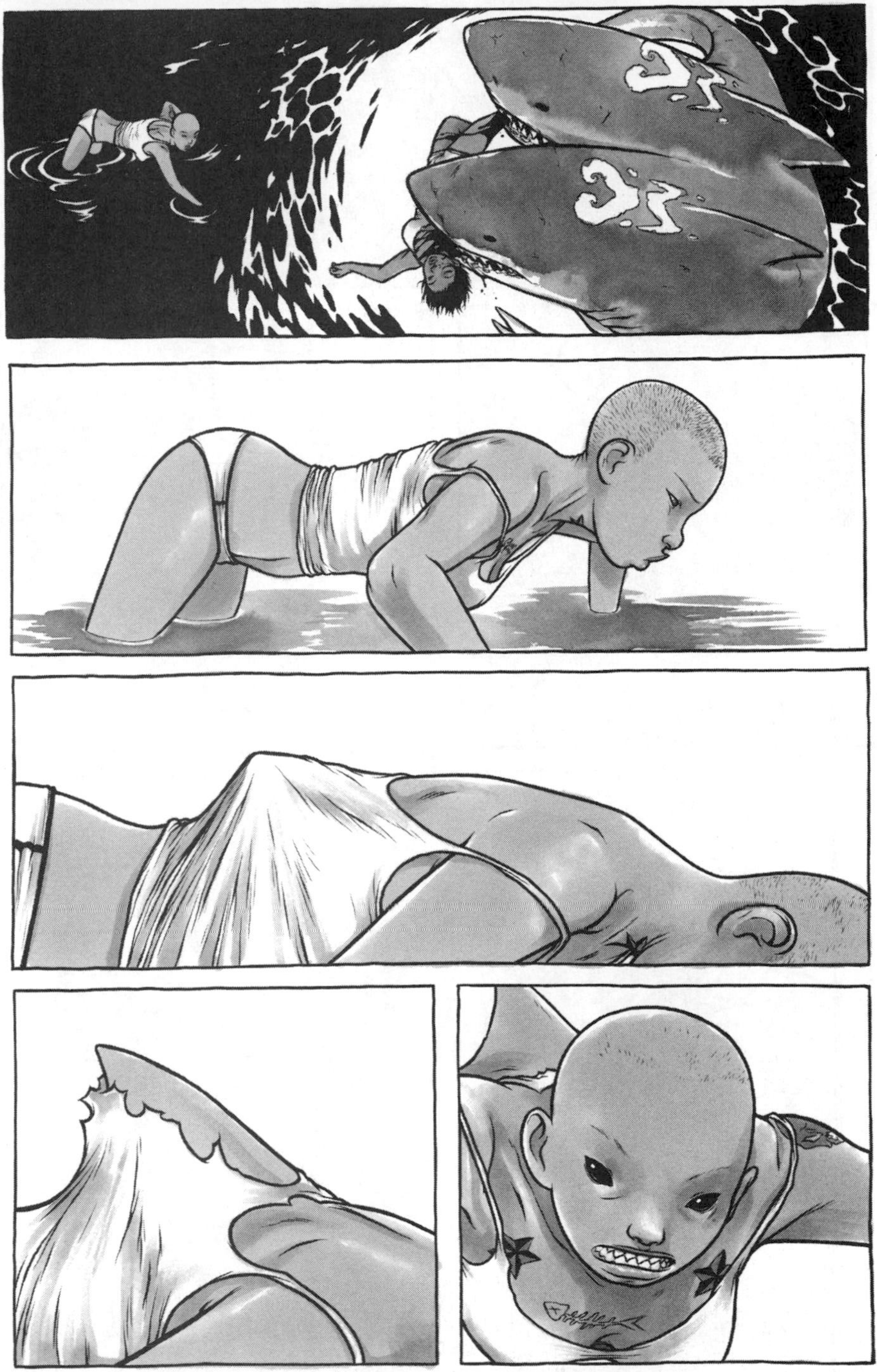

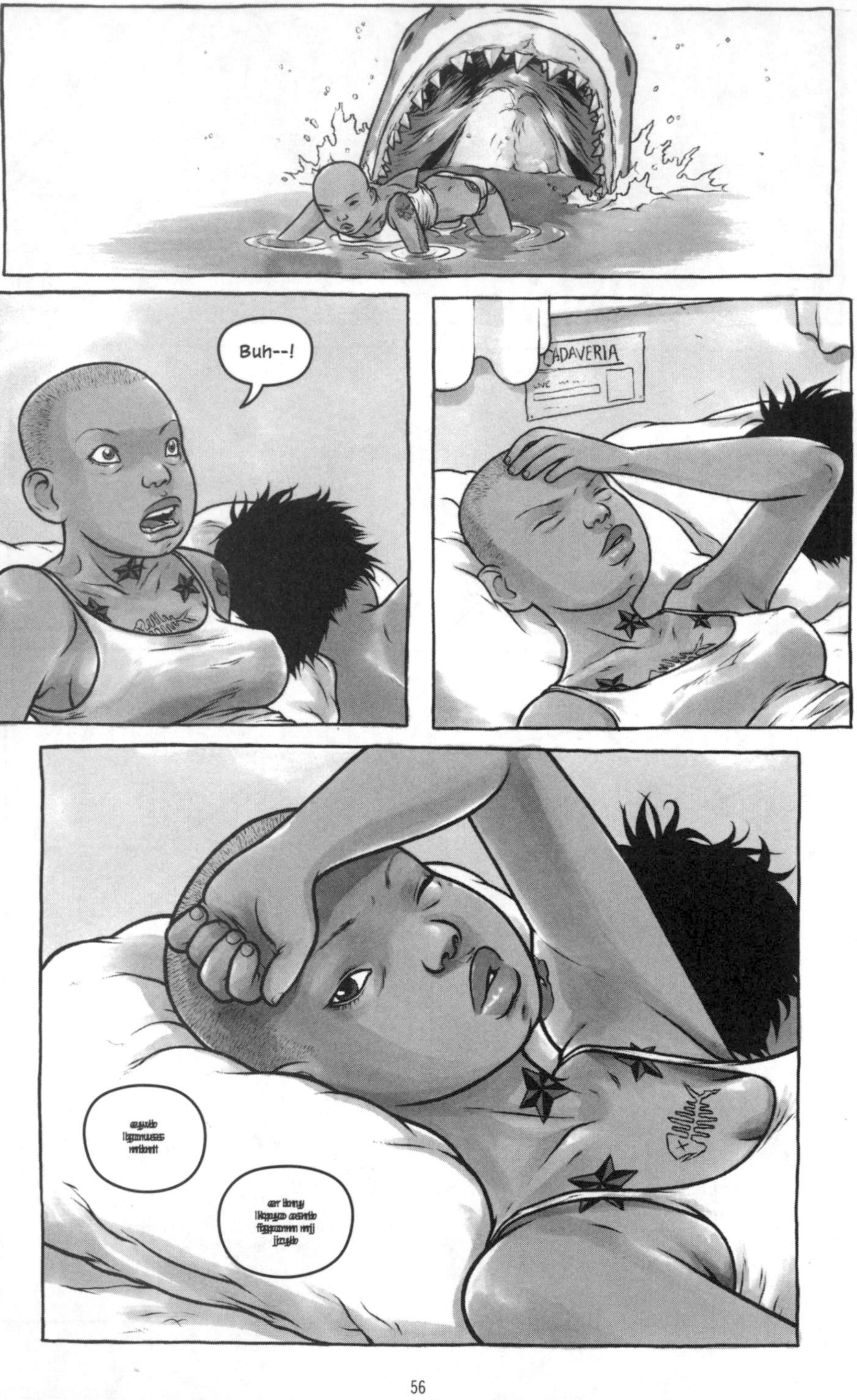
Buh--!
ADAVERIA

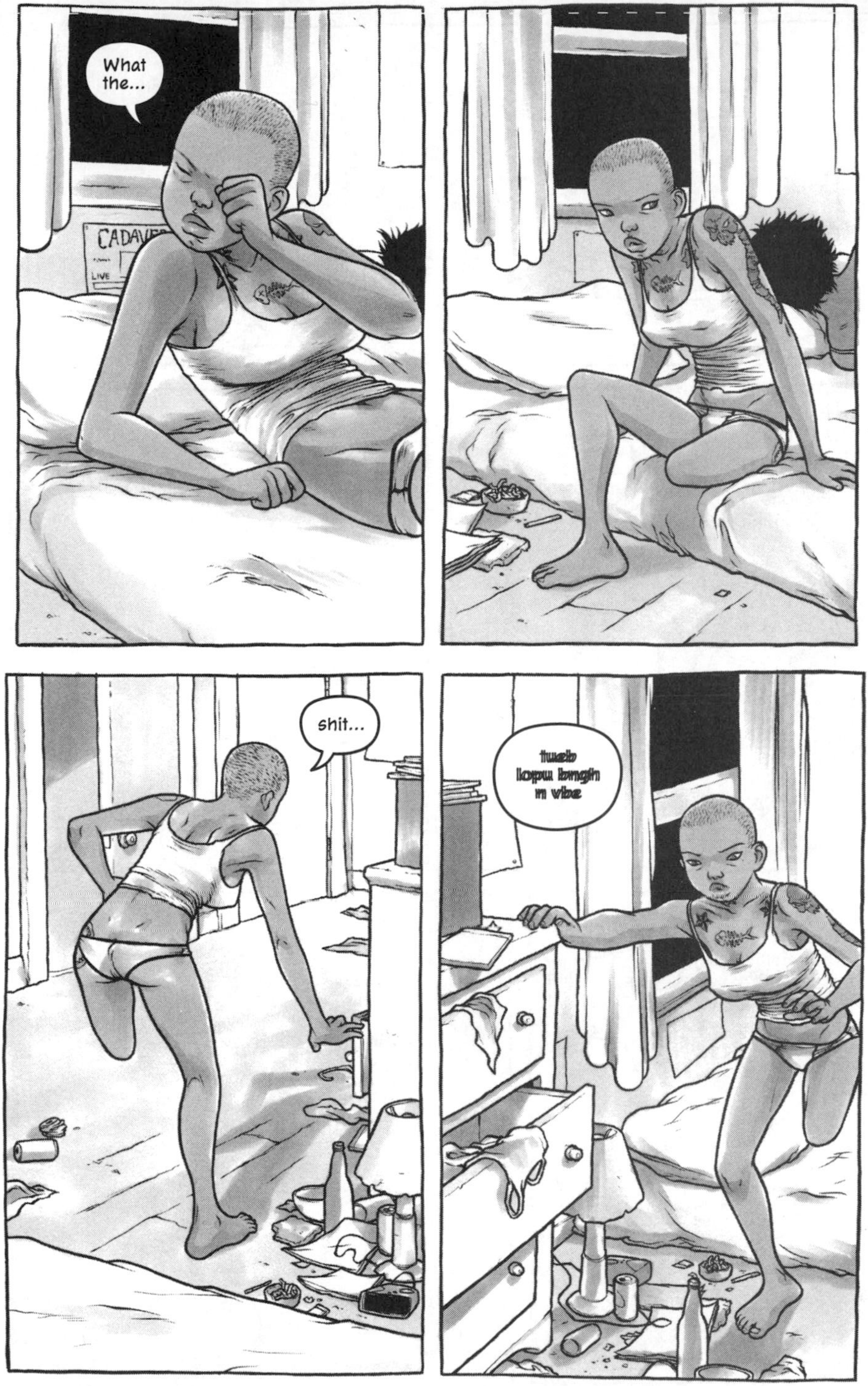
What the...
shit...
twelb lopu lmgin m vibe

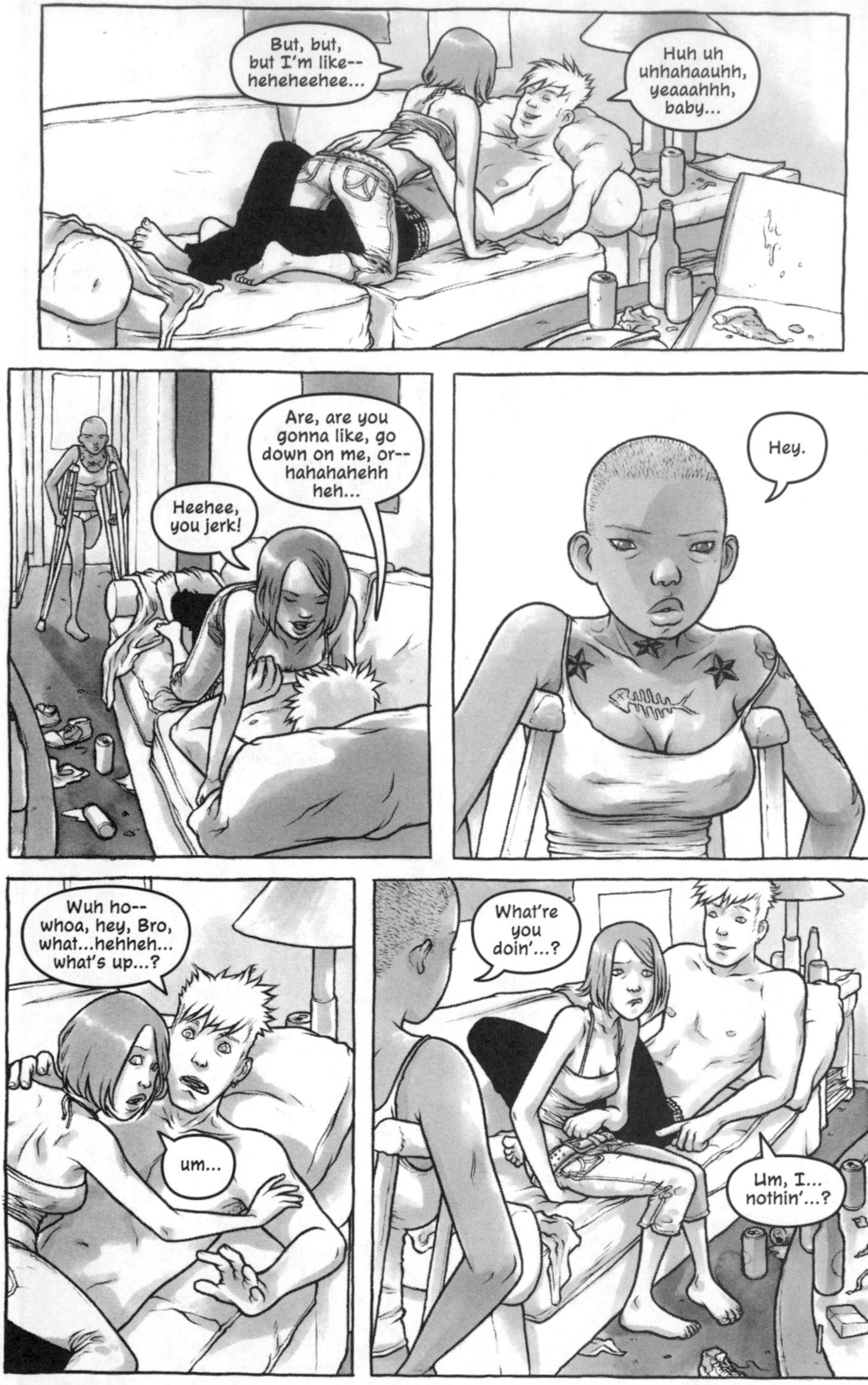
But, but, but I'm like-- heheheehee...
Huh uh uhhahaauhh, yeaaahhh, baby...
Are, are you gonna like, go down on me, or-- hahahahehh heh...
Heehee, you jerk!
Hey.
Wuh ho-- whoa, hey, Bro, what...hehheh... what's up...?
um...
What're you doin'...?
Um, I... nothin'...?

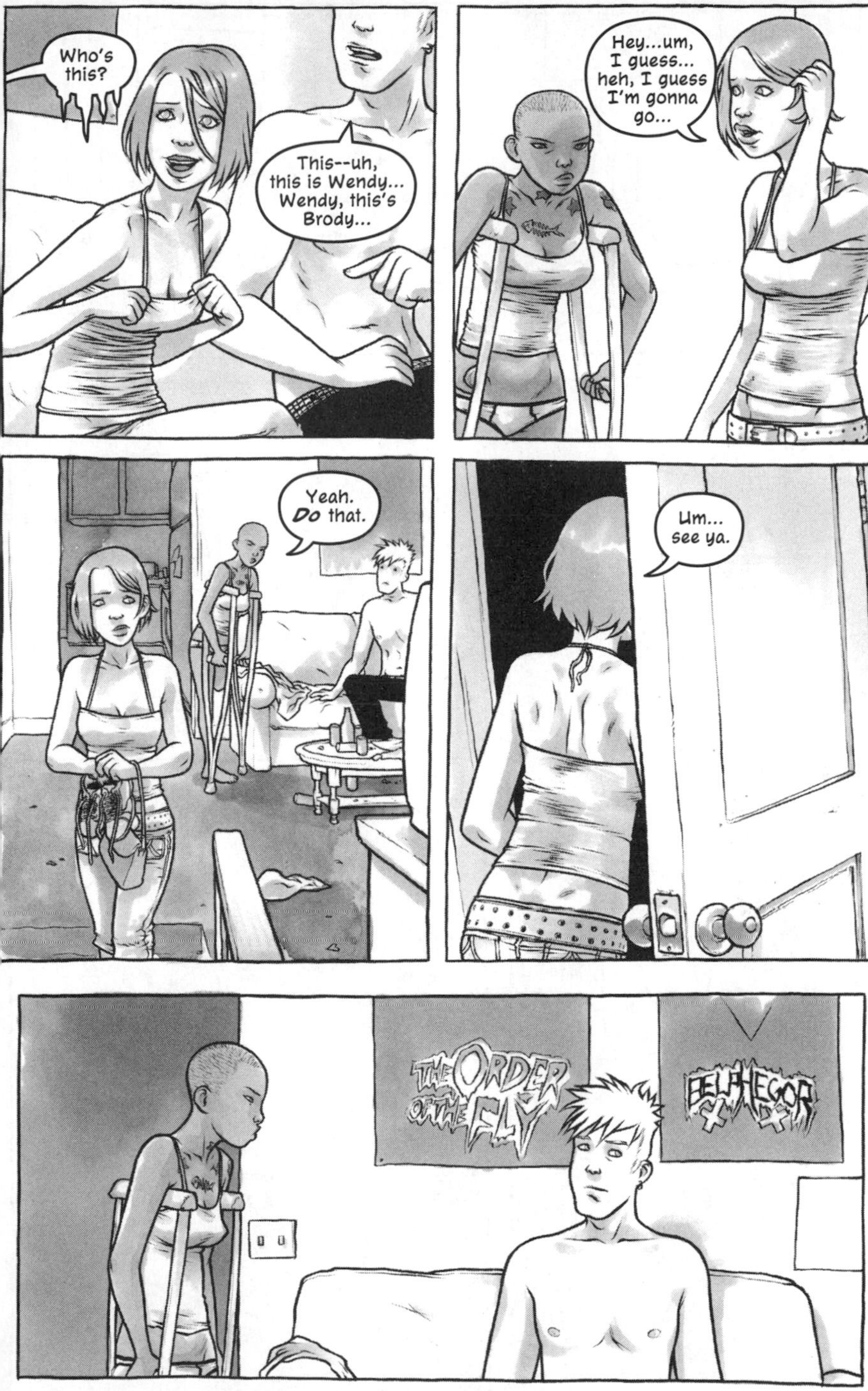
Who's this?
This--uh, this is Wendy... Wendy, this's Brody...
Hey...um, I guess... heh, I guess I'm gonna go...
Yeah. *Do* that.
Um... see ya.
THE ORDER OF THE FLY
BELPHEGOR

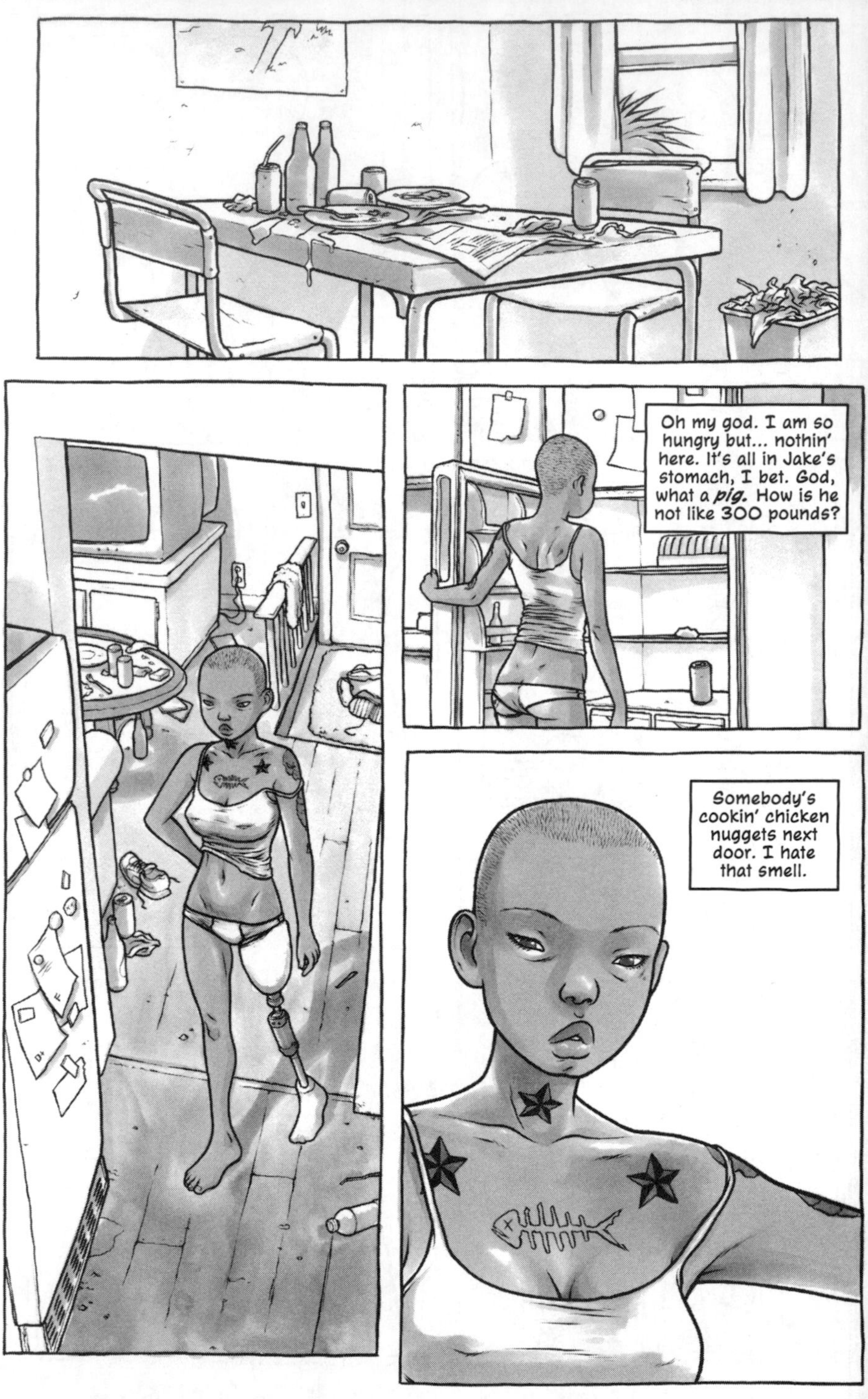
Oh my god. I am so hungry but... nothin' here. It's all in Jake's stomach, I bet. God, what a *pig.* How is he not like 300 pounds?
Somebody's cookin' chicken nuggets next door. I hate that smell.

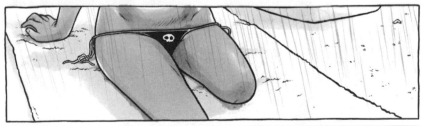

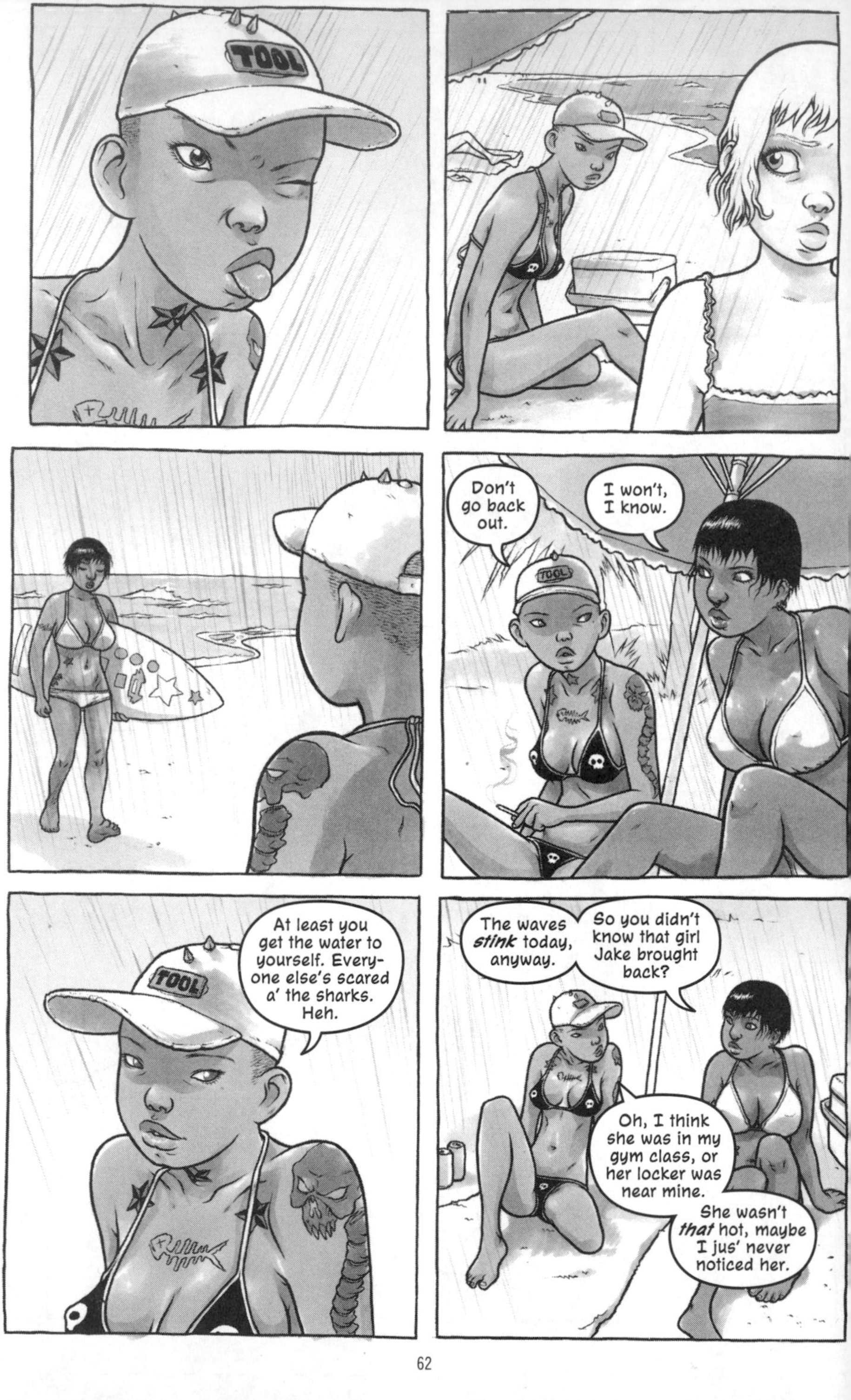
TOOL
Don't go back out.
I won't, I know.
At least you get the water to yourself. Every-one else's scared a' the sharks. Heh.
The waves *stink* today, anyway.
So you didn't know that girl Jake brought back?
Oh, I think she was in my gym class, or her locker was near mine.
She wasn't *that* hot, maybe I jus' never noticed her.

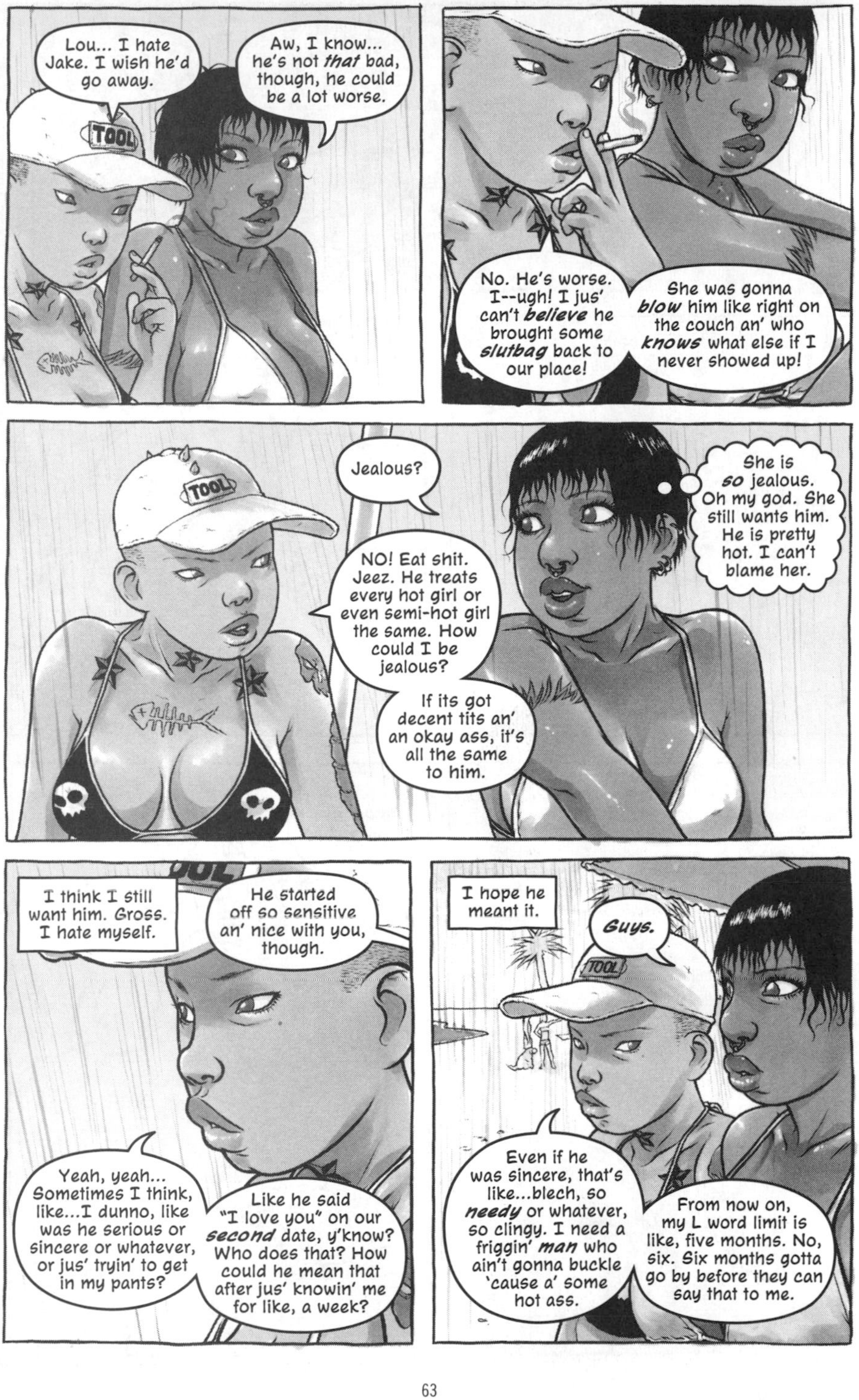

Lou... I hate Jake. I wish he'd go away.
Aw, I know... he's not *that* bad, though, he could be a lot worse.
TOOL
No. He's worse. I--ugh! I jus' can't **believe** he brought some **slutbag** back to our place!
She was gonna **blow** him like right on the couch an' who **knows** what else if I never showed up!
Jealous?
TOOL
NO! Eat shit. Jeez. He treats every hot girl or even semi-hot girl the same. How could I be jealous?
She is **so** jealous. Oh my god. She still wants him. He is pretty hot. I can't blame her.
If its got decent tits an' an okay ass, it's all the same to him.
I think I still want him. Gross. I hate myself.
He started off so sensitive an' nice with you, though.
Yeah, yeah... Sometimes I think, like...I dunno, like was he serious or sincere or whatever, or jus' tryin' to get in my pants?
Like he said "I love you" on our **second** date, y'know? Who does that? How could he mean that after jus' knowin' me for like, a week?
I hope he meant it.
Guys.
TOOL
Even if he was sincere, that's like...blech, so **needy** or whatever, so clingy. I need a friggin' **man** who ain't gonna buckle 'cause a' some hot ass.
From now on, my L word limit is like, five months. No, six. Six months gotta go by before they can say that to me.

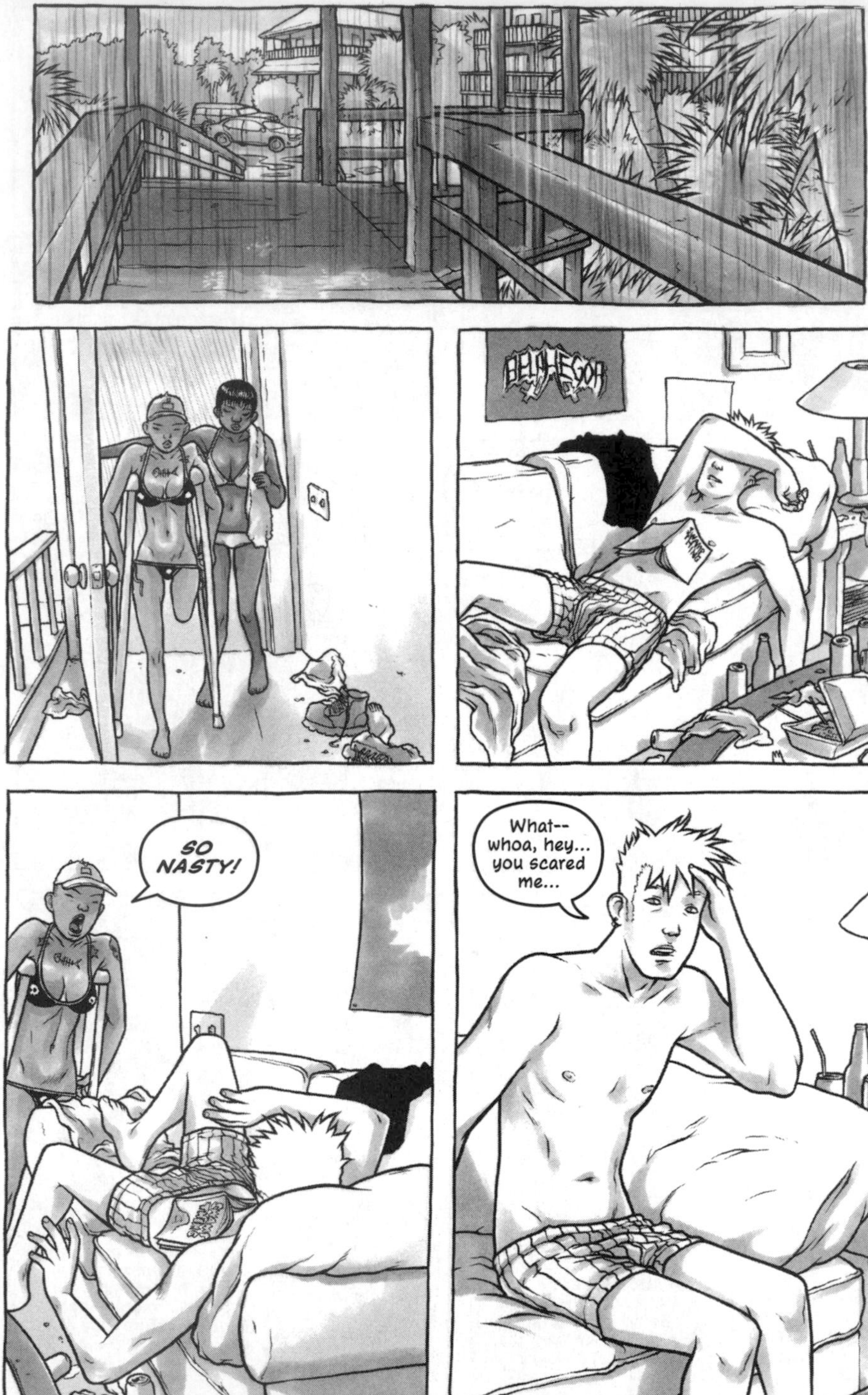
SO NASTY!
What-- whoa, hey... you scared me...

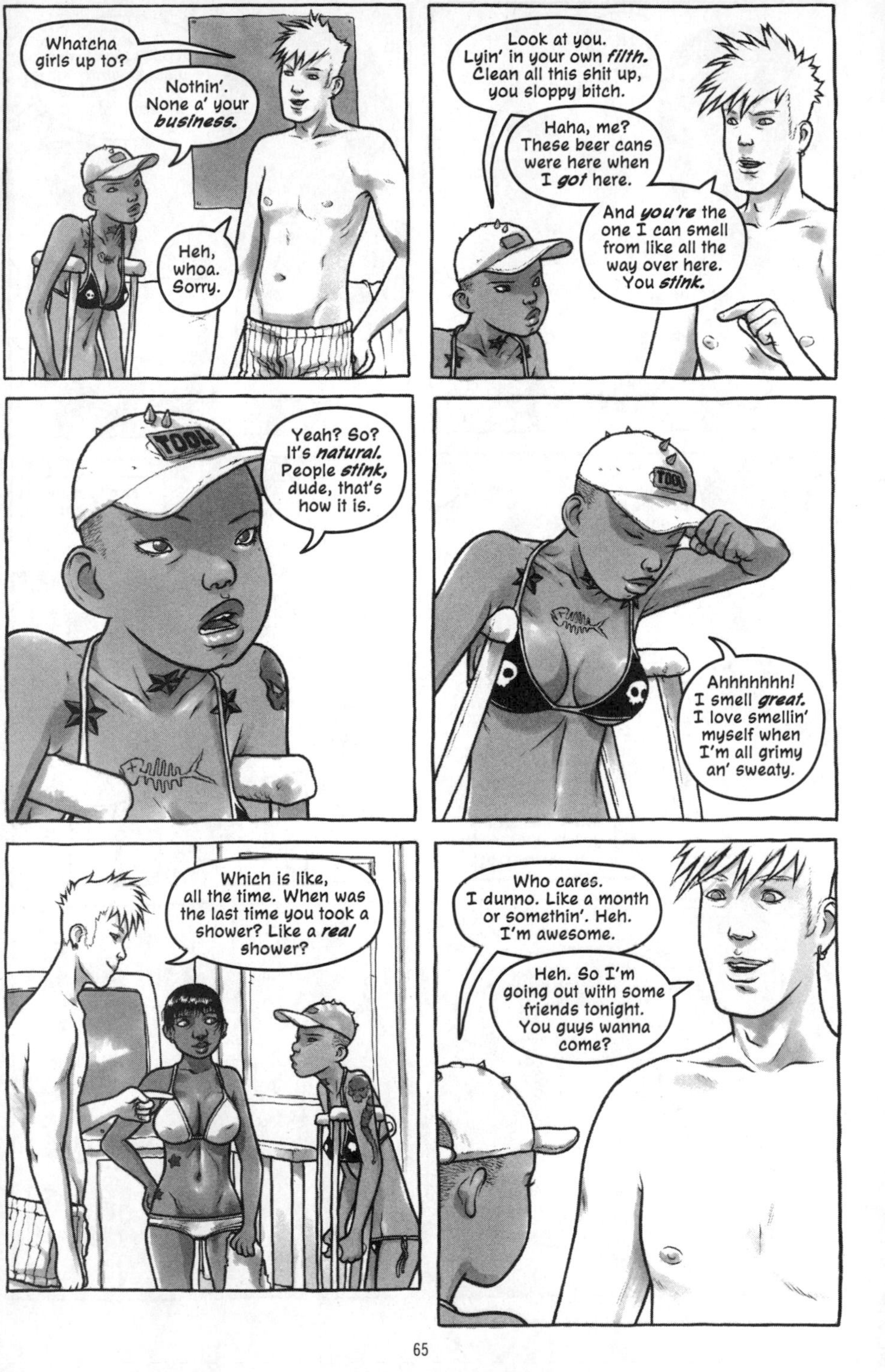
Whatcha girls up to?
Nothin'. None a' your business.
Heh, whoa. Sorry.
Look at you. Lyin' in your own filth. Clean all this shit up, you sloppy bitch.
Haha, me? These beer cans were here when I got here.
And you're the one I can smell from like all the way over here. You stink.
TOOL
Yeah? So? It's natural. People stink, dude, that's how it is.
TOOL
Ahhhhhhh! I smell great. I love smellin' myself when I'm all grimy an' sweaty.
Which is like, all the time. When was the last time you took a shower? Like a real shower?
Who cares. I dunno. Like a month or somethin'. Heh. I'm awesome.
Heh. So I'm going out with some friends tonight. You guys wanna come?

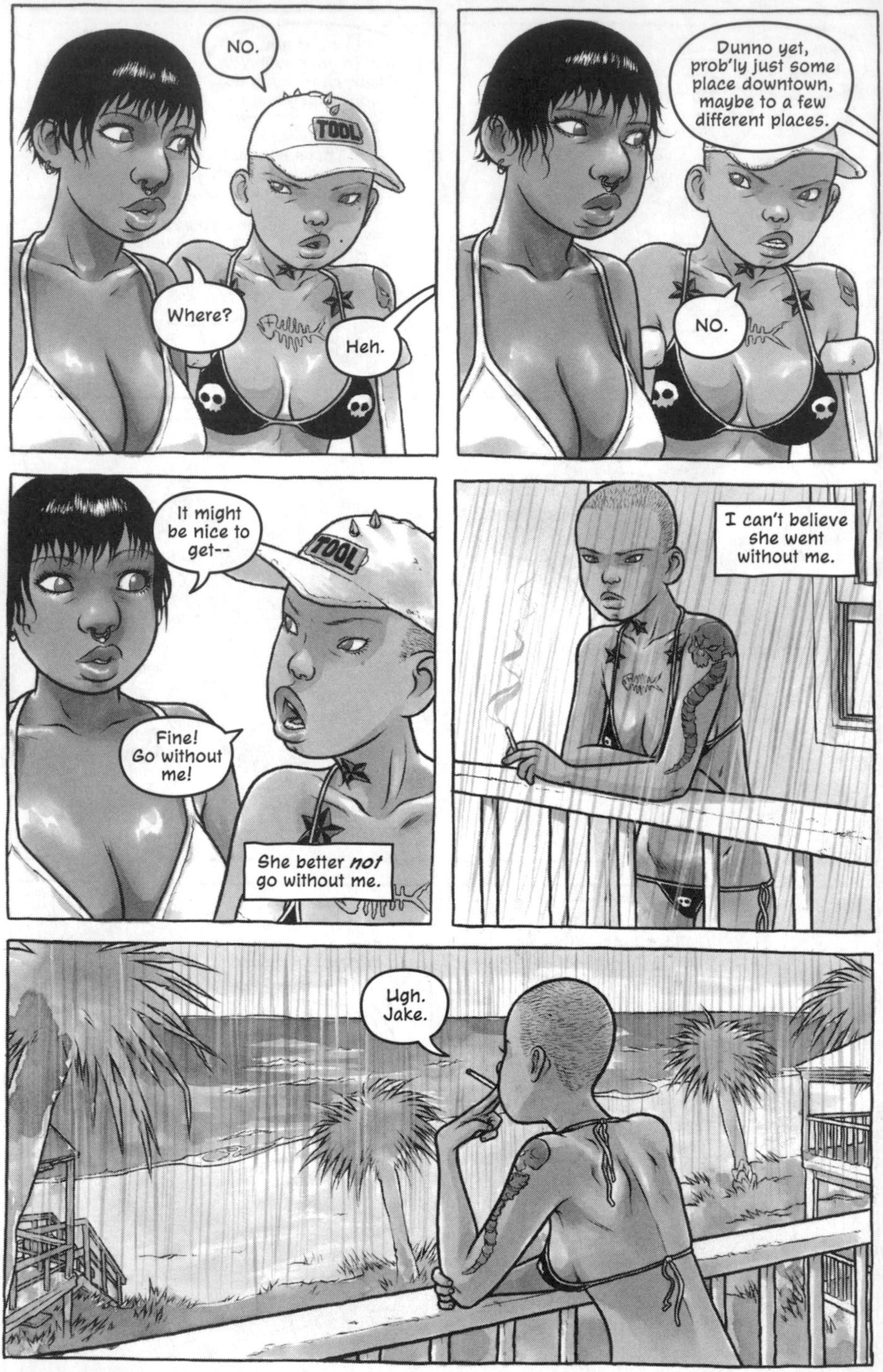
NO.
Where?
Heh.
Dunno yet, prob'ly just some place downtown, maybe to a few different places.
NO.
It might be nice to get--
Fine! Go without me!
She better *not* go without me.
I can't believe she went without me.
Ugh. Jake.

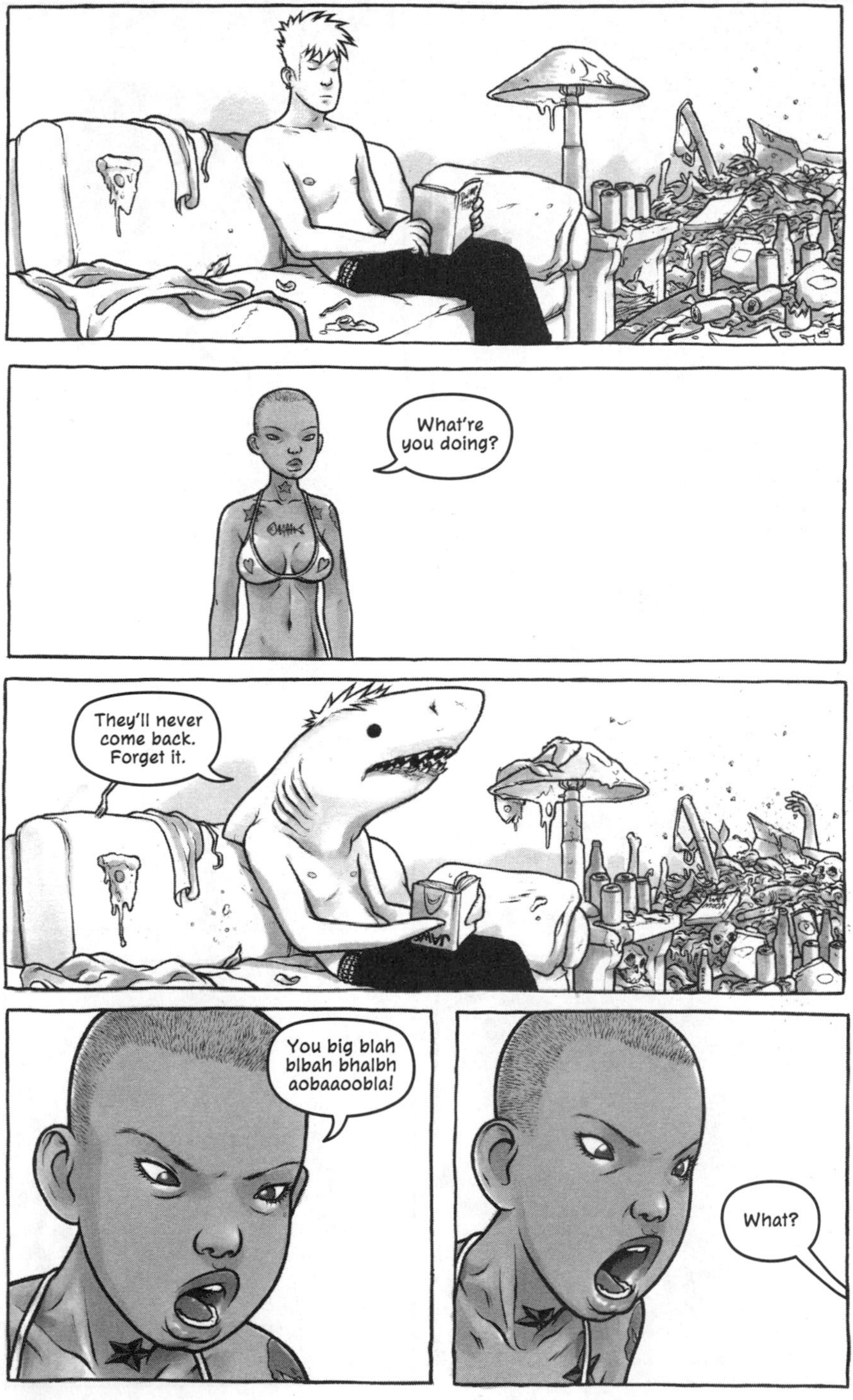
What're you doing?
They'll never come back. Forget it.
You big blah blbah bhalbh aobaaoobla!
What?

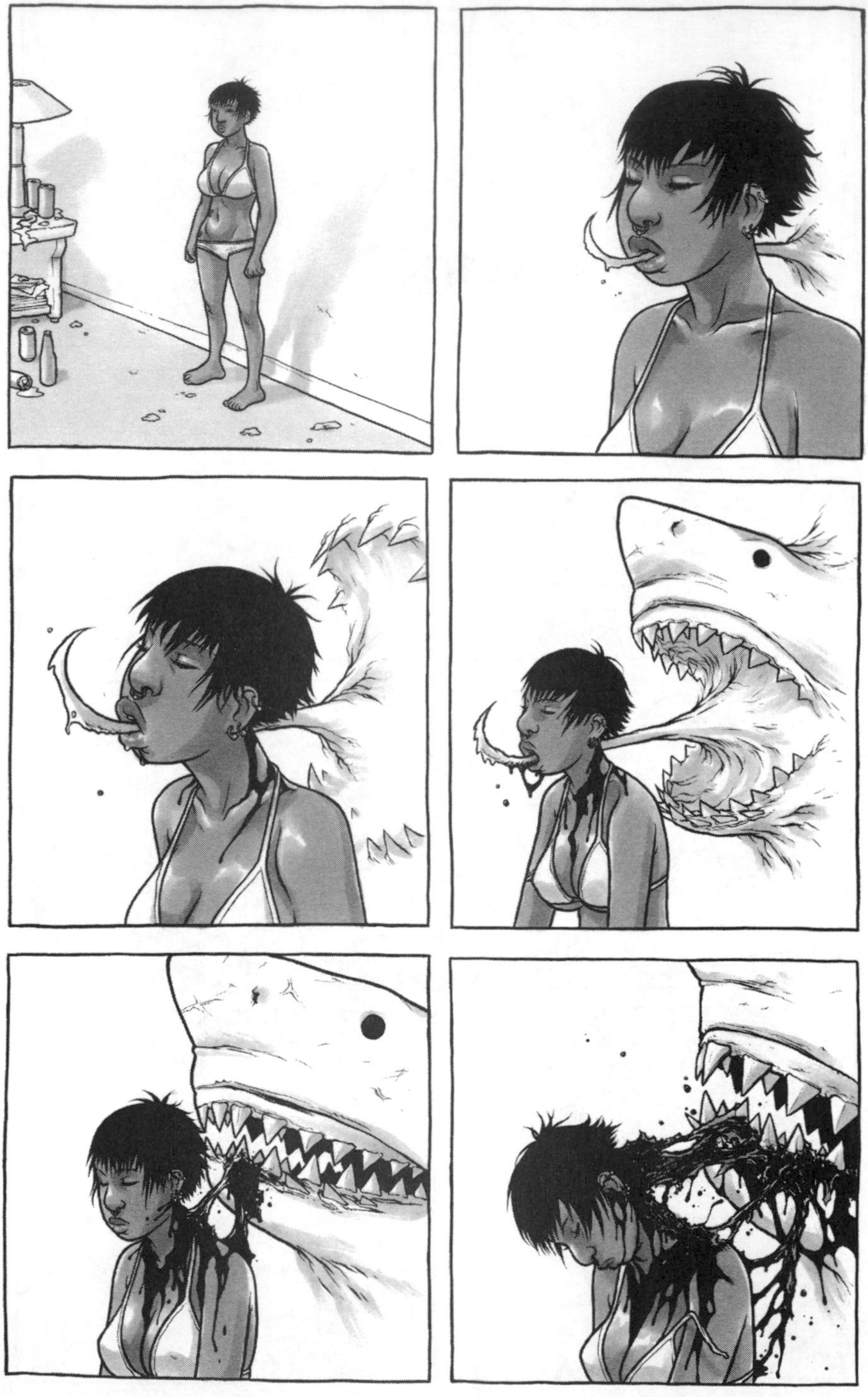

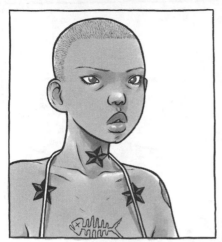

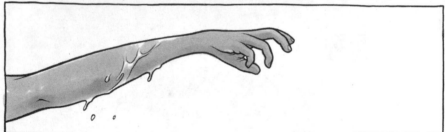

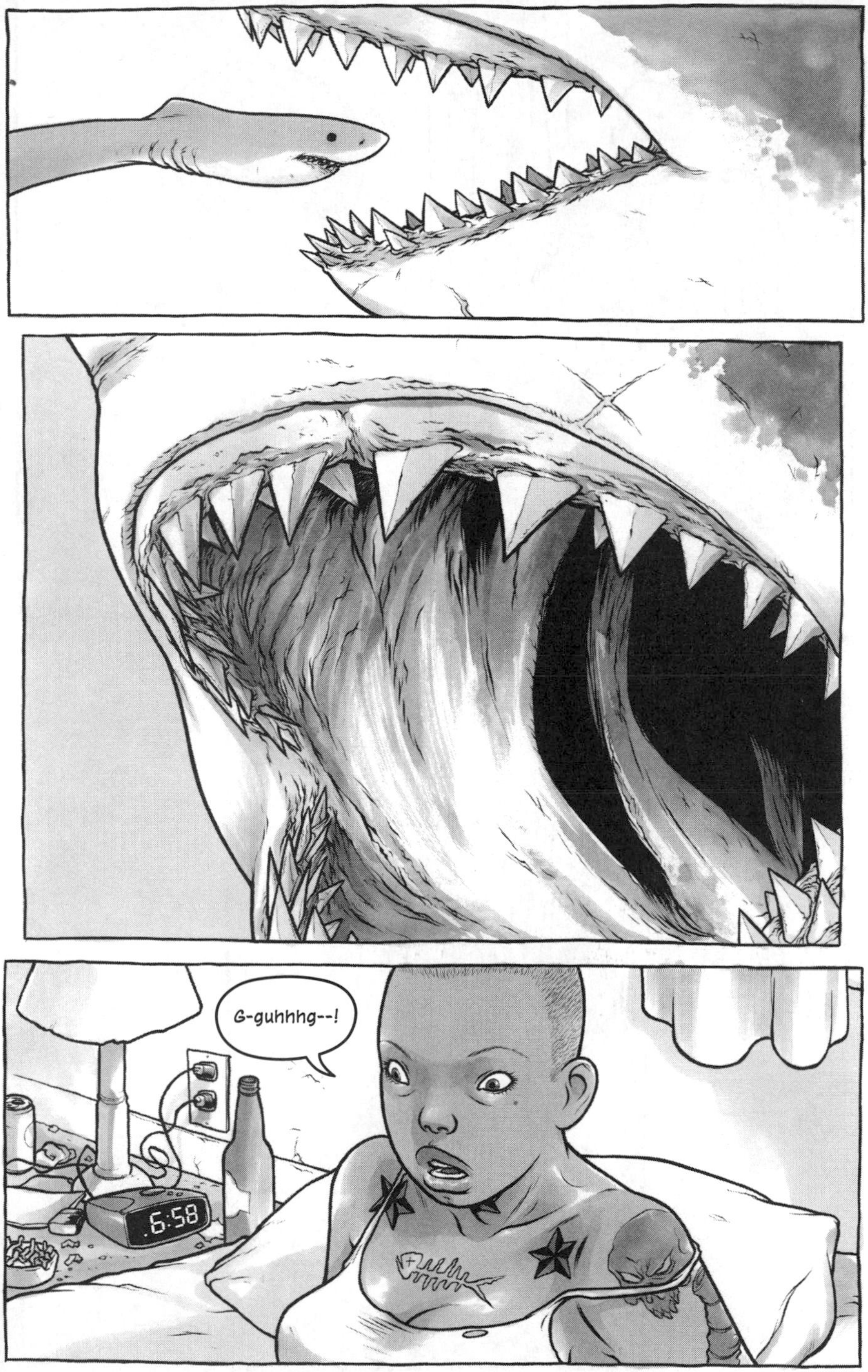
G-guhhhg--!
6:58

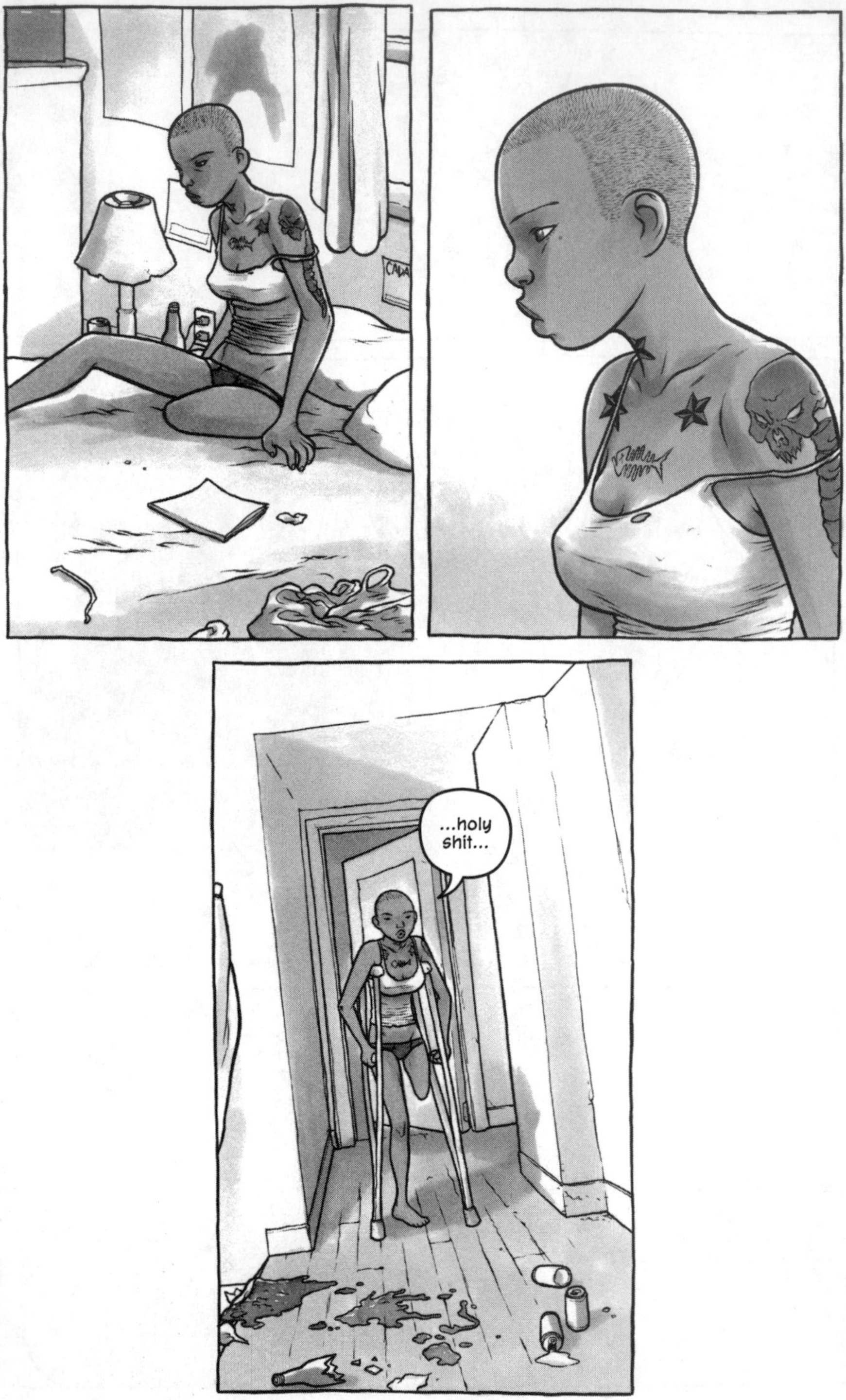
...holy shit...

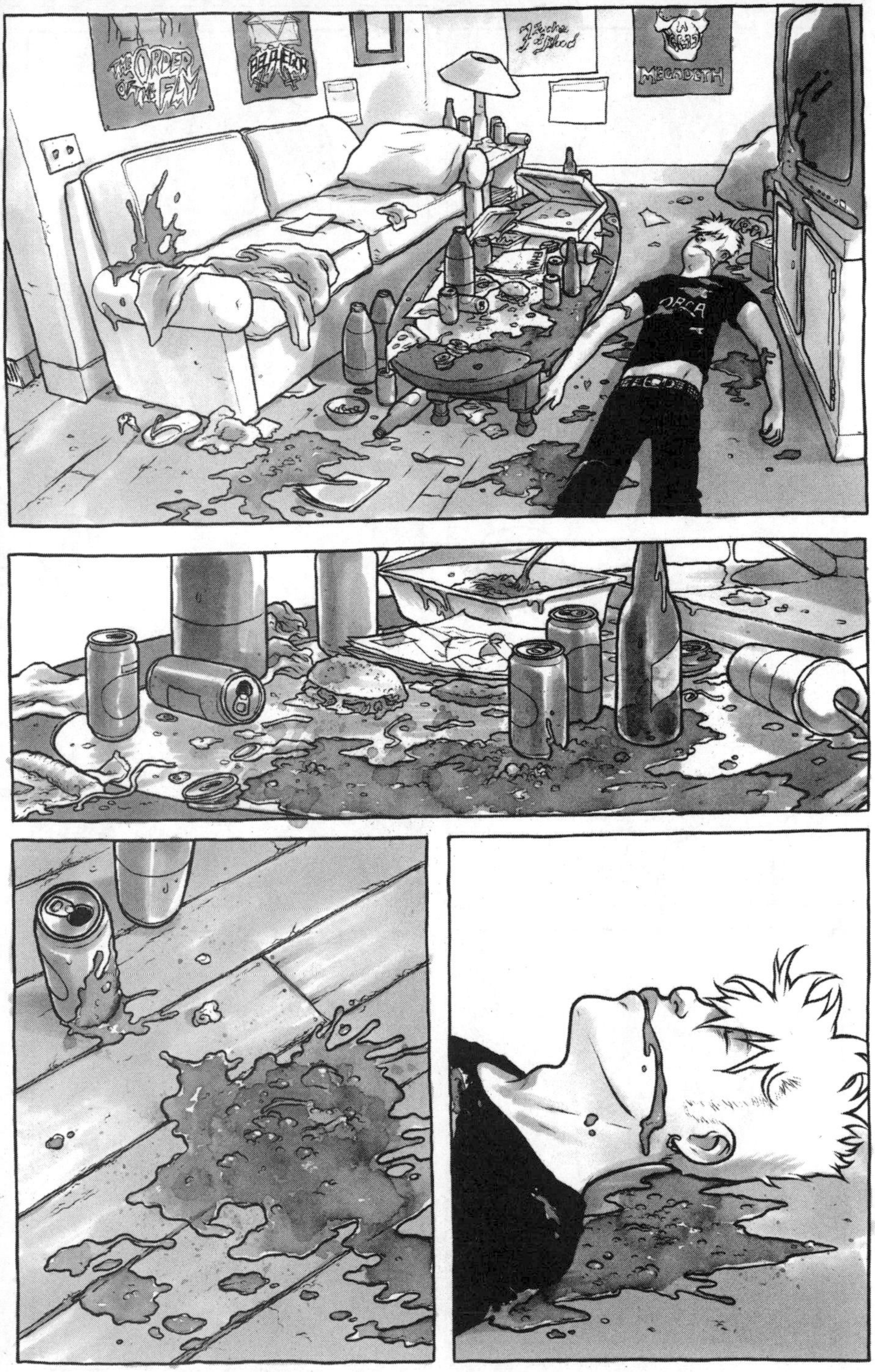
THE ORDER OF THE FLY
MEGADETH

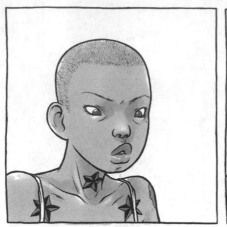

Jake.

JAKE.

JAKE!

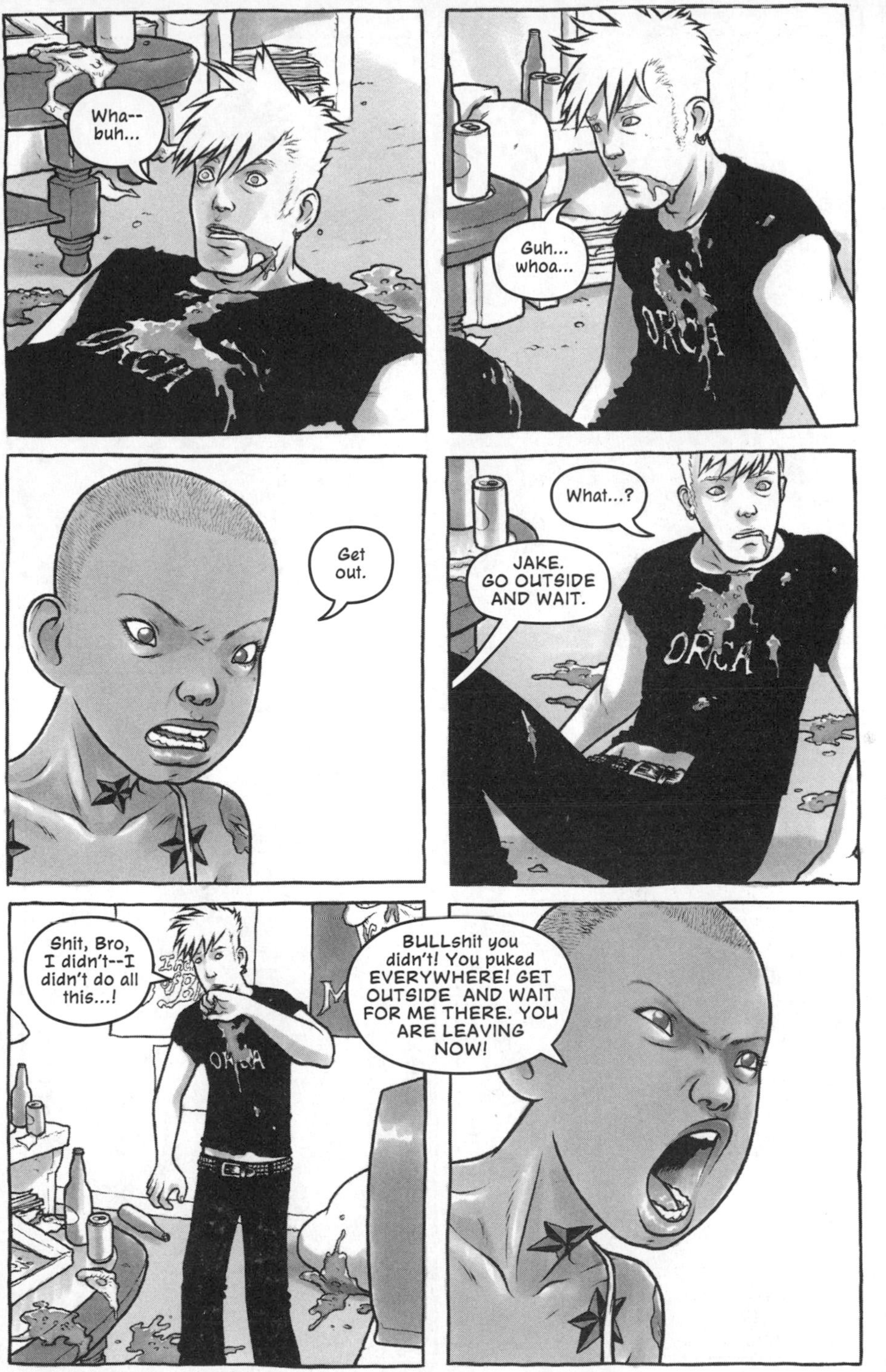
Wha--
buh...
Guh...
whoa...
Get
out.
What...?
JAKE.
GO OUTSIDE
AND WAIT.
Shit, Bro,
I didn't--I
didn't do all
this...!
BULLshit you
didn't! You puked
EVERYWHERE! GET
OUTSIDE AND WAIT
FOR ME THERE. YOU
ARE LEAVING
NOW!

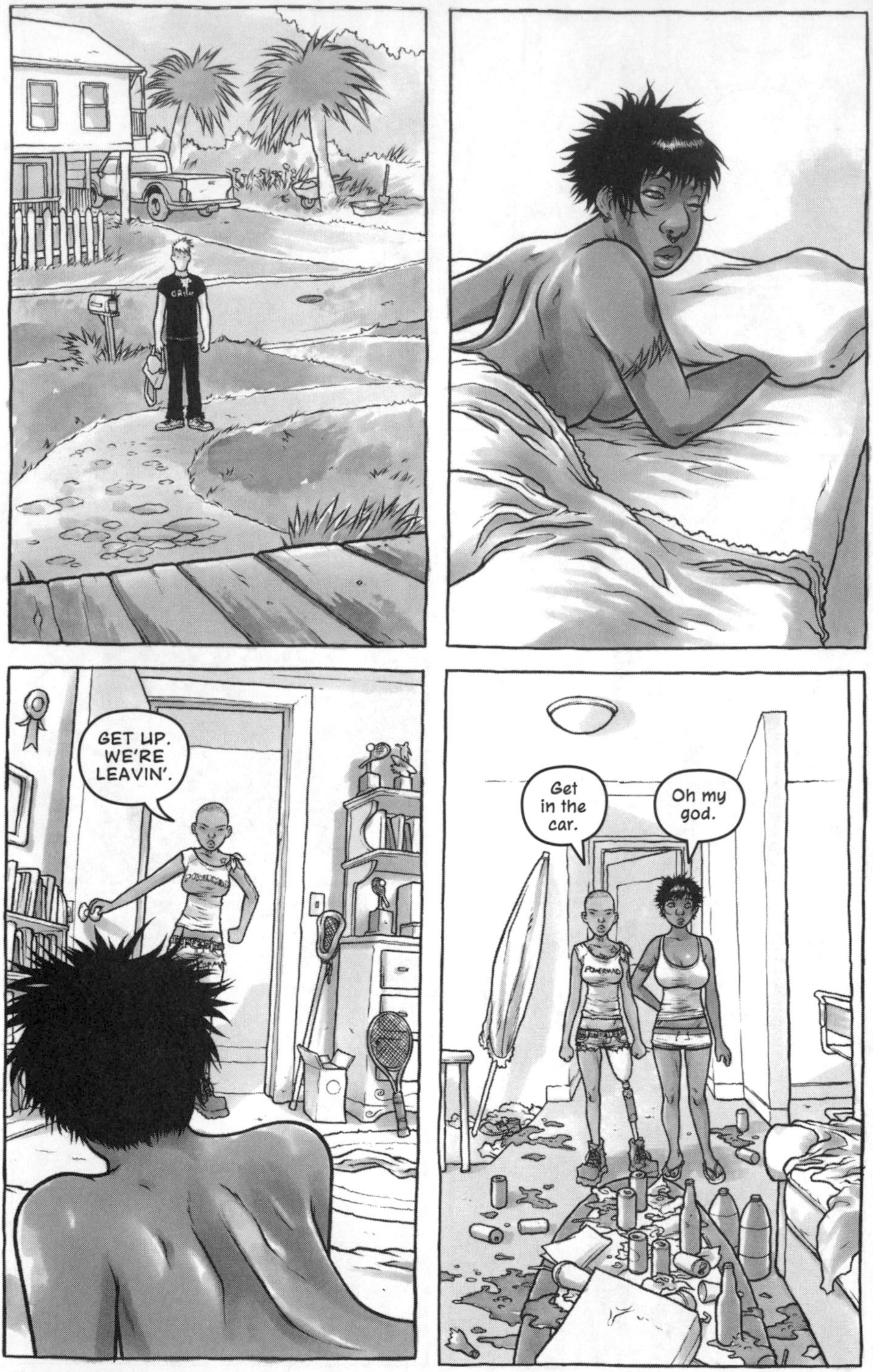
GET UP. WE'RE LEAVIN'.
Get in the car.
Oh my god.

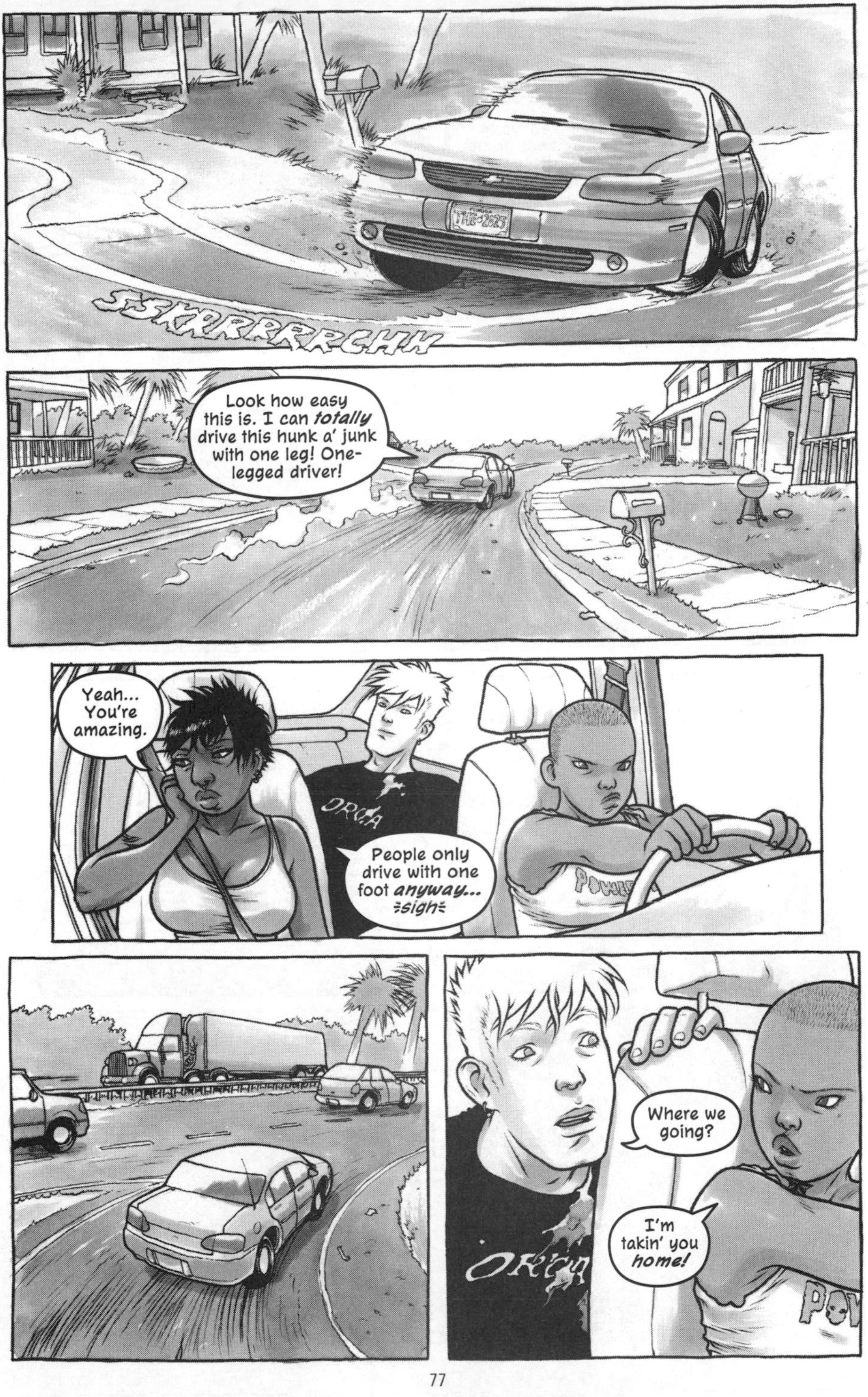
SSKRRRRRRCHH
Look how easy this is. I can *totally* drive this hunk a' junk with one leg! One-legged driver!
Yeah... You're amazing.
People only drive with one foot *anyway...* *sigh*
Where we going?
I'm takin' you *home!*

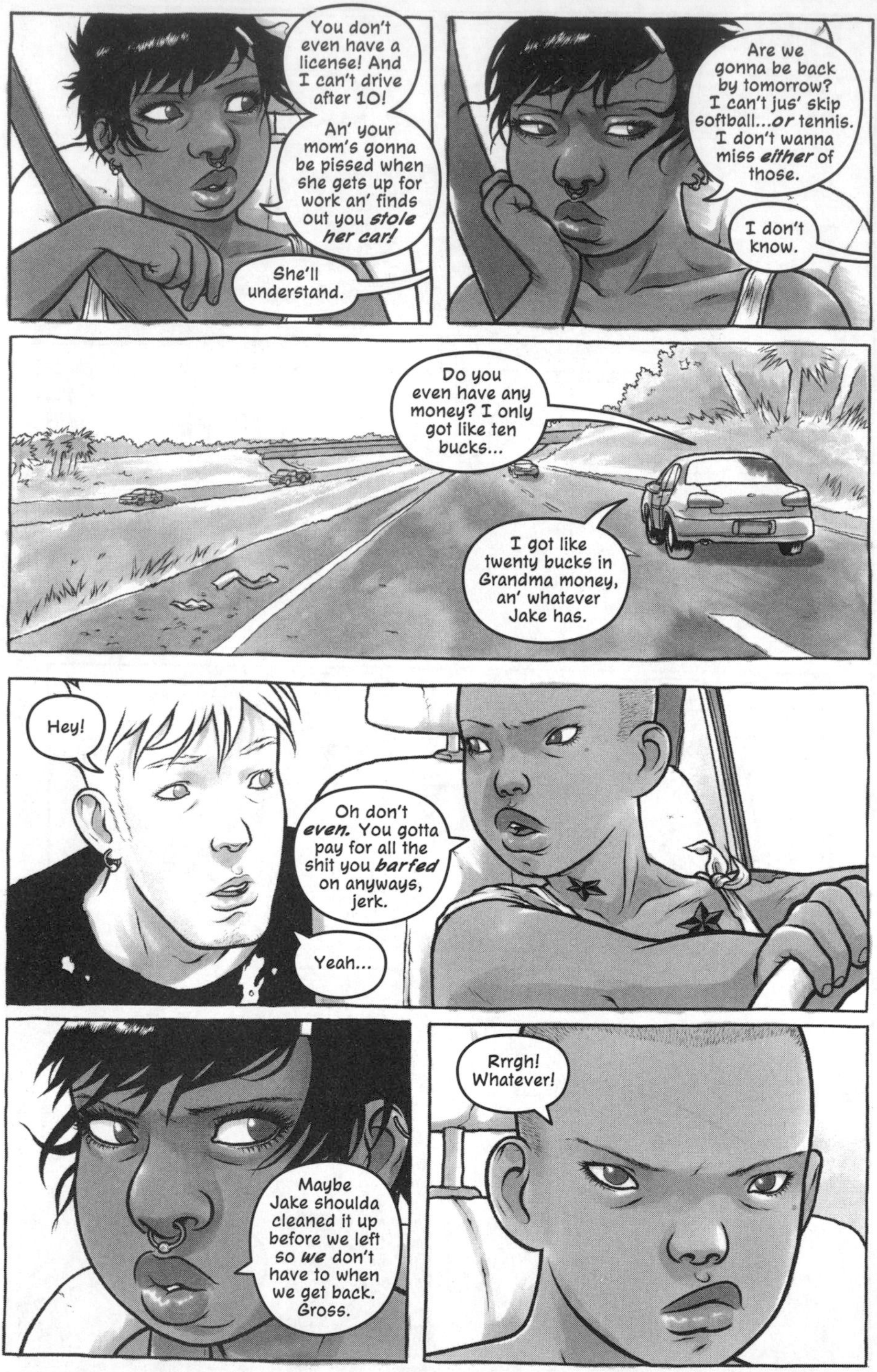
You don't even have a license! And I can't drive after 10!
An' your mom's gonna be pissed when she gets up for work an' finds out you *stole her car!*
She'll understand.
Are we gonna be back by tomorrow? I can't jus' skip softball...*or* tennis. I don't wanna miss *either* of those.
I don't know.
Do you even have any money? I only got like ten bucks...
I got like twenty bucks in Grandma money, an' whatever Jake has.
Hey!
Oh don't *even.* You gotta pay for all the shit you *barfed* on anyways, jerk.
Yeah...
Maybe Jake shoulda cleaned it up before we left so *we* don't have to when we get back. Gross.
Rrrgh! Whatever!

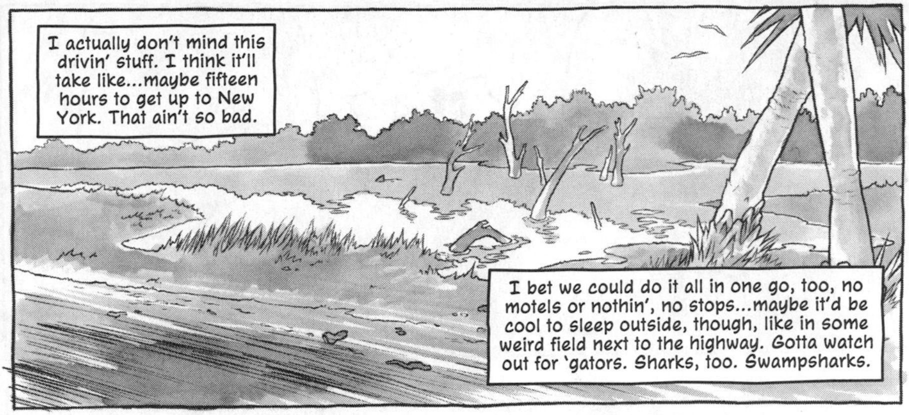
I actually don't mind this drivin' stuff. I think it'll take like...maybe fifteen hours to get up to New York. That ain't so bad.
I bet we could do it all in one go, too, no motels or nothin', no stops...maybe it'd be cool to sleep outside, though, like in some weird field next to the highway. Gotta watch out for 'gators. Sharks, too. Swampsharks.

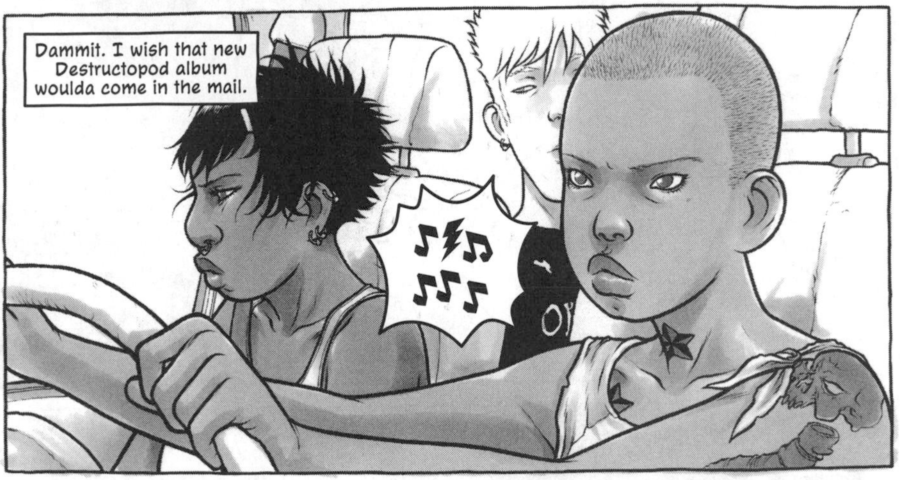
Dammit. I wish that new Destructopod album woulda come in the mail.

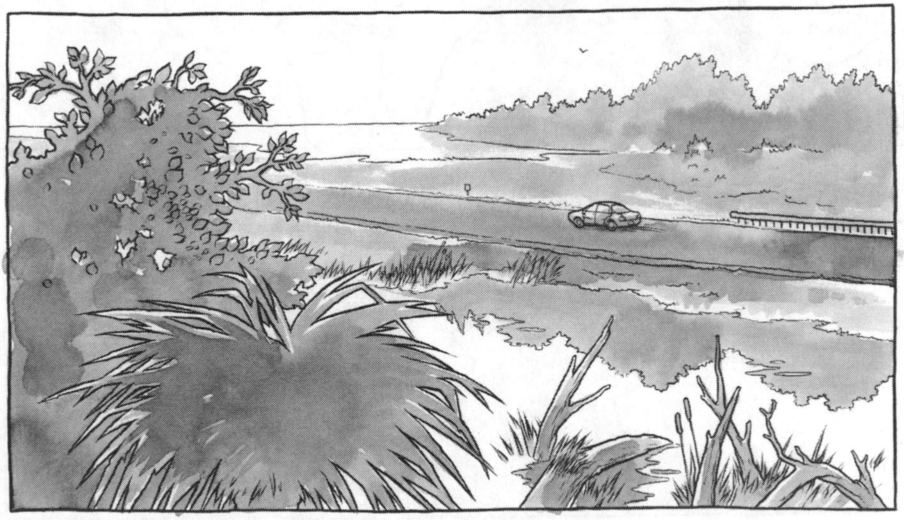

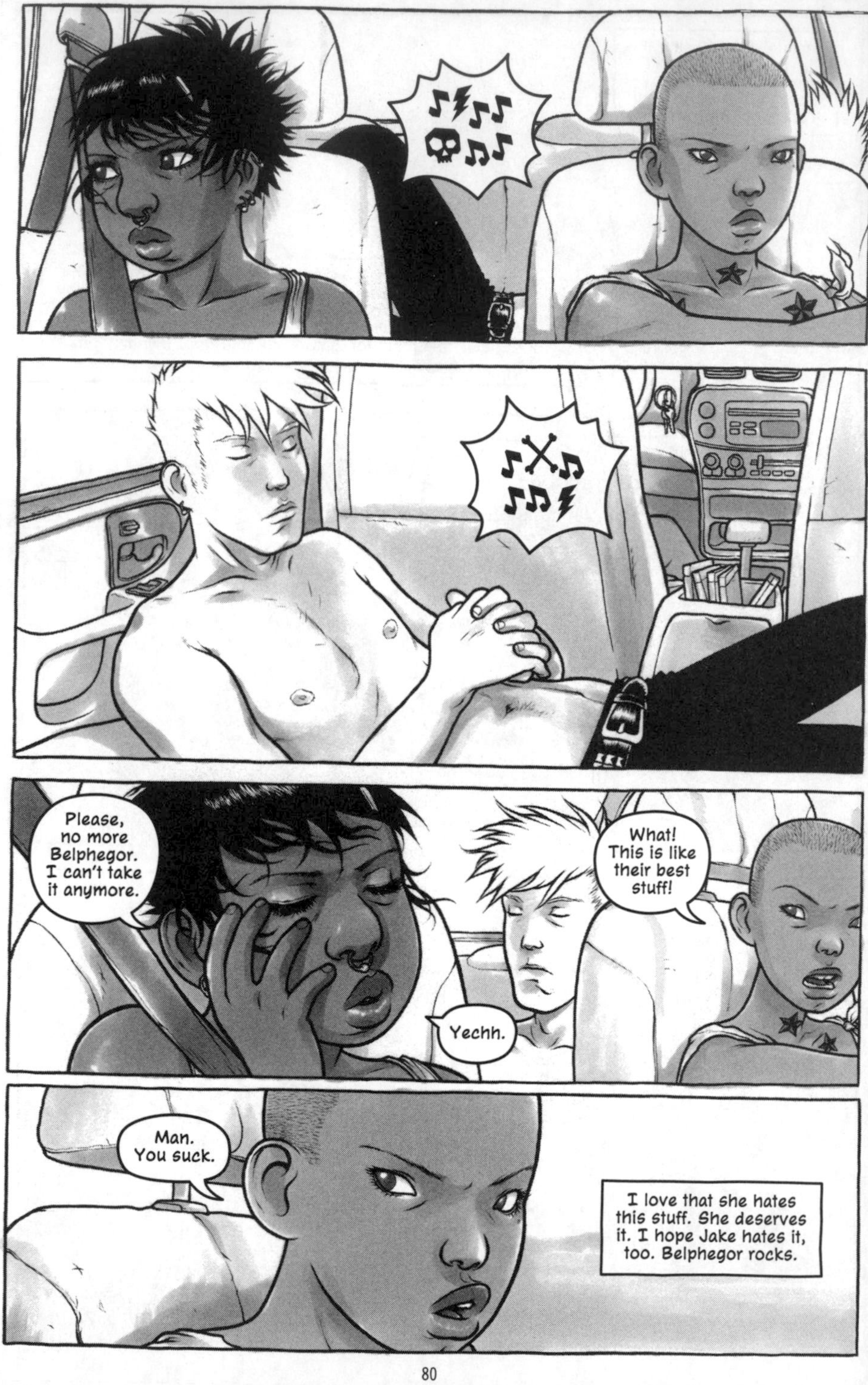
Please, no more Belphegor. I can't take it anymore.
What! This is like their best stuff!
Yechh.
Man. You suck.
I love that she hates this stuff. She deserves it. I hope Jake hates it, too. Belphegor rocks.

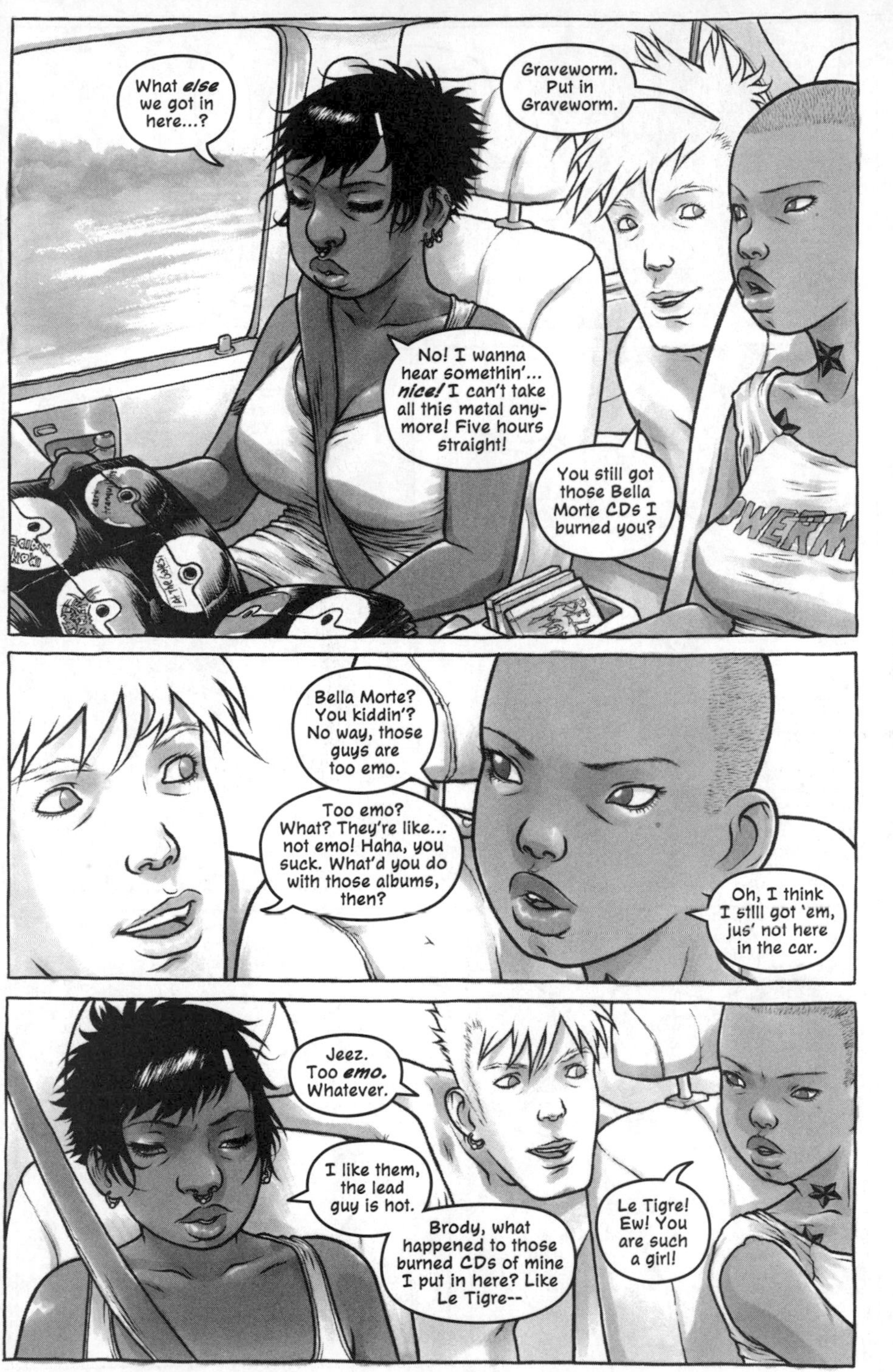
What *else* we got in here...?
Graveworm. Put in Graveworm.
No! I wanna hear somethin'... *nice!* I can't take all this metal any-more! Five hours straight!
You still got those Bella Morte CDs I burned you?
Bella Morte? You kiddin'? No way, those guys are too emo.
Too emo? What? They're like... not emo! Haha, you suck. What'd you do with those albums, then?
Oh, I think I still got 'em, jus' not here in the car.
Jeez. Too *emo.* Whatever.
I like them, the lead guy is hot.
Brody, what happened to those burned CDs of mine I put in here? Like Le Tigre--
Le Tigre! Ew! You are such a girl!

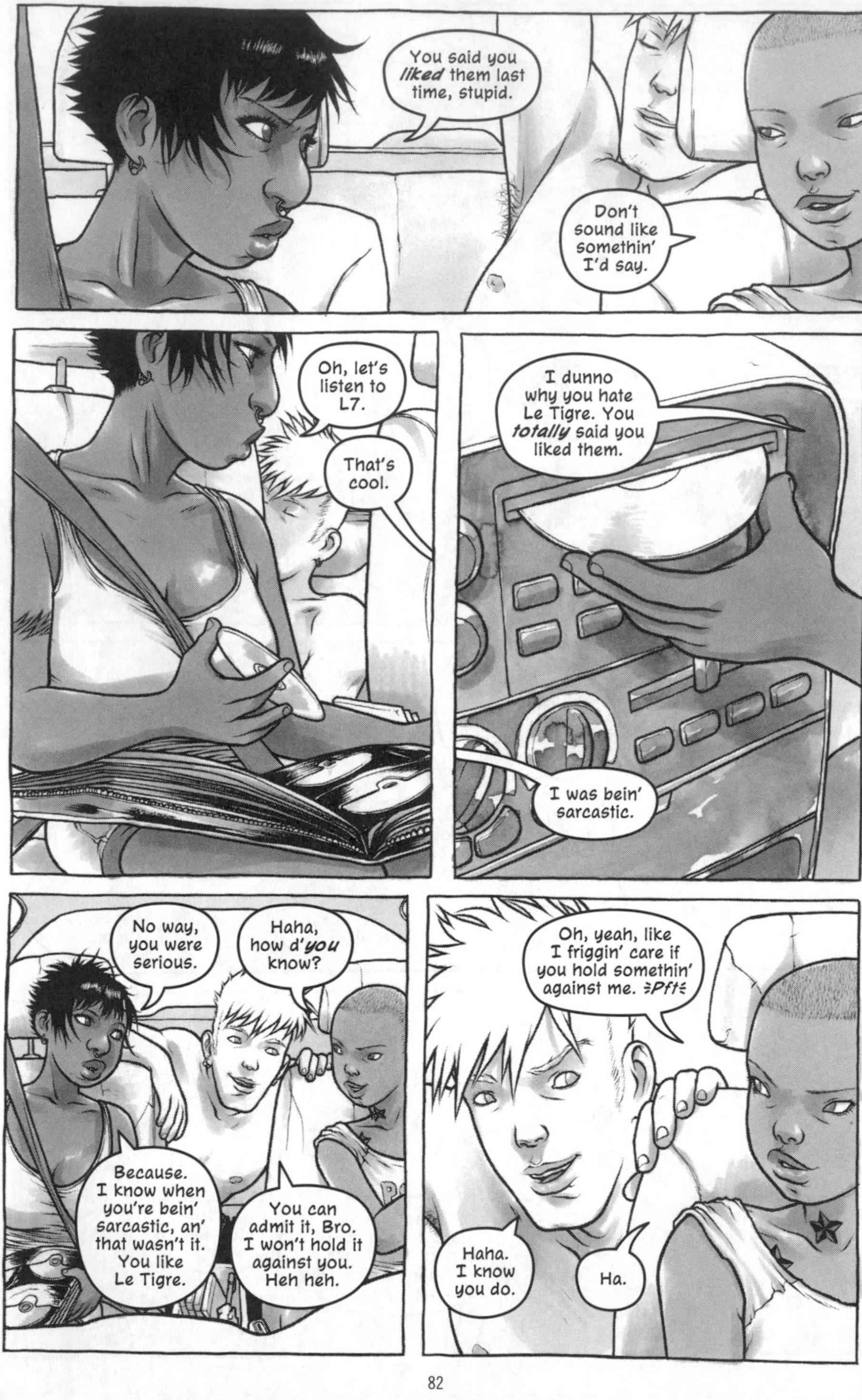
You said you *liked* them last time, stupid.
Don't sound like somethin' I'd say.
Oh, let's listen to L7.
That's cool.
I dunno why you hate Le Tigre. You *totally* said you liked them.
I was bein' sarcastic.
No way, you were serious.
Haha, how d'*you* know?
Because. I know when you're bein' sarcastic, an' that wasn't it. You like Le Tigre.
You can admit it, Bro. I won't hold it against you. Heh heh.
Oh, yeah, like I friggin' care if you hold somethin' against me. *Pft*
Haha. I know you do.
Ha.

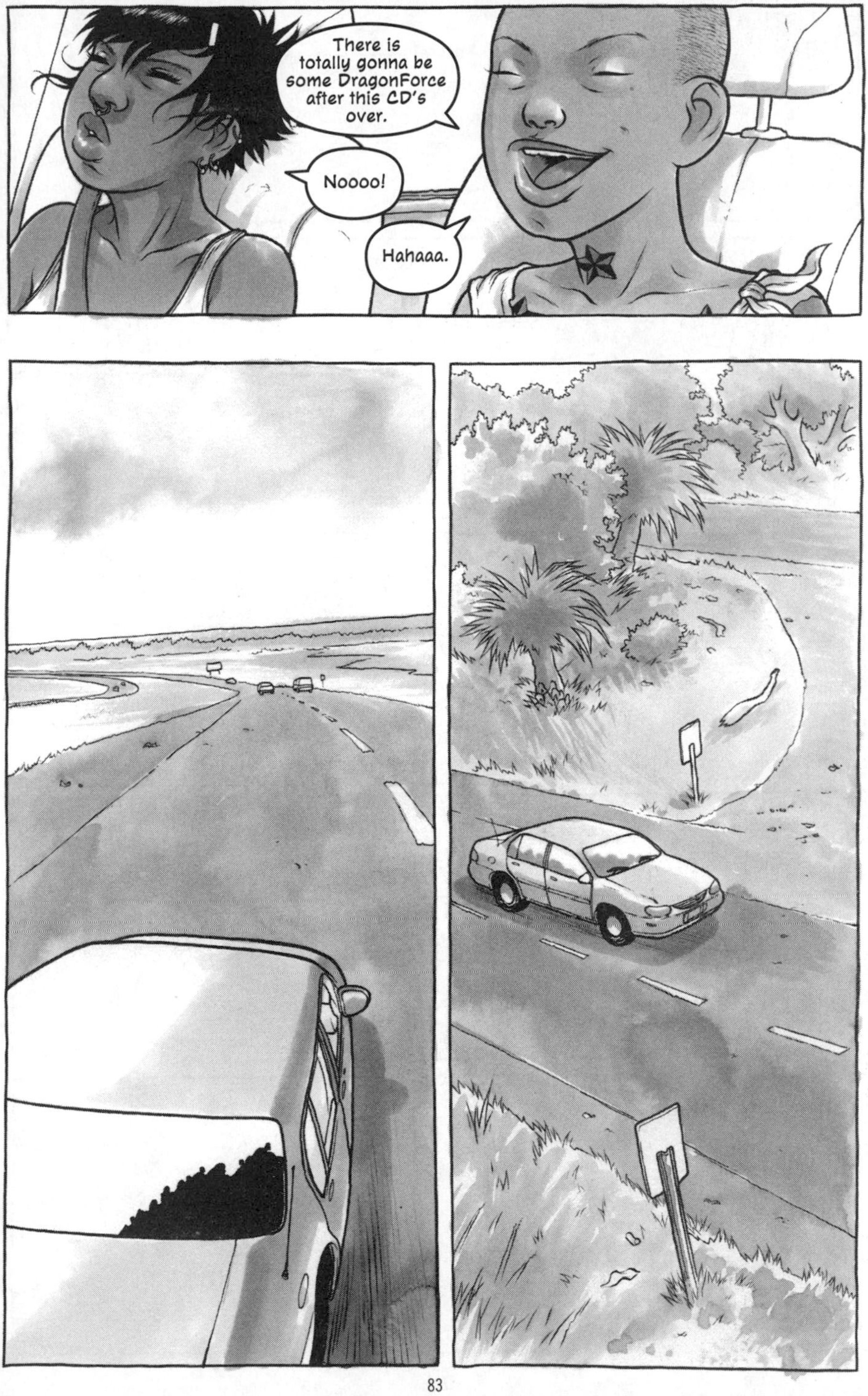
There is totally gonna be some DragonForce after this CD's over.
Noooo!
Hahaaa.

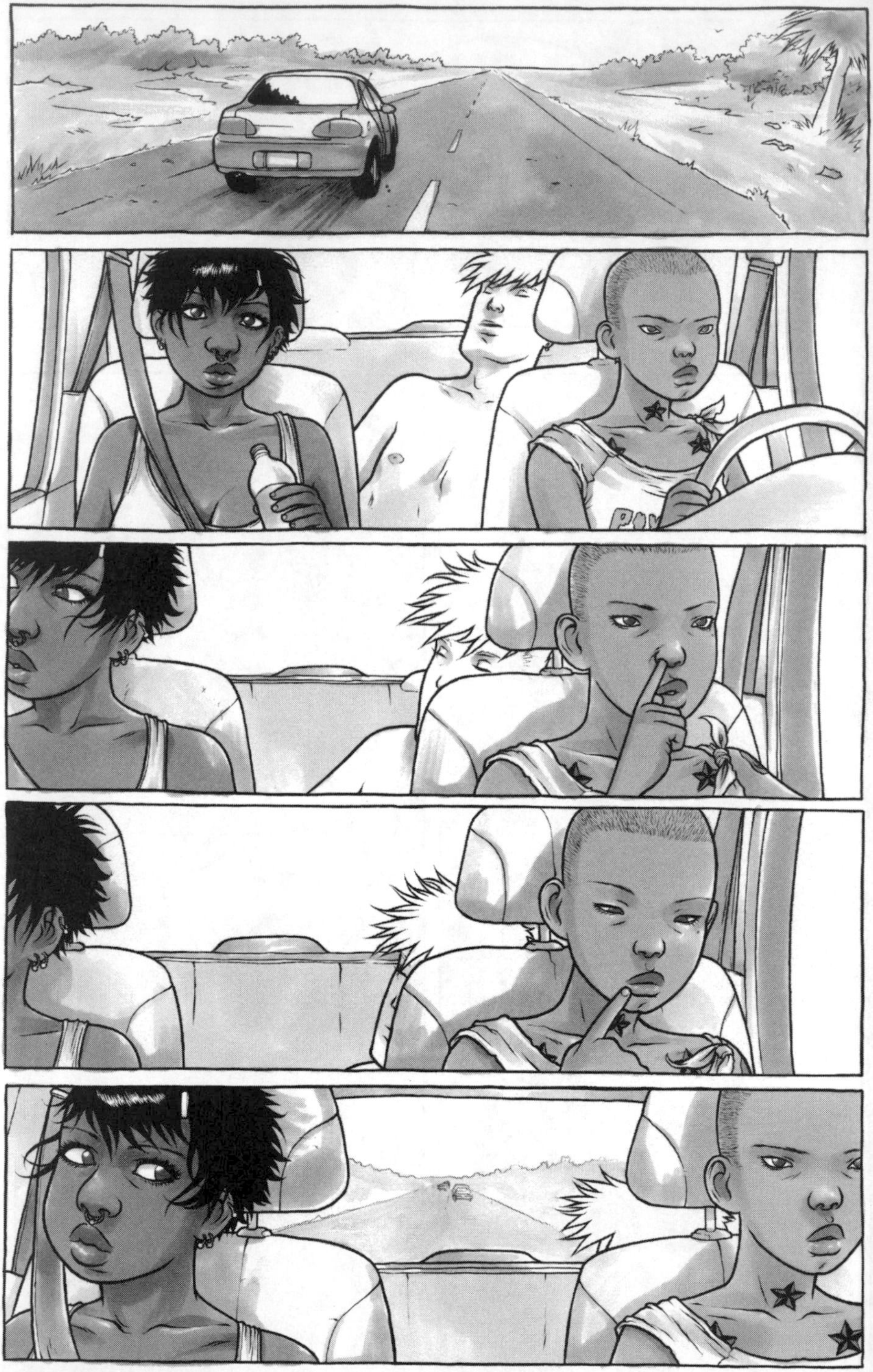

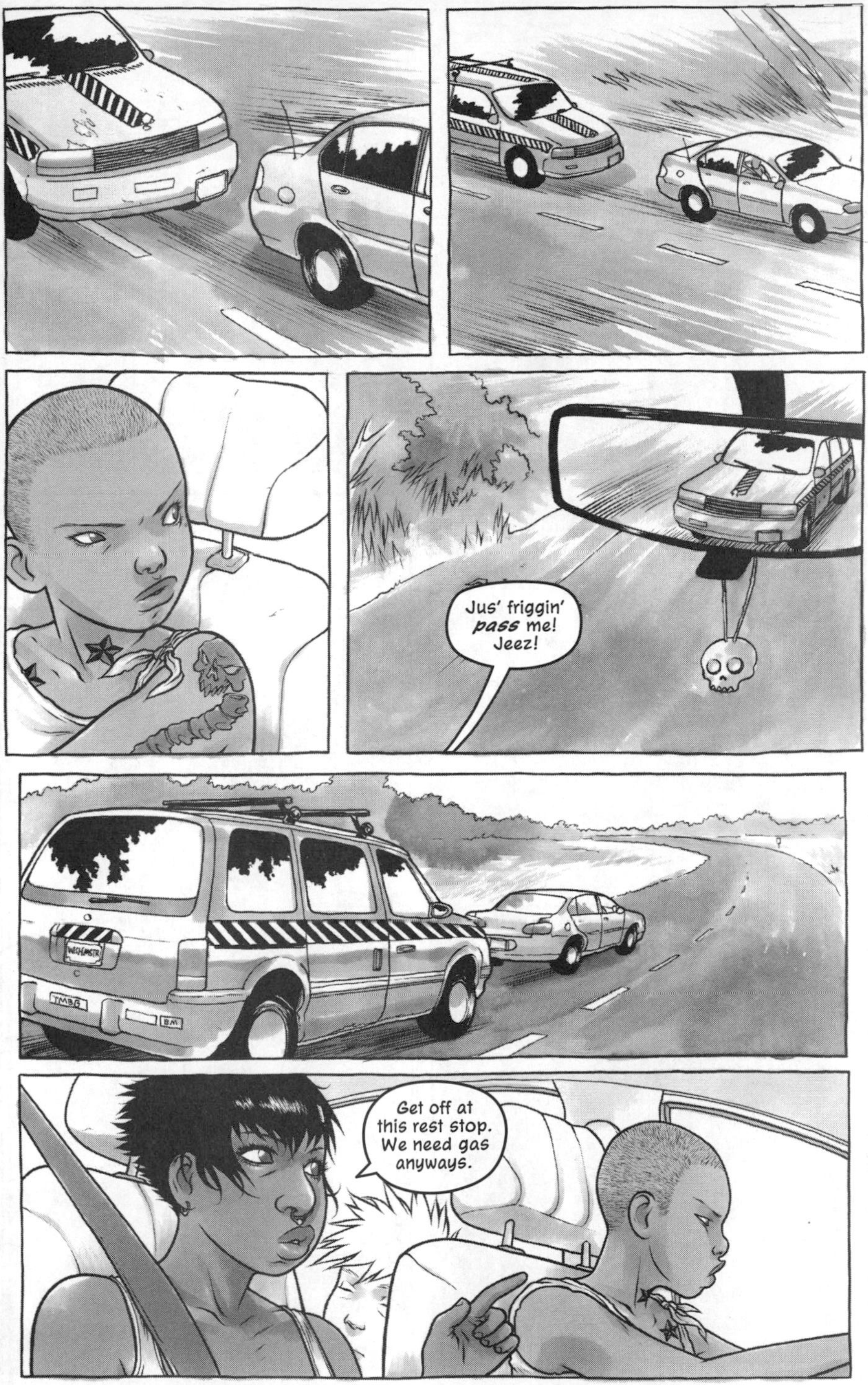
Jus' friggin' *pass* me! Jeez!
Get off at this rest stop. We need gas anyways.

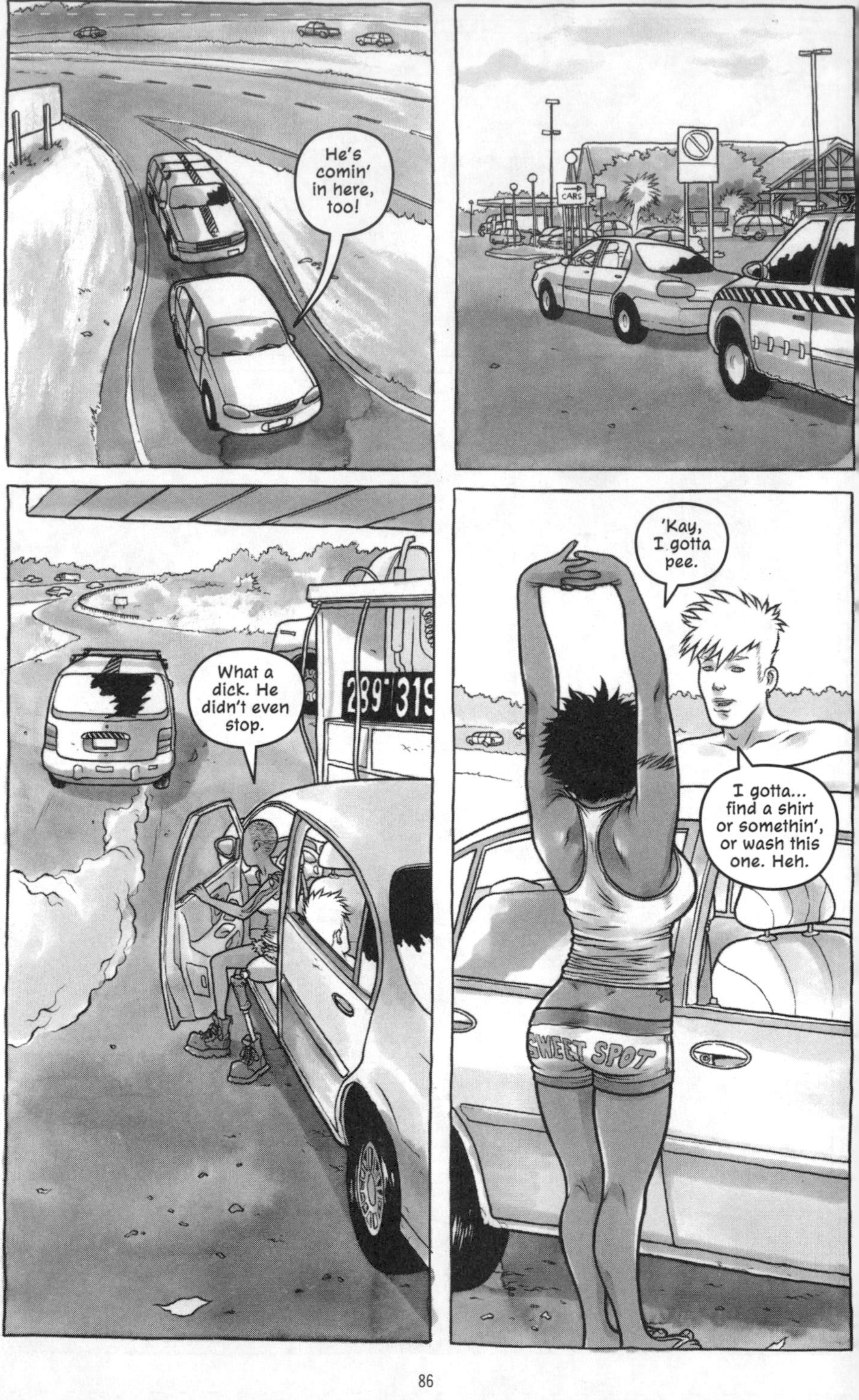
He's comin' in here, too!
CARS
What a dick. He didn't even stop.
'Kay, I gotta pee.
I gotta... find a shirt or somethin', or wash this one. Heh.
SWEET SPOT

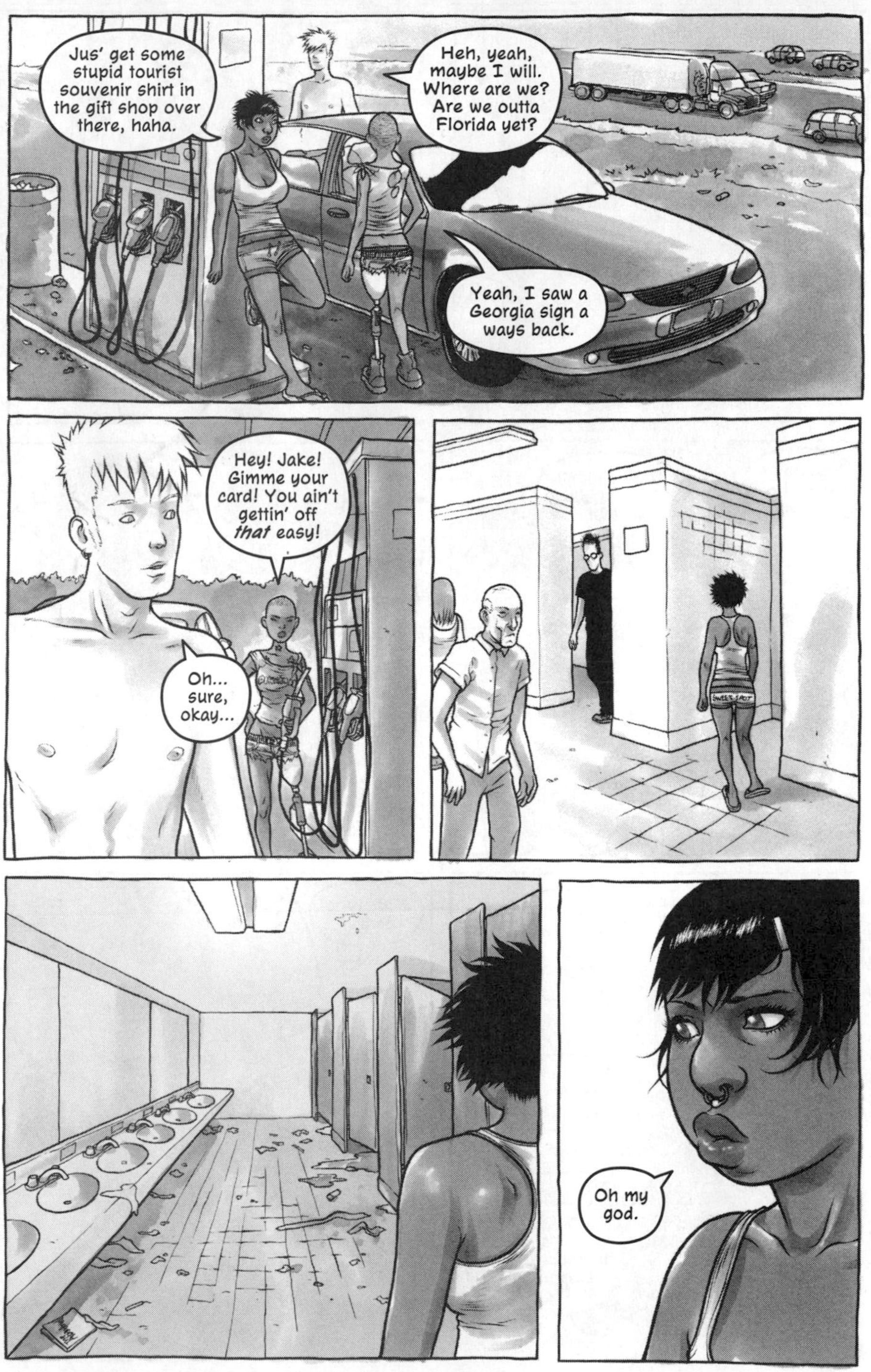
Jus' get some stupid tourist souvenir shirt in the gift shop over there, haha.
Heh, yeah, maybe I will. Where are we? Are we outta Florida yet?
Yeah, I saw a Georgia sign a ways back.
Hey! Jake! Gimme your card! You ain't gettin' off *that* easy!
Oh... sure, okay...
Oh my god.

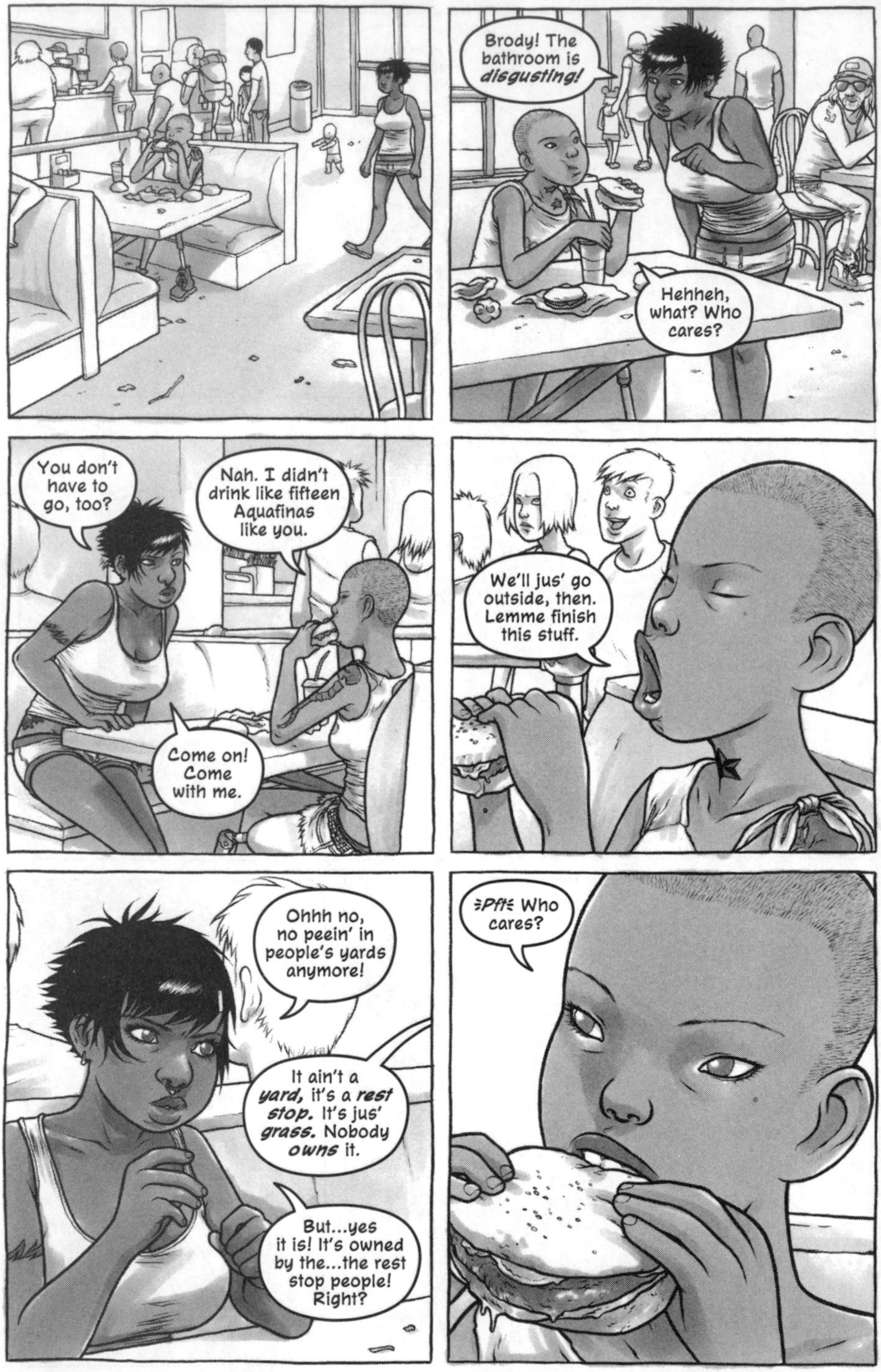
Brody! The bathroom is *disgusting!*
Hehheh, what? Who cares?
You don't have to go, too?
Nah. I didn't drink like fifteen Aquafinas like you.
Come on! Come with me.
We'll jus' go outside, then. Lemme finish this stuff.
Ohhh no, no peein' in people's yards anymore!
It ain't a *yard,* it's a *rest stop.* It's jus' *grass.* Nobody *owns* it.
But...yes it is! It's owned by the...the rest stop people! Right?
Pft Who cares?

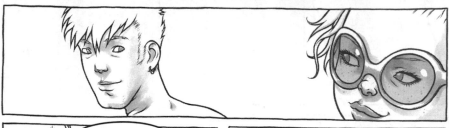

Hi! You just come from swimmin' or somethin'?

Heh heh, no... um, I just spilled um, engine oil all over my shirt, so I'm in here getting a new one.

Ah. Here, get this one...

I like the *peach,* isn't it cute?

GEORGIA ON MY MIND

89

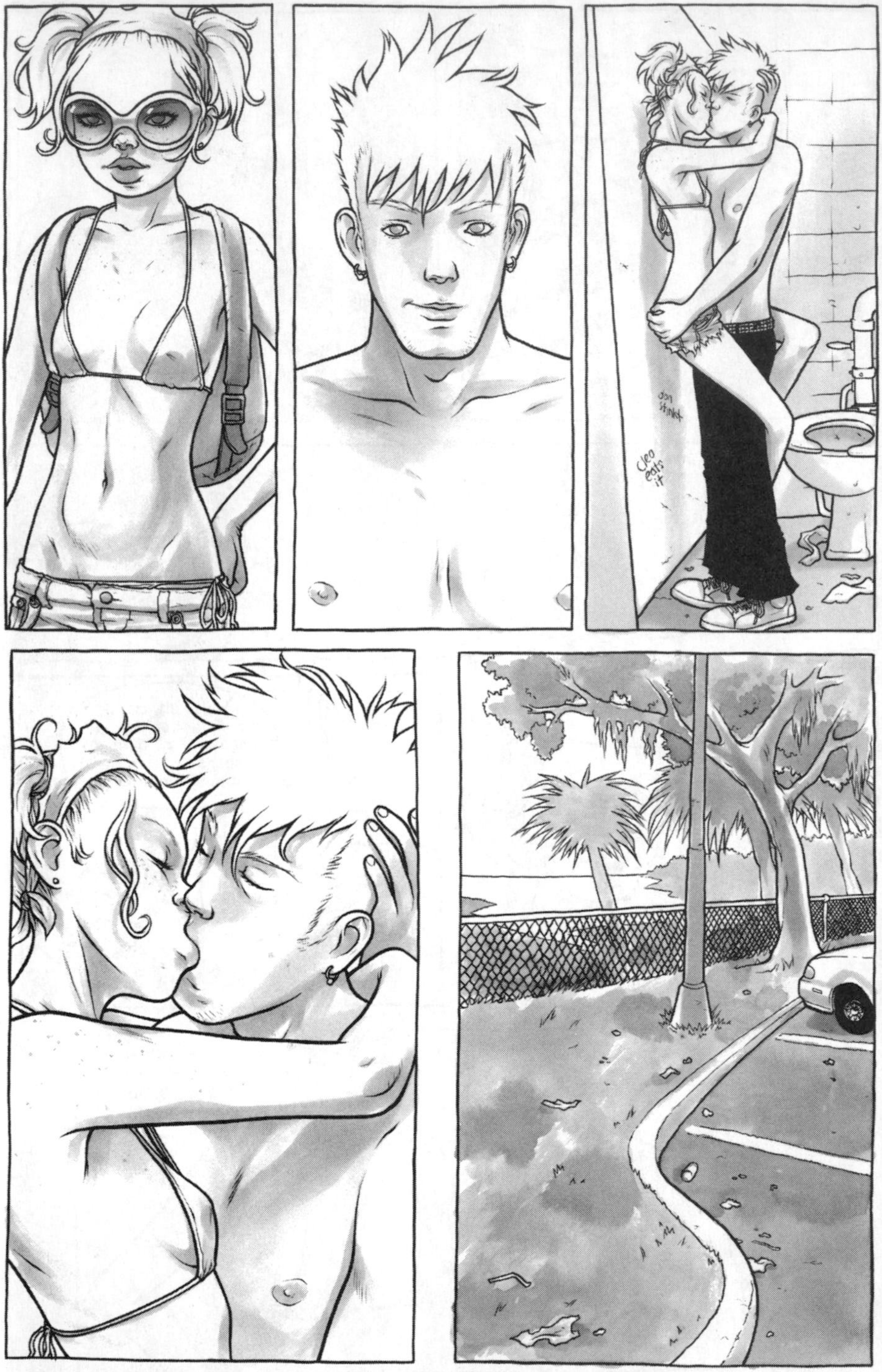
Cleo eats it

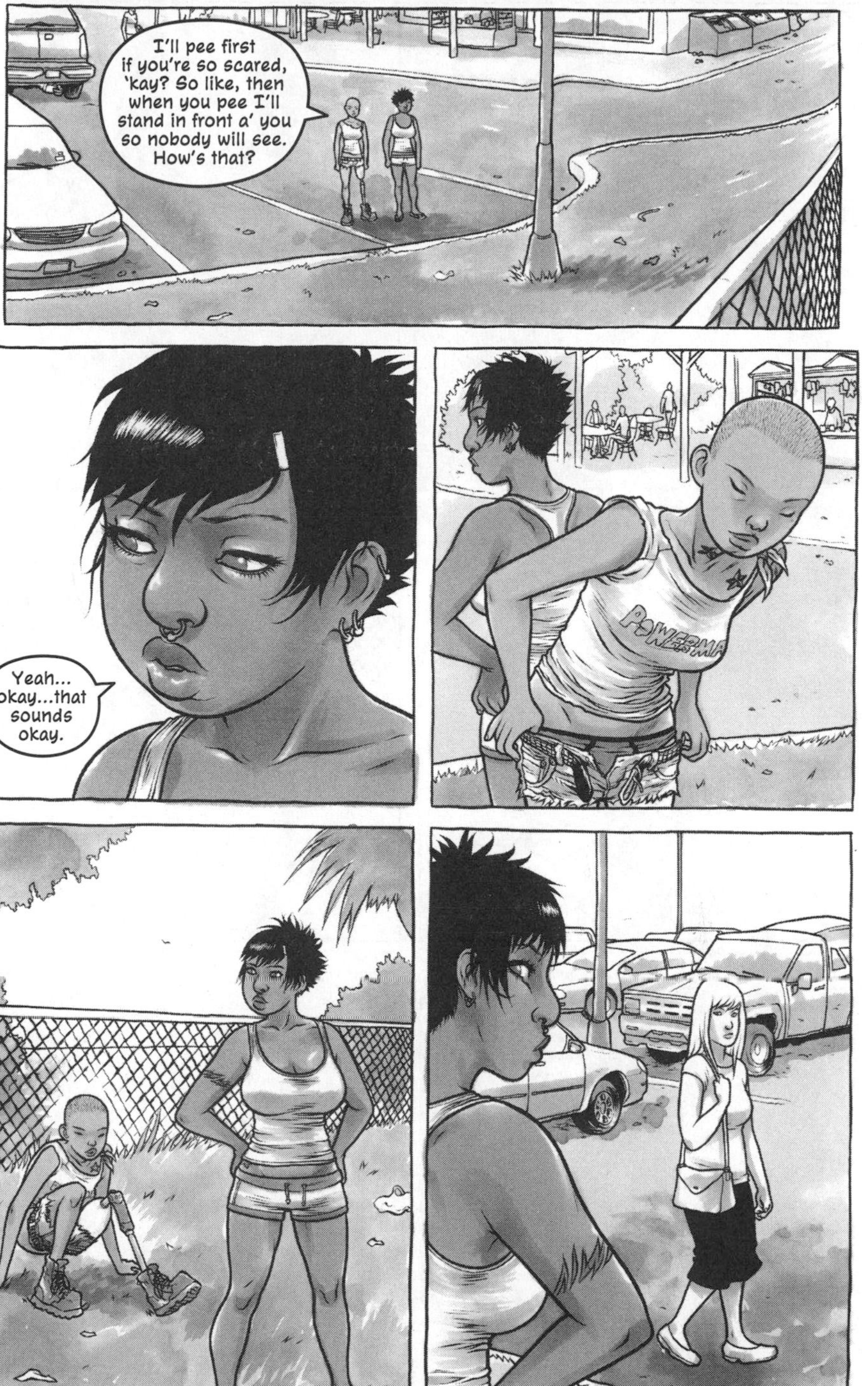
I'll pee first if you're so scared, 'kay? So like, then when you pee I'll stand in front a' you so nobody will see. How's that?
Yeah... okay...that sounds okay.
POWERMA

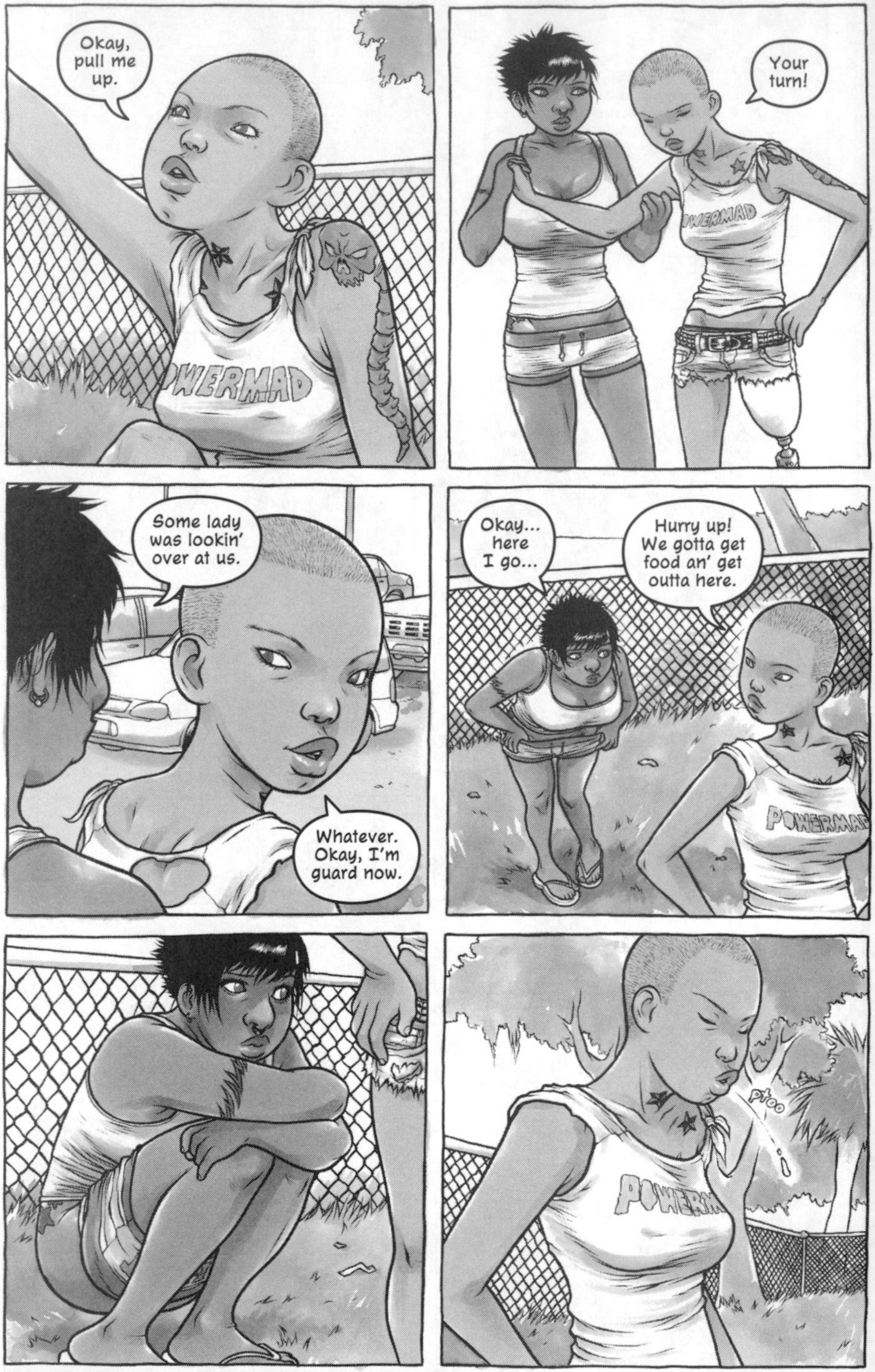
Okay, pull me up.
Your turn!
Some lady was lookin' over at us.
Whatever. Okay, I'm guard now.
Okay... here I go...
Hurry up! We gotta get food an' get outta here.
ptoo

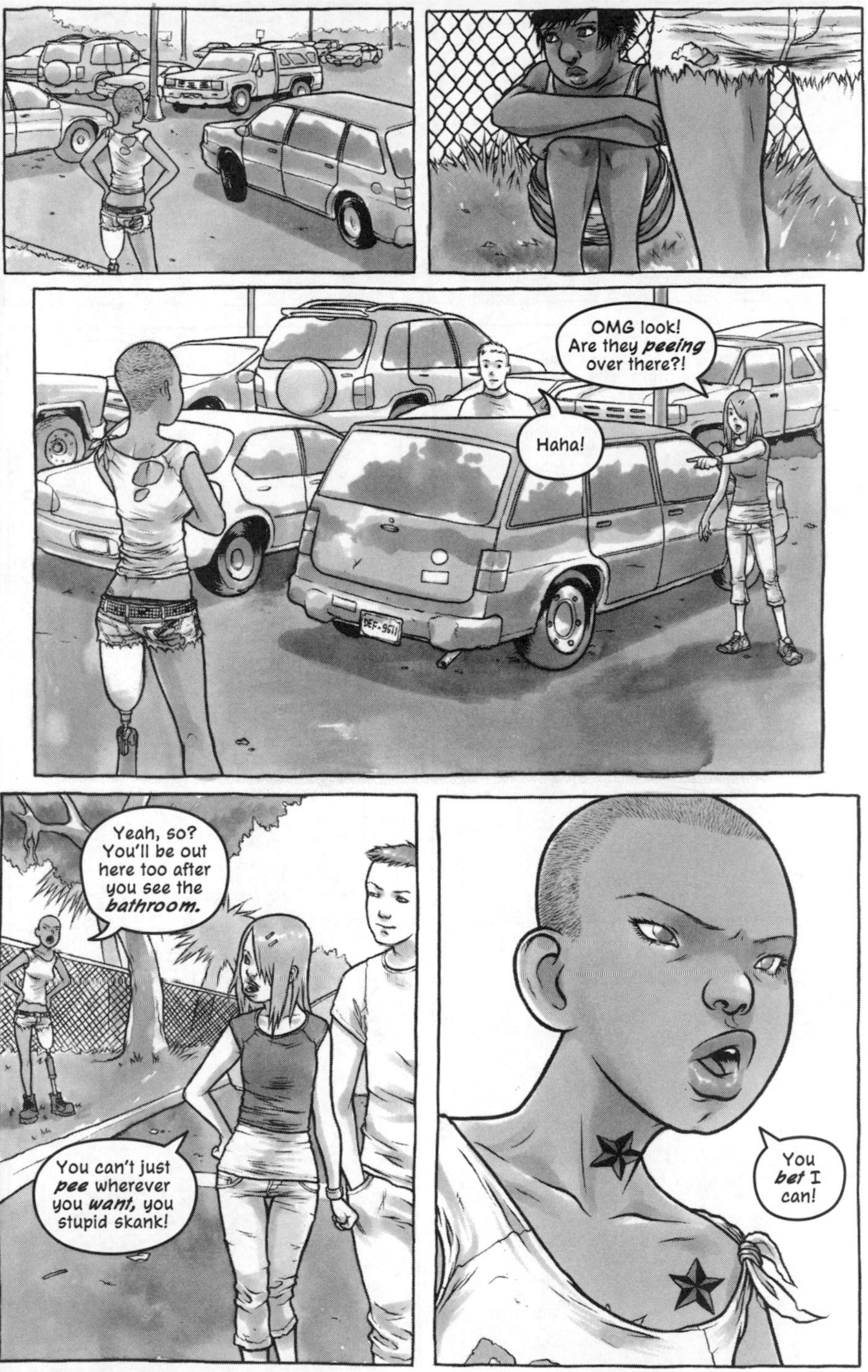
OMG look! Are they *peeing* over there?!
Haha!
Yeah, so? You'll be out here too after you see the *bathroom.*
You can't just *pee* wherever you *want,* you stupid skank!
You *bet* I can!

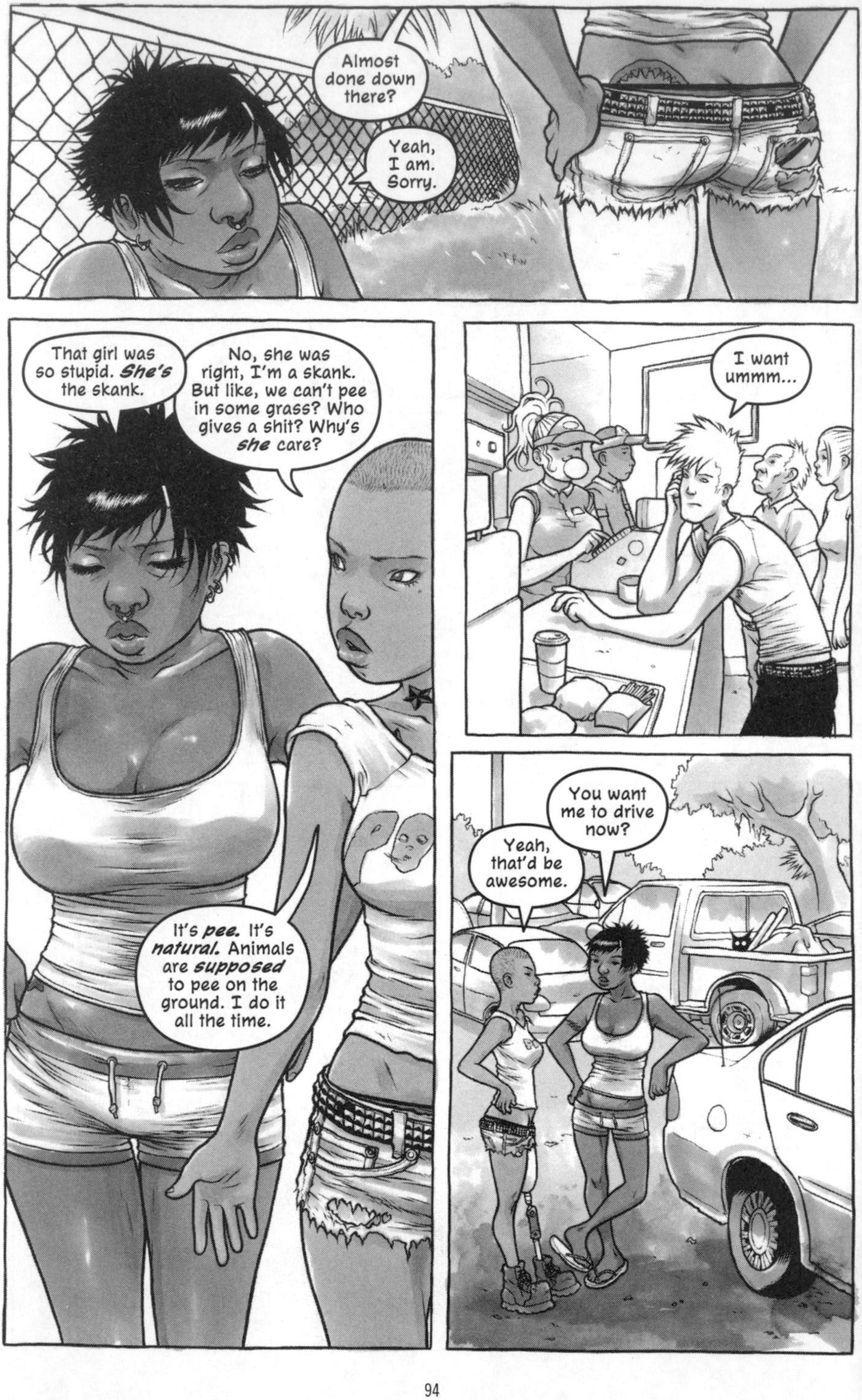
Almost done down there?
Yeah, I am. Sorry.
That girl was so stupid. *She's* the skank.
No, she was right, I'm a skank. But like, we can't pee in some grass? Who gives a shit? Why's *she* care?
It's *pee.* It's *natural.* Animals are *supposed* to pee on the ground. I do it all the time.
I want ummm...
You want me to drive now?
Yeah, that'd be awesome.

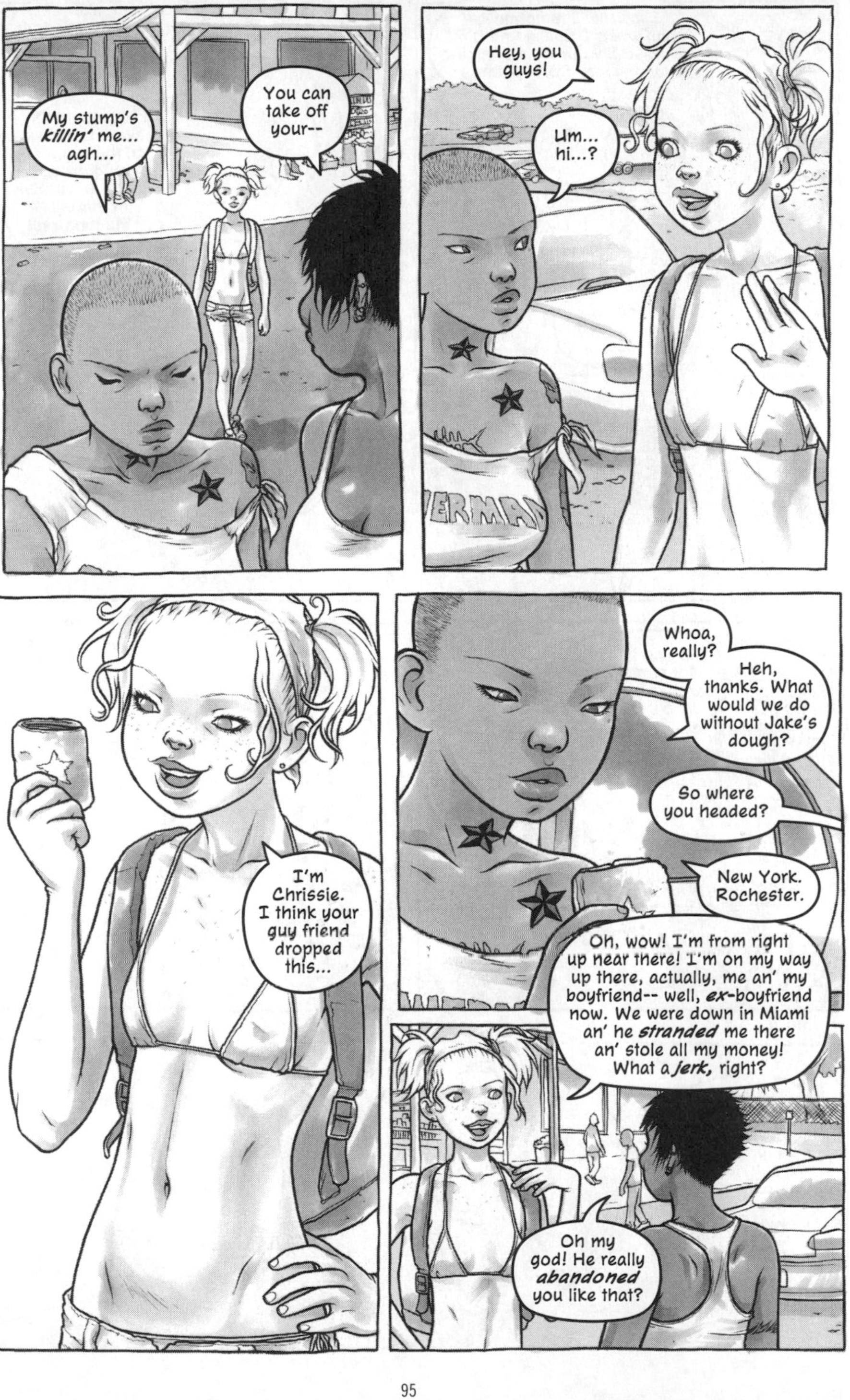
My stump's *killin'* me... agh...
You can take off your--
Hey, you guys!
Um... hi...?
I'm Chrissie. I think your guy friend dropped this...
Whoa, really?
Heh, thanks. What would we do without Jake's dough?
So where you headed?
New York. Rochester.
Oh, wow! I'm from right up near there! I'm on my way up there, actually, me an' my boyfriend-- well, *ex*-boyfriend now. We were down in Miami an' he *stranded* me there an' stole all my money! What a *jerk,* right?
Oh my god! He really *abandoned* you like that?

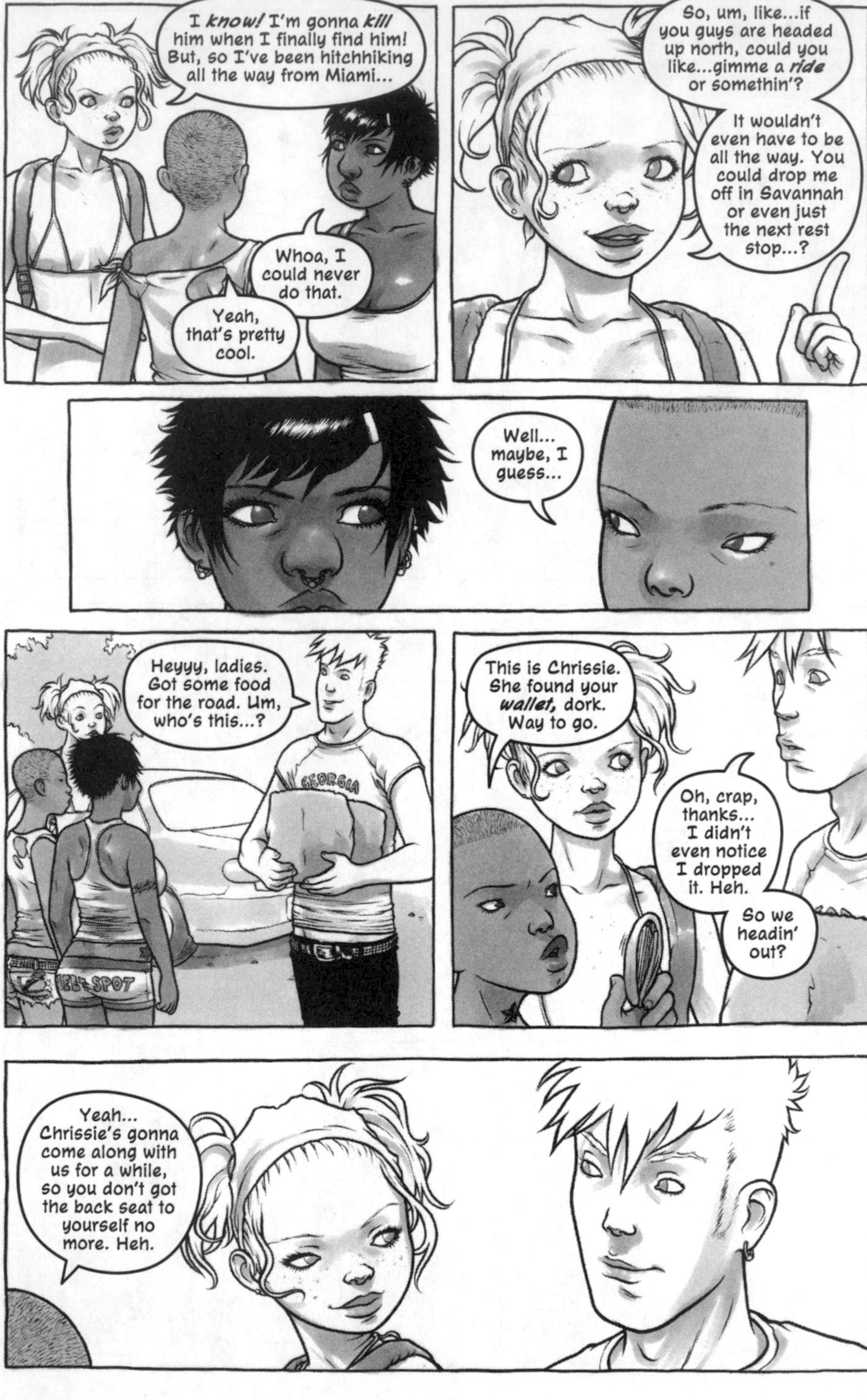
I know! I'm gonna kill him when I finally find him! But, so I've been hitchhiking all the way from Miami...
Whoa, I could never do that.
Yeah, that's pretty cool.
So, um, like...if you guys are headed up north, could you like...gimme a ride or somethin'?
It wouldn't even have to be all the way. You could drop me off in Savannah or even just the next rest stop...?
Well... maybe, I guess...
Heyyy, ladies. Got some food for the road. Um, who's this...?
GEORGIA
This is Chrissie. She found your wallet, dork. Way to go.
Oh, crap, thanks... I didn't even notice I dropped it. Heh.
So we headin' out?
Yeah... Chrissie's gonna come along with us for a while, so you don't got the back seat to yourself no more. Heh.

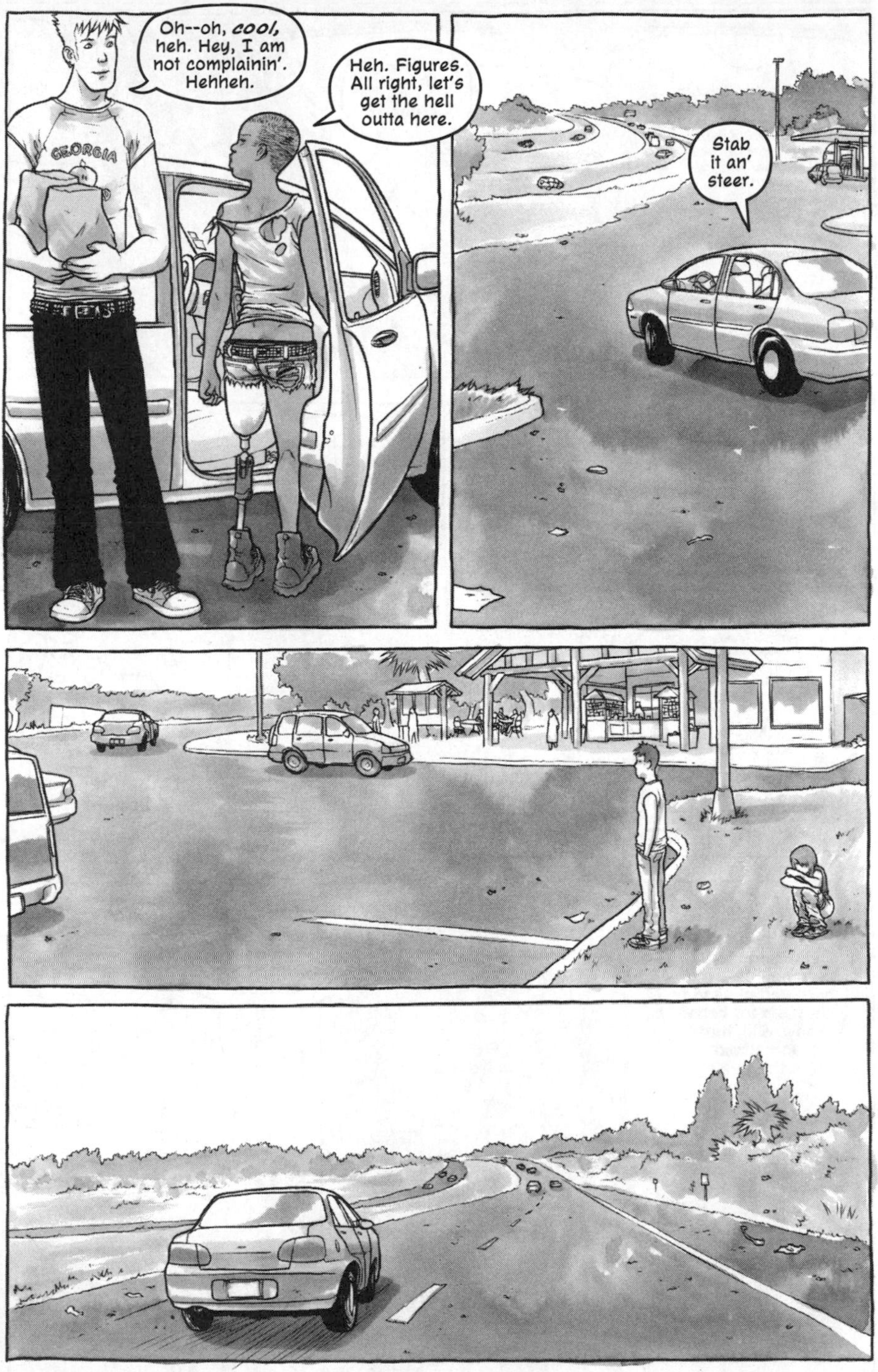

Oh--oh, *cool,* heh. Hey, I am not complainin'. Hehheh.
Heh. Figures. All right, let's get the hell outta here.
Stab it an' steer.

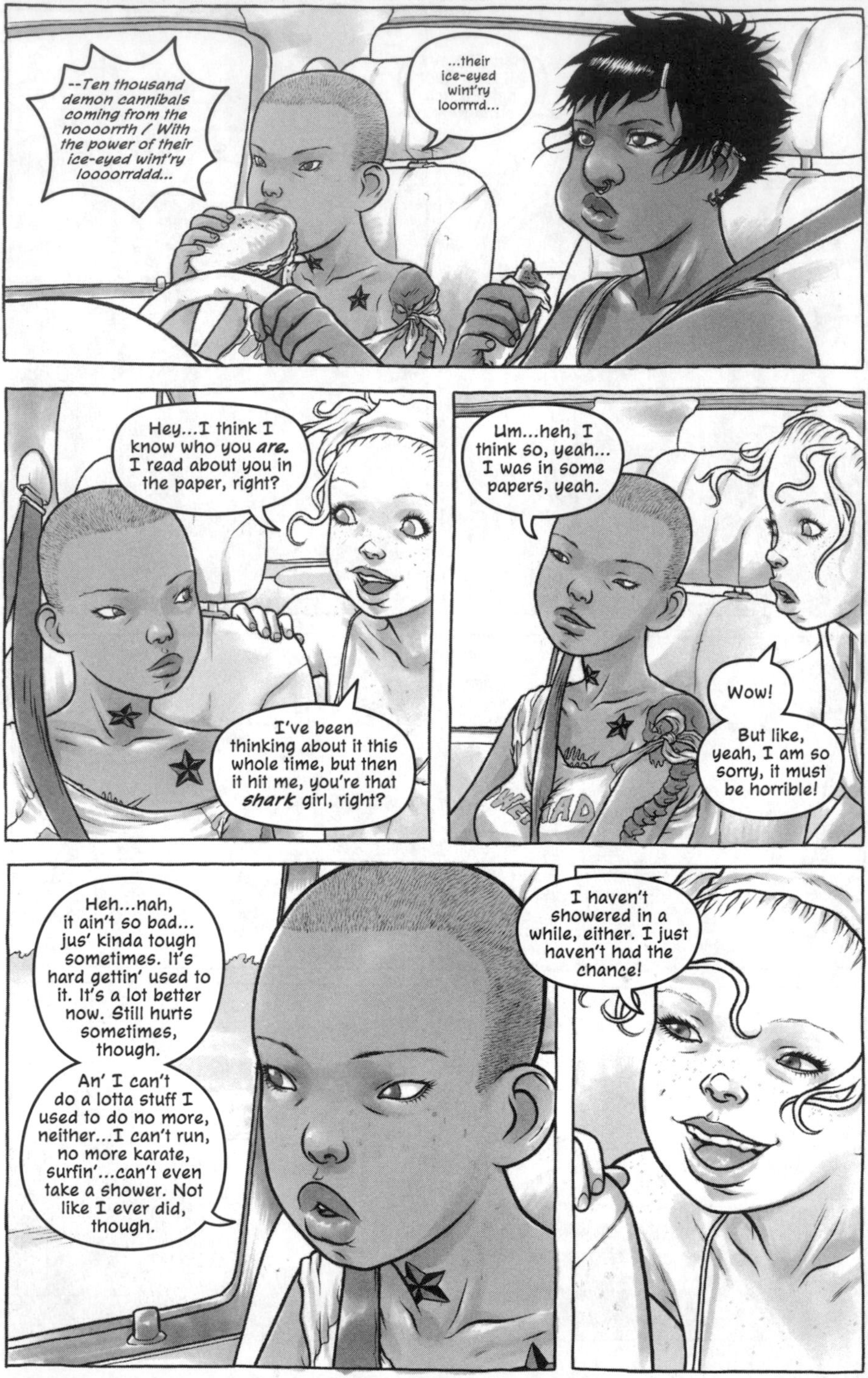
--Ten thousand demon cannibals coming from the noooorrth / With the power of their ice-eyed wint'ry loooorrddd...
...their ice-eyed wint'ry loorrrrd...
Hey...I think I know who you *are.* I read about you in the paper, right?
I've been thinking about it this whole time, but then it hit me, you're that *shark* girl, right?
Um...heh, I think so, yeah... I was in some papers, yeah.
Wow!
But like, yeah, I am so sorry, it must be horrible!
Heh...nah, it ain't so bad... jus' kinda tough sometimes. It's hard gettin' used to it. It's a lot better now. Still hurts sometimes, though.
An' I can't do a lotta stuff I used to do no more, neither...I can't run, no more karate, surfin'...can't even take a shower. Not like I ever did, though.
I haven't showered in a while, either. I just haven't had the chance!

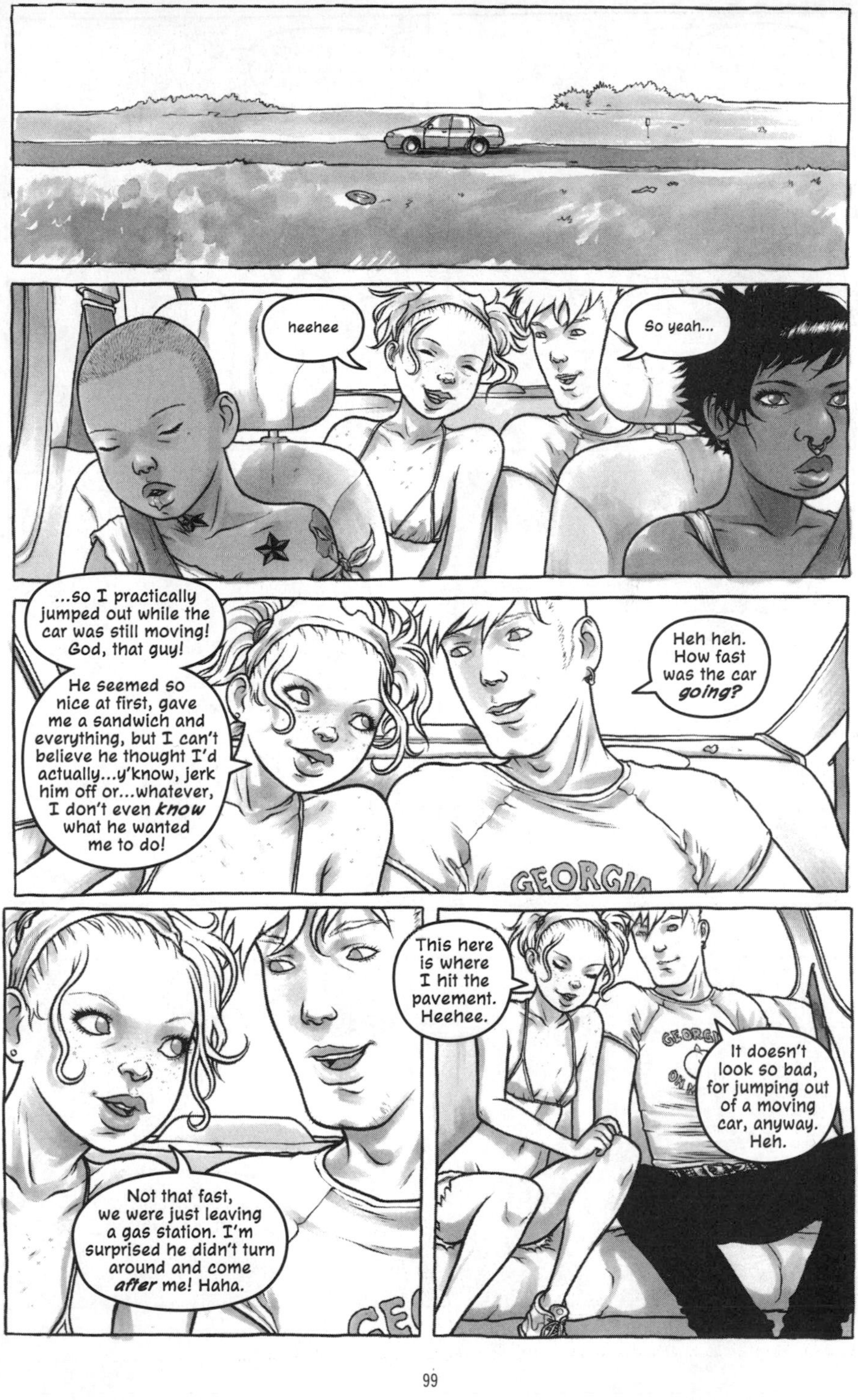
heehee
So yeah...
...so I practically jumped out while the car was still moving! God, that guy!
He seemed so nice at first, gave me a sandwich and everything, but I can't believe he thought I'd actually...y'know, jerk him off or...whatever, I don't even *know* what he wanted me to do!
Heh heh. How fast was the car *going?*
GEORGIA
Not that fast, we were just leaving a gas station. I'm surprised he didn't turn around and come *after* me! Haha.
This here is where I hit the pavement. Heehee.
It doesn't look so bad, for jumping out of a moving car, anyway. Heh.

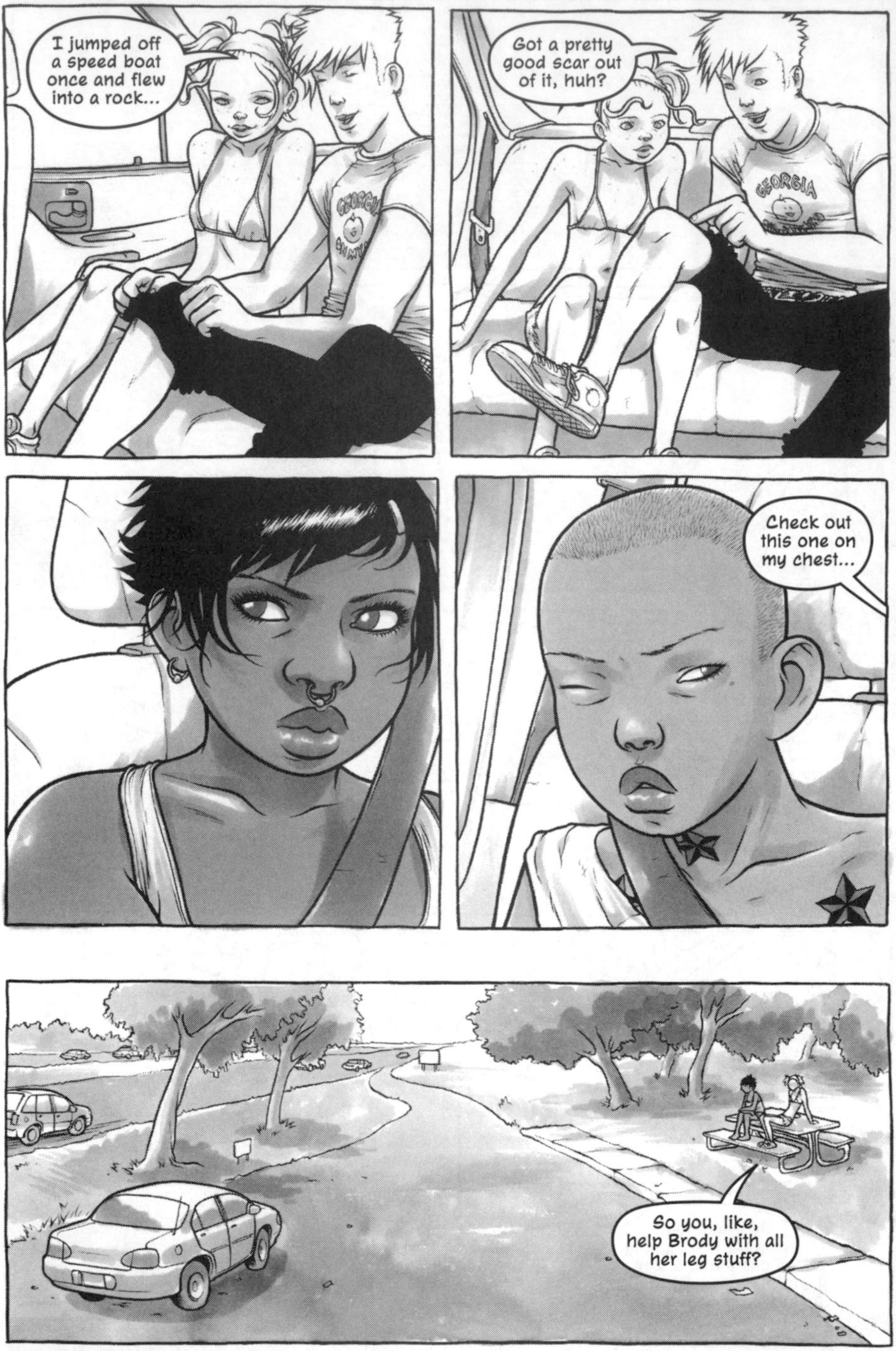
I jumped off a speed boat once and flew into a rock...
Got a pretty good scar out of it, huh?
GEORGIA
Check out this one on my chest...
So you, like, help Brody with all her leg stuff?

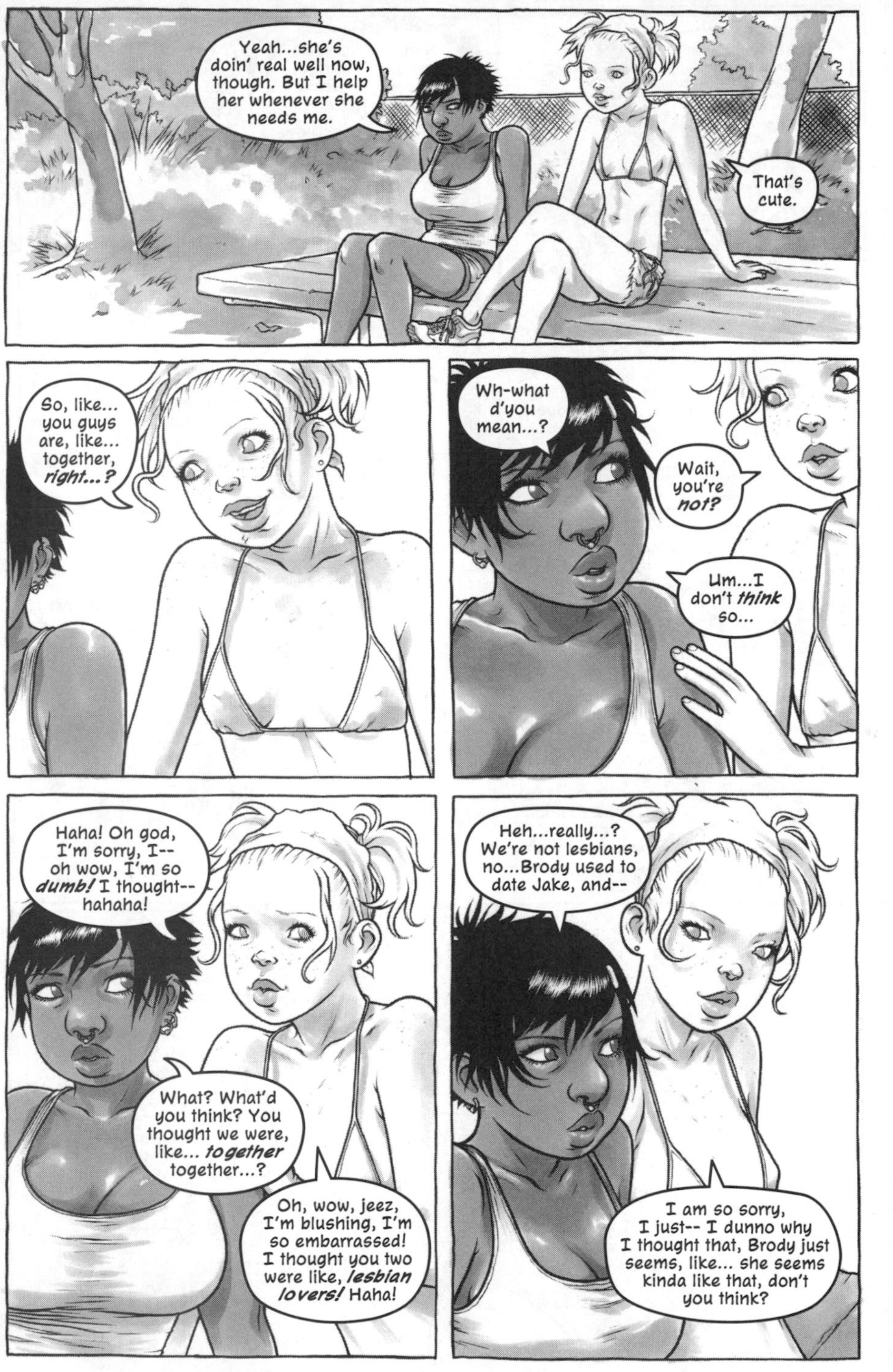
Yeah...she's doin' real well now, though. But I help her whenever she needs me.
That's cute.
So, like... you guys are, like... together, **right...?**
Wh-what d'you mean...?
Wait, you're **not?**
Um...I don't **think** so...
Haha! Oh god, I'm sorry, I-- oh wow, I'm so **dumb!** I thought-- hahaha!
What? What'd you think? You thought we were, like... **together** together...?
Oh, wow, jeez, I'm blushing, I'm so embarrassed! I thought you two were like, **lesbian lovers!** Haha!
Heh...really...? We're not lesbians, no...Brody used to date Jake, and--
I am so sorry, I just-- I dunno why I thought that, Brody just seems, like... she seems kinda like that, don't you think?

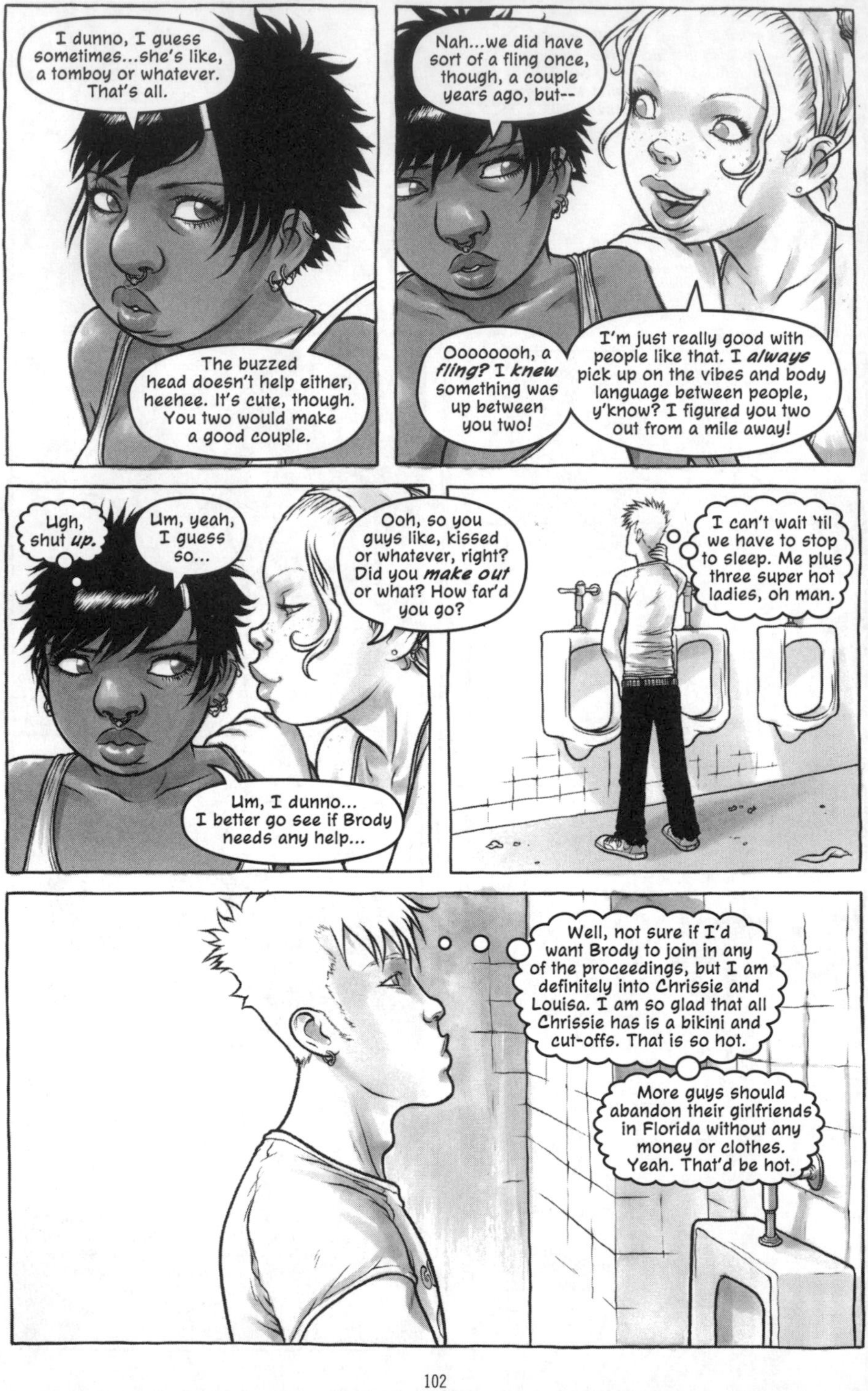
I dunno, I guess sometimes...she's like, a tomboy or whatever. That's all.
The buzzed head doesn't help either, heehee. It's cute, though. You two would make a good couple.
Nah...we did have sort of a fling once, though, a couple years ago, but--
Ooooooh, a *fling?* I *knew* something was up between you two!
I'm just really good with people like that. I *always* pick up on the vibes and body language between people, y'know? I figured you two out from a mile away!
Ugh, shut *up.*
Um, yeah, I guess so...
Ooh, so you guys like, kissed or whatever, right? Did you *make out* or what? How far'd you go?
Um, I dunno... I better go see if Brody needs any help...
I can't wait 'til we have to stop to sleep. Me plus three super hot ladies, oh man.
Well, not sure if I'd want Brody to join in any of the proceedings, but I am definitely into Chrissie and Louisa. I am so glad that all Chrissie has is a bikini and cut-offs. That is so hot.
More guys should abandon their girlfriends in Florida without any money or clothes. Yeah. That'd be hot.

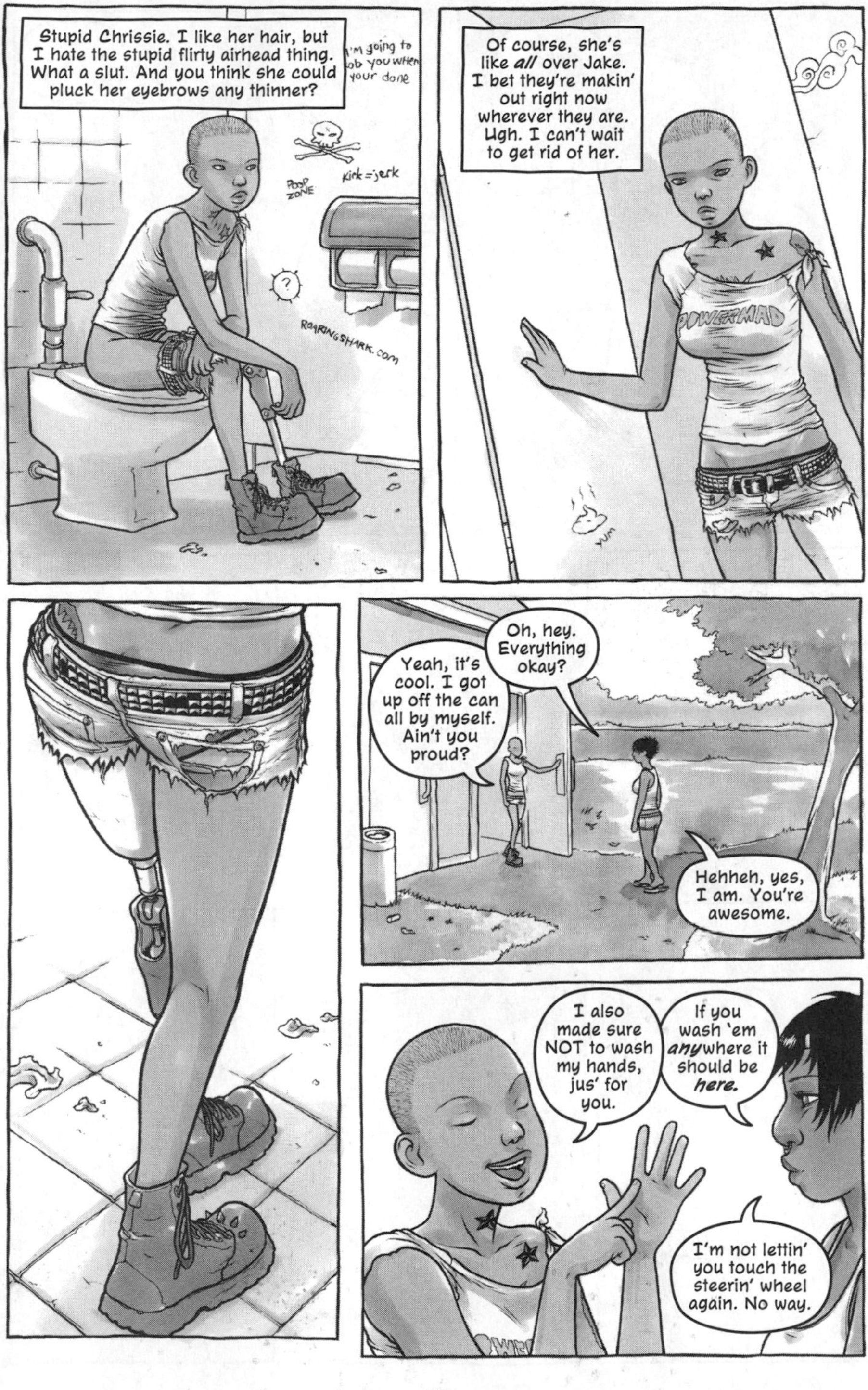
Stupid Chrissie. I like her hair, but I hate the stupid flirty airhead thing. What a slut. And you think she could pluck her eyebrows any thinner?
POOP ZONE
Kirk = jerk
ROARINGSHARK.COM
Of course, she's like *all* over Jake. I bet they're makin' out right now wherever they are. Ugh. I can't wait to get rid of her.
POWERMAD
YUM
Oh, hey. Everything okay?
Yeah, it's cool. I got up off the can all by myself. Ain't you proud?
Hehheh, yes, I am. You're awesome.
I also made sure NOT to wash my hands, jus' for you.
If you wash 'em *any*where it should be *here.*
I'm not lettin' you touch the steerin' wheel again. No way.

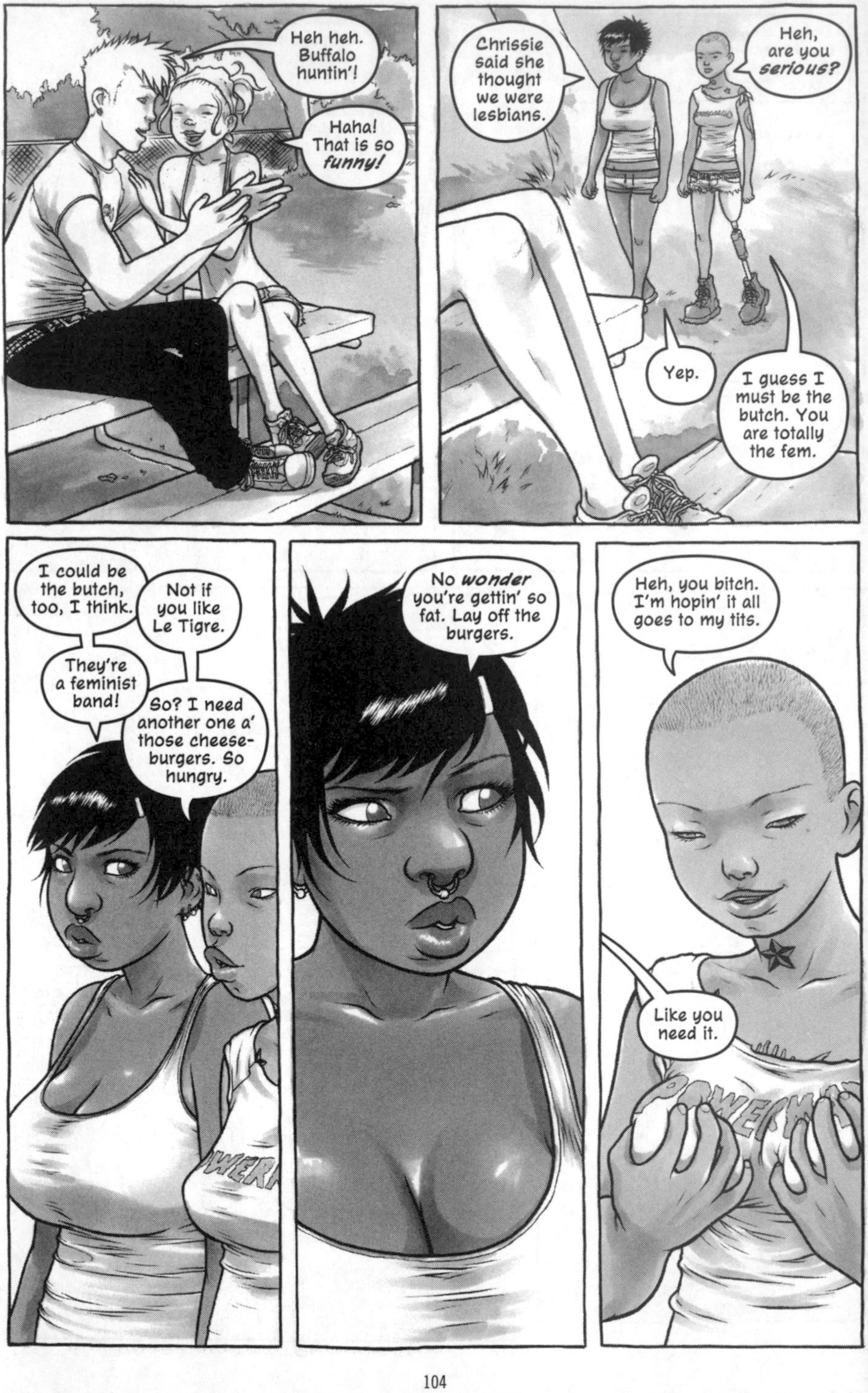
Heh heh. Buffalo huntin'!
Haha! That is so *funny!*
Chrissie said she thought we were lesbians.
Heh, are you *serious?*
Yep.
I guess I must be the butch. You are totally the fem.
I could be the butch, too, I think.
Not if you like Le Tigre.
They're a feminist band!
So? I need another one a' those cheese-burgers. So hungry.
No *wonder* you're gettin' so fat. Lay off the burgers.
Heh, you bitch. I'm hopin' it all goes to my tits.
Like you need it.

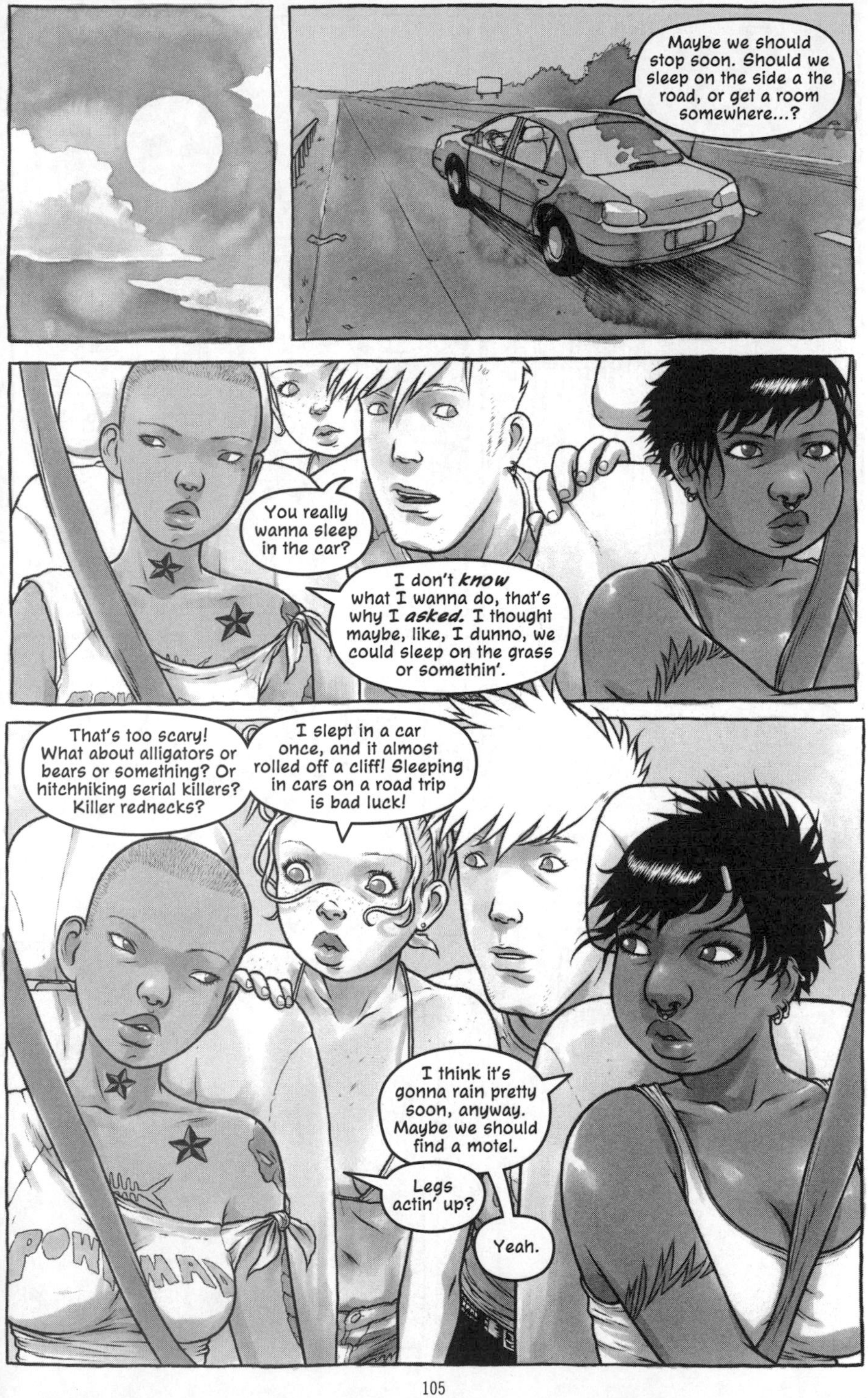
Maybe we should stop soon. Should we sleep on the side a the road, or get a room somewhere...?
You really wanna sleep in the car?
I don't ***know*** what I wanna do, that's why I ***asked.*** I thought maybe, like, I dunno, we could sleep on the grass or somethin'.
That's too scary! What about alligators or bears or something? Or hitchhiking serial killers? Killer rednecks?
I slept in a car once, and it almost rolled off a cliff! Sleeping in cars on a road trip is bad luck!
I think it's gonna rain pretty soon, anyway. Maybe we should find a motel.
Legs actin' up?
Yeah.

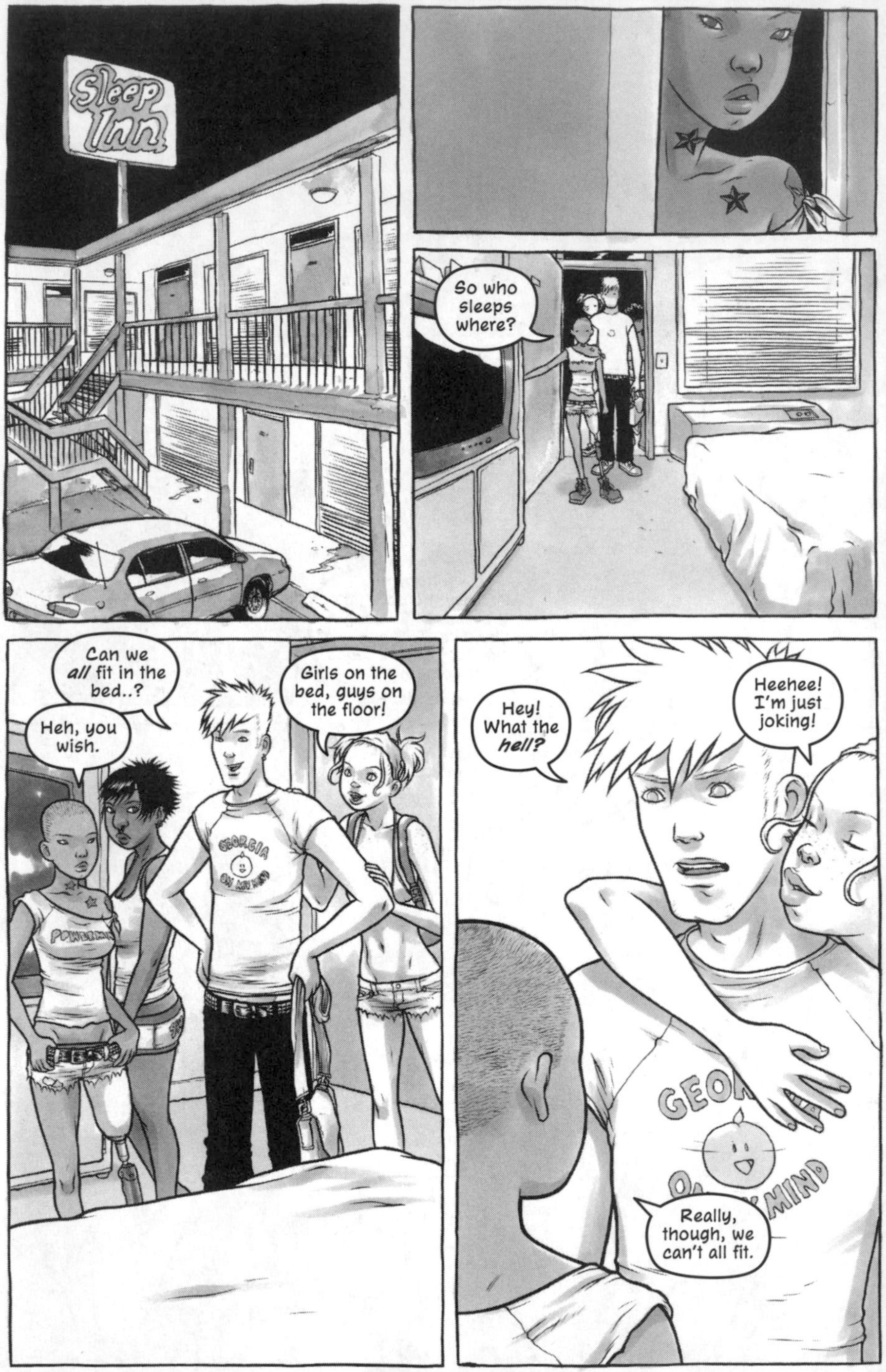
Sleep Inn
So who sleeps where?
Can we *all* fit in the bed..?
Heh, you wish.
Girls on the bed, guys on the floor!
Hey! What the *hell?*
Heehee! I'm just joking!
Really, though, we can't all fit.

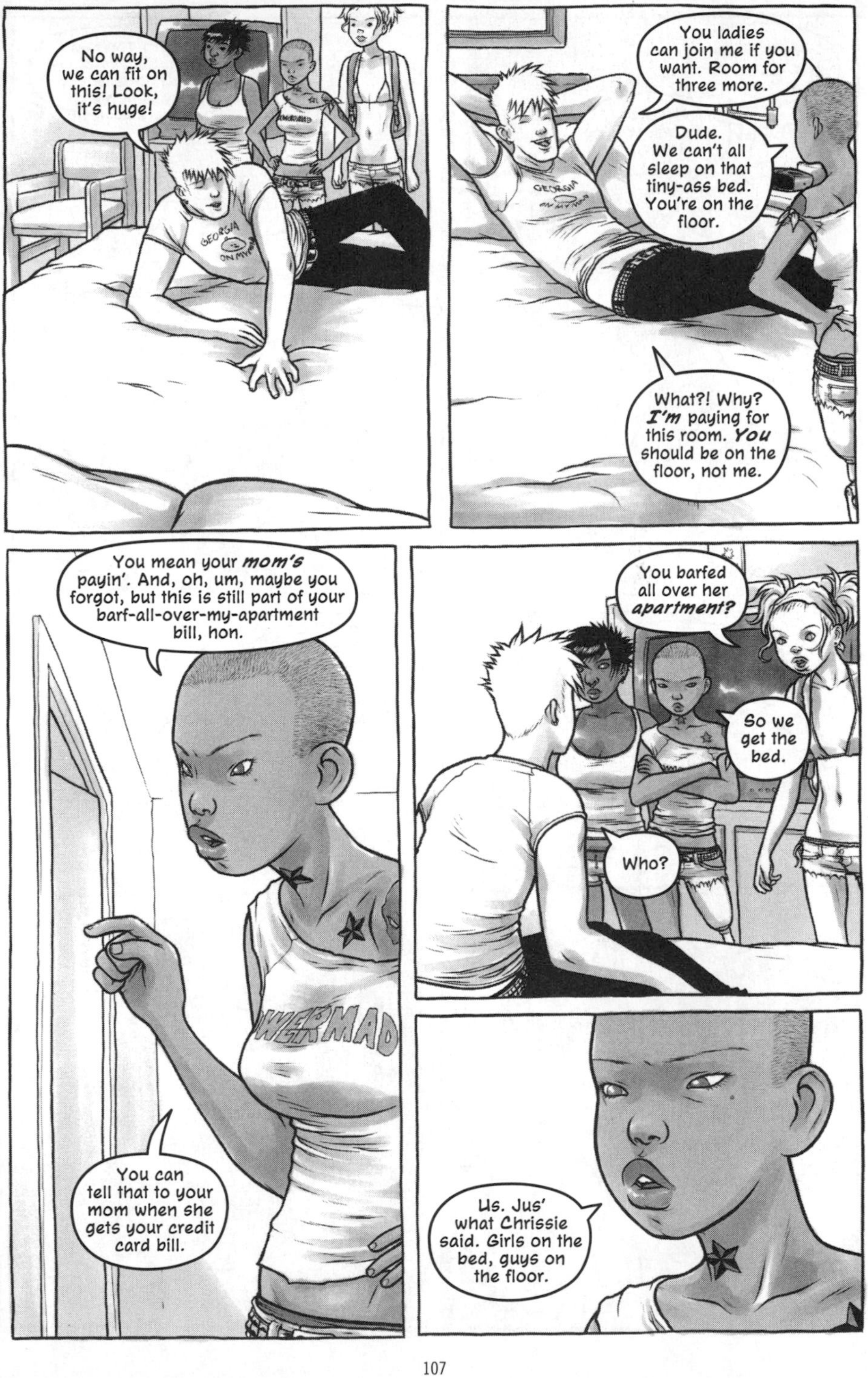

No way, we can fit on this! Look, it's huge!
You ladies can join me if you want. Room for three more.
Dude. We can't all sleep on that tiny-ass bed. You're on the floor.
What?! Why? *I'm* paying for this room. *You* should be on the floor, not me.
You mean your *mom's* payin'. And, oh, um, maybe you forgot, but this is still part of your barf-all-over-my-apartment bill, hon.
You can tell that to your mom when she gets your credit card bill.
You barfed all over her *apartment?*
So we get the bed.
Who?
Us. Jus' what Chrissie said. Girls on the bed, guys on the floor.

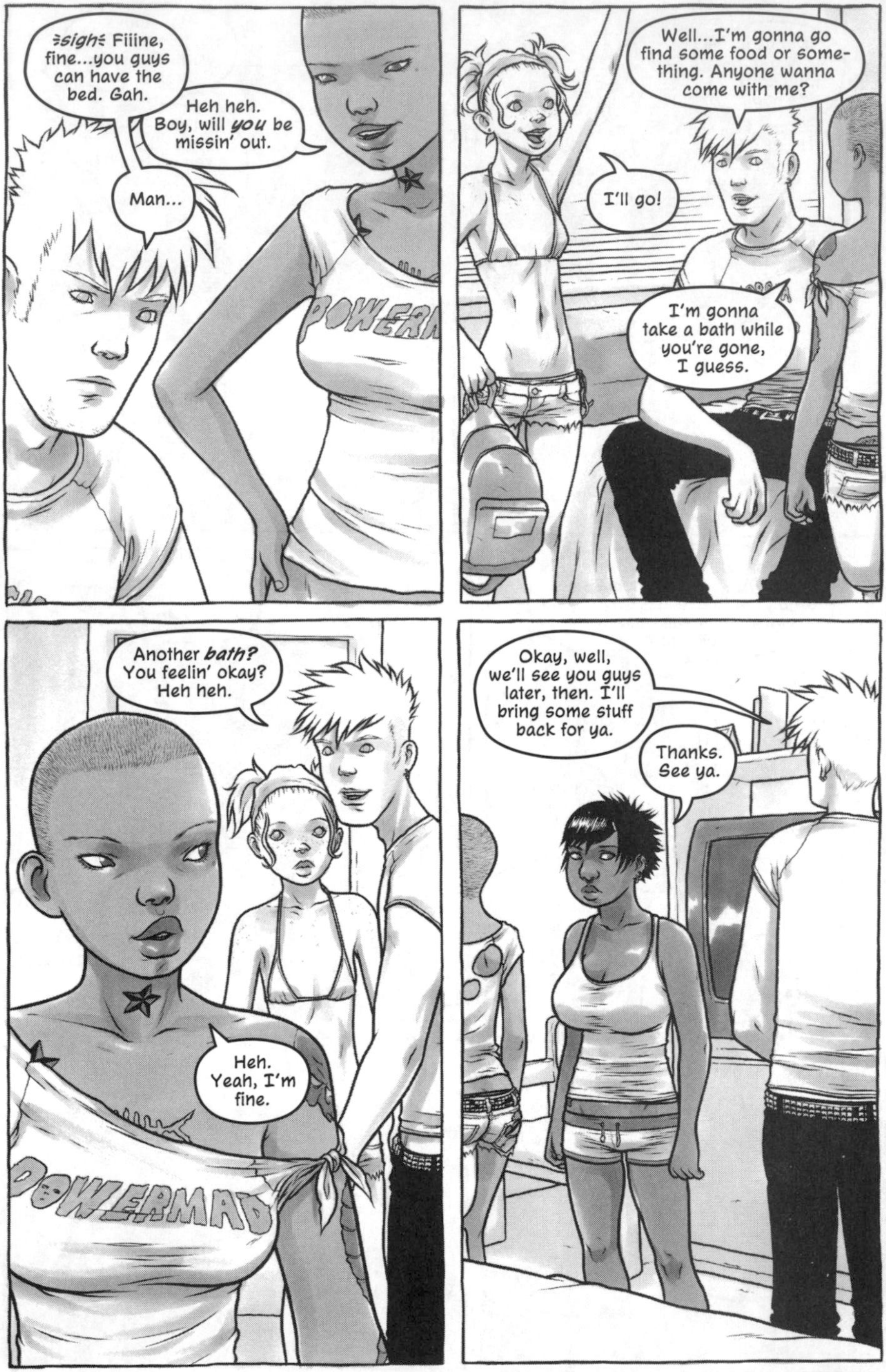
sigh Fiiine, fine...you guys can have the bed. Gah.
Heh heh. Boy, will *you* be missin' out.
Man...
Well...I'm gonna go find some food or something. Anyone wanna come with me?
I'll go!
I'm gonna take a bath while you're gone, I guess.
Another *bath?* You feelin' okay? Heh heh.
Heh. Yeah, I'm fine.
Okay, well, we'll see you guys later, then. I'll bring some stuff back for ya.
Thanks. See ya.
POWERMAD

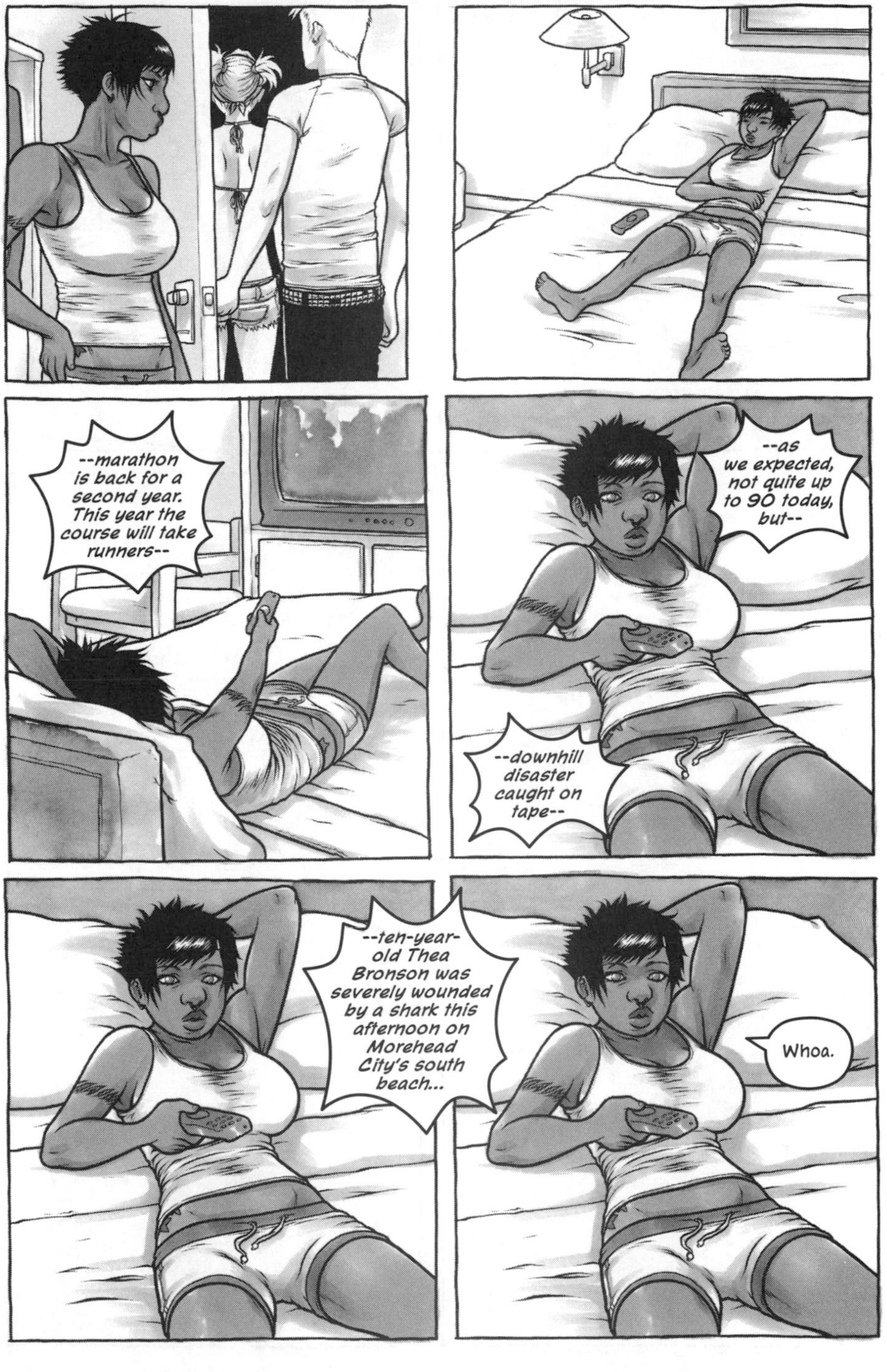
--marathon is back for a second year. This year the course will take runners--
--as we expected, not quite up to 90 today, but--
--downhill disaster caught on tape--
--ten-year-old Thea Bronson was severely wounded by a shark this afternoon on Morehead City's south beach...
Whoa.

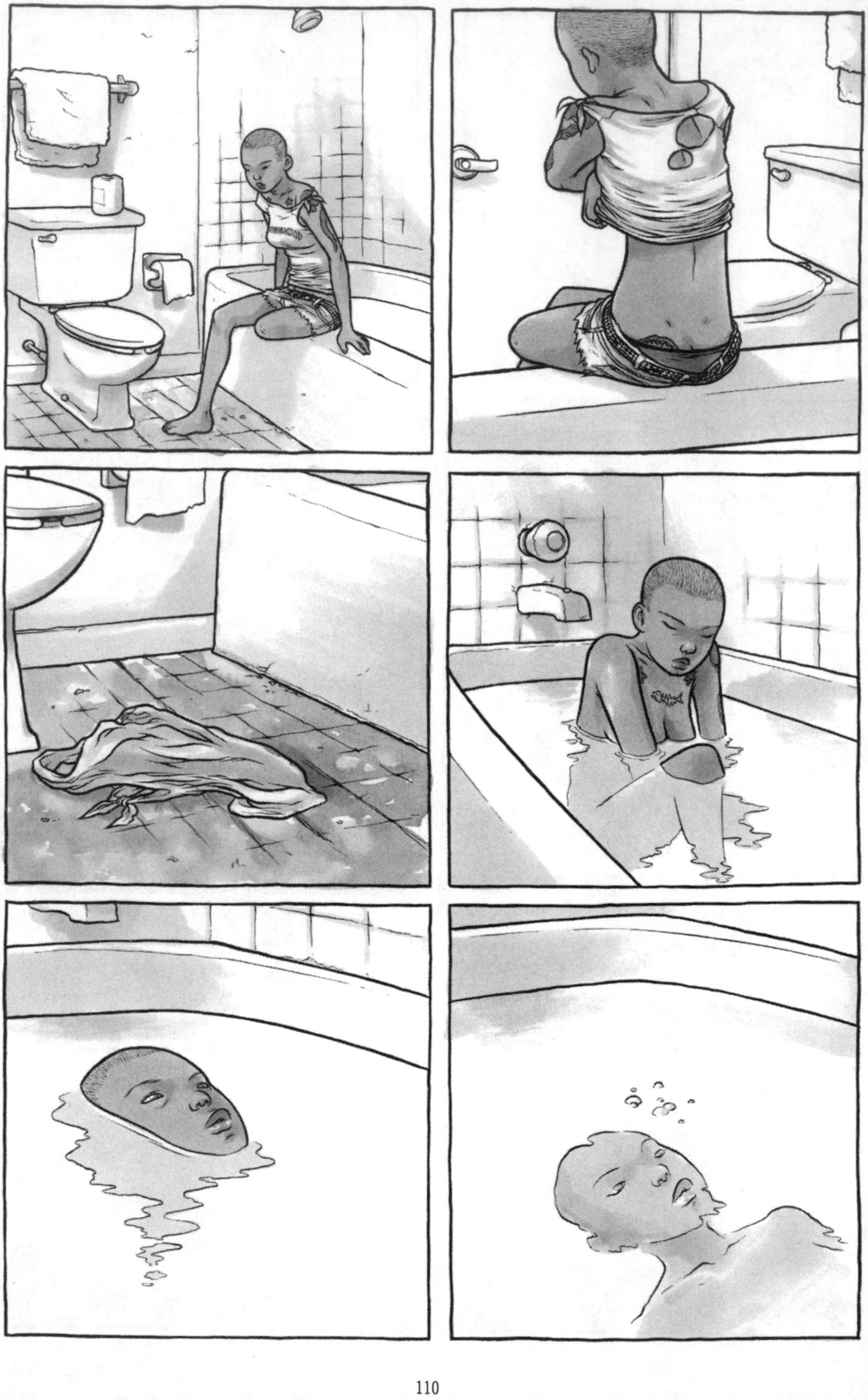

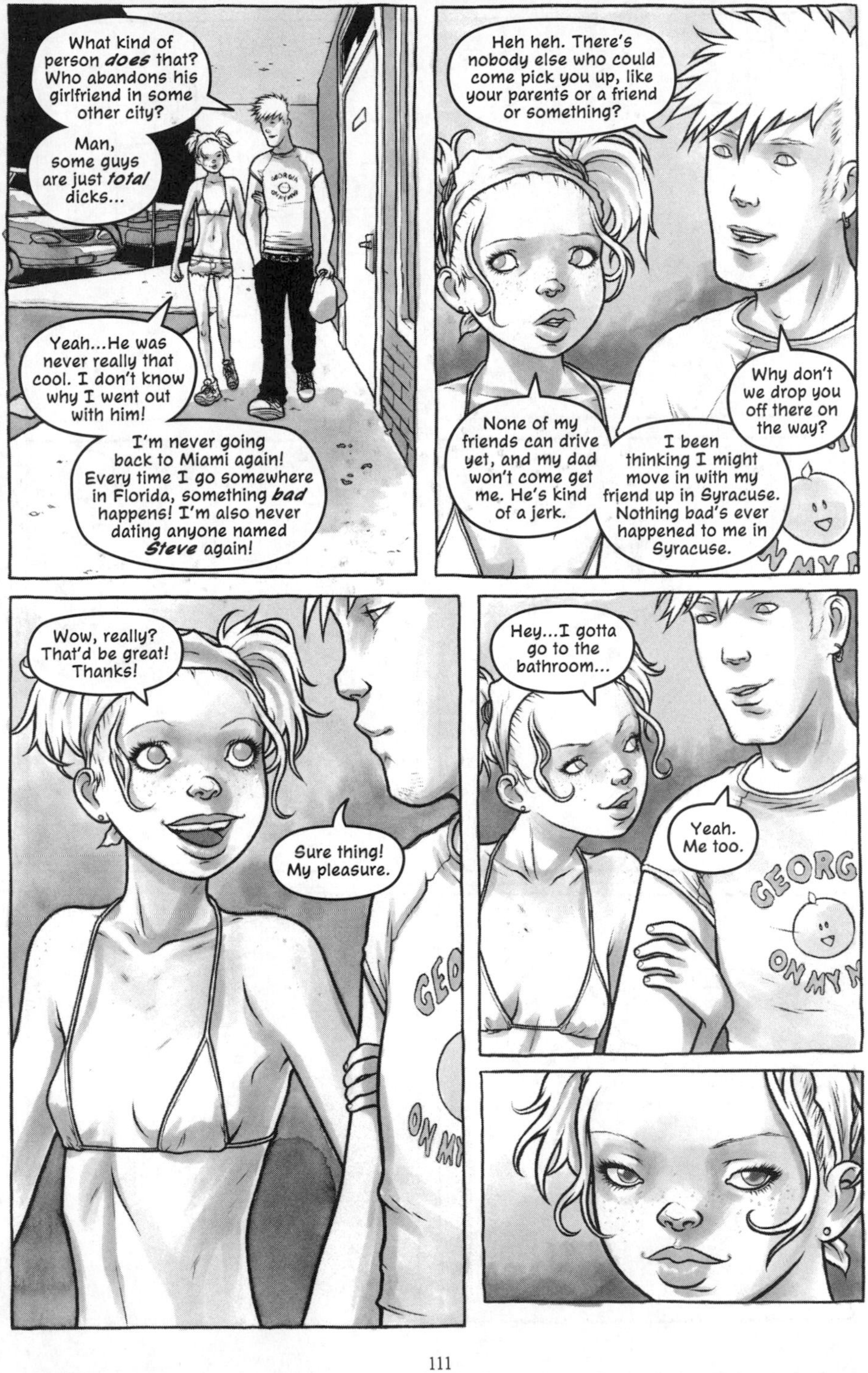
What kind of person *does* that? Who abandons his girlfriend in some other city?
Man, some guys are just *total* dicks...
Yeah...He was never really that cool. I don't know why I went out with him!
I'm never going back to Miami again! Every time I go somewhere in Florida, something *bad* happens! I'm also never dating anyone named *Steve* again!
Heh heh. There's nobody else who could come pick you up, like your parents or a friend or something?
None of my friends can drive yet, and my dad won't come get me. He's kind of a jerk.
I been thinking I might move in with my friend up in Syracuse. Nothing bad's ever happened to me in Syracuse.
Why don't we drop you off there on the way?
Wow, really? That'd be great! Thanks!
Sure thing! My pleasure.
Hey...I gotta go to the bathroom...
Yeah. Me too.

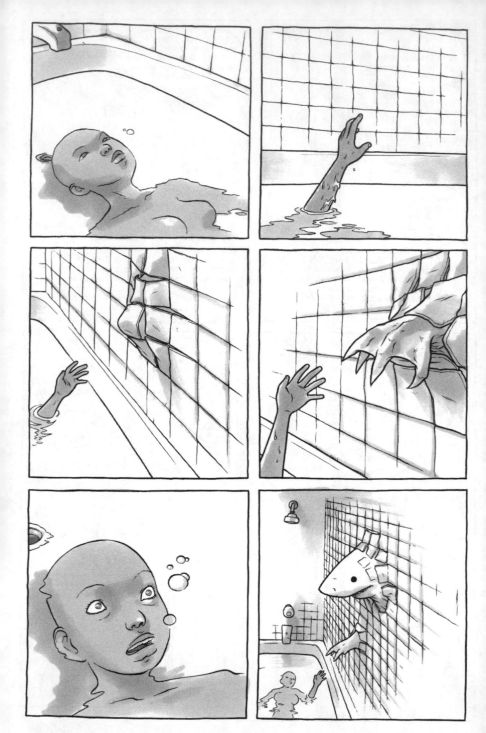

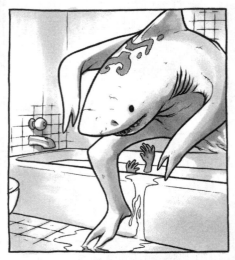

113

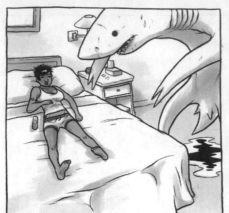

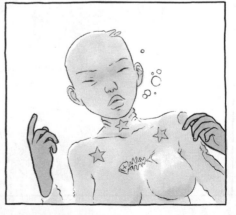

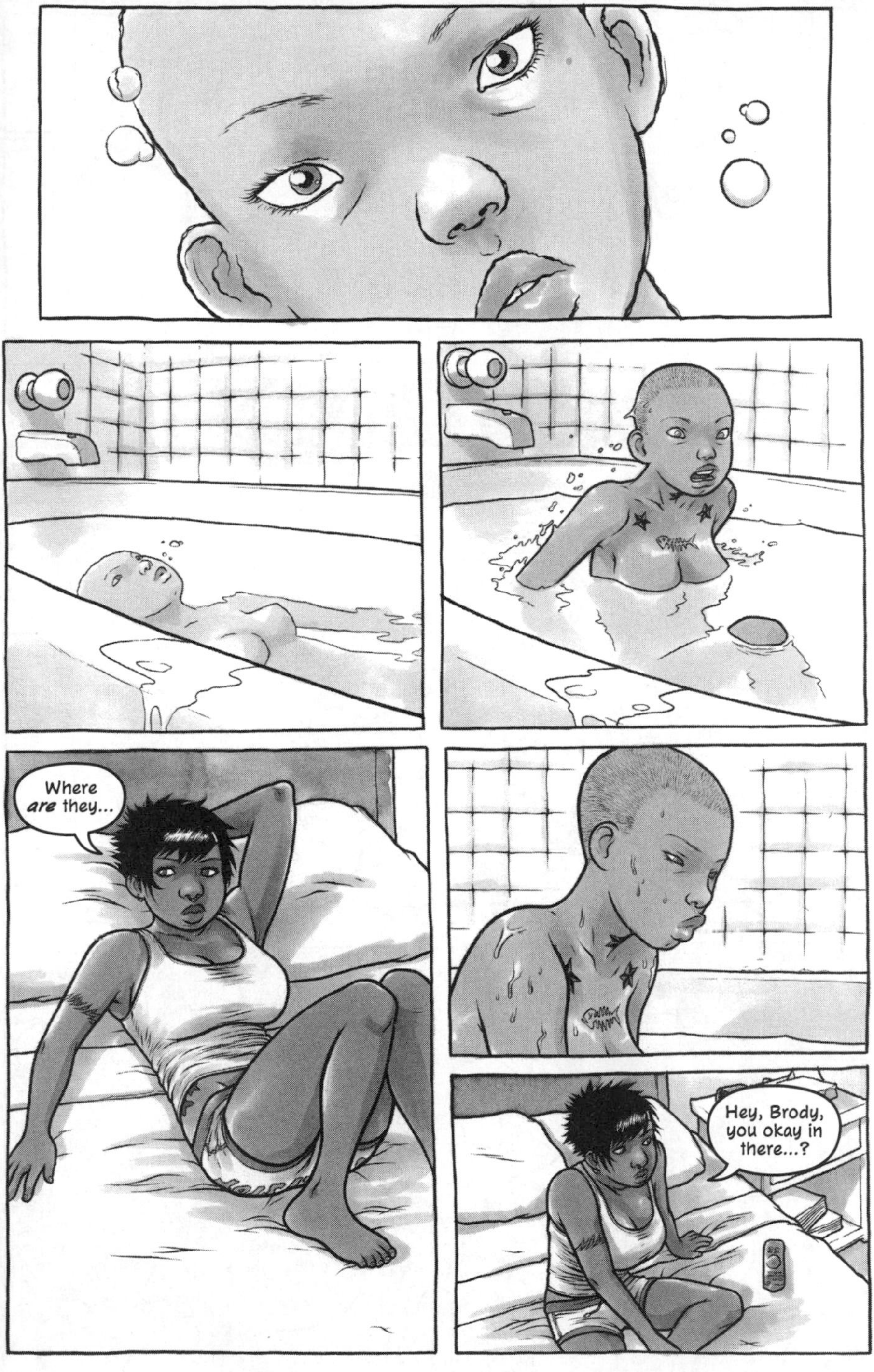
Where *are* they...
Hey, Brody, you okay in there...?

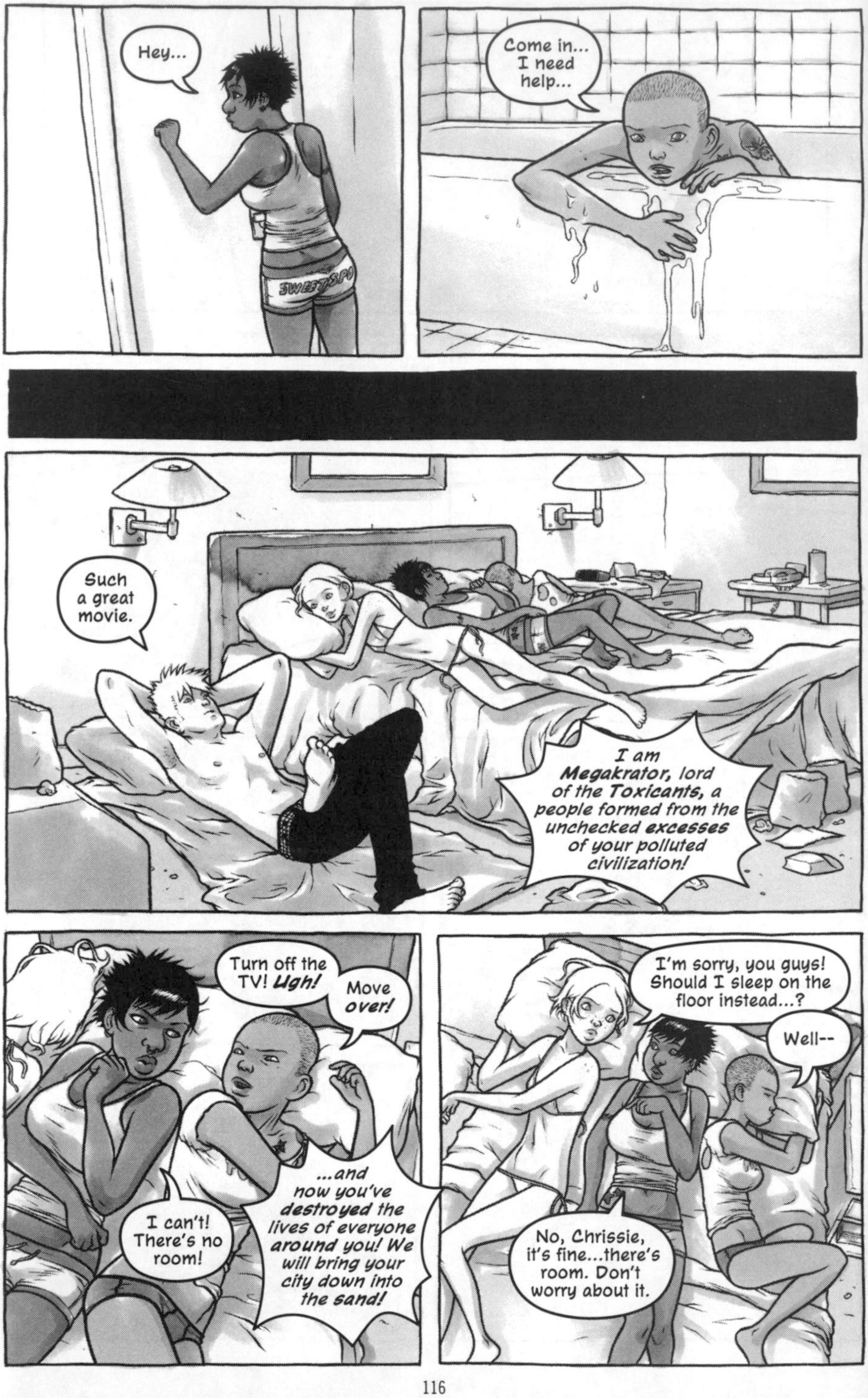
Hey...
Come in... I need help...
SWEETSPO
Such a great movie.
I am Megakrator, lord of the Toxicants, a people formed from the unchecked excesses of your polluted civilization!
Turn off the TV! Ugh!
Move over!
I can't! There's no room!
...and now you've destroyed the lives of everyone around you! We will bring your city down into the sand!
I'm sorry, you guys! Should I sleep on the floor instead...?
Well--
No, Chrissie, it's fine...there's room. Don't worry about it.

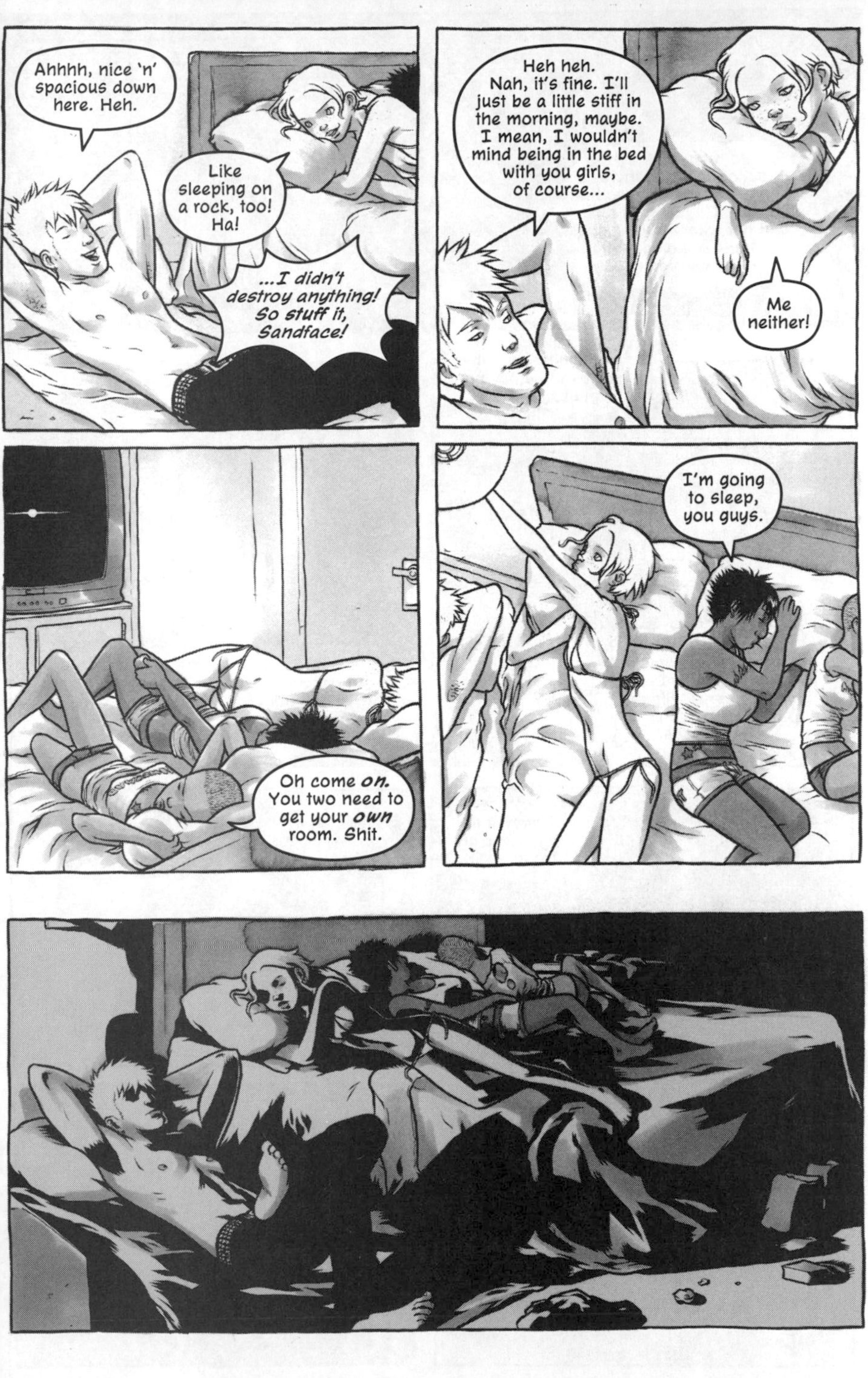

Ahhhh, nice 'n' spacious down here. Heh.
Like sleeping on a rock, too! Ha!
...I didn't destroy anything! So stuff it, Sandface!
Heh heh. Nah, it's fine. I'll just be a little stiff in the morning, maybe. I mean, I wouldn't mind being in the bed with you girls, of course...
Me neither!
Oh come on. You two need to get your own room. Shit.
I'm going to sleep, you guys.

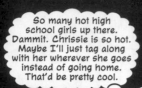

So many hot high school girls up there. Dammit. Chrissie is so hot. Maybe I'll just tag along with her wherever she goes instead of going home. That'd be pretty cool.

I feel bad about Louisa getting dragged along on this whole thing, but she seems to be having an okay time...

...even though it's all her idea, I kinda feel bad about Brody, too. I don't know why she's flipping out so bad. Teenage girls are nuts.

What is with Chrissie? She's got her arm around me an' everything, but then she's all over Jake...I don't know.

She's bad news, I think. I want this trip to be over with, everything is so awkward.

I want it to be jus' me an' Brody again.

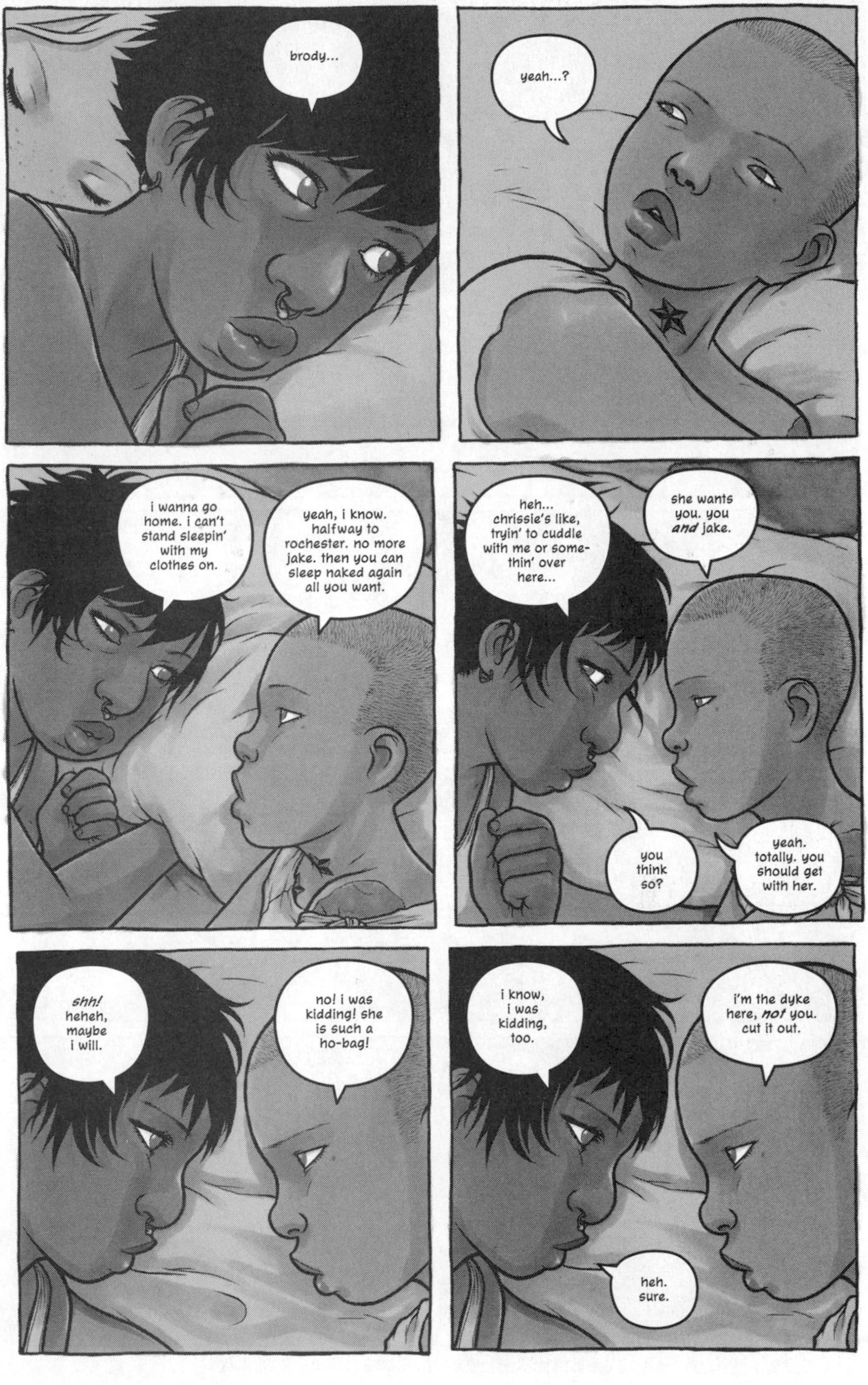
brody...
yeah...?
i wanna go home. i can't stand sleepin' with my clothes on.
yeah, i know. halfway to rochester. no more jake. then you can sleep naked again all you want.
heh... chrissie's like, tryin' to cuddle with me or some-thin' over here...
she wants you. you *and* jake.
you think so?
yeah. totally. you should get with her.
shh! heheh, maybe i will.
no! i was kidding! she is such a ho-bag!
i know, i was kidding, too.
i'm the dyke here, *not* you. cut it out.
heh. sure.

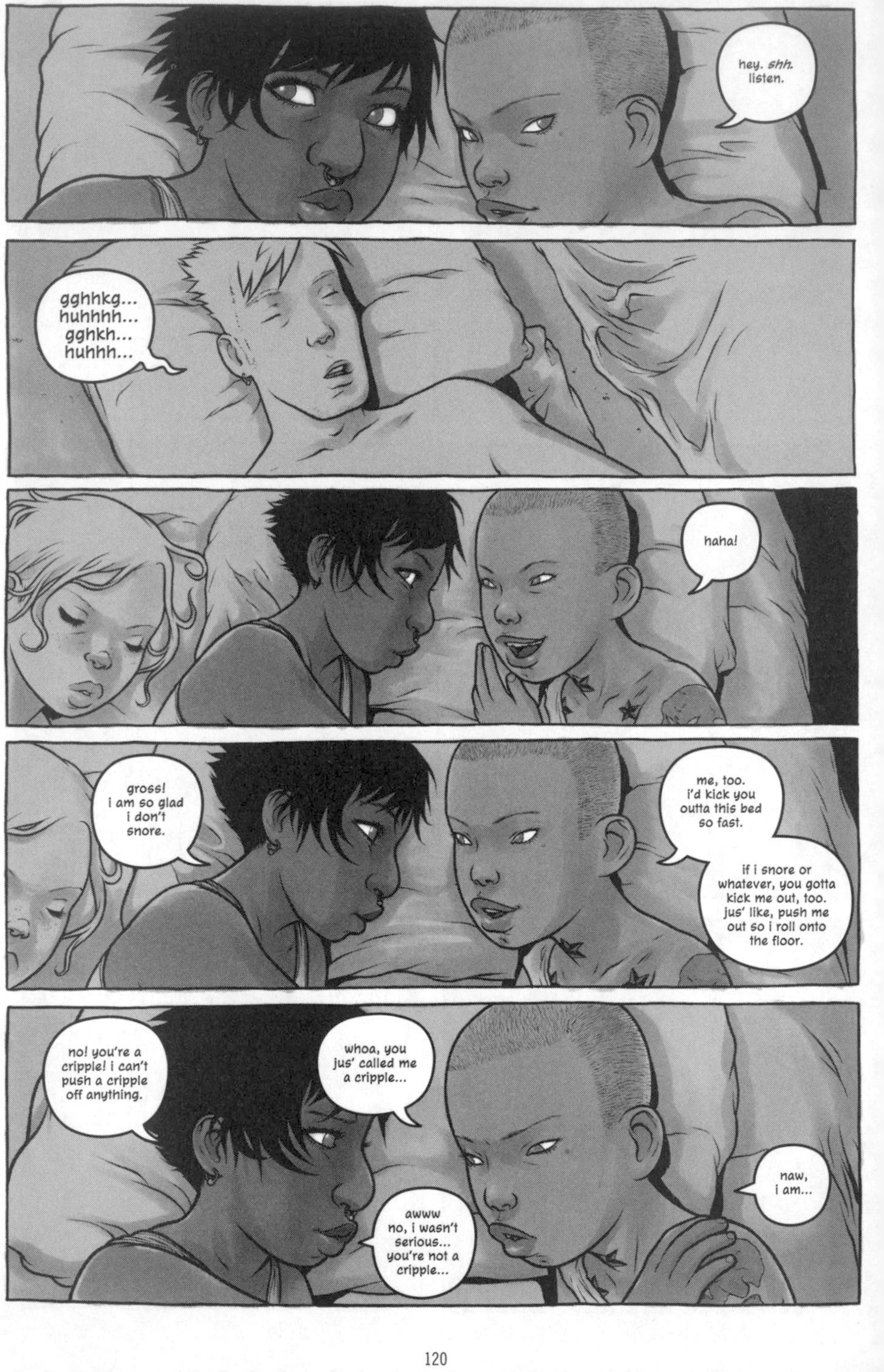
hey. *shh.* listen.
gghhkg... huhhhh... gghkh... huhhh...
haha!
gross! i am so glad i don't snore.
me, too. i'd kick you outta this bed so fast.
if i snore or whatever, you gotta kick me out, too. jus' like, push me out so i roll onto the floor.
no! you're a cripple! i can't push a cripple off anything.
whoa, you jus' called me a cripple...
naw, i am...
awww no, i wasn't serious... you're not a cripple...

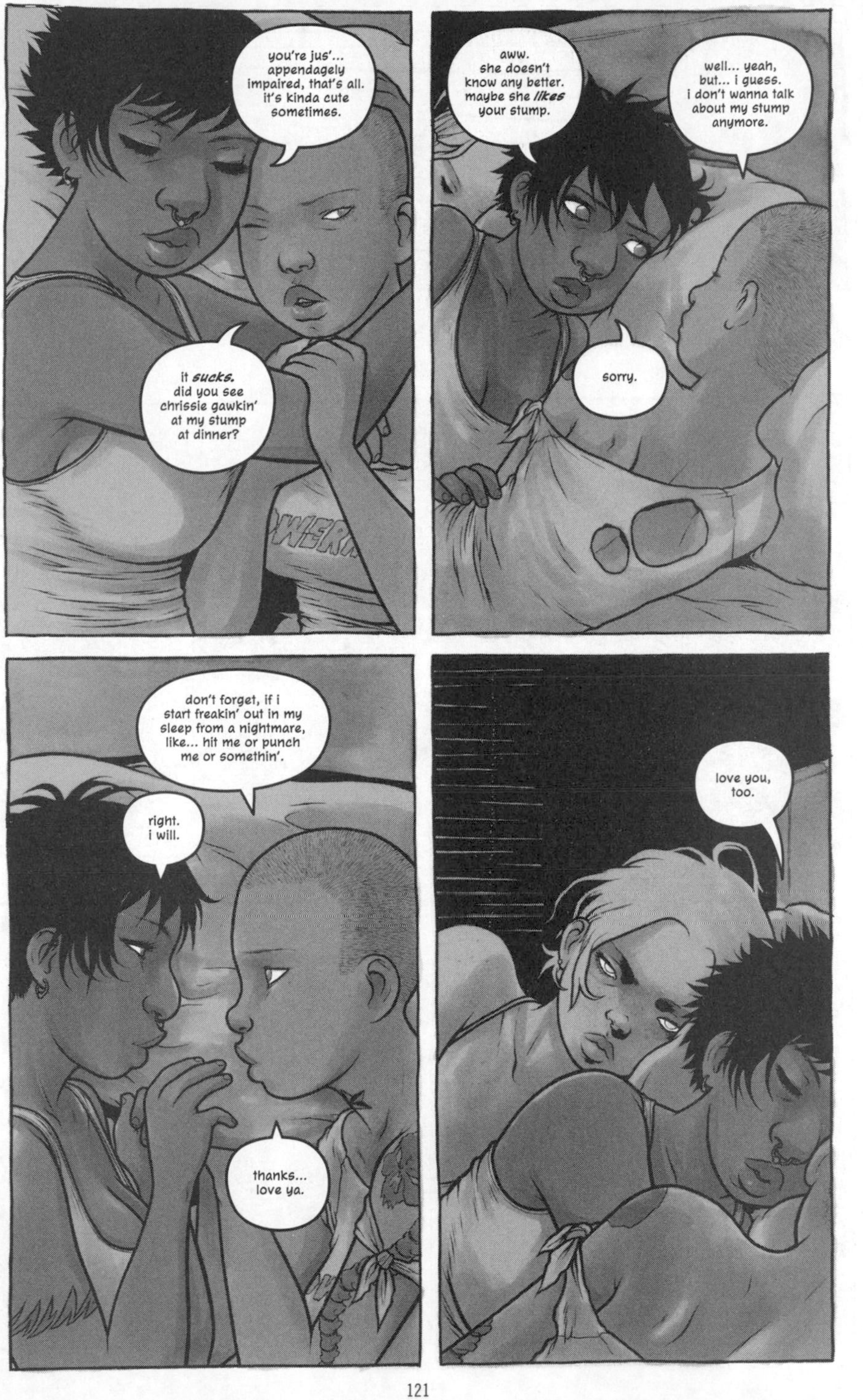
you're jus'... appendagely impaired, that's all. it's kinda cute sometimes.
it *sucks.* did you see chrissie gawkin' at my stump at dinner?
aww. she doesn't know any better. maybe she *likes* your stump.
well... yeah, but... i guess. i don't wanna talk about my stump anymore.
sorry.
don't forget, if i start freakin' out in my sleep from a nightmare, like... hit me or punch me or somethin'.
right. i will.
thanks... love ya.
love you, too.

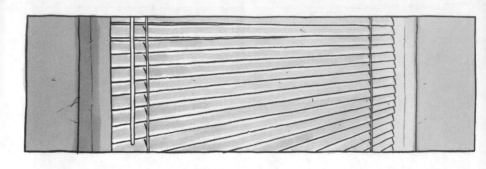

guhh...

Hey, you guys! Rise and shine! Got some donuts!

unnggghh... whaaat...

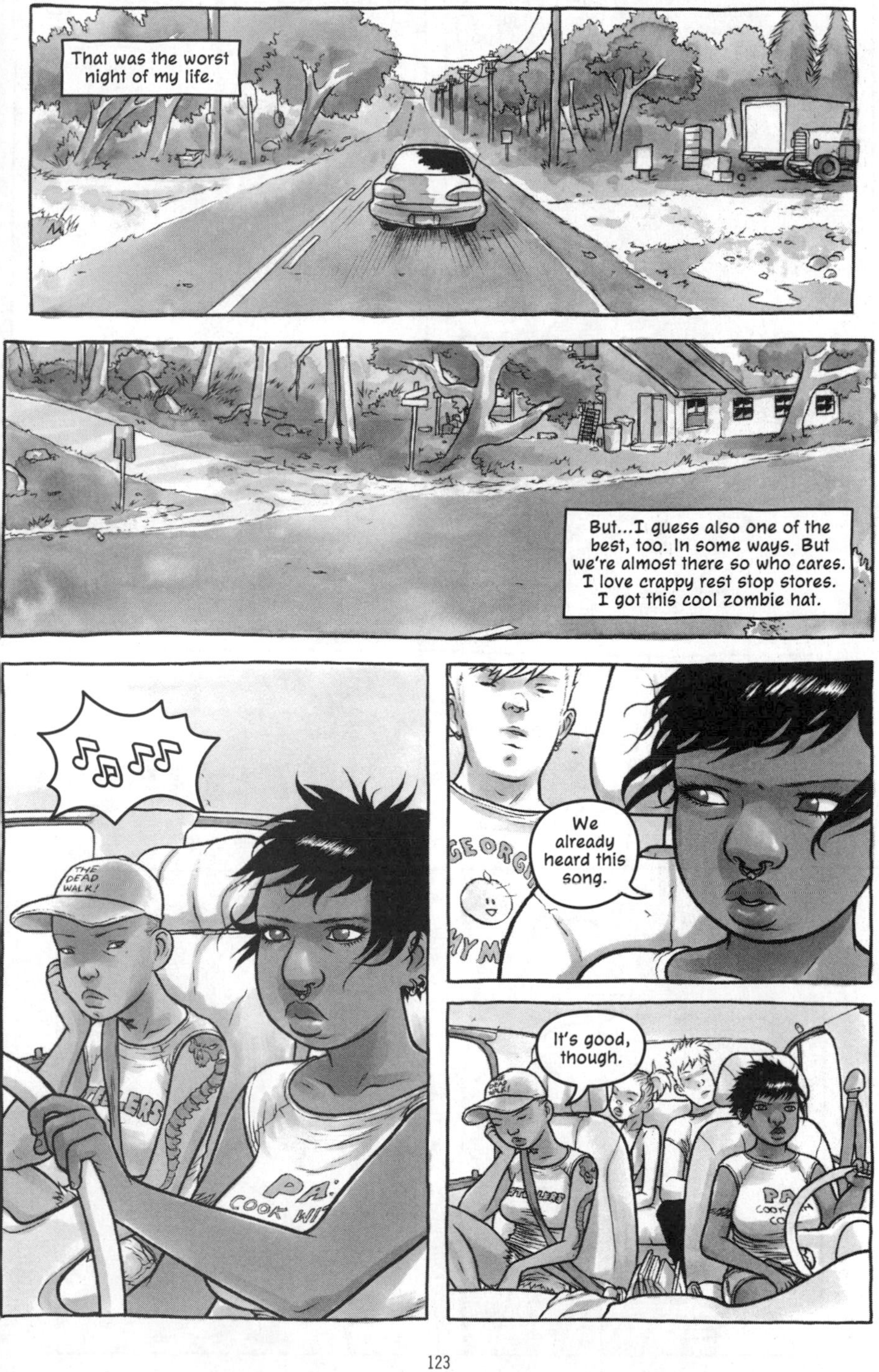

That was the worst night of my life.
But...I guess also one of the best, too. In some ways. But we're almost there so who cares. I love crappy rest stop stores. I got this cool zombie hat.
THE DEAD WALK!
We already heard this song.
It's good, though.

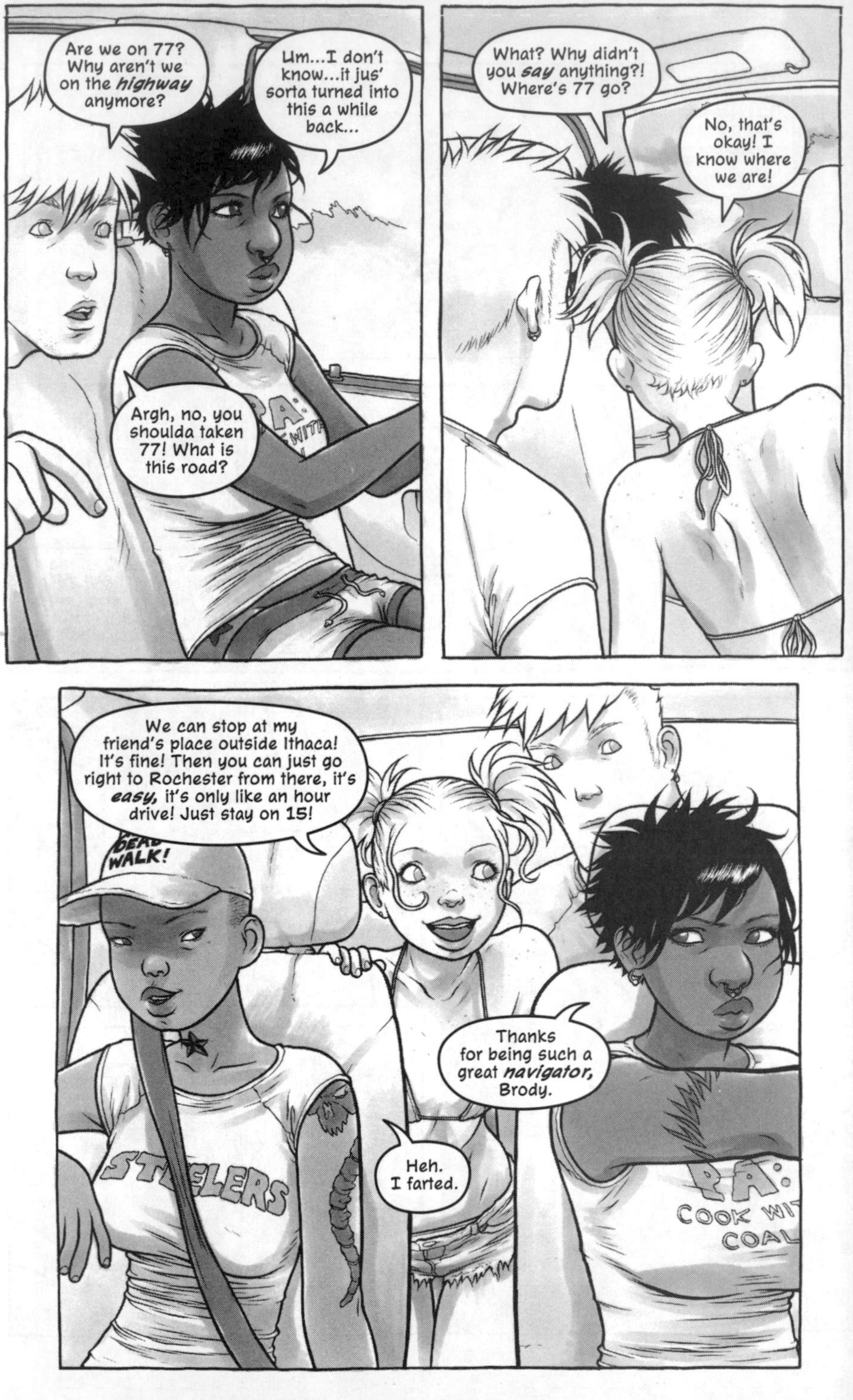
Are we on 77? Why aren't we on the *highway* anymore?
Um...I don't know...it jus' sorta turned into this a while back...
Argh, no, you shoulda taken 77! What is this road?
What? Why didn't you *say* anything?! Where's 77 go?
No, that's okay! I know where we are!
We can stop at my friend's place outside Ithaca! It's fine! Then you can just go right to Rochester from there, it's *easy,* it's only like an hour drive! Just stay on 15!
Thanks for being such a great *navigator,* Brody.
Heh. I farted.

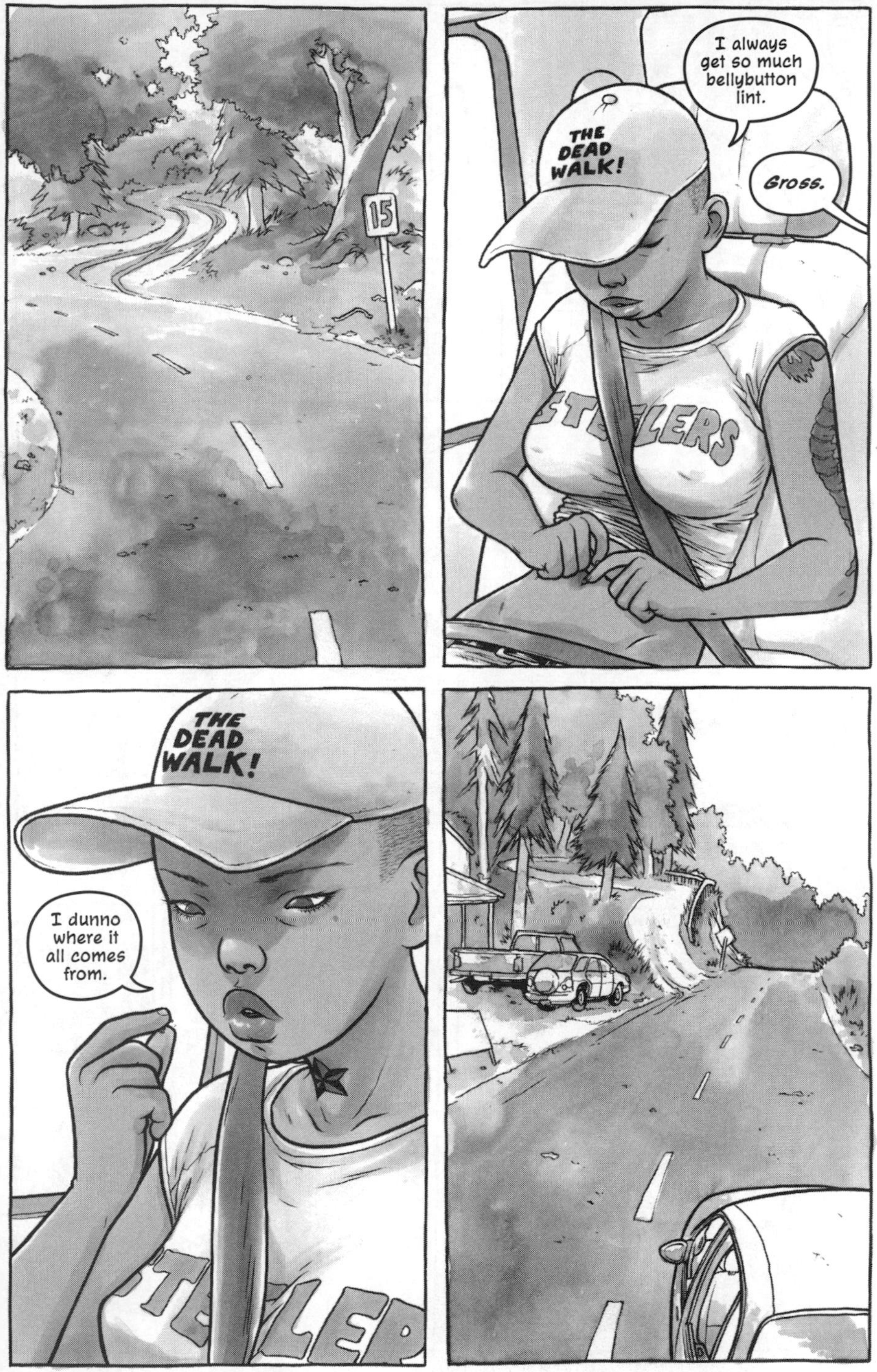
15
THE DEAD WALK!
I always get so much bellybutton lint.
Gross.
THE DEAD WALK!
I dunno where it all comes from.

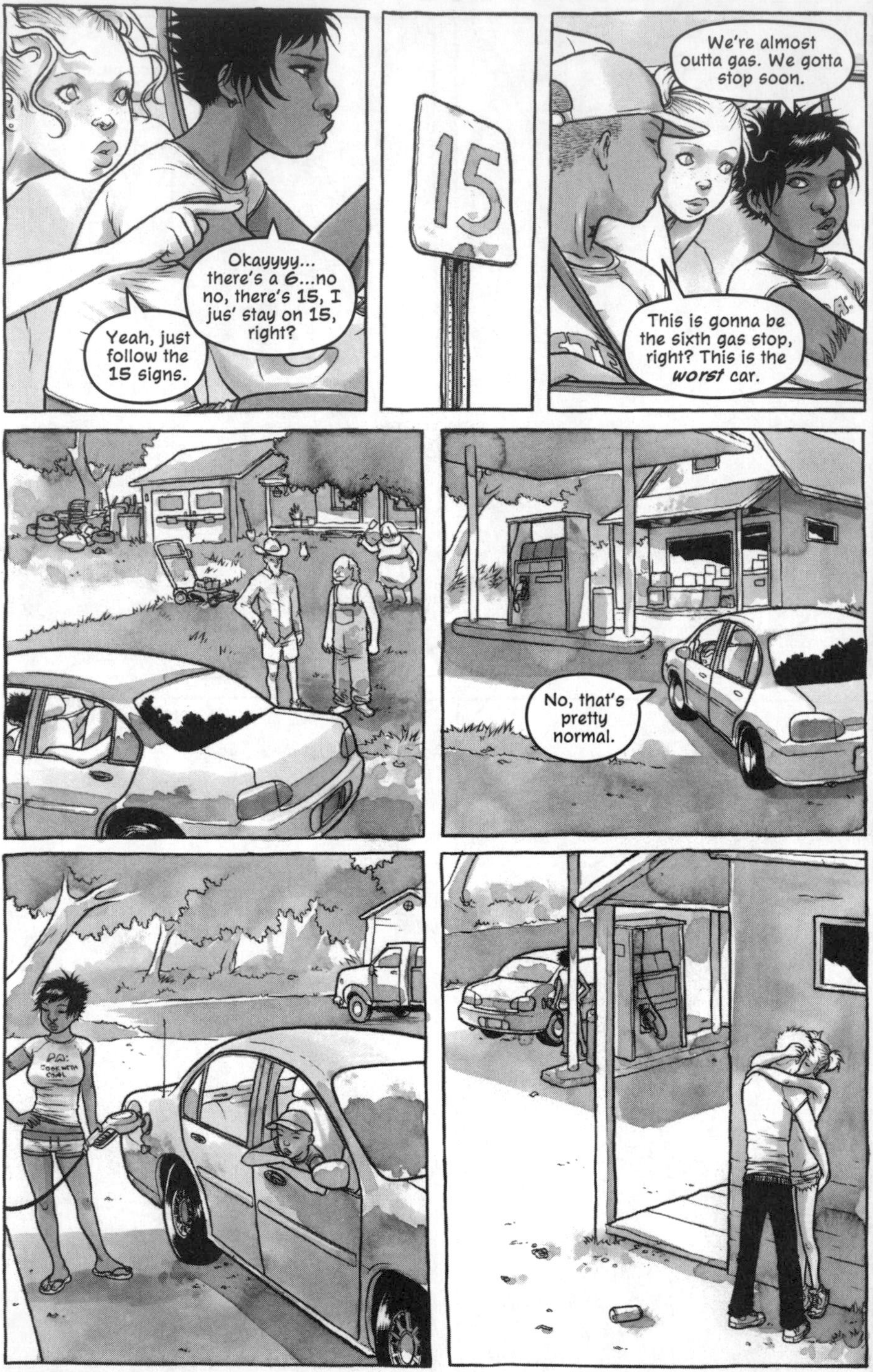
Okayyyy... there's a 6...no no, there's 15, I jus' stay on 15, right?
Yeah, just follow the 15 signs.
15
We're almost outta gas. We gotta stop soon.
This is gonna be the sixth gas stop, right? This is the *worst* car.
No, that's pretty normal.

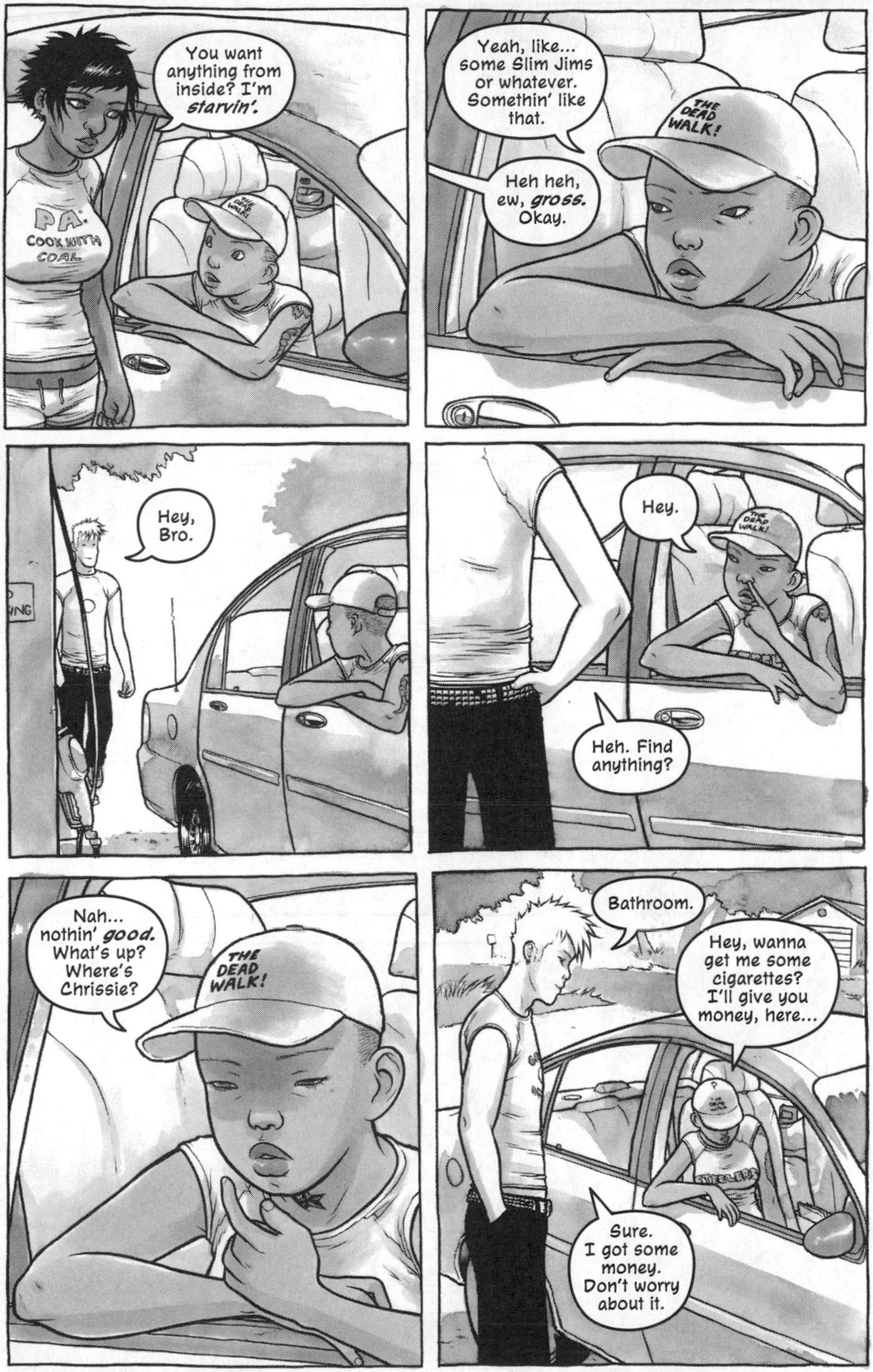

PA: COOK WITH COAL
You want anything from inside? I'm *starvin'.*
THE DEAD WALK!
Yeah, like... some Slim Jims or whatever. Somethin' like that.
Heh heh, ew, *gross.* Okay.
THE DEAD WALK!
Hey, Bro.
Hey.
THE DEAD WALK!
Heh. Find anything?
Nah... nothin' *good.* What's up? Where's Chrissie?
THE DEAD WALK!
Bathroom.
Hey, wanna get me some cigarettes? I'll give you money, here...
Sure. I got some money. Don't worry about it.

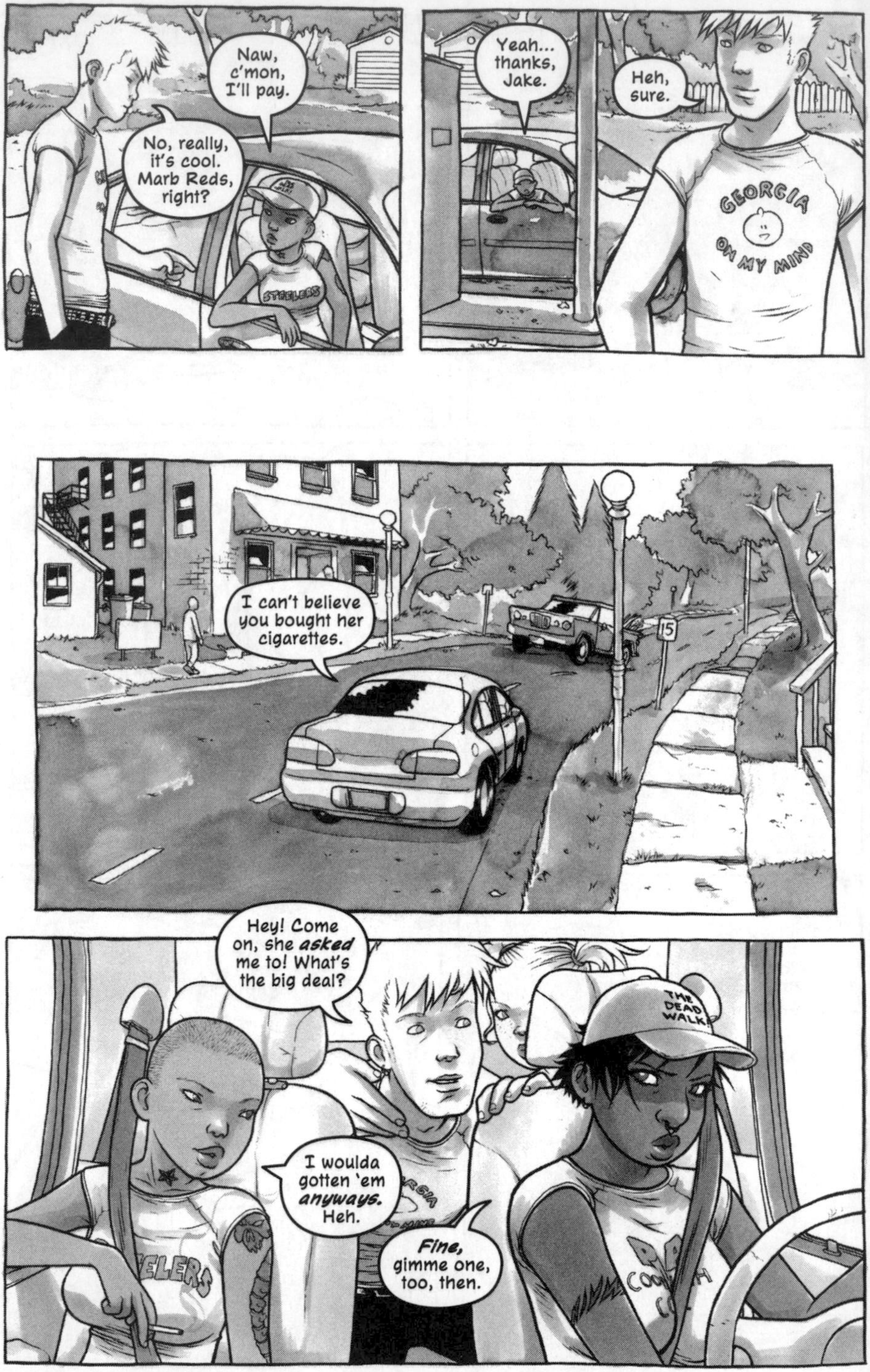

Naw, c'mon, I'll pay.
No, really, it's cool. Marb Reds, right?
Yeah... thanks, Jake.
Heh, sure.
GEORGIA ON MY MIND
STEELERS
15
I can't believe you bought her cigarettes.
Hey! Come on, she *asked* me to! What's the big deal?
THE DEAD WALK!
I woulda gotten 'em *anyways.* Heh.
Fine, gimme one, too, then.

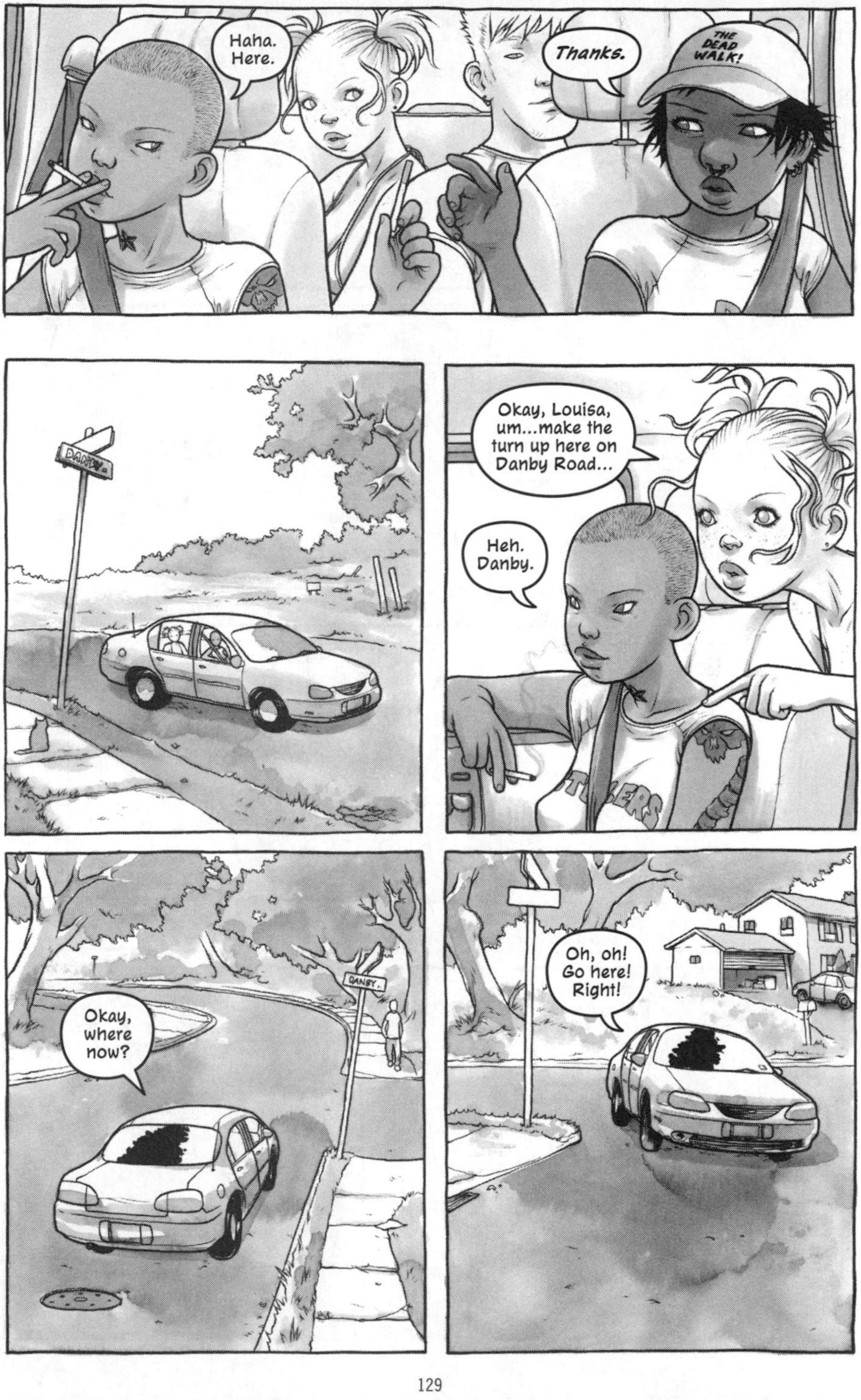
Haha. Here.
Thanks.
THE DEAD WALK!
DANBY
Okay, Louisa, um...make the turn up here on Danby Road...
Heh. Danby.
Okay, where now?
DANBY
Oh, oh! Go here! Right!

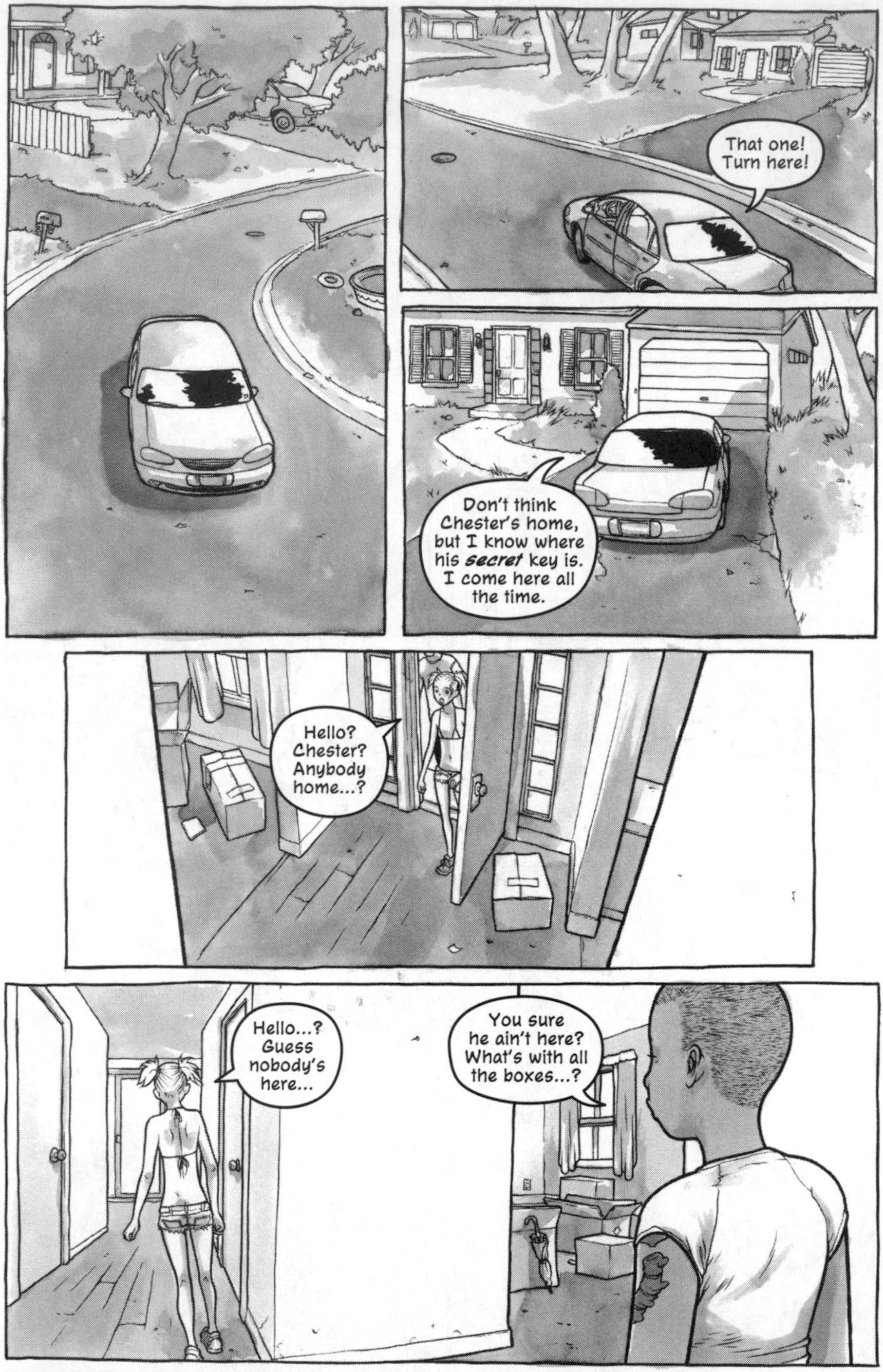
That one! Turn here!
Don't think Chester's home, but I know where his *secret* key is. I come here all the time.
Hello? Chester? Anybody home...?
Hello...? Guess nobody's here...
You sure he ain't here? What's with all the boxes...?

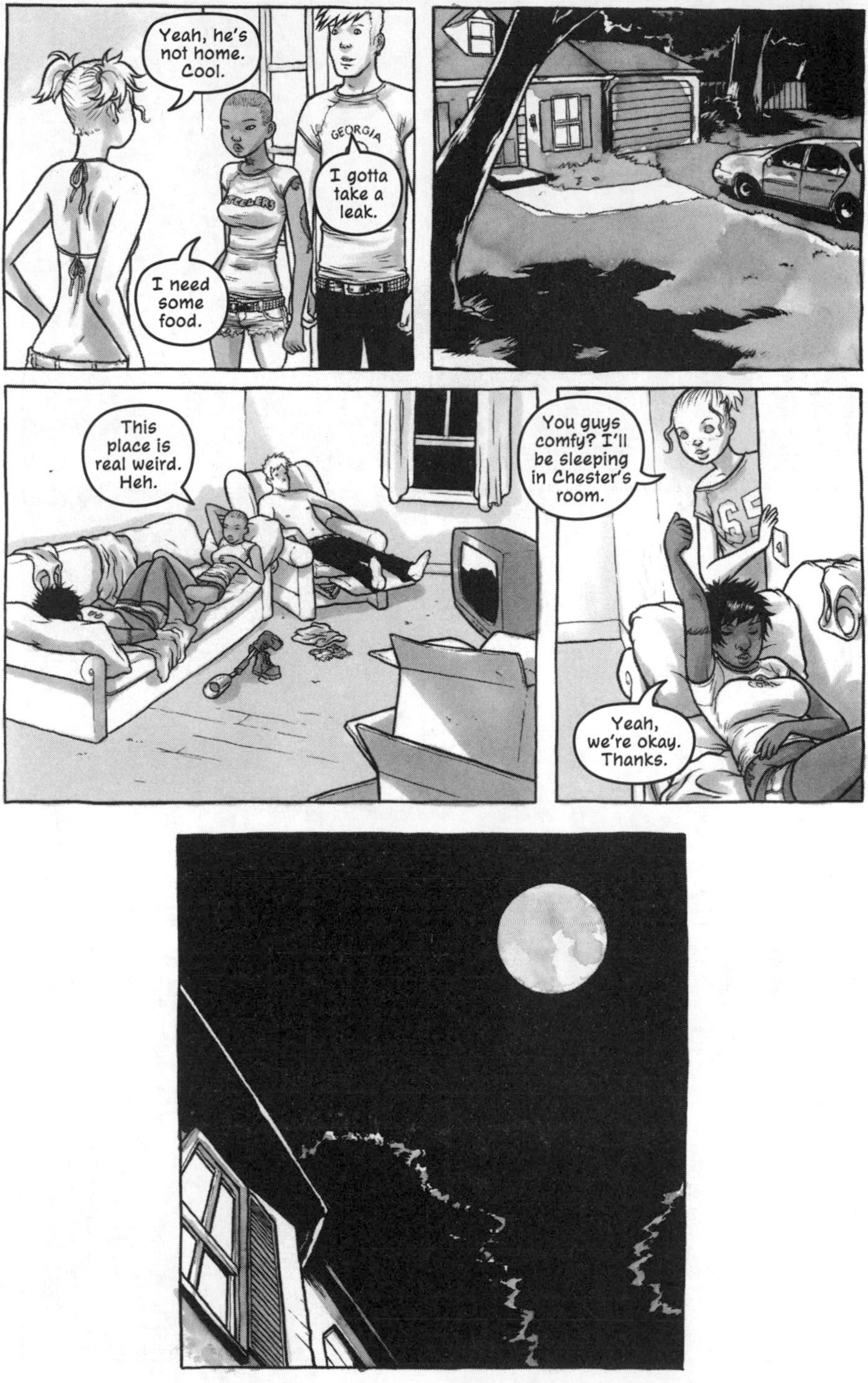
Yeah, he's not home. Cool.
GEORGIA
I gotta take a leak.
I need some food.
This place is real weird. Heh.
You guys comfy? I'll be sleeping in Chester's room.
Yeah, we're okay. Thanks.

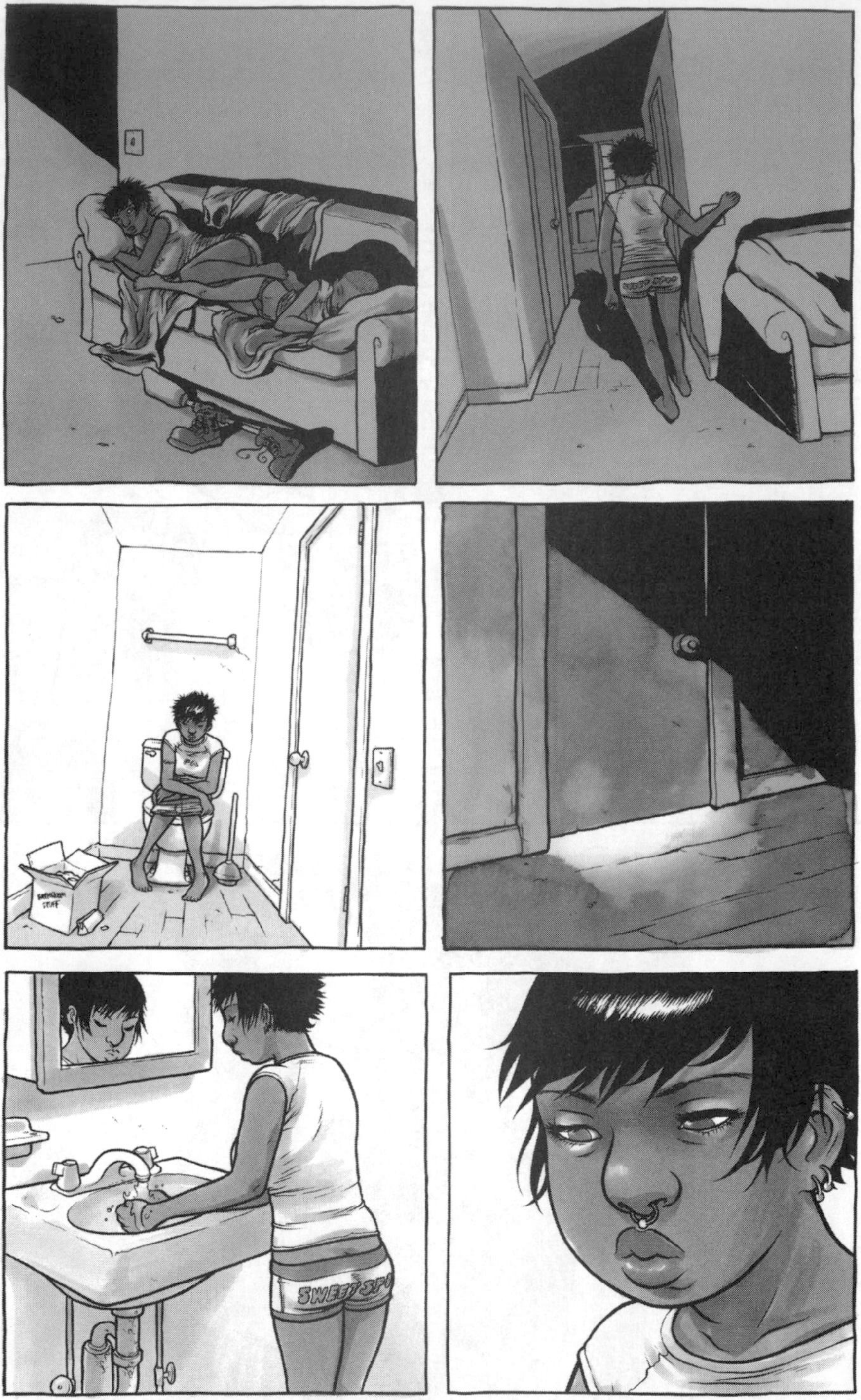

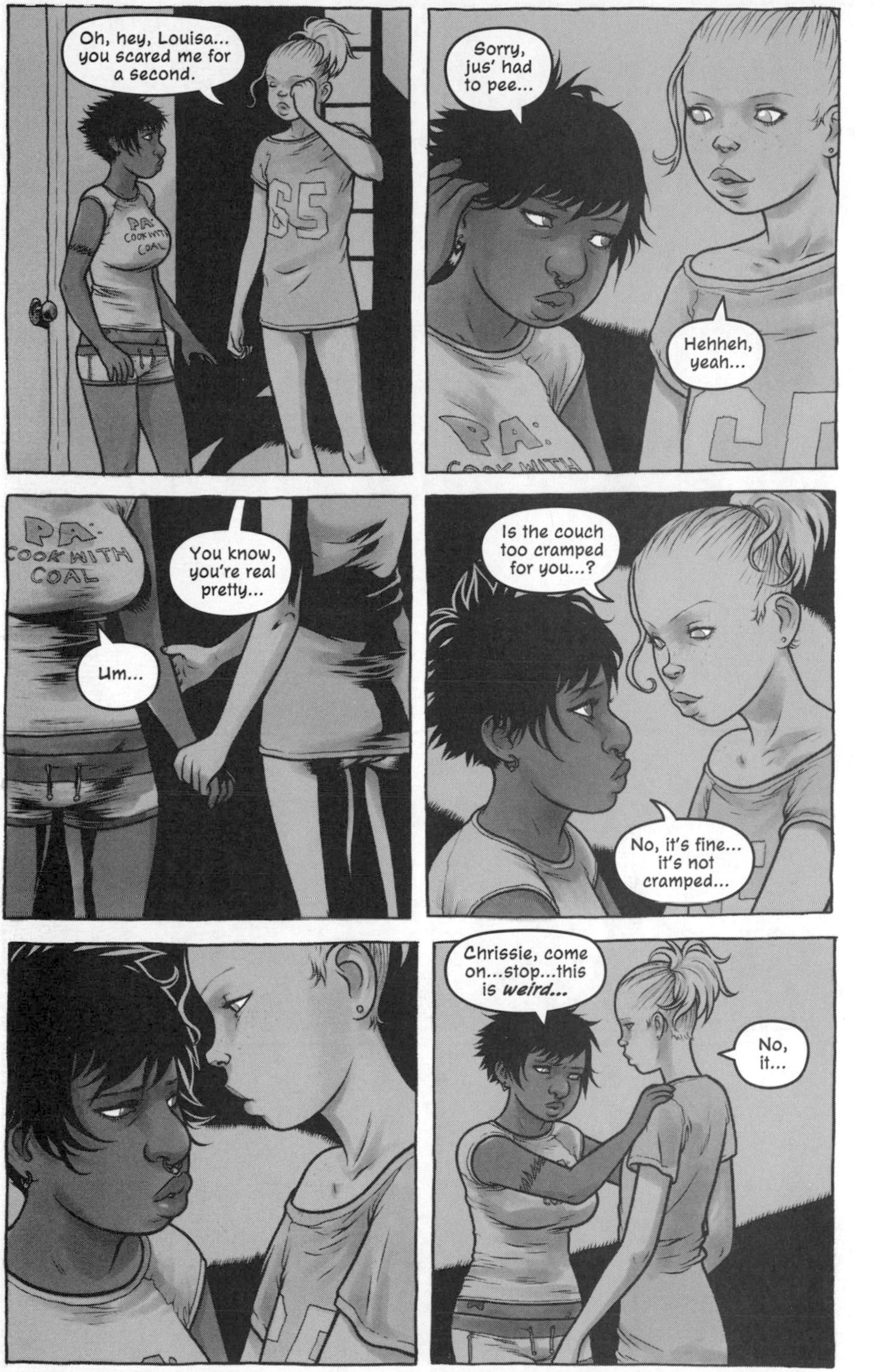
Oh, hey, Louisa... you scared me for a second.
PA: COOK WITH COAL
65
Sorry, jus' had to pee...
Hehheh, yeah...
PA: COOK WITH COAL
You know, you're real pretty...
Um...
Is the couch too cramped for you...?
No, it's fine... it's not cramped...
Chrissie, come on...stop...this is *weird...*
No, it...

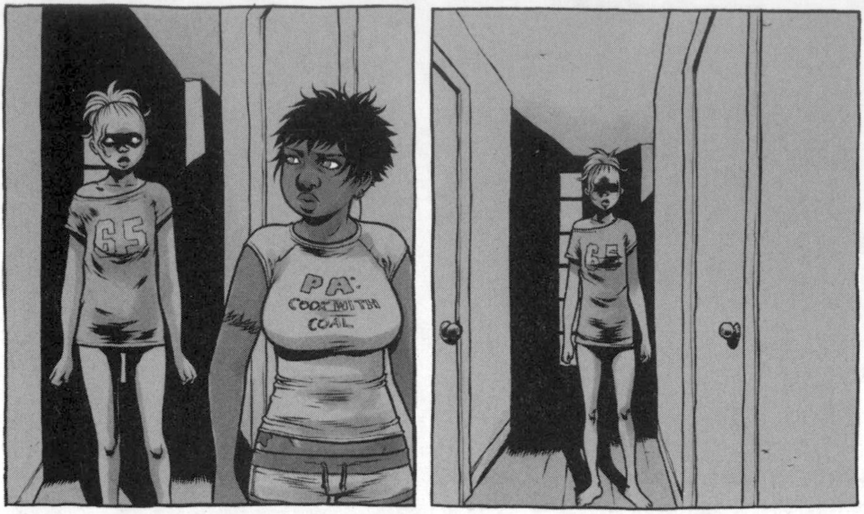
PA:
COOK WITH
COAL

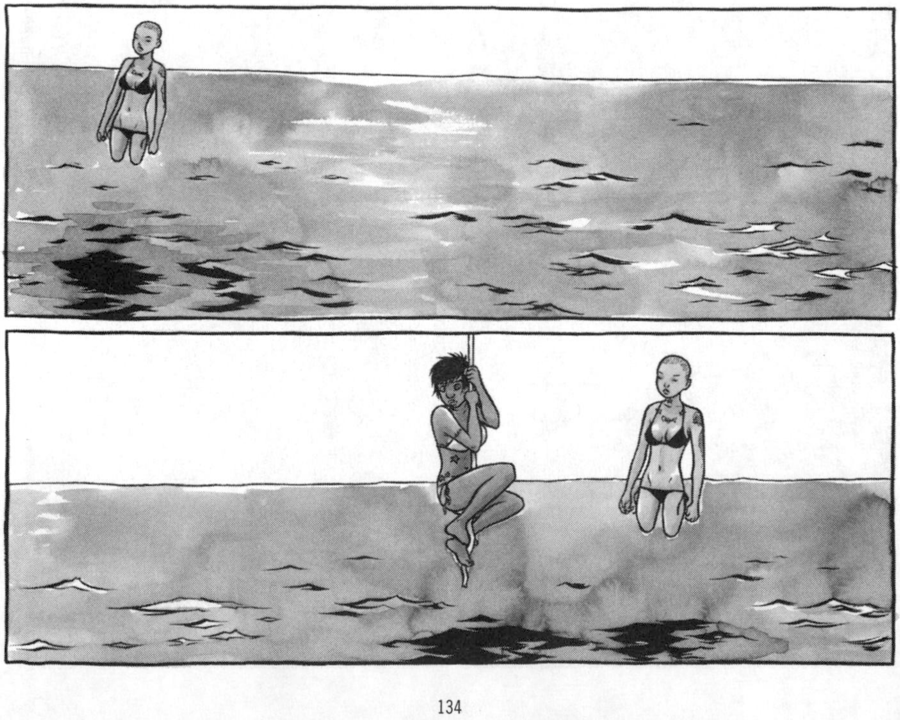

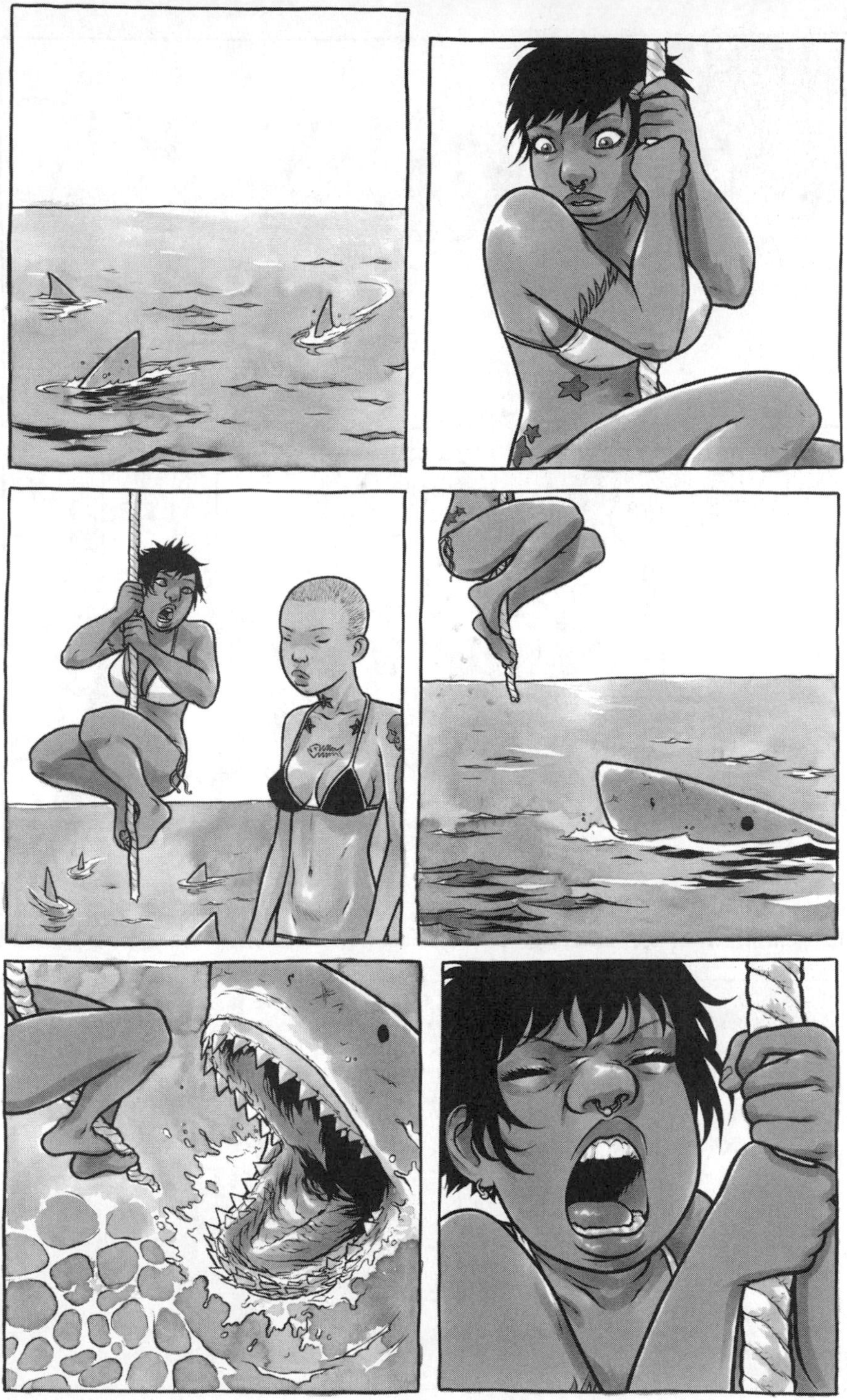

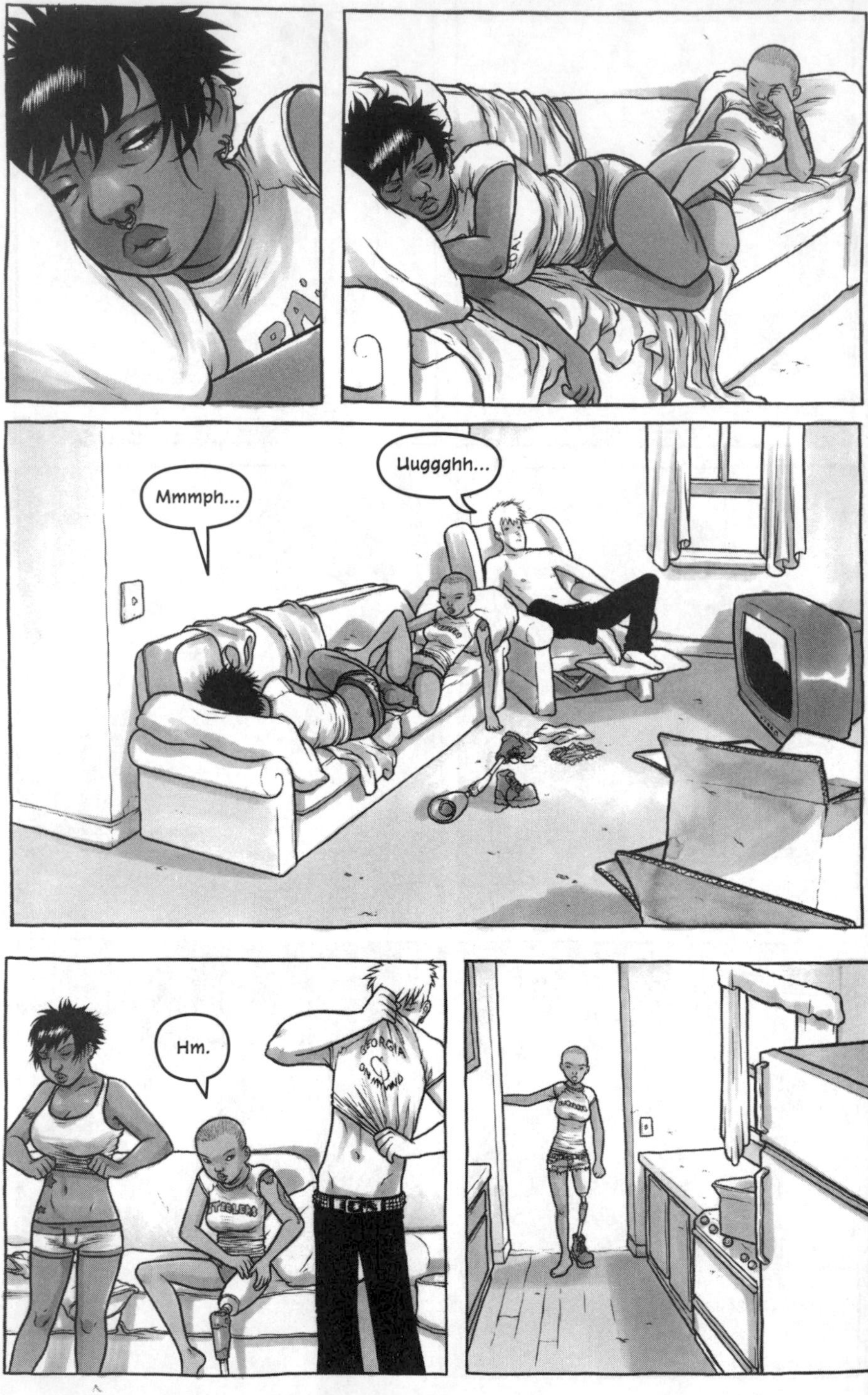

Mmmph...
Uuggghh...
Hm.

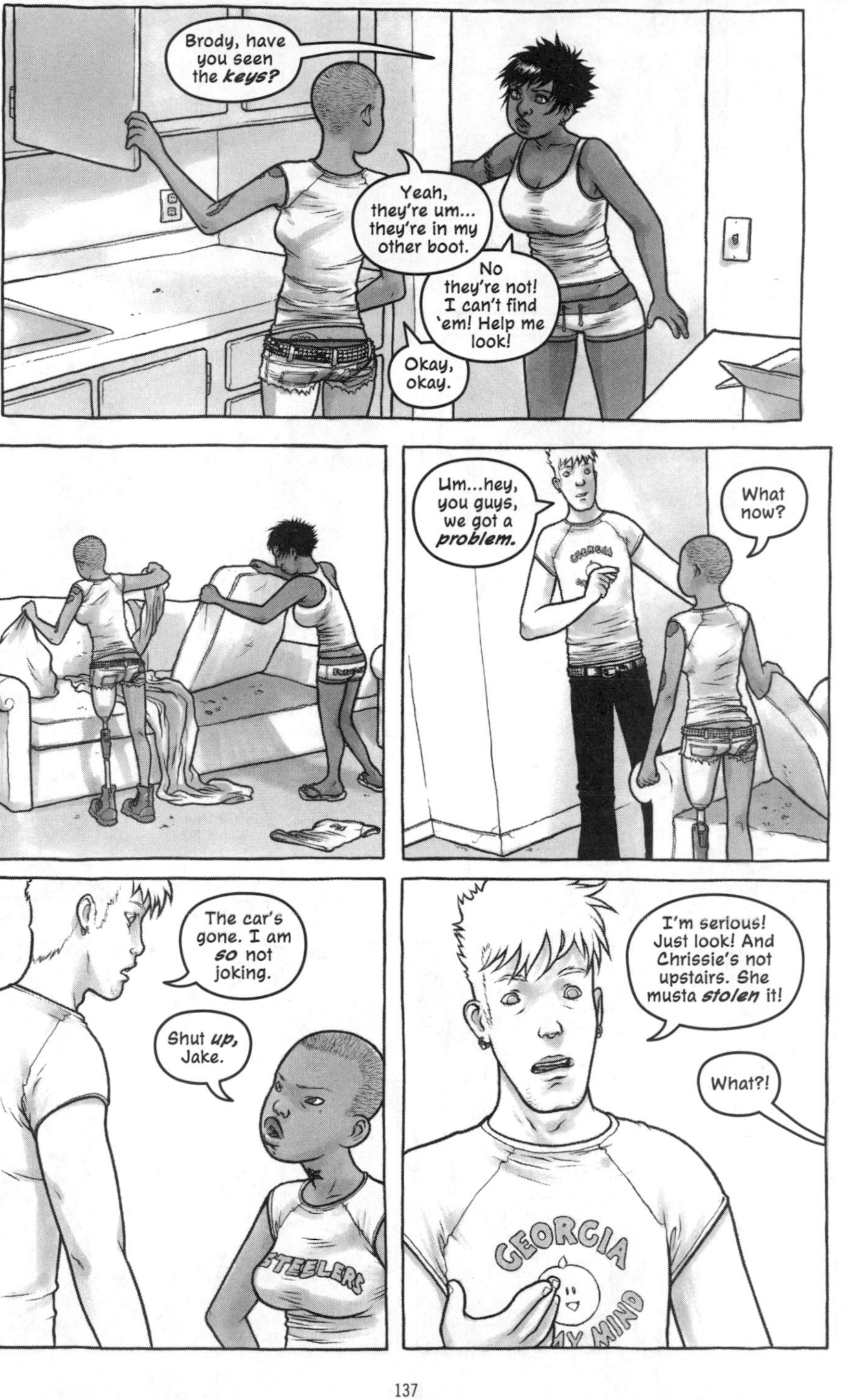
Brody, have you seen the *keys?*
Yeah, they're um... they're in my other boot.
No they're not! I can't find 'em! Help me look!
Okay, okay.
Um...hey, you guys, we got a *problem.*
What now?
GEORGIA
The car's gone. I am *so* not joking.
Shut *up,* Jake.
STEELERS
I'm serious! Just look! And Chrissie's not upstairs. She musta *stolen* it!
What?!
GEORGIA
MY MIND

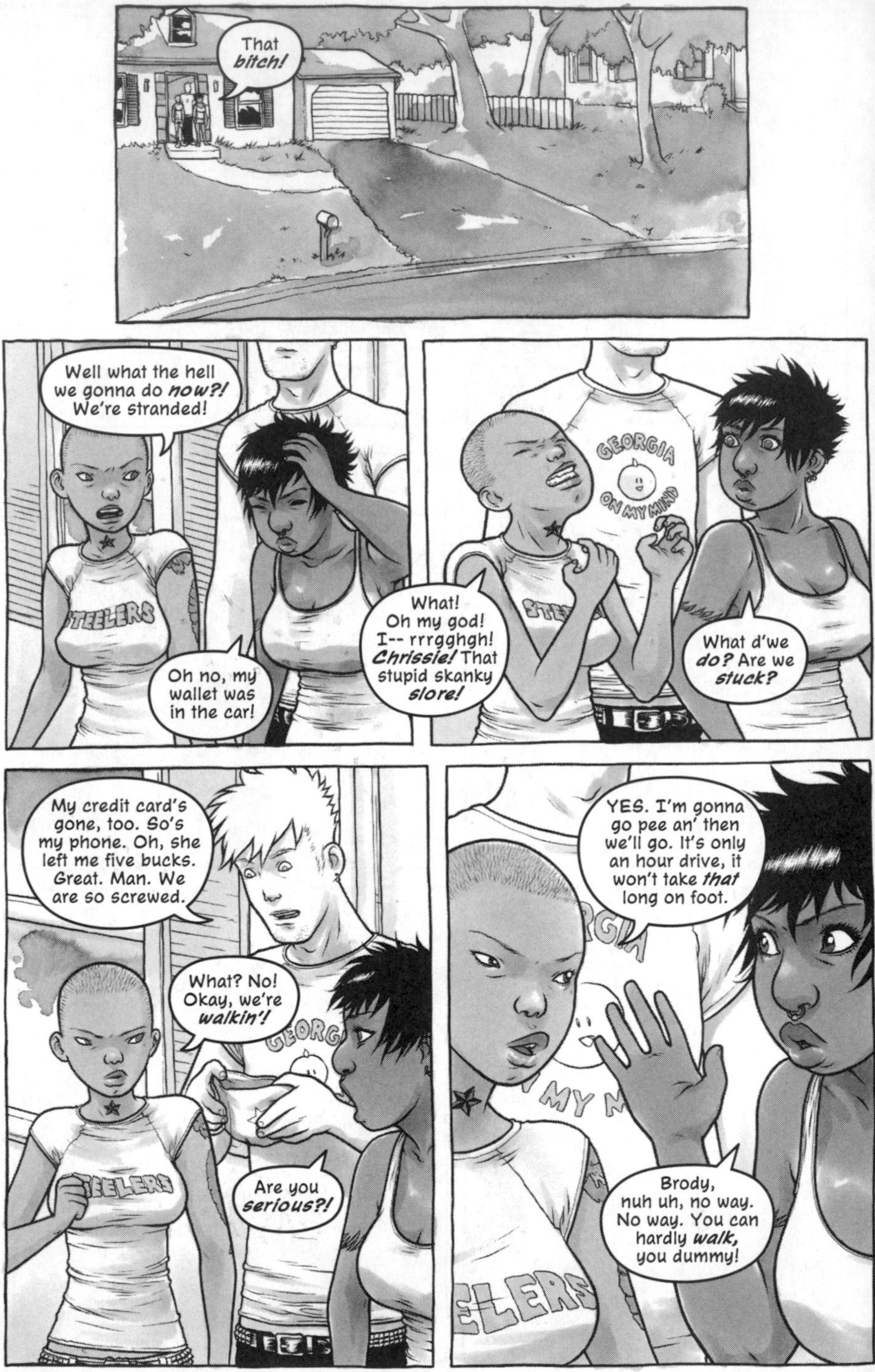

That *bitch!*
Well what the hell we gonna do *now?!* We're stranded!
Oh no, my wallet was in the car!
What! Oh my god! I-- rrrgghgh! *Chrissie!* That stupid skanky *slore!*
What d'we *do?* Are we *stuck?*
GEORGIA ON MY MIND
STEELERS
My credit card's gone, too. So's my phone. Oh, she left me five bucks. Great. Man. We are so screwed.
What? No! Okay, we're *walkin'!*
Are you *serious?!*
YES. I'm gonna go pee an' then we'll go. It's only an hour drive, it won't take *that* long on foot.
Brody, nuh uh, no way. No way. You can hardly *walk,* you dummy!

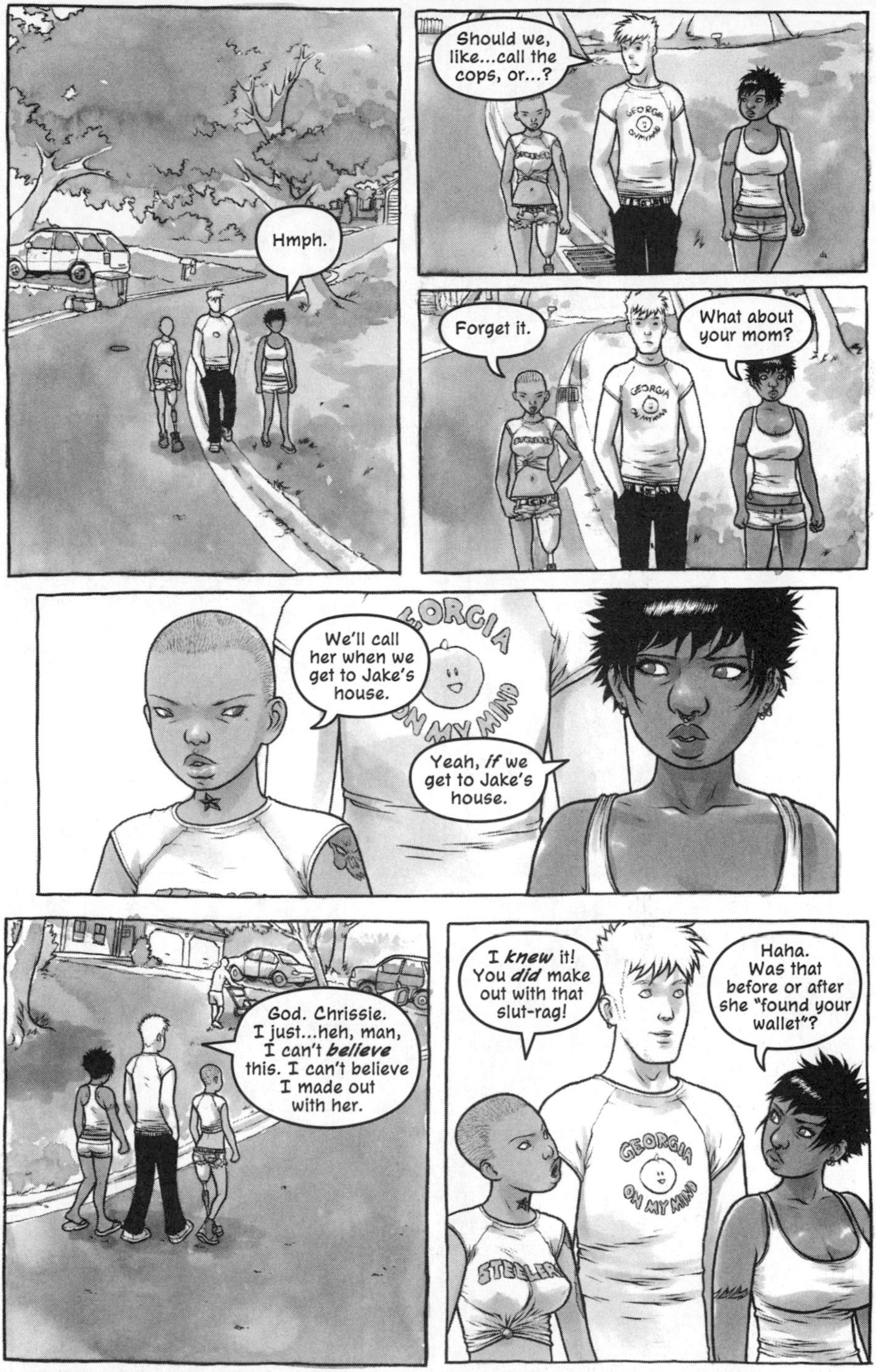
Hmph.
Should we, like...call the cops, or...?
Forget it.
What about your mom?
We'll call her when we get to Jake's house.
Yeah, *if* we get to Jake's house.
God. Chrissie. I just...heh, man, I can't ***believe*** this. I can't believe I made out with her.
I ***knew*** it! You ***did*** make out with that slut-rag!
Haha. Was that before or after she "found your wallet"?

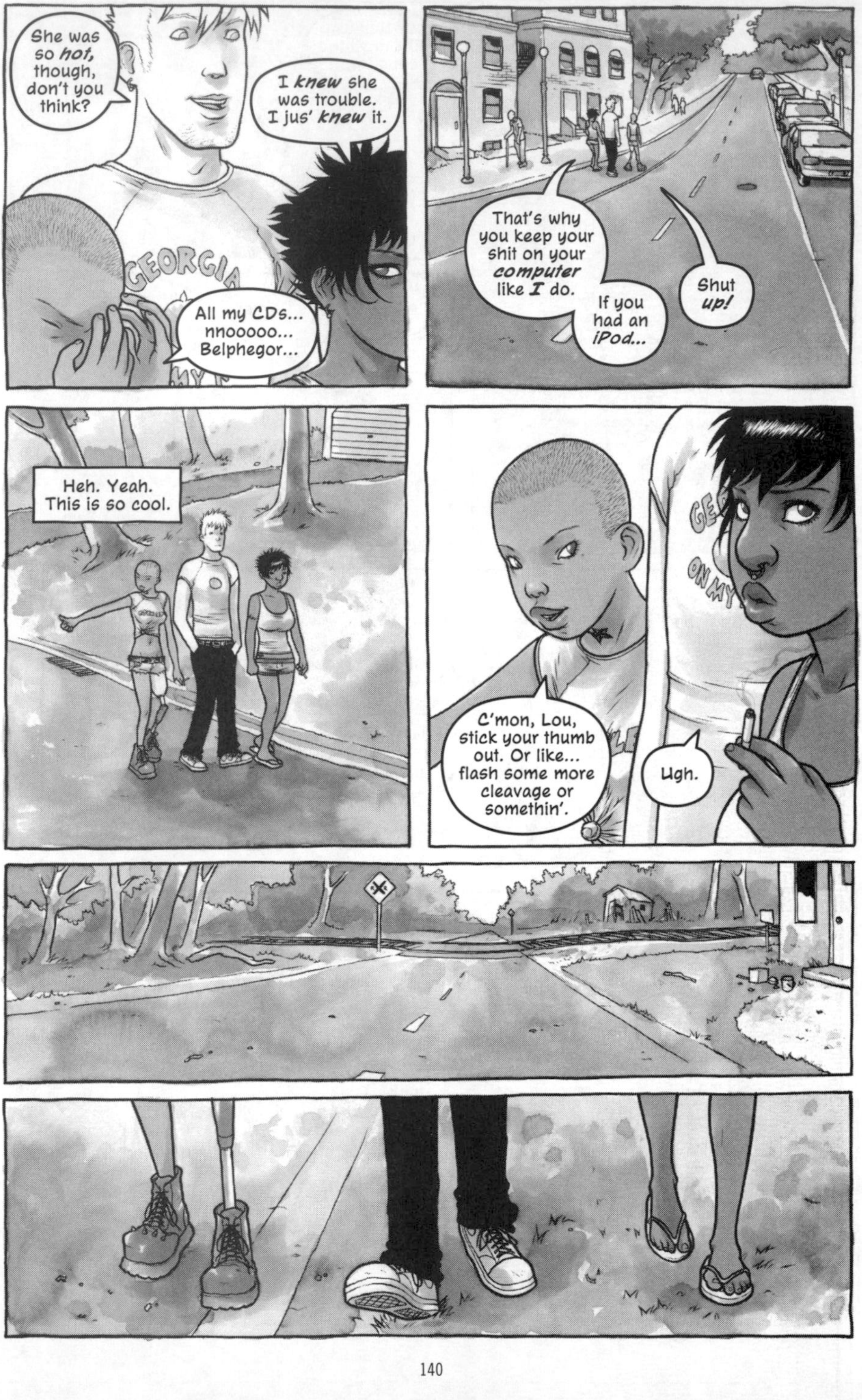

She was so *hot,* though, don't you think?
I ***knew*** she was trouble. I jus' ***knew*** it.
All my CDs... nnooooo... Belphegor...
That's why you keep your shit on your ***computer*** like ***I*** do.
If you had an *iPod...*
Shut *up!*
Heh. Yeah. This is so cool.
C'mon, Lou, stick your thumb out. Or like... flash some more cleavage or somethin'.
Ugh.

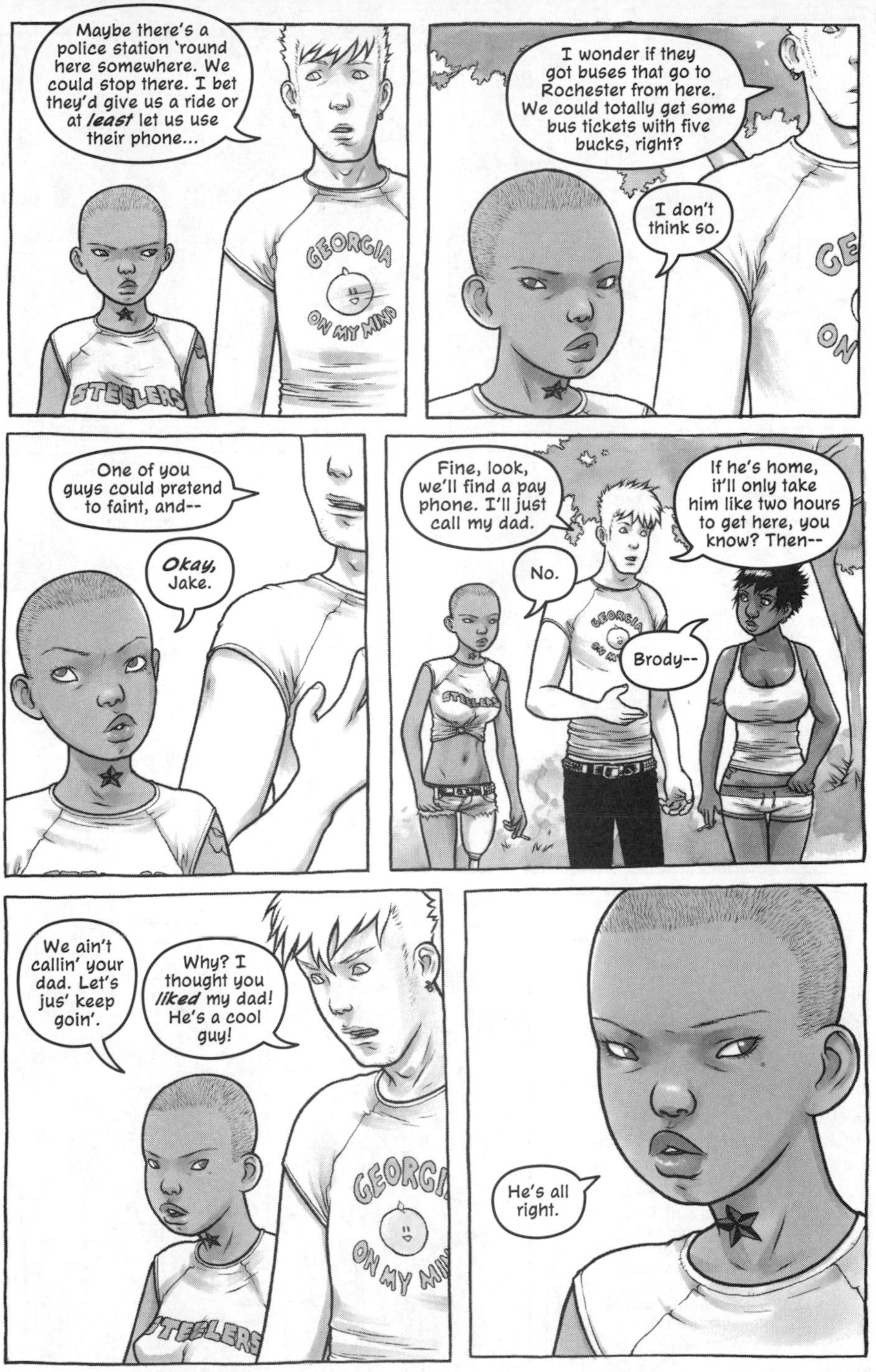

Maybe there's a police station 'round here somewhere. We could stop there. I bet they'd give us a ride or at *least* let us use their phone...
GEORGIA ON MY MIND
STEELERS
I wonder if they got buses that go to Rochester from here. We could totally get some bus tickets with five bucks, right?
I don't think so.
One of you guys could pretend to faint, and--
Okay, Jake.
Fine, look, we'll find a pay phone. I'll just call my dad.
If he's home, it'll only take him like two hours to get here, you know? Then--
No.
Brody--
We ain't callin' your dad. Let's jus' keep goin'.
Why? I thought you *liked* my dad! He's a cool guy!
He's all right.

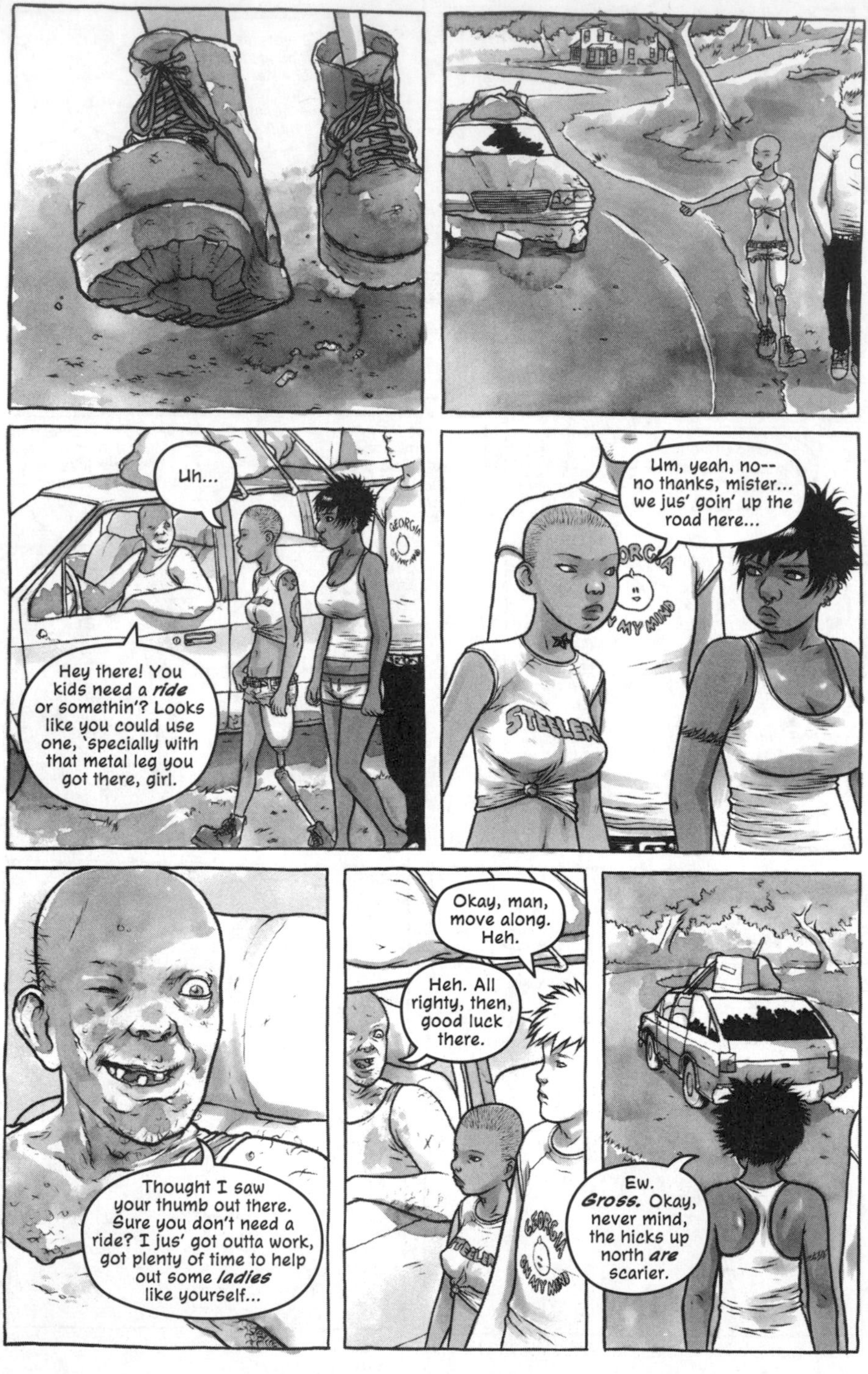
Uh...
Hey there! You kids need a *ride* or somethin'? Looks like you could use one, 'specially with that metal leg you got there, girl.
Um, yeah, no-- no thanks, mister... we jus' goin' up the road here...
STEELERS
Thought I saw your thumb out there. Sure you don't need a ride? I jus' got outta work, got plenty of time to help out some *ladies* like yourself...
Okay, man, move along. Heh.
Heh. All righty, then, good luck there.
Ew. ***Gross.*** Okay, never mind, the hicks up north *are* scarier.

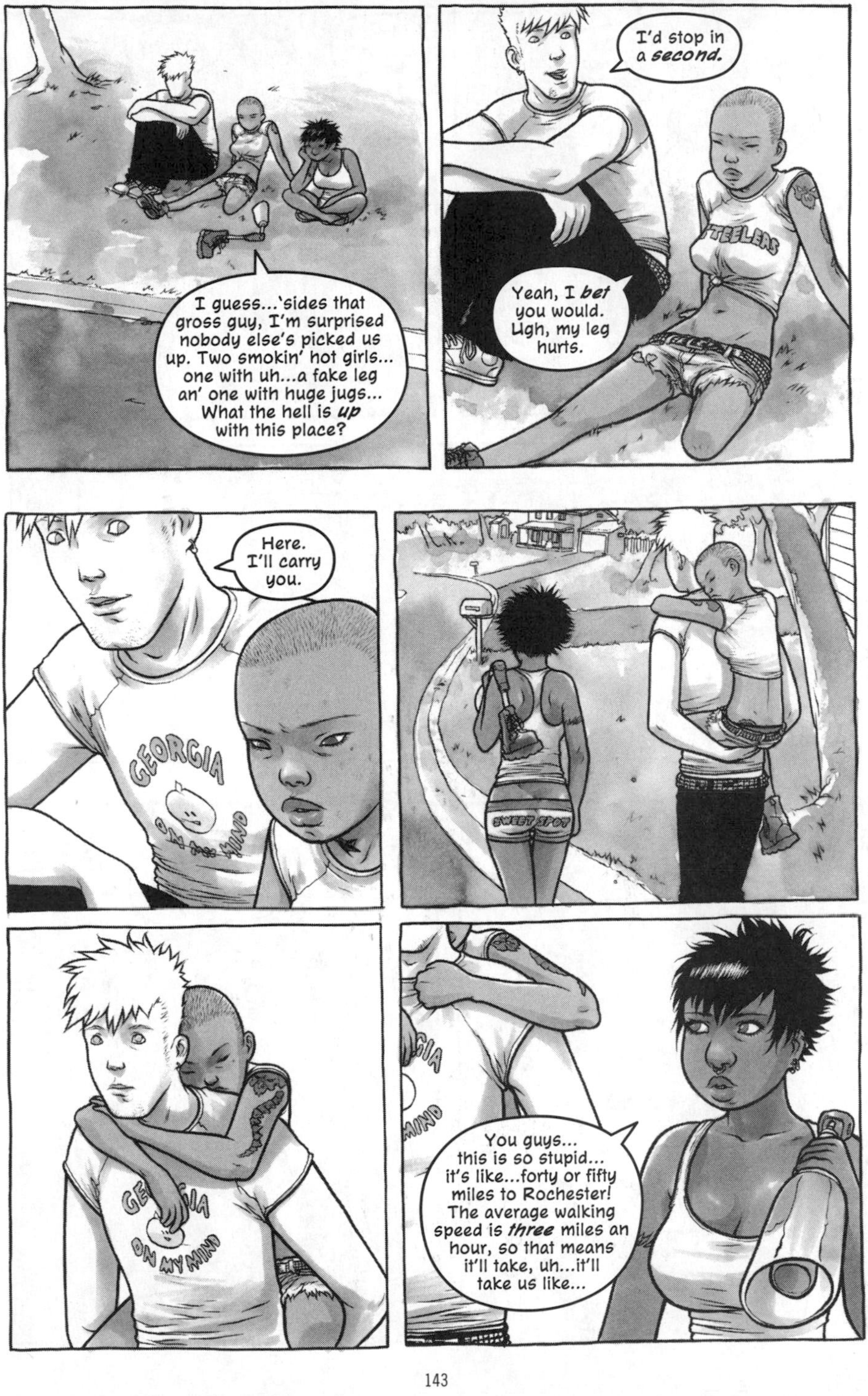
I guess...'sides that gross guy, I'm surprised nobody else's picked us up. Two smokin' hot girls... one with uh...a fake leg an' one with huge jugs... What the hell is *up* with this place?
I'd stop in a *second.*
Yeah, I *bet* you would. Ugh, my leg hurts.
STEELERS
Here. I'll carry you.
GEORGIA
SWEET SPOT
GEORGIA ON MY MIND
You guys... this is so stupid... it's like...forty or fifty miles to Rochester! The average walking speed is *three* miles an hour, so that means it'll take, uh...it'll take us like...

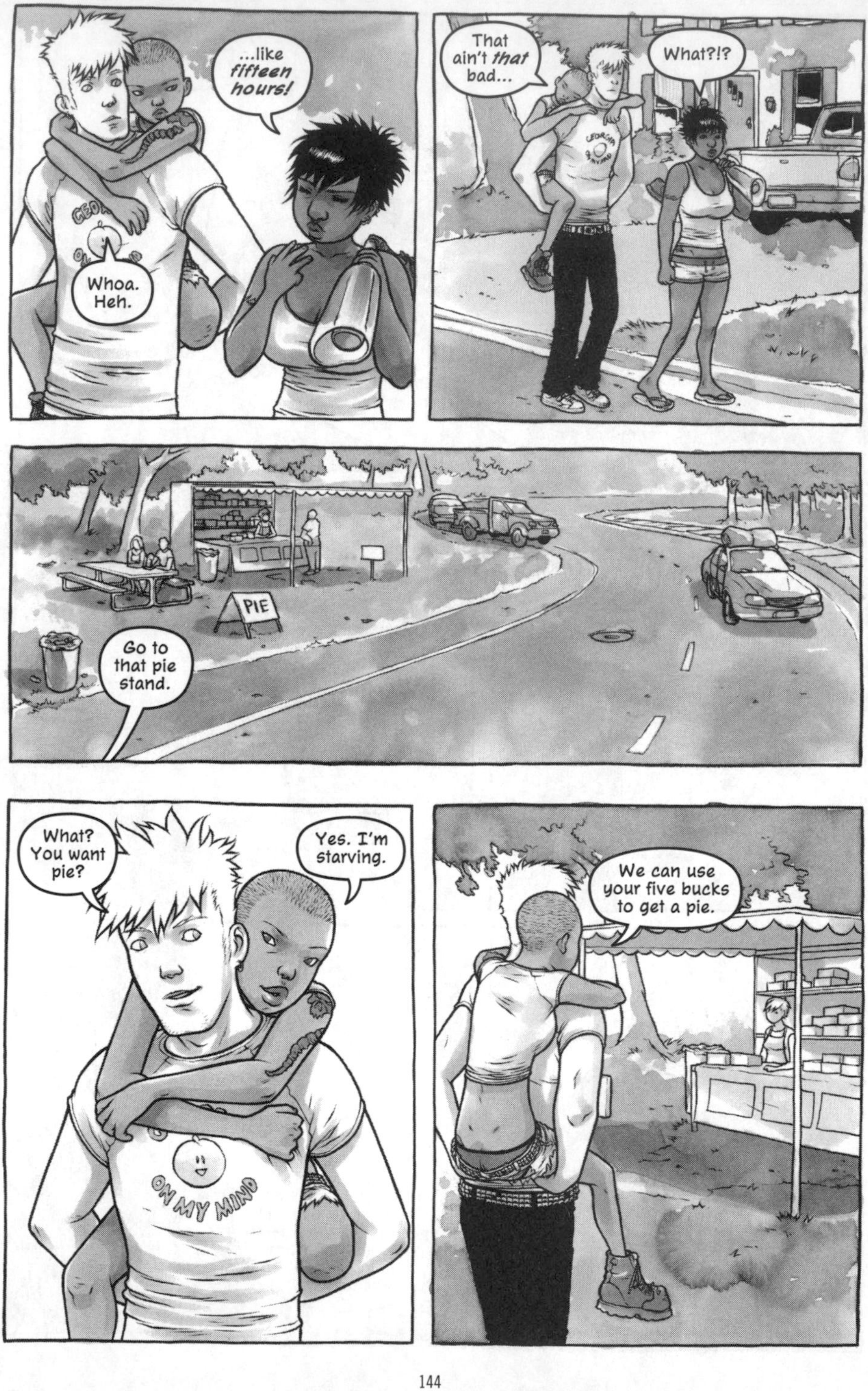
...like *fifteen hours!*
Whoa. Heh.
That ain't *that* bad...
What?!?
PIE
Go to that pie stand.
What? You want pie?
Yes. I'm starving.
ON MY MIND
We can use your five bucks to get a pie.

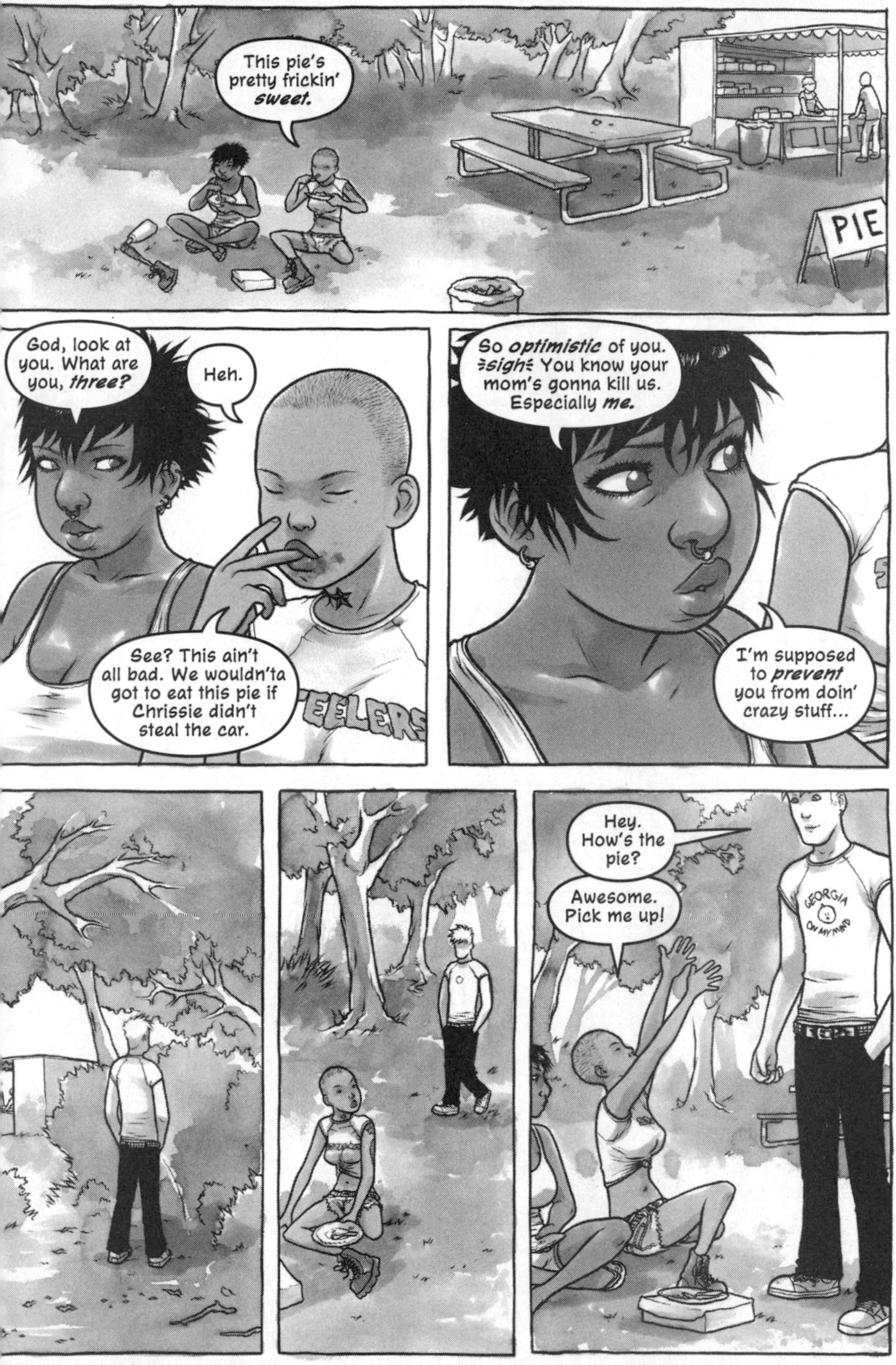
This pie's pretty frickin' *sweet.*
PIE
God, look at you. What are you, *three?*
Heh.
See? This ain't all bad. We wouldn'ta got to eat this pie if Chrissie didn't steal the car.
So *optimistic* of you. ≶*sigh*≶ You know your mom's gonna kill us. Especially *me.*
I'm supposed to *prevent* you from doin' crazy stuff...
Hey. How's the pie?
Awesome. Pick me up!
GEORGIA ON MY MIND

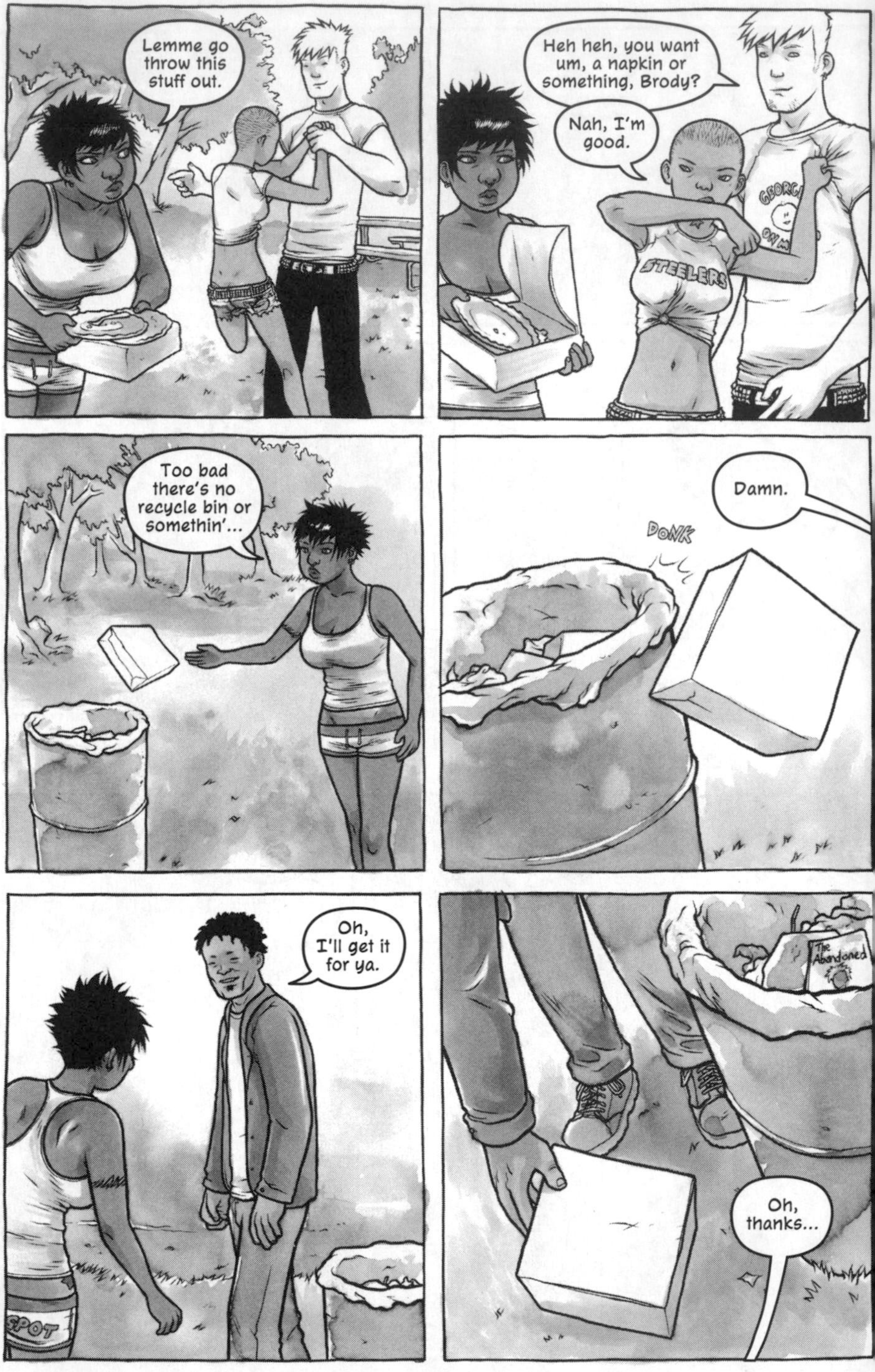
Lemme go throw this stuff out.
Heh heh, you want um, a napkin or something, Brody?
Nah, I'm good.
STEELERS
Too bad there's no recycle bin or somethin'...
Damn.
DONK
Oh, I'll get it for ya.
SPOT
The Abandoned
Oh, thanks...

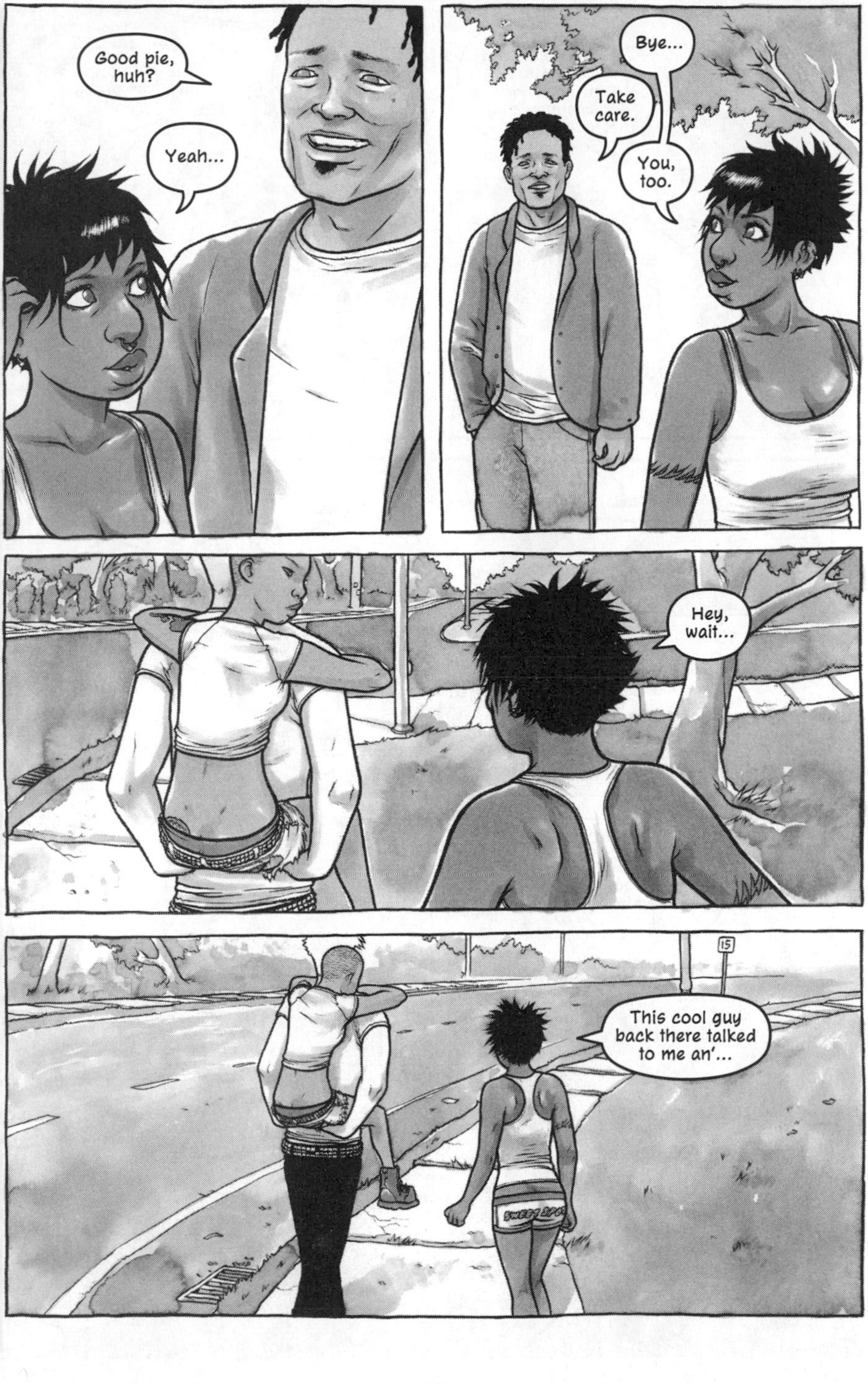
Good pie, huh?
Yeah...
Bye...
Take care.
You, too.
Hey, wait...
15
This cool guy back there talked to me an'...

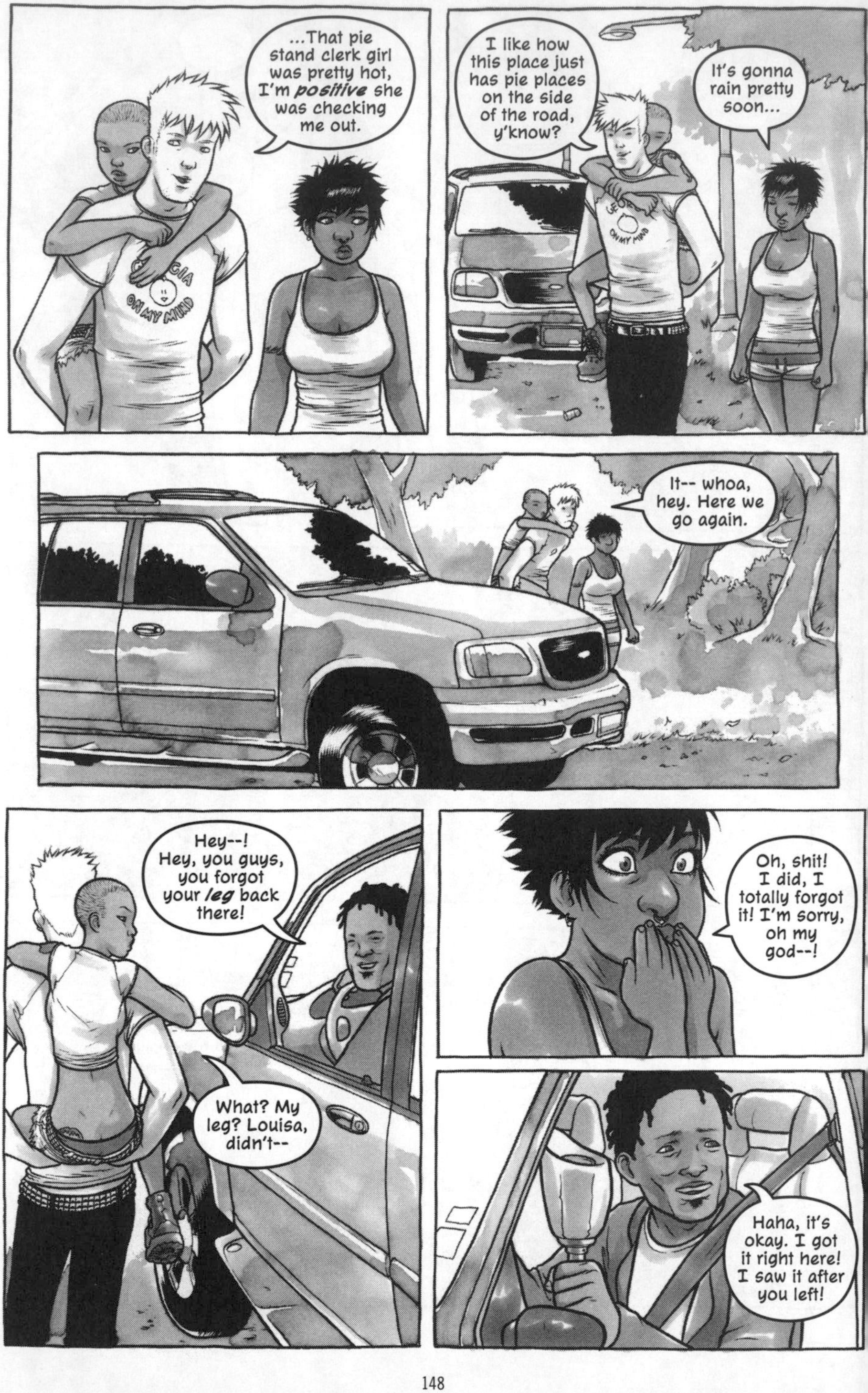
...That pie stand clerk girl was pretty hot, I'm ***positive*** she was checking me out.
I like how this place just has pie places on the side of the road, y'know?
It's gonna rain pretty soon...
It-- whoa, hey. Here we go again.
Hey--! Hey, you guys, you forgot your ***leg*** back there!
What? My leg? Louisa, didn't--
Oh, shit! I did, I totally forgot it! I'm sorry, oh my god--!
Haha, it's okay. I got it right here! I saw it after you left!

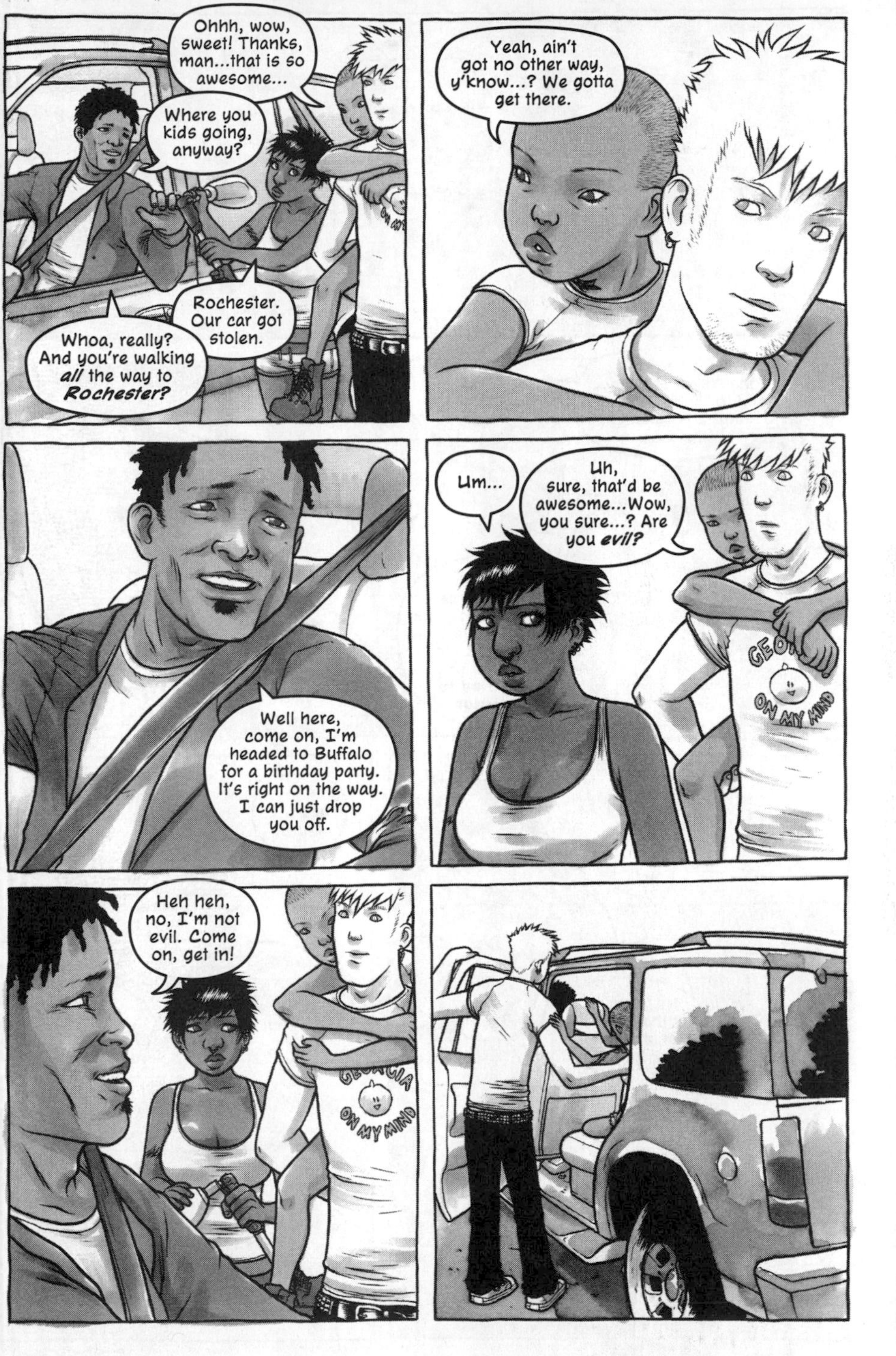

Ohhh, wow, sweet! Thanks, man...that is so awesome...
Where you kids going, anyway?
Rochester. Our car got stolen.
Whoa, really? And you're walking *all* the way to **Rochester?**
Yeah, ain't got no other way, y'know...? We gotta get there.
Well here, come on, I'm headed to Buffalo for a birthday party. It's right on the way. I can just drop you off.
Um...
Uh, sure, that'd be awesome...Wow, you sure...? Are you *evil?*
GEORGIA ON MY MIND
Heh heh, no, I'm not evil. Come on, get in!
GEORGIA ON MY MIND

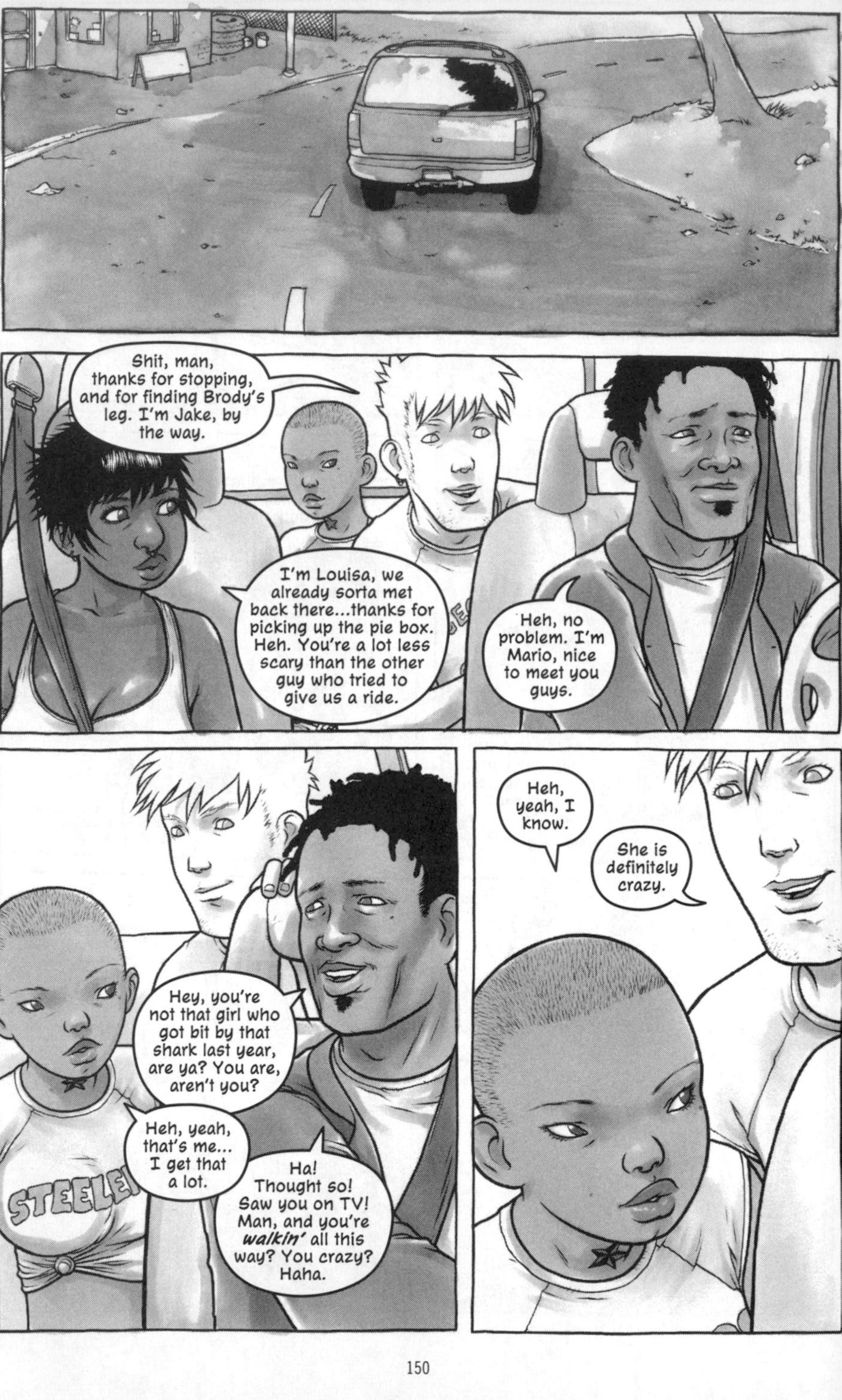
Shit, man, thanks for stopping, and for finding Brody's leg. I'm Jake, by the way.
I'm Louisa, we already sorta met back there...thanks for picking up the pie box. Heh. You're a lot less scary than the other guy who tried to give us a ride.
Heh, no problem. I'm Mario, nice to meet you guys.
Hey, you're not that girl who got bit by that shark last year, are ya? You are, aren't you?
Heh, yeah, that's me... I get that a lot.
Ha! Thought so! Saw you on TV! Man, and you're *walkin'* all this way? You crazy? Haha.
Heh, yeah, I know.
She is definitely crazy.

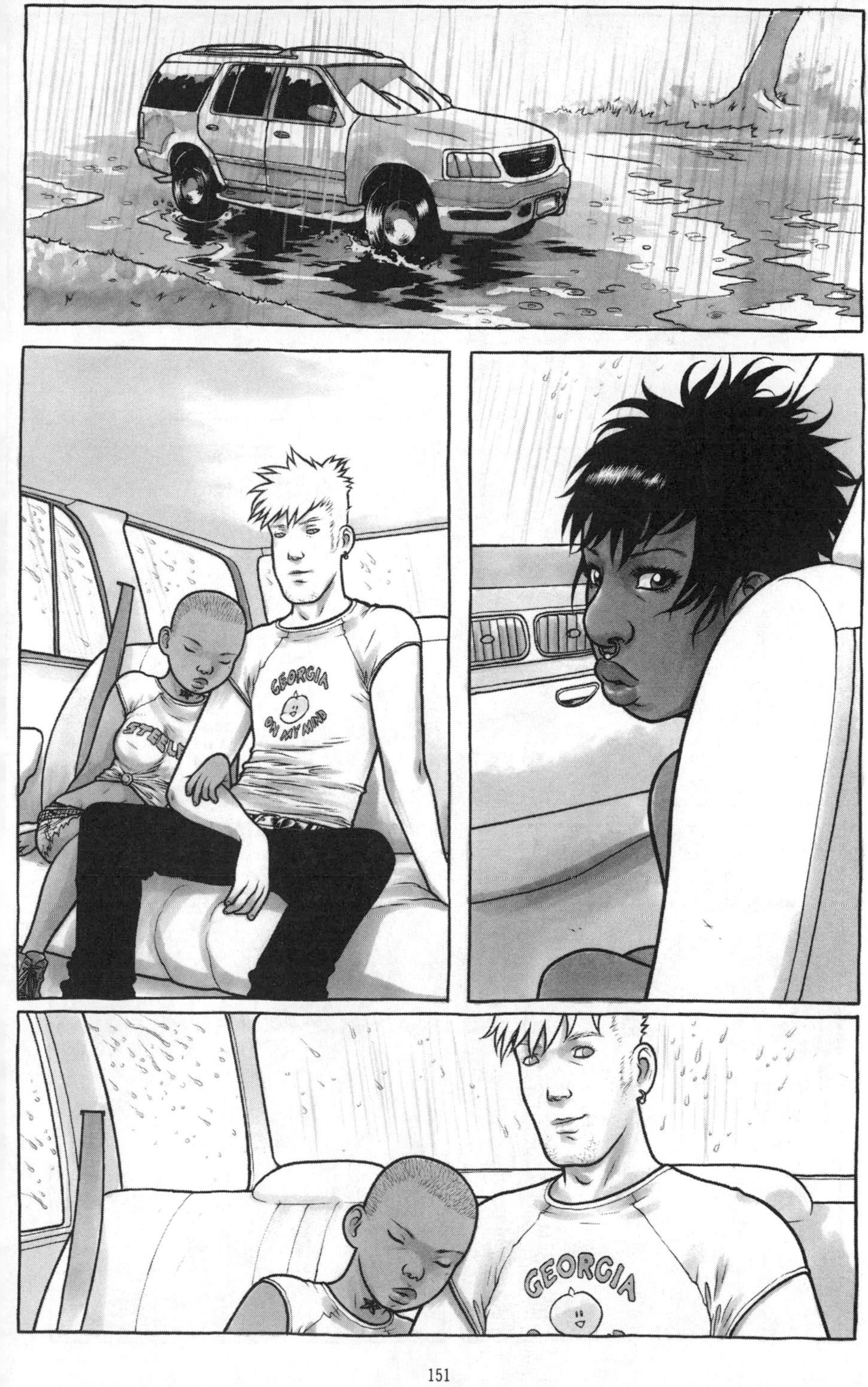
GEORGIA
ON MY MIND
GEORGIA

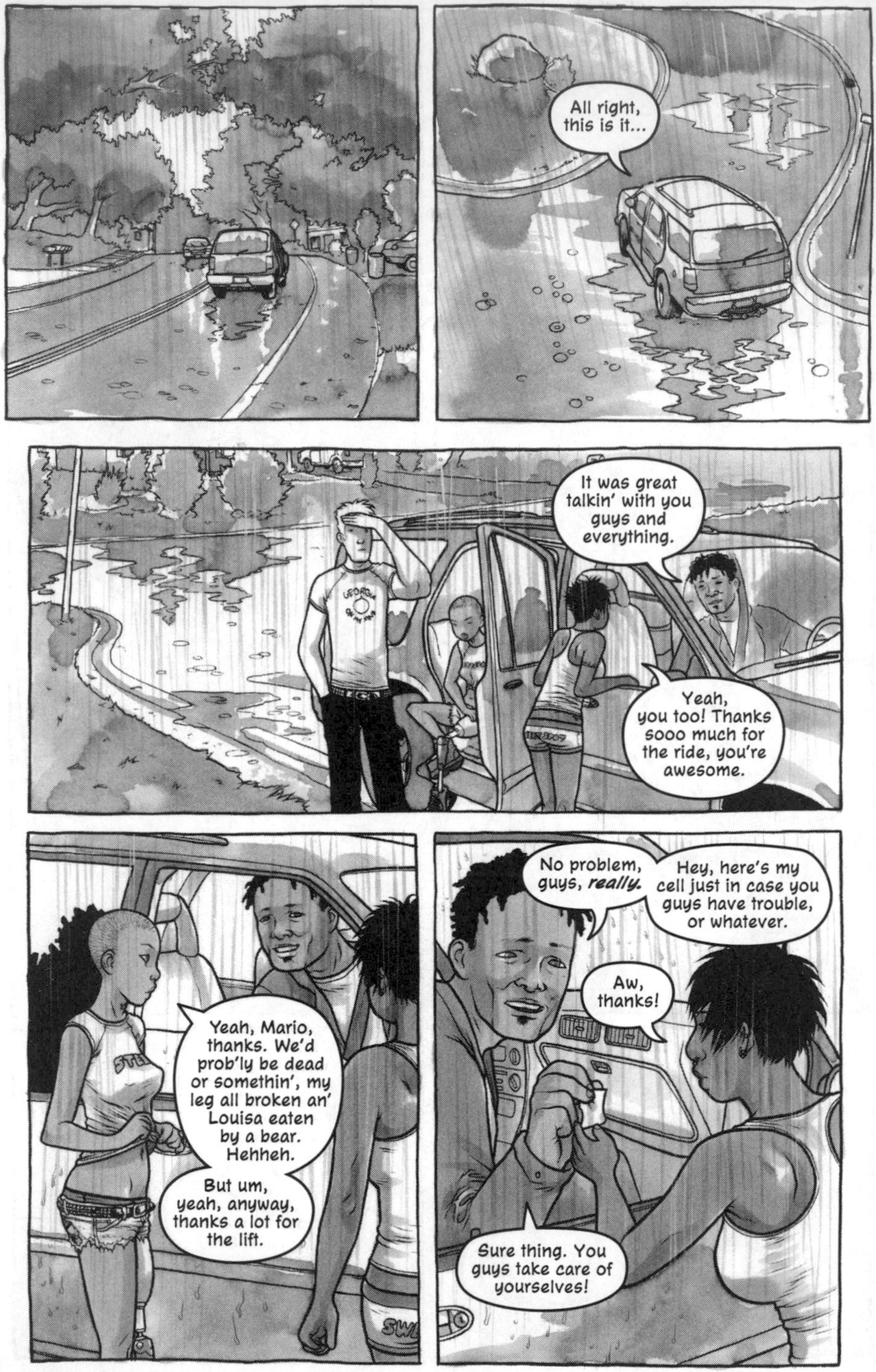
All right, this is it...
It was great talkin' with you guys and everything.
Yeah, you too! Thanks sooo much for the ride, you're awesome.
Yeah, Mario, thanks. We'd prob'ly be dead or somethin', my leg all broken an' Louisa eaten by a bear. Hehheh.
But um, yeah, anyway, thanks a lot for the lift.
No problem, guys, ***really.***
Hey, here's my cell just in case you guys have trouble, or whatever.
Aw, thanks!
Sure thing. You guys take care of yourselves!

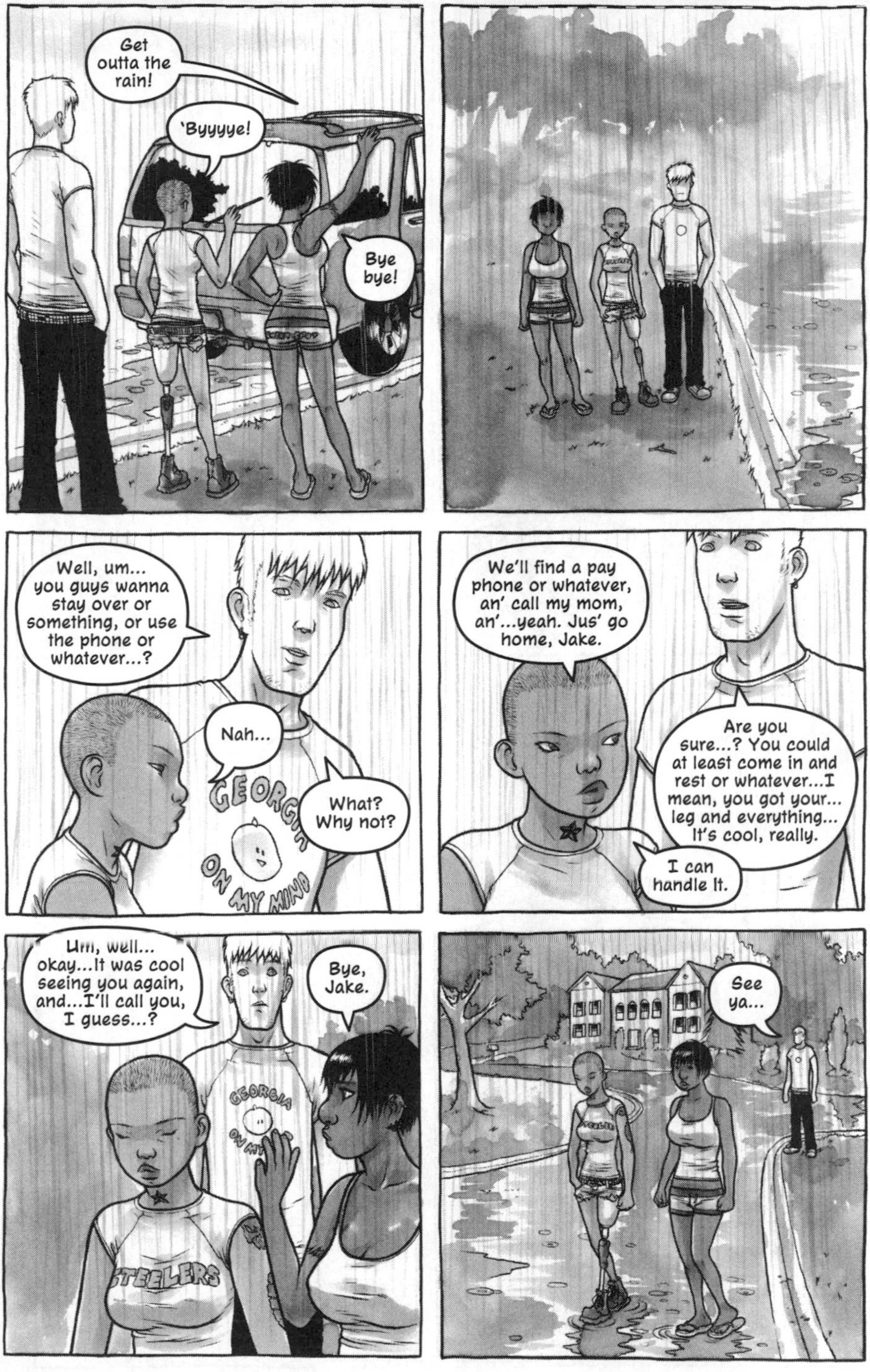
Get outta the rain!
'Byyyye!
Bye bye!
Well, um... you guys wanna stay over or something, or use the phone or whatever...?
Nah...
What? Why not?
GEORGIA ON MY MIND
We'll find a pay phone or whatever, an' call my mom, an'...yeah. Jus' go home, Jake.
Are you sure...? You could at least come in and rest or whatever...I mean, you got your... leg and everything... It's cool, really.
I can handle it.
Um, well... okay...It was cool seeing you again, and...I'll call you, I guess...?
Bye, Jake.
STEELERS
See ya...

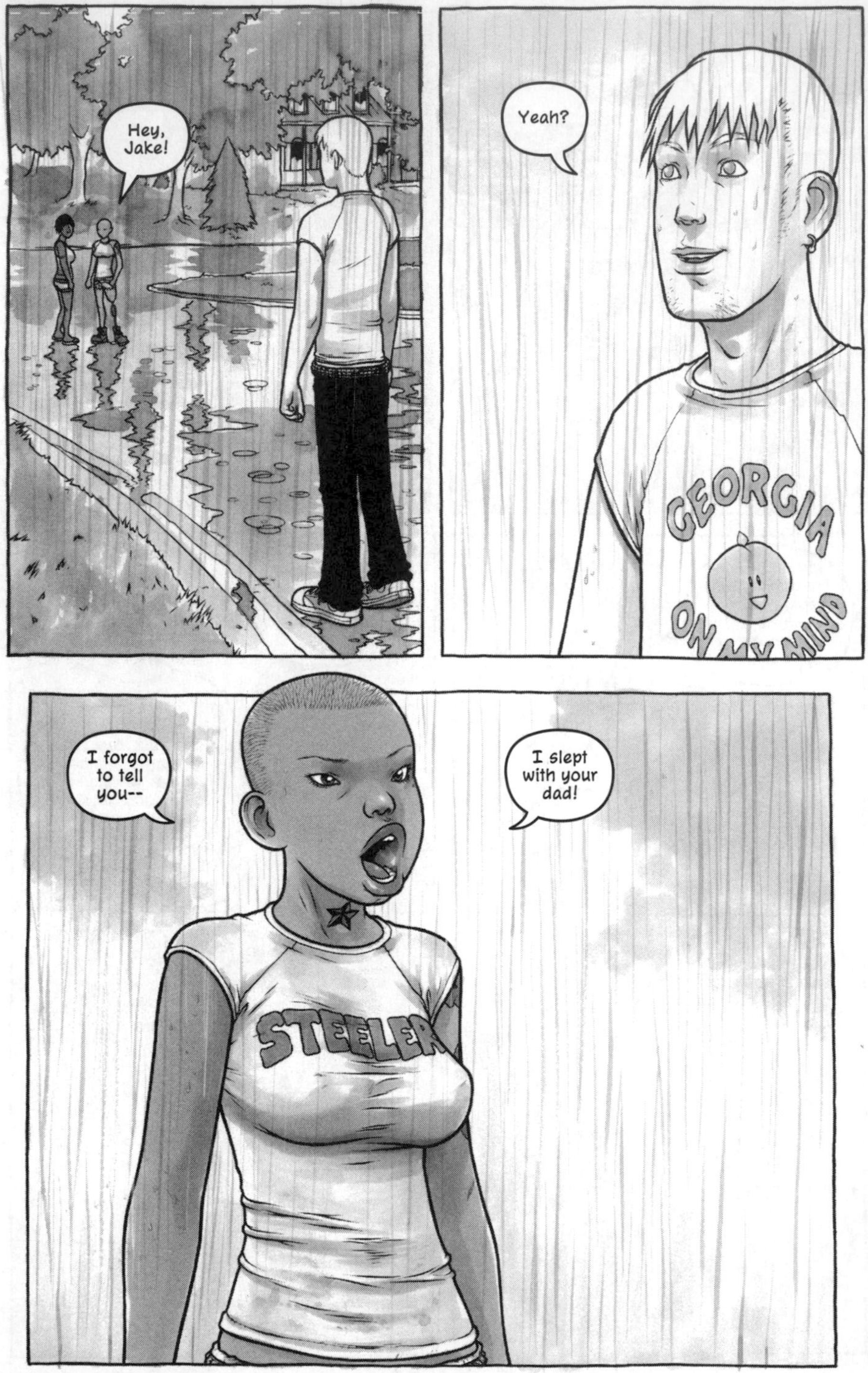
Hey, Jake!
Yeah?
GEORGIA
I forgot to tell you--
I slept with your dad!

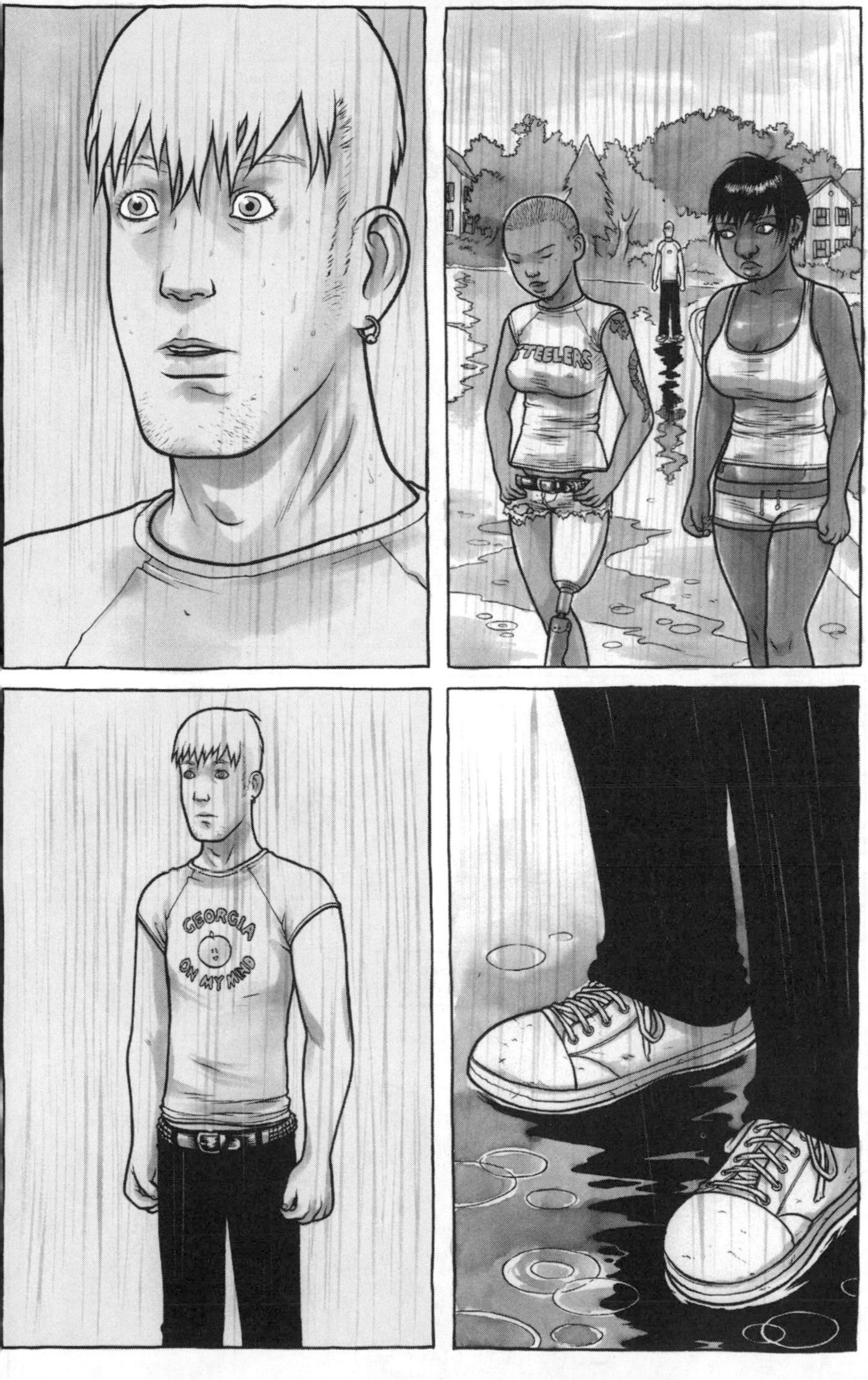
STEELERS
GEORGIA
ON MY MIND

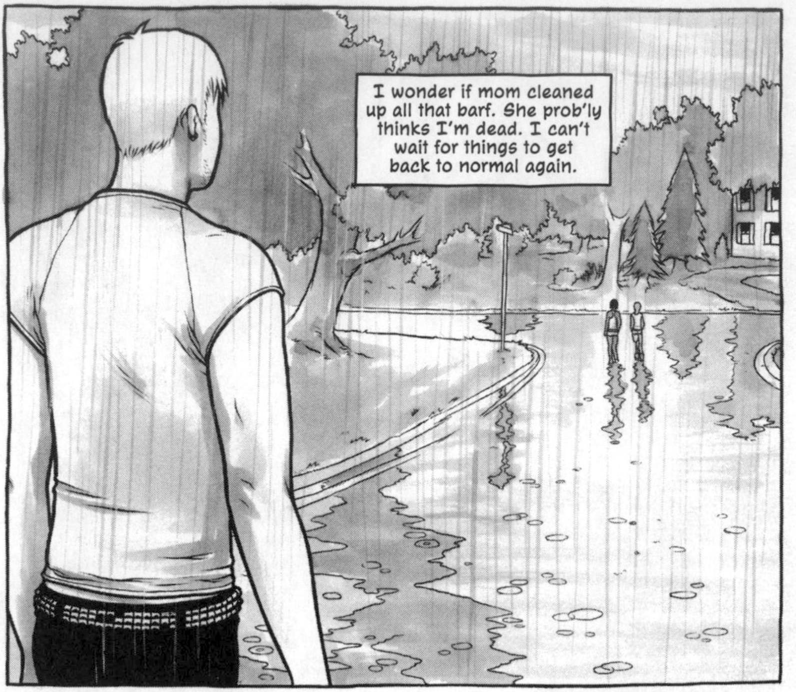
I wonder if mom cleaned up all that barf. She prob'ly thinks I'm dead. I can't wait for things to get back to normal again.

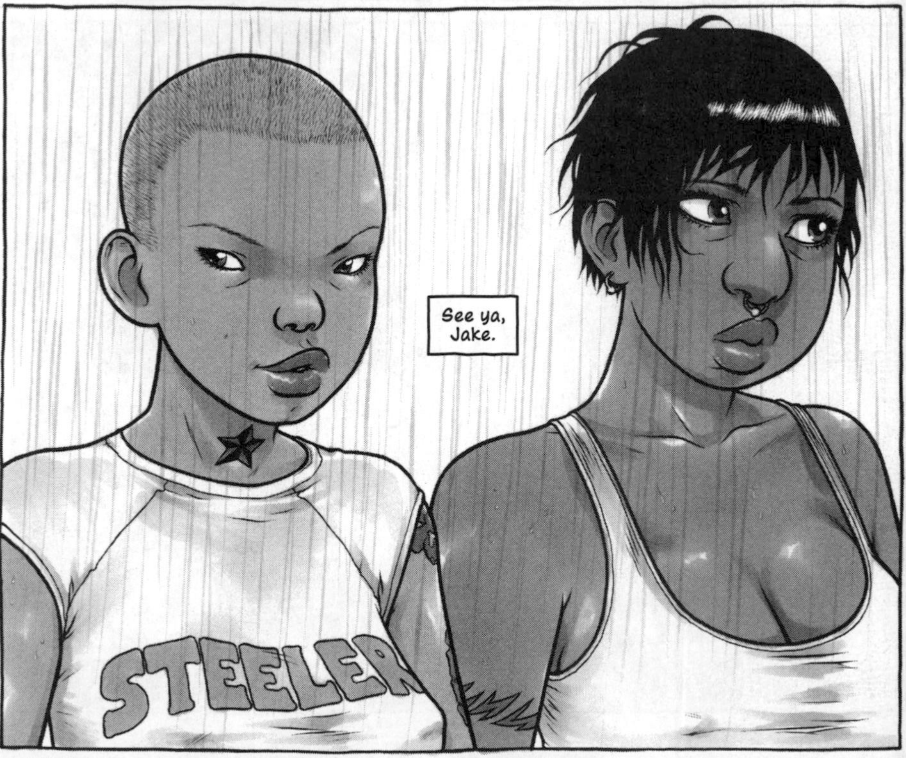
See ya, Jake.
STEELER

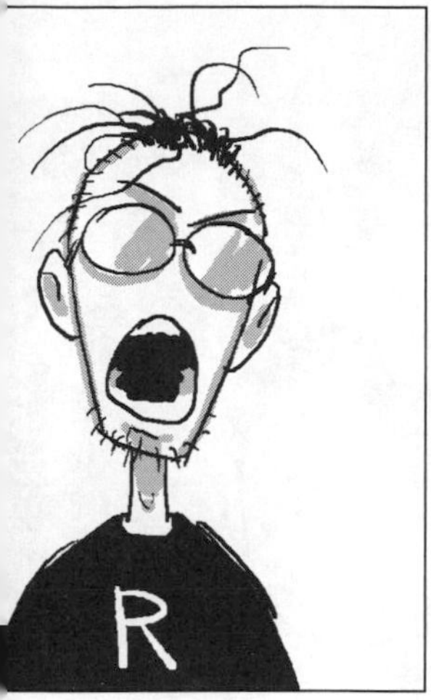
R

ROSS CAMPBELL

Ross is an art monk who currently lives in Rochester, New York. His first published work was for White Wolf Publishing's Exalted RPG books, which he continues to do illustrations for today. He made his comics debut doing the flashbacks in *Too Much Hopeless Savages* and then illustrated *Spooked* (written by Antony Johnston), both published by Oni Press. The first volume of his flagship series, *Wet Moon*, was released in 2005 (Oni Press), followed by *The Abandoned* (Tokyopop) and *Wet Moon 2*. Ross spends his time working and not much else, but he gets some time off to watch a movie or two every Friday. His personal website is www.greenoblivion.com, and his deviantArt gallery is at mooncalfe.deviantart.com.

He likes monsters, zombies, horror movies, Tifa Lockhart, rednecks, Fefe Dobson, barbarian warriors, alien terror, tea, and cats. He hates neighbors, ketchup, frogs, any type of lawncare machine, and wizards (except for the wizard in *Conan*).

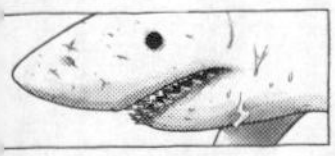

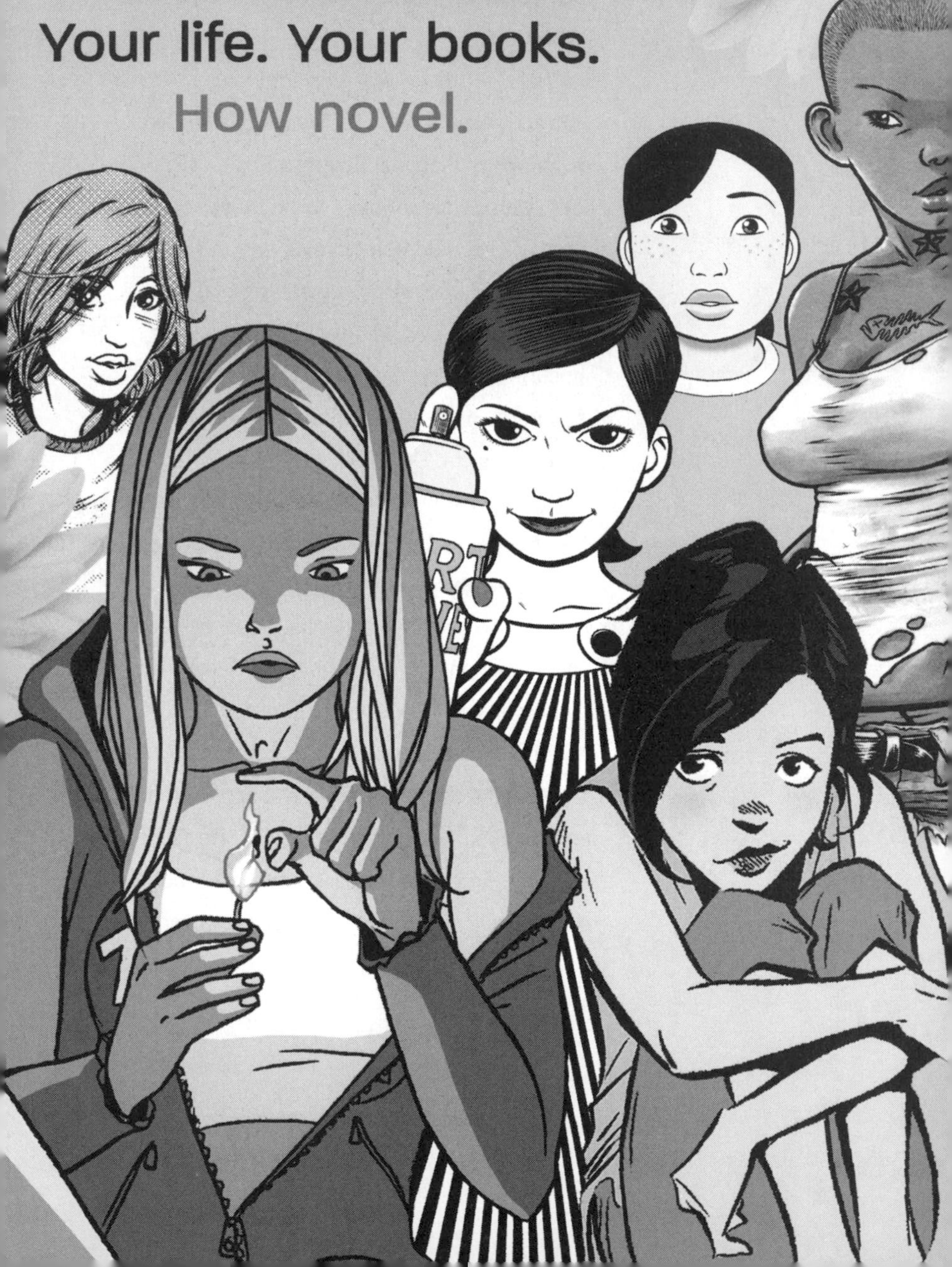

When Danni and her mom move in with her mom's alcoholic boyfriend,

Danni develops a fierce crush on Haskell, her soon-to-be stepbrother,

who's a hardcore environmentalist. Desperate and confused, Danni wrestles

with what she's willing to sacrifice as she confronts first love, family secrets

and the politics of ecoterrorism — set against the lush backdrop of

the Pacific Northwest.

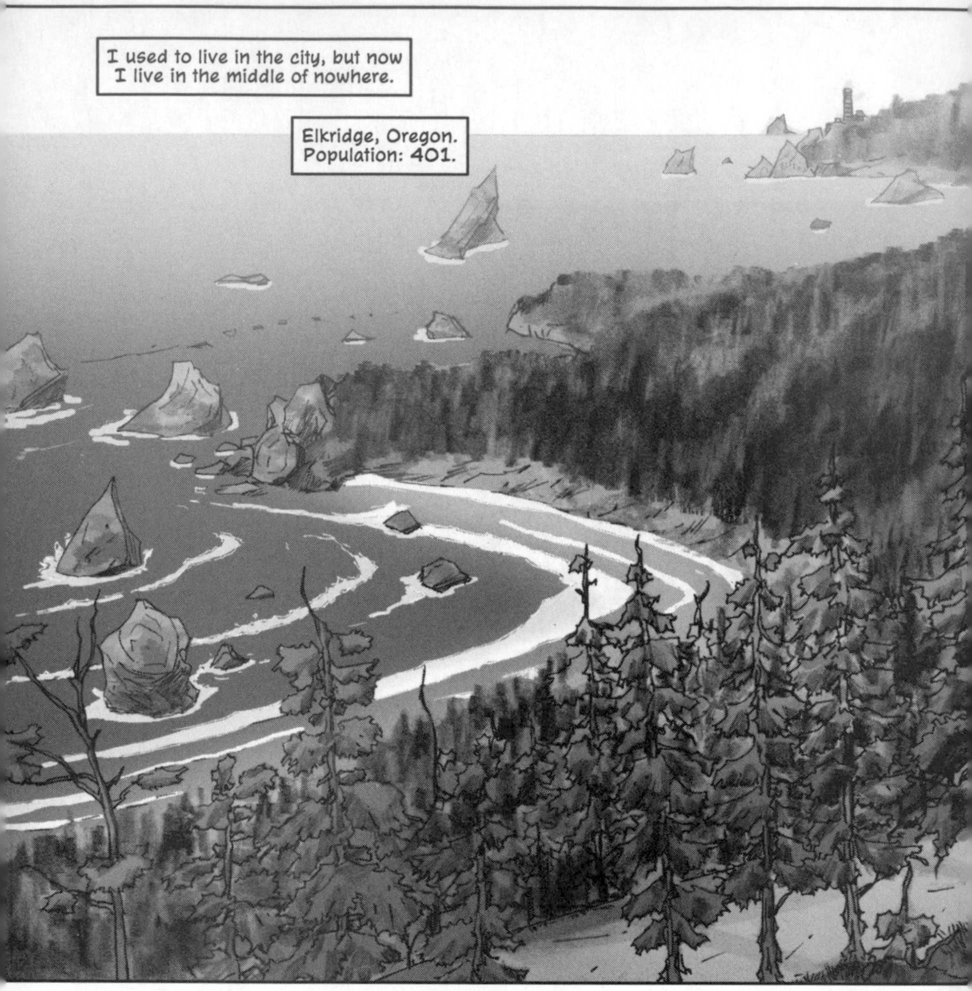
I used to live in the city, but now I live in the middle of nowhere.
Elkridge, Oregon. Population: 401.

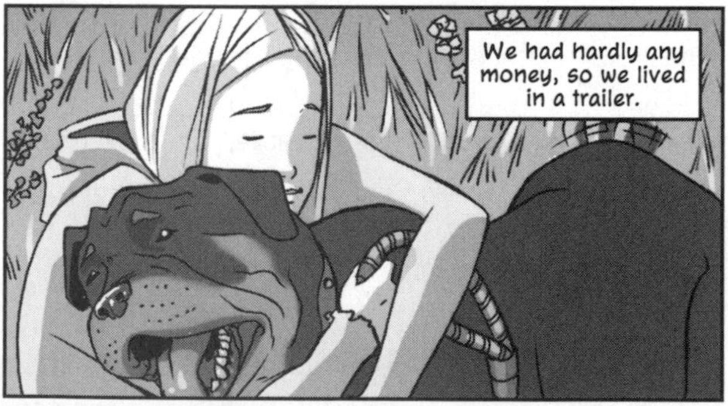
We had hardly any money, so we lived in a trailer.

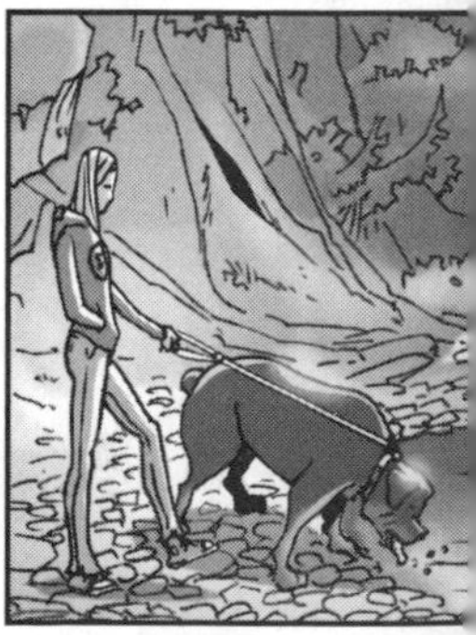

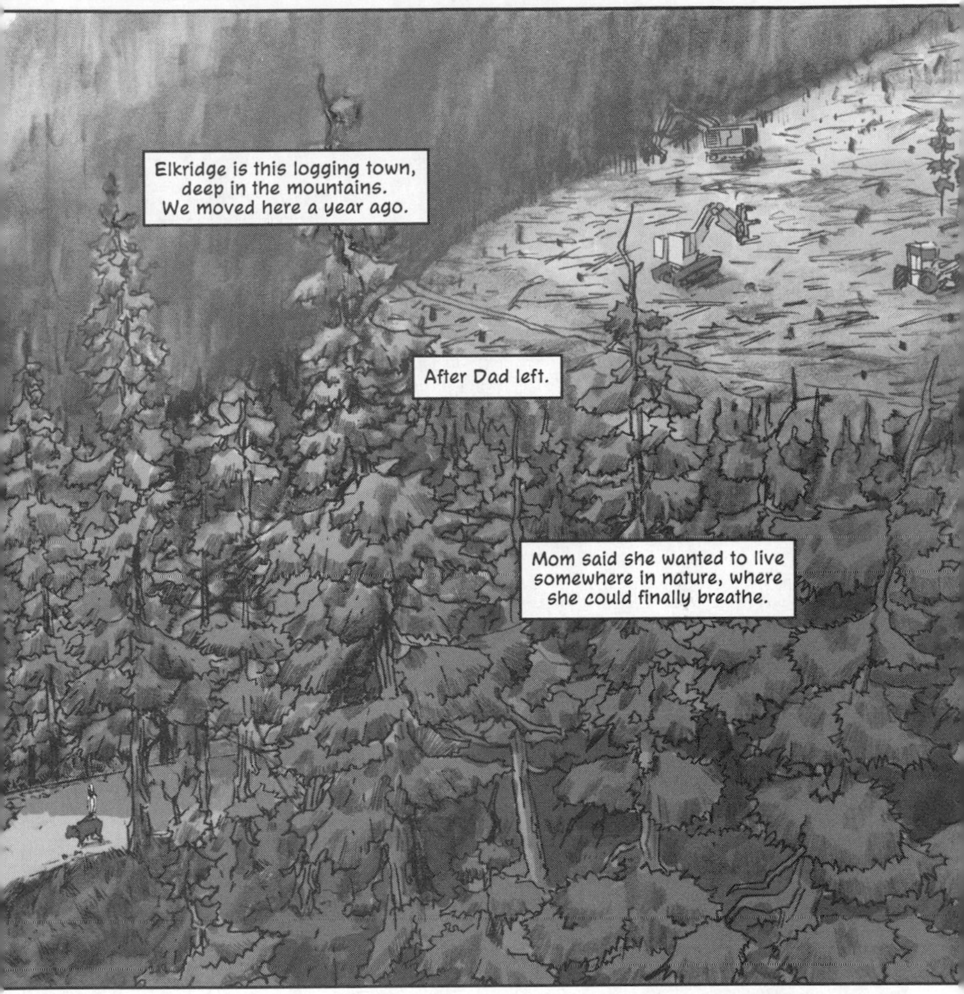
Elkridge is this logging town, deep in the mountains. We moved here a year ago.
After Dad left.
Mom said she wanted to live somewhere in nature, where she could finally breathe.

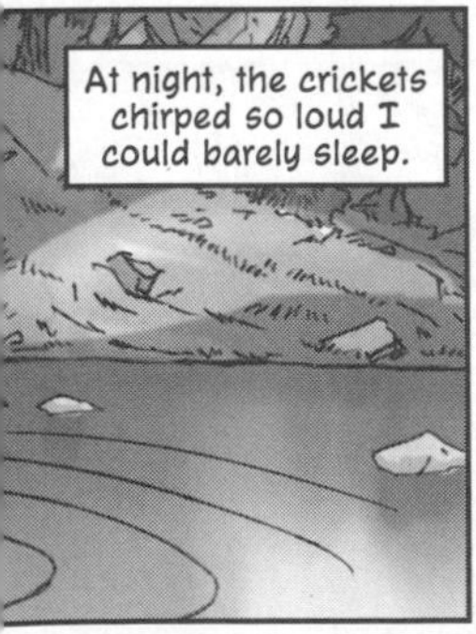
At night, the crickets chirped so loud I could barely sleep.

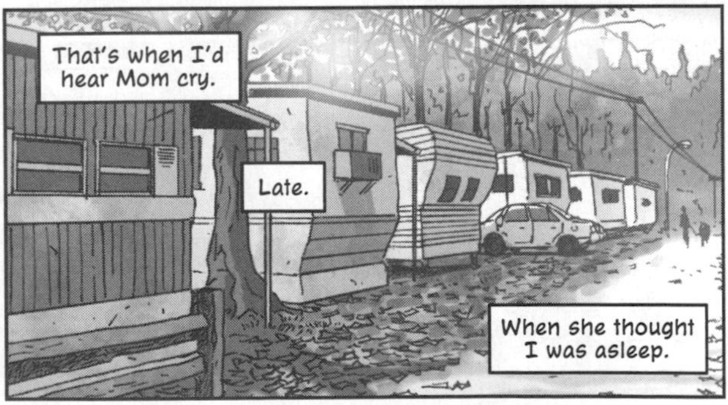
That's when I'd hear Mom cry.
Late.
When she thought I was asleep.

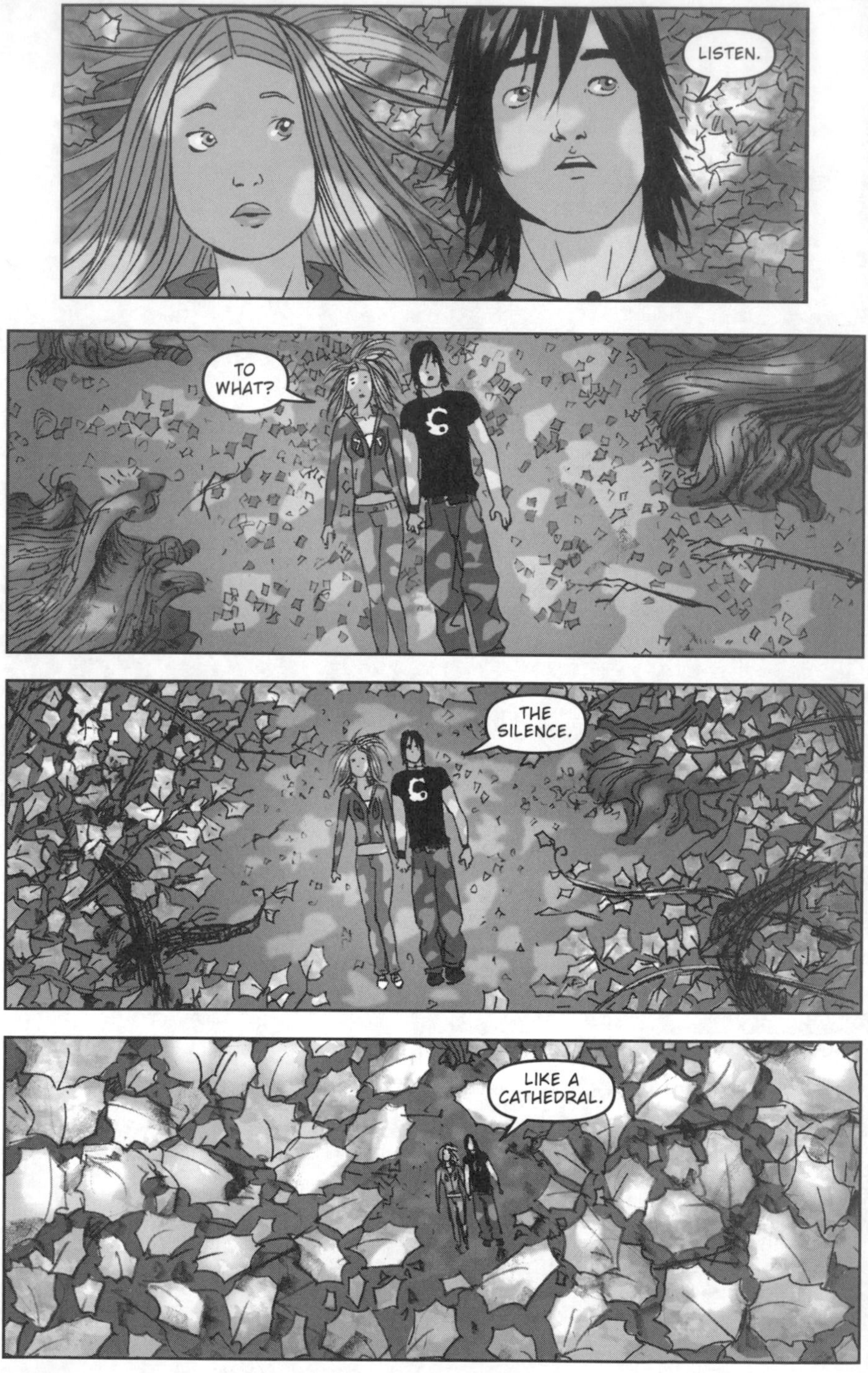
LISTEN.
TO WHAT?
THE SILENCE.
LIKE A CATHEDRAL.

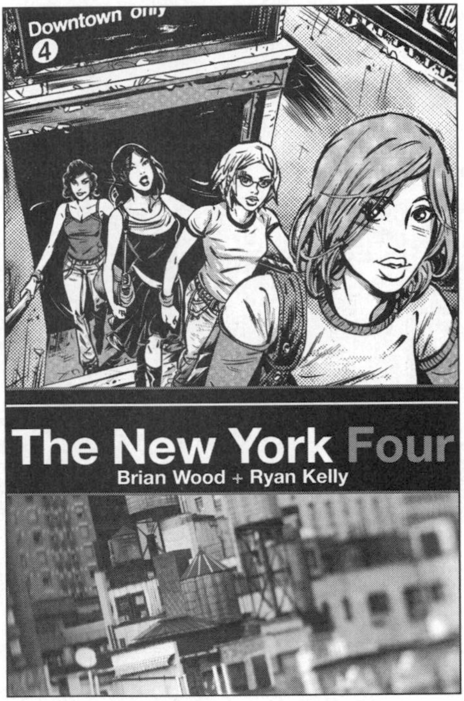
Downtown only
4
The New York Four
Brian Wood + Ryan Kelly

Written by multiple Eisner Award nominee/Indie icon BRIAN WOOD

Experience New York City through the eyes of Riley, a shy, almost reclusive straight-A student who convinces three other NYU freshmen to join a research group to earn extra money.

As the girls become fast friends, two things complicate what should be the greatest time of Riley's life: connecting with her arty, estranged older sister and having a mysterious online crush on a guy known only as "sneakerfreak."

Will Riley be able to balance new relationships with academics and her stuffy literati parents as the intensity of her secret romance threatens to unravel everything?

By BRIAN WOOD & RYAN KELLY

AVAILABLE IN JULY ■ Read on.

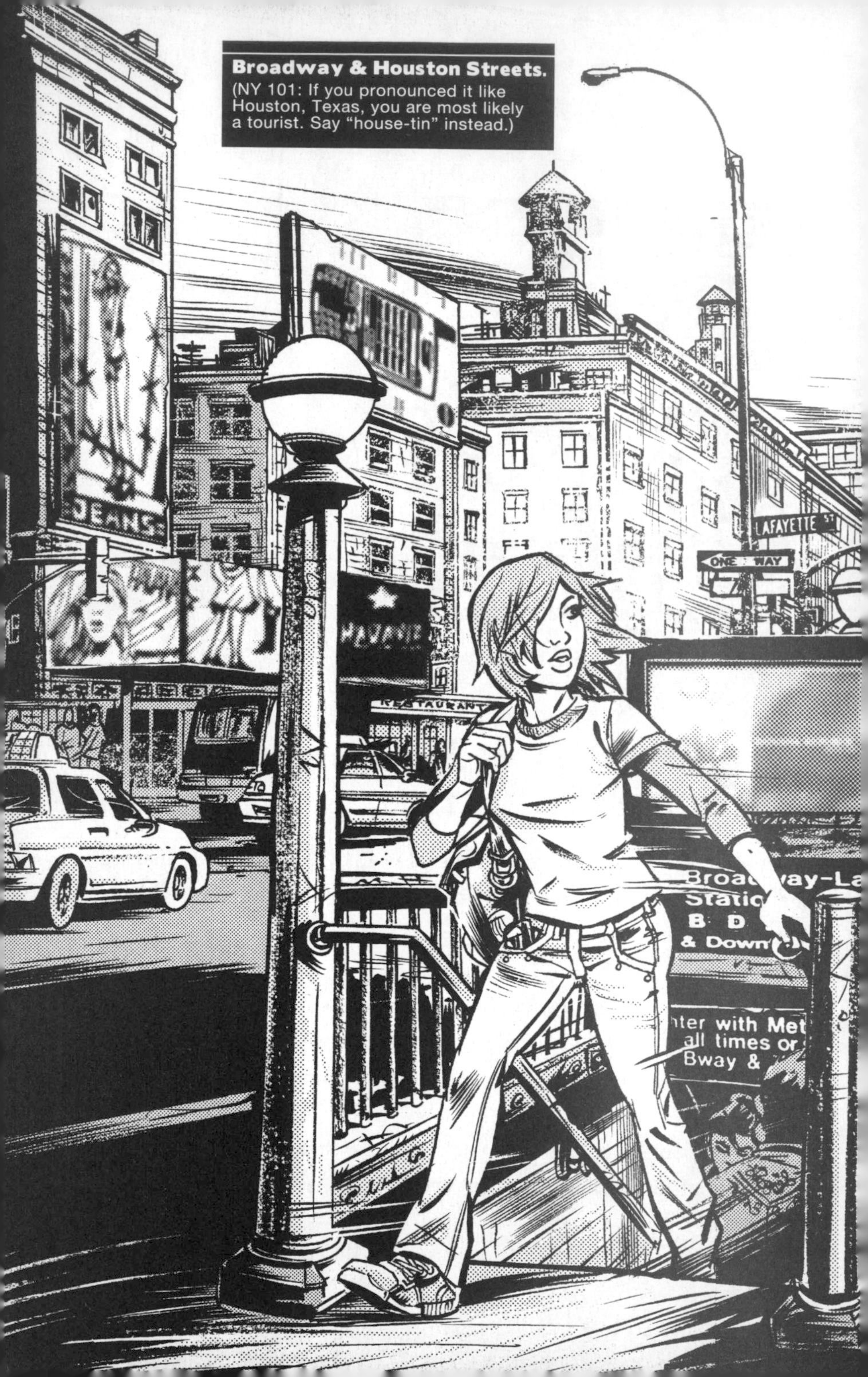
Broadway & Houston Streets.
(NY 101: If you pronounced it like Houston, Texas, you are most likely a tourist. Say "house-tin" instead.)
JEANS
LAFAYETTE ST
ONE WAY
RESTAURANT

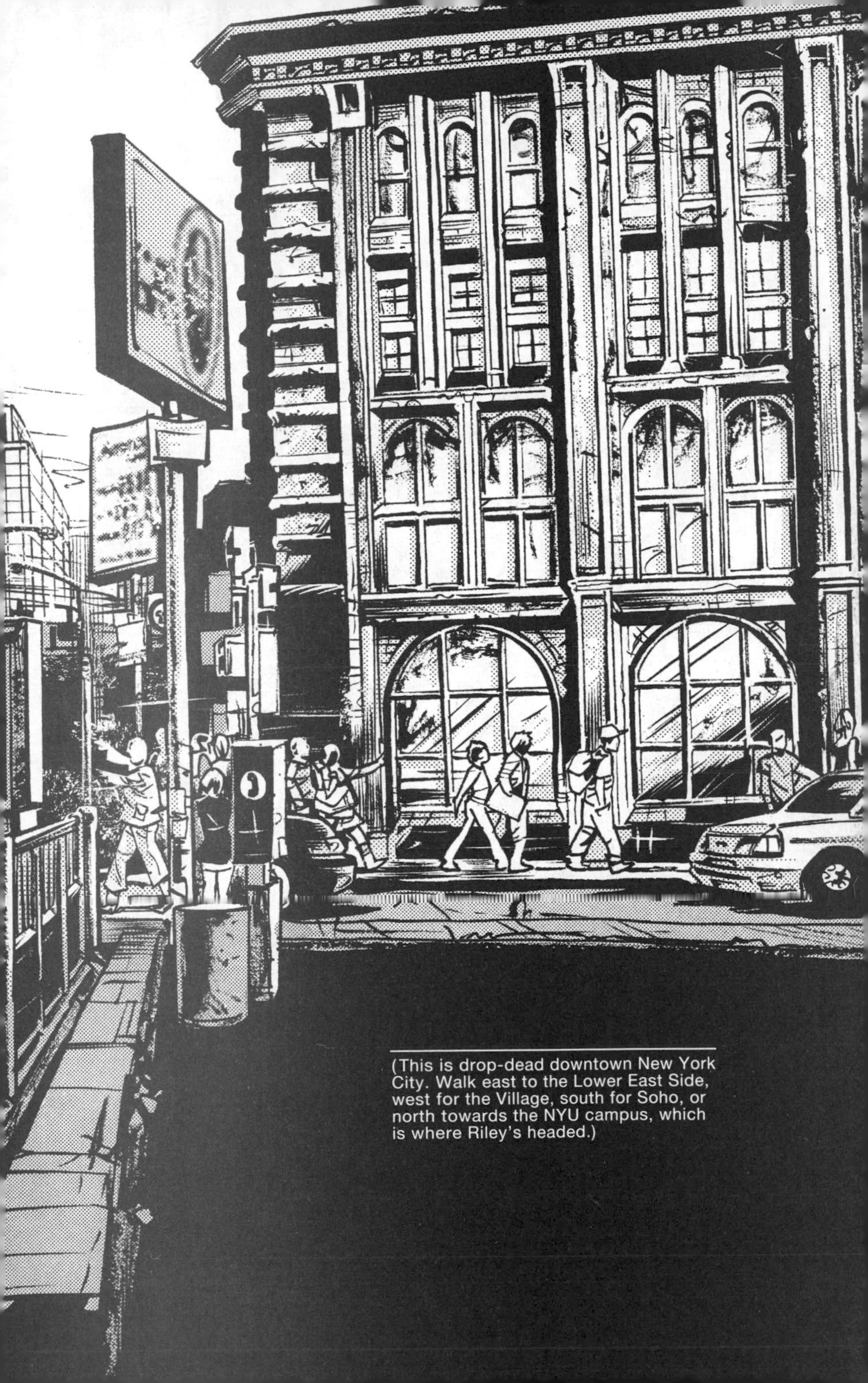
(This is drop-dead downtown New York City. Walk east to the Lower East Side, west for the Village, south for Soho, or north towards the NYU campus, which is where Riley's headed.)

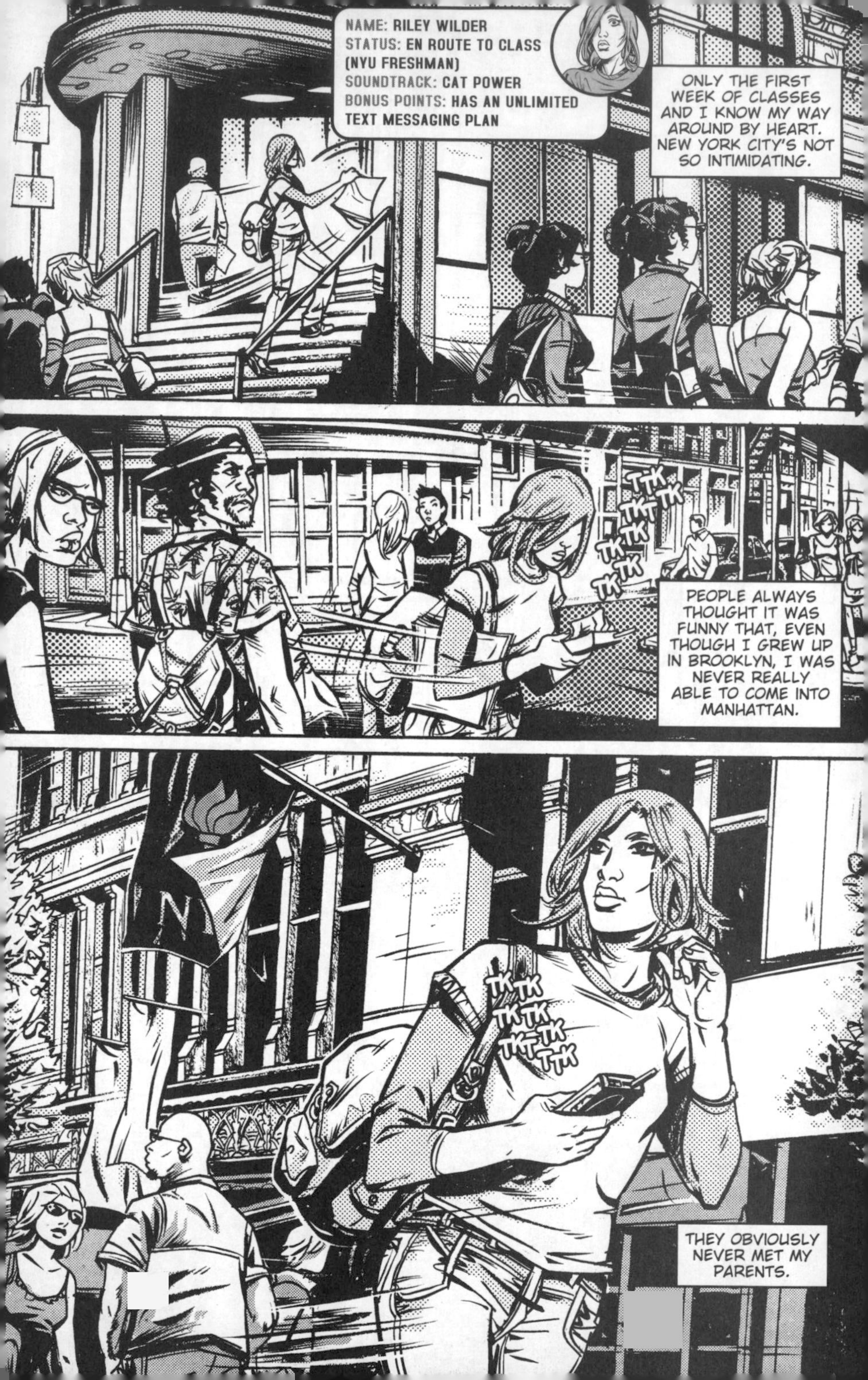
NAME: RILEY WILDER
STATUS: EN ROUTE TO CLASS
(NYU FRESHMAN)
SOUNDTRACK: CAT POWER
BONUS POINTS: HAS AN UNLIMITED TEXT MESSAGING PLAN
ONLY THE FIRST WEEK OF CLASSES AND I KNOW MY WAY AROUND BY HEART. NEW YORK CITY'S NOT SO INTIMIDATING.
TK TK TK TK TK TK TK TK TK TK
PEOPLE ALWAYS THOUGHT IT WAS FUNNY THAT, EVEN THOUGH I GREW UP IN BROOKLYN, I WAS NEVER REALLY ABLE TO COME INTO MANHATTAN.
TK TK TK TK TK TK TK TK TK TK
THEY OBVIOUSLY NEVER MET MY PARENTS.

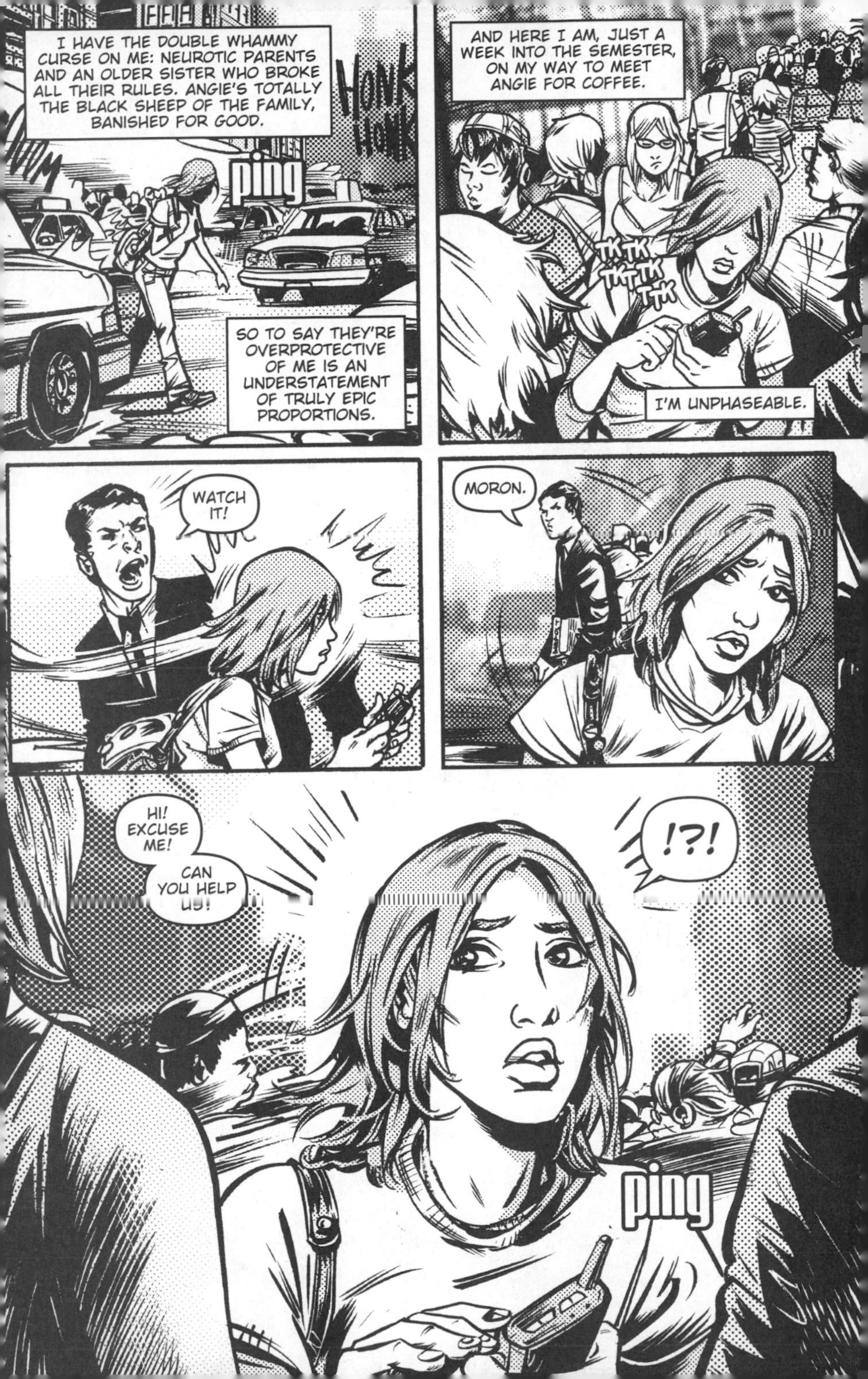
I HAVE THE DOUBLE WHAMMY CURSE ON ME: NEUROTIC PARENTS AND AN OLDER SISTER WHO BROKE ALL THEIR RULES. ANGIE'S TOTALLY THE BLACK SHEEP OF THE FAMILY, BANISHED FOR GOOD.
HONK HONK
ping
SO TO SAY THEY'RE OVERPROTECTIVE OF ME IS AN UNDERSTATEMENT OF TRULY EPIC PROPORTIONS.
AND HERE I AM, JUST A WEEK INTO THE SEMESTER, ON MY WAY TO MEET ANGIE FOR COFFEE.
TK TK TK TK TK TK
I'M UNPHASEABLE.
WATCH IT!
MORON.
HI! EXCUSE ME!
CAN YOU HELP US?
!?!
ping

By the highly acclaimed author of *Boy Proof* and *Beige*

JANES in LOVE

by CECIL CASTELLUCCI and JIM RUGG

ART SAVE

Praise for *The Plain Janes*:

"Thought-provoking....absolutely engaging..."
——Booklist, Starred review

Starred review in Publishers Weekly

Washington Post Best of 2007 pick

Included in The New York Public Library's Books for the Teen Age 2008

The second title in the PLAIN JANES series finds the coolest clique of misfits playing cupid and becoming entangled in the affairs of the heart.

P.L.A.I.N., People Loving Art In Neighborhoods, goes global once the art gang procures a spot in the Metro City Museum of Modern Art contest.

And the girls will discover that in art and in love, general rules don't often apply.

By CECIL CASTELLUCCI & JIM RUGG
AVAILABLE IN SEPTEMBER ■ Read on.

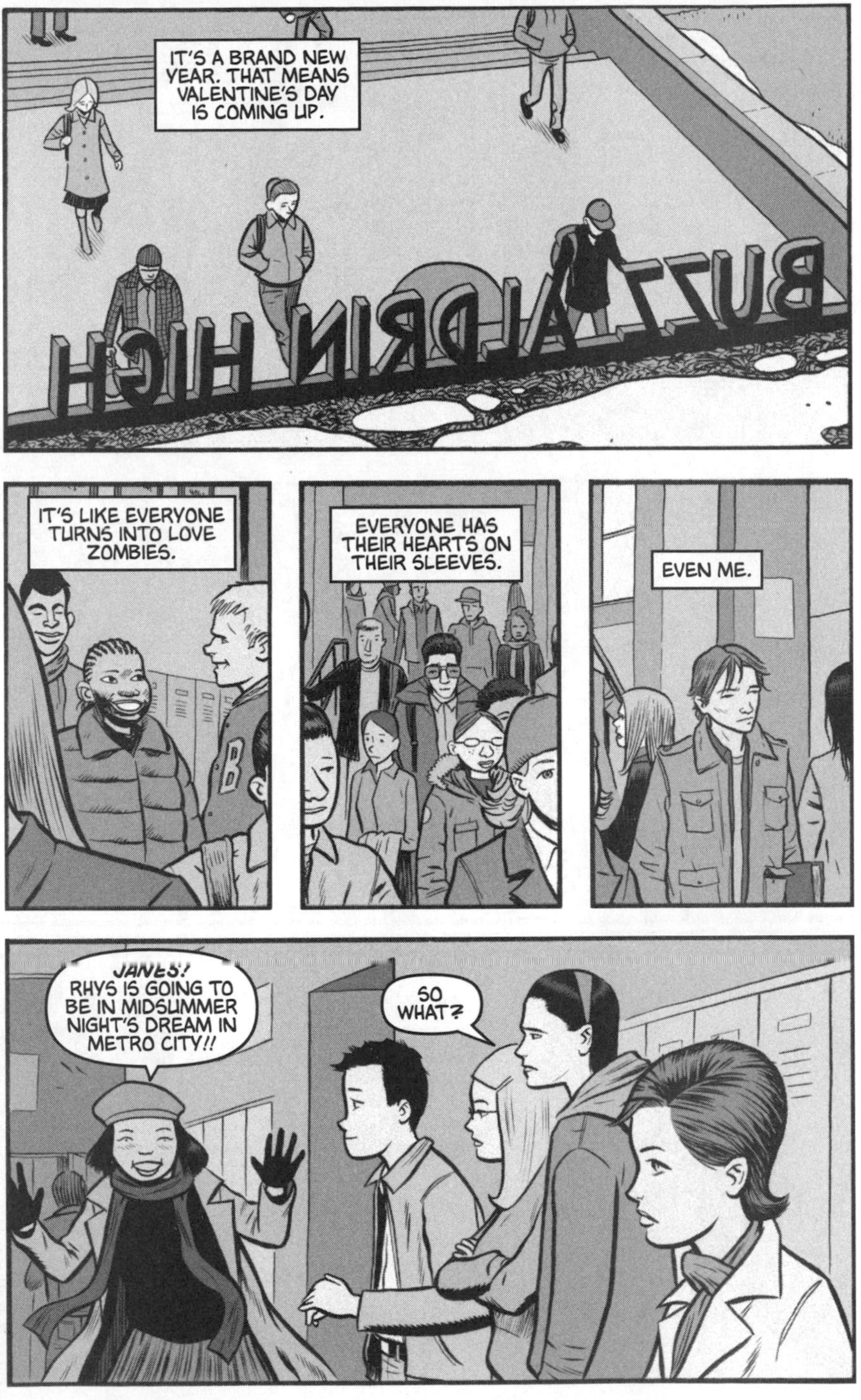
IT'S A BRAND NEW YEAR. THAT MEANS VALENTINE'S DAY IS COMING UP.
BUZZ ALDRIN HIGH
IT'S LIKE EVERYONE TURNS INTO LOVE ZOMBIES.
EVERYONE HAS THEIR HEARTS ON THEIR SLEEVES.
EVEN ME.
JANES! RHYS IS GOING TO BE IN MIDSUMMER NIGHT'S DREAM IN METRO CITY!!
SO WHAT?

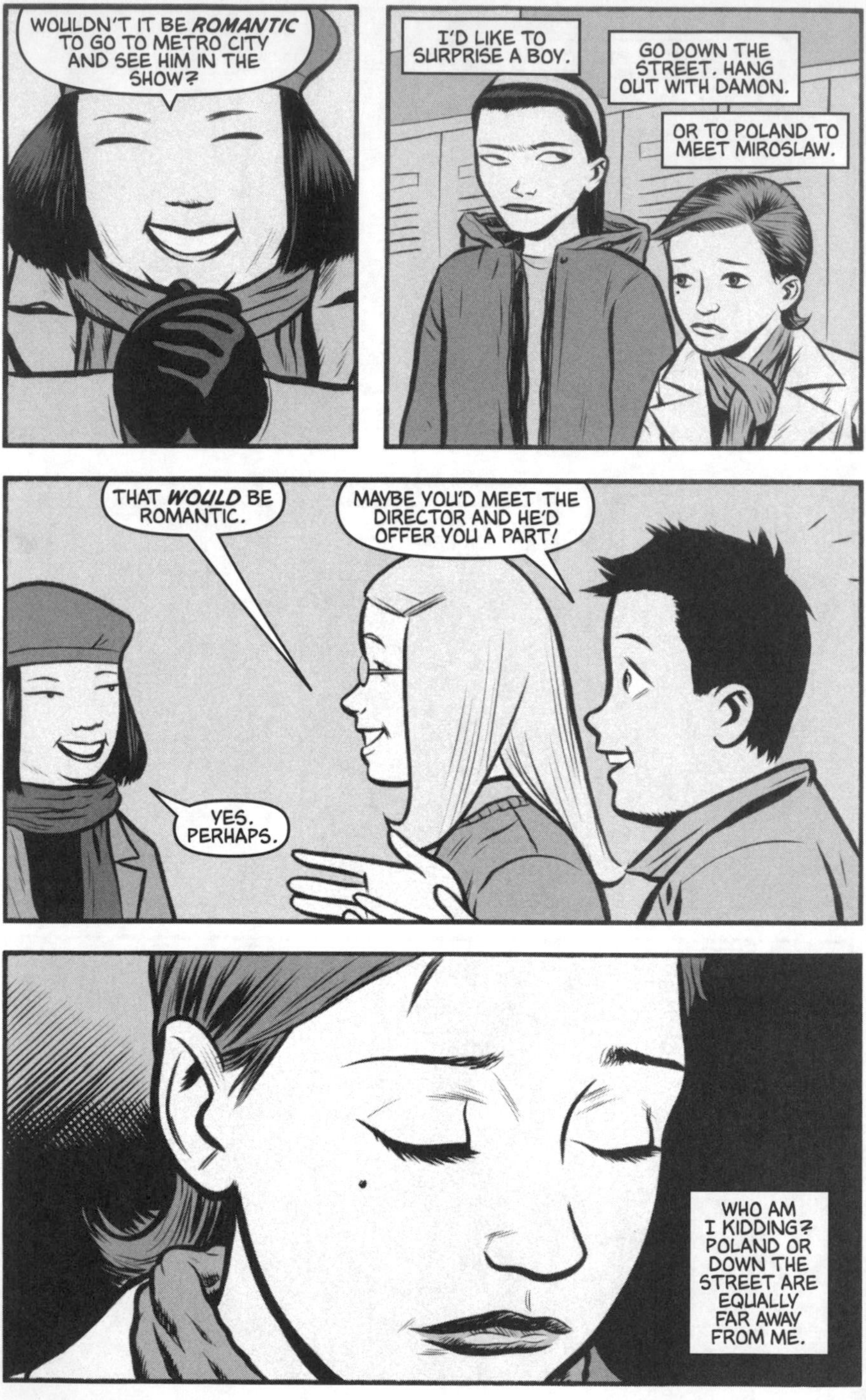

WOULDN'T IT BE ROMANTIC TO GO TO METRO CITY AND SEE HIM IN THE SHOW?
I'D LIKE TO SURPRISE A BOY.
GO DOWN THE STREET. HANG OUT WITH DAMON.
OR TO POLAND TO MEET MIROSLAW.
THAT WOULD BE ROMANTIC.
MAYBE YOU'D MEET THE DIRECTOR AND HE'D OFFER YOU A PART!
YES. PERHAPS.
WHO AM I KIDDING? POLAND OR DOWN THE STREET ARE EQUALLY FAR AWAY FROM ME.

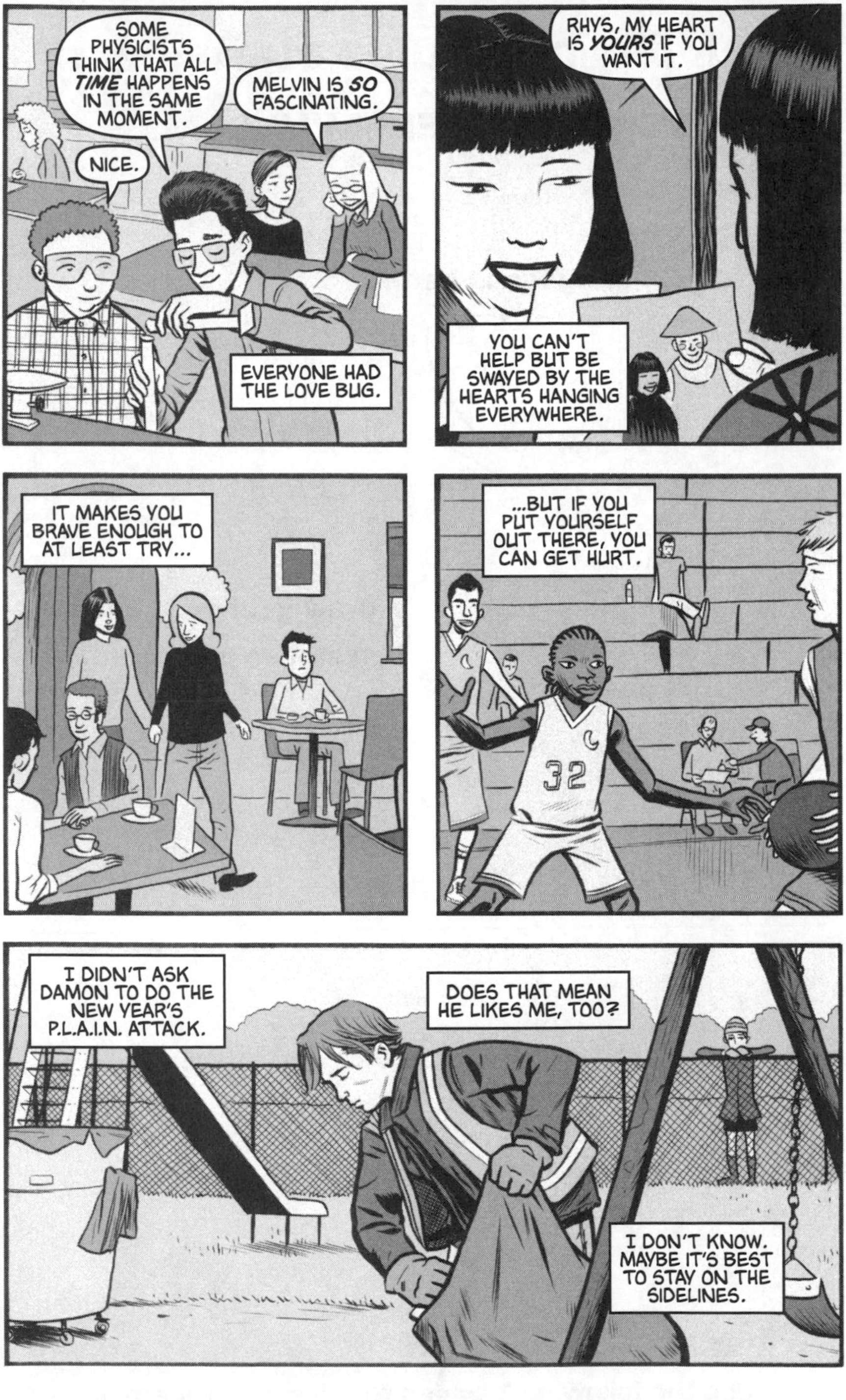
SOME PHYSICISTS THINK THAT ALL TIME HAPPENS IN THE SAME MOMENT.
MELVIN IS SO FASCINATING.
NICE.
EVERYONE HAD THE LOVE BUG.
RHYS, MY HEART IS YOURS IF YOU WANT IT.
YOU CAN'T HELP BUT BE SWAYED BY THE HEARTS HANGING EVERYWHERE.
IT MAKES YOU BRAVE ENOUGH TO AT LEAST TRY...
...BUT IF YOU PUT YOURSELF OUT THERE, YOU CAN GET HURT.
32
I DIDN'T ASK DAMON TO DO THE NEW YEAR'S P.L.A.I.N. ATTACK.
DOES THAT MEAN HE LIKES ME, TOO?
I DON'T KNOW. MAYBE IT'S BEST TO STAY ON THE SIDELINES.

Your life in pictures starts here!

~A DO-IT YOURSELF MINI COMIC~

Write your story ideas here:

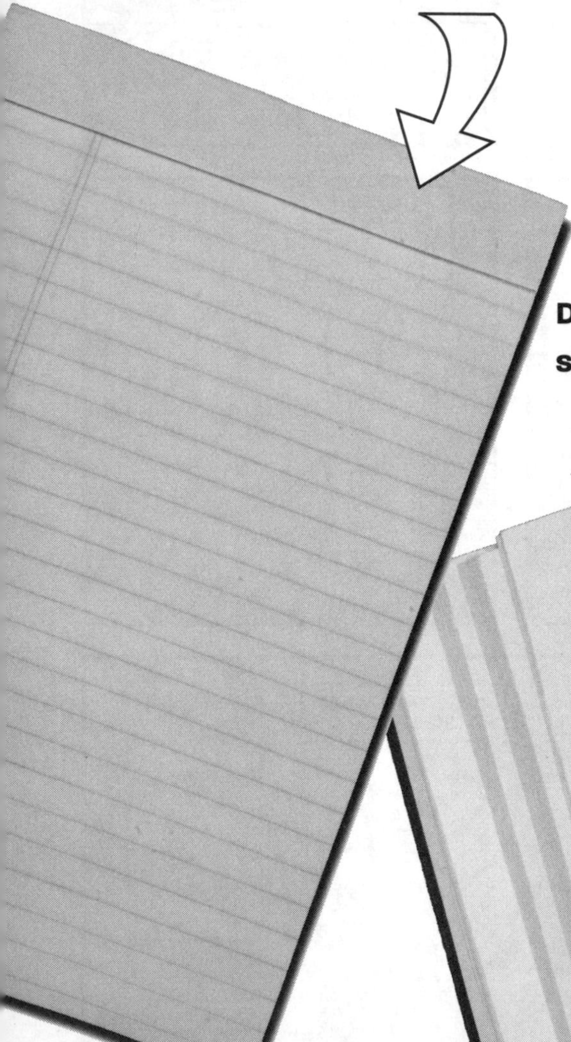

Draw your main character sketches here:

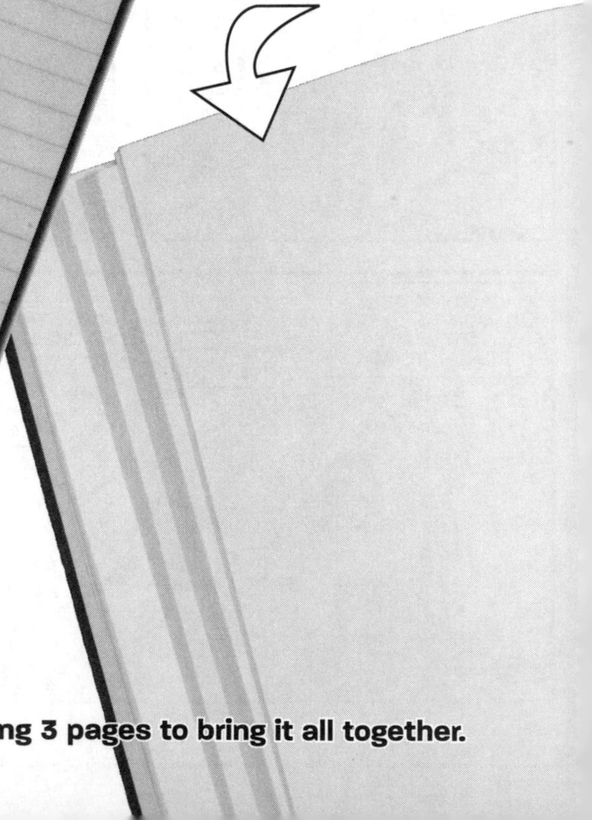

Use the following 3 pages to bring it all together.

TITLE: BY:

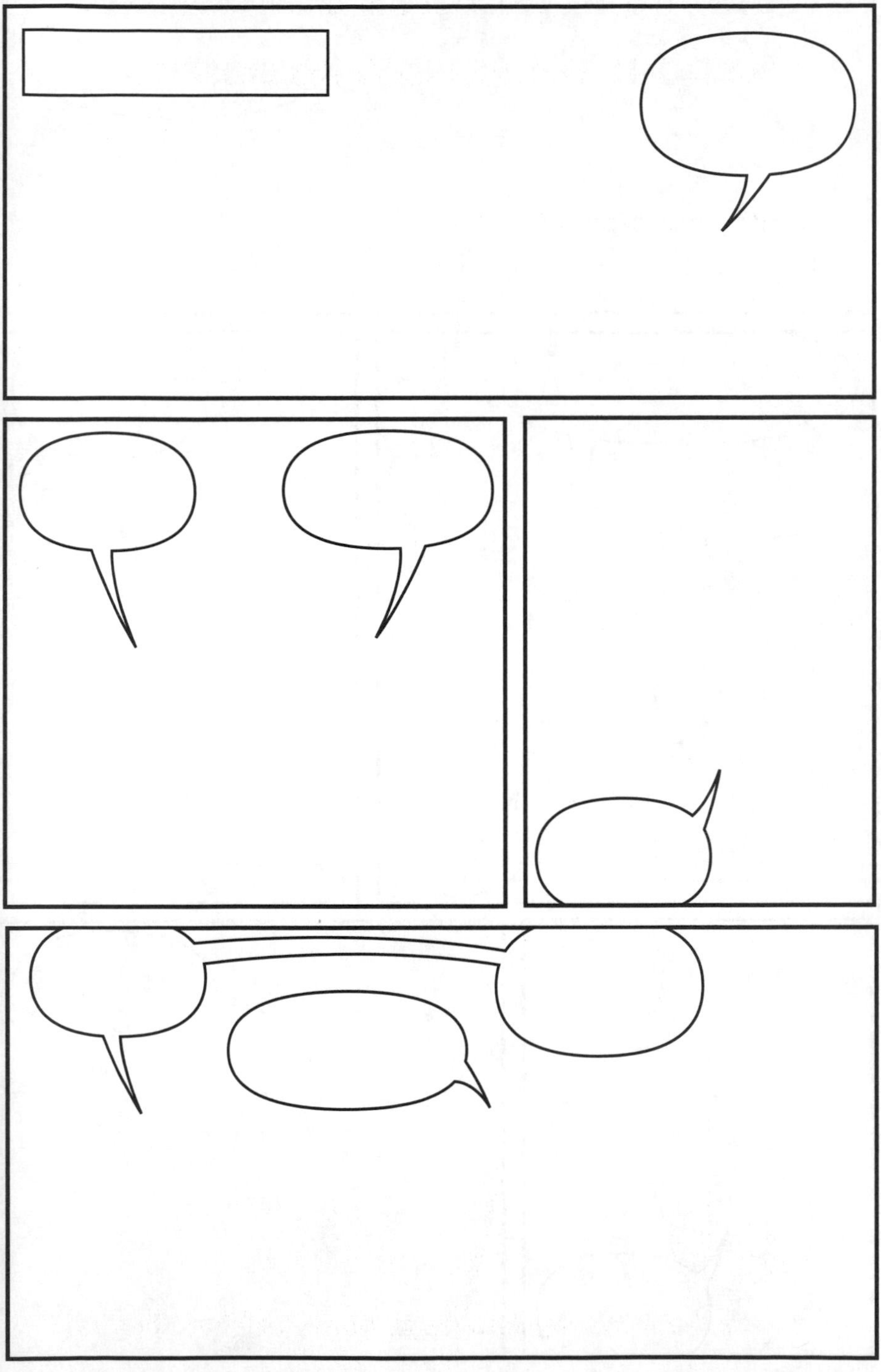

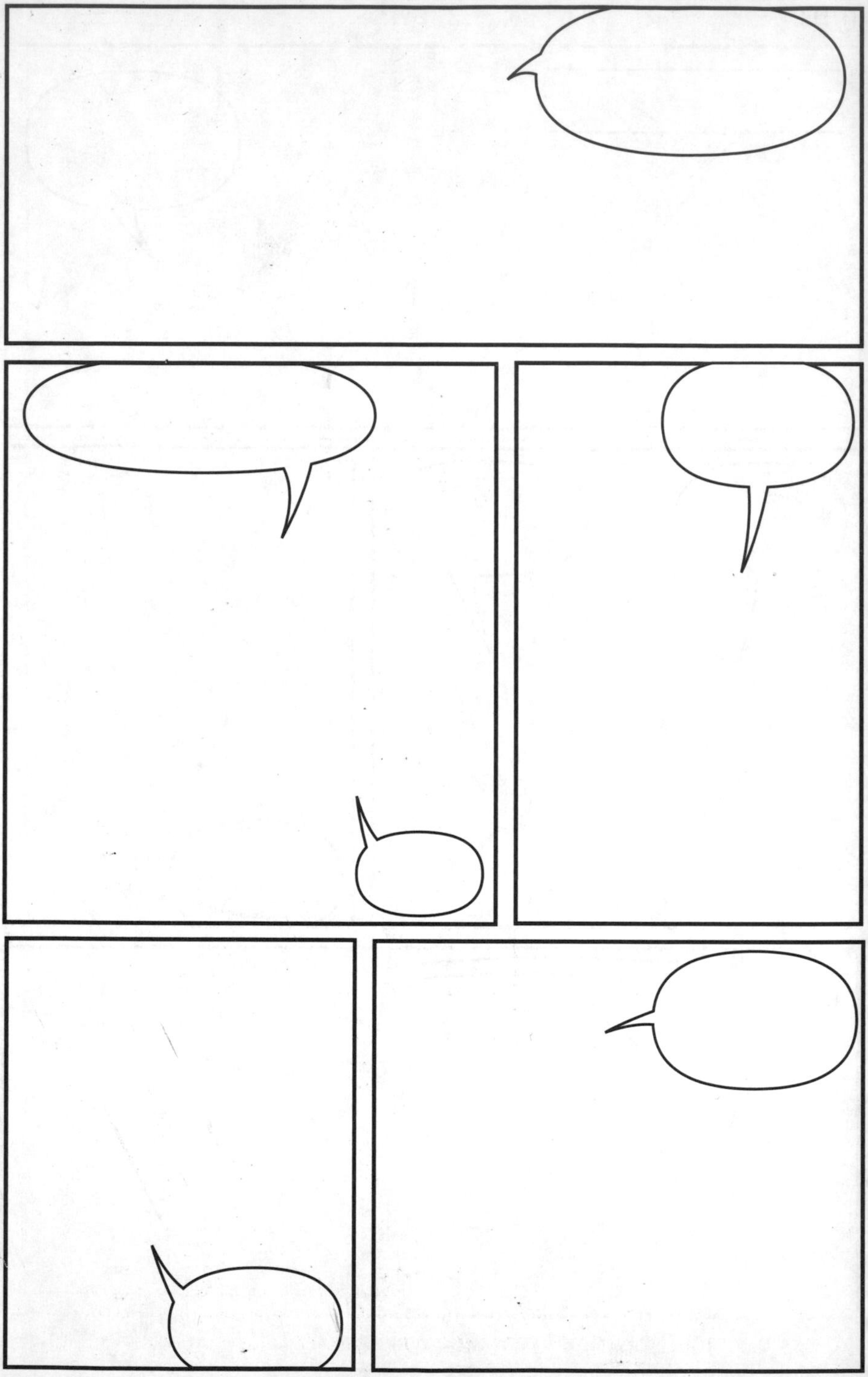